Charles Peter Mason

English Grammar

Including the principles of grammatical analysis, enlarged and thoroughly revised

Charles Peter Mason

English Grammar

Including the principles of grammatical analysis, enlarged and thoroughly revised

ISBN/EAN: 9783337312794

Printed in Europe, USA, Canada, Australia, Japan

Cover: Foto ©Paul-Georg Meister /pixelio.de

More available books at **www.hansebooks.com**

Authorized by the Minister of Education.

ENGLISH GRAMMAR,

INCLUDING

THE PRINCIPLES OF GRAMMATICAL ANALYSIS.

BY

C. P. MASON, B.A., F.C.P.,

FELLOW OF UNIVERSITY COLLEGE, LONDON.

ENLARGED AND THOROUGHLY REVISED.

WITH EXAMINATION PAPERS ADDED,

BY

W. HOUSTON, M.A.

Twenty-Second Edition.

TORONTO:
ADAM MILLER AND CO.
1877.

Entered according to Act of Parliament of Canada, in the year 1876, by
ADAM MILLER & CO.,
In the Office of the Minister of Agriculture.

PREFACE.

It is hardly necessary to repeat here the acknowledgments which I have already made in previous editions of the extent to which my "English Grammar" in its present form is indebted to the splendid works of Mätzner and Koch, the latter of whom has traced the development of English with such care and fulness that later systematic grammars contain little of consequence on this subject beyond what is already to be found in his pages. I have made special reference to his work from time to time by way of reminding the reader of the source of the information given. The few instances in which I have been beholden to Dr. Morris's "Historical Outlines of English Accidence" for materials not already contained in Koch's grammar have been scrupulously noticed. In the present edition the Exercises have been somewhat modified by the excision of some which are already to be found in my more elementary works, and are only needed by beginners, so as to make room for some additional help towards the understanding of the more difficult constructions.

The study of English has made rapid advances of late years, and no grammar, intended for pupils in the upper classes of schools that make any pretensions to teaching of a high character, can be deemed satisfactory, which does not go far beyond the mere statement of the current forms and idioms of our language. My aim in this work has been to write a manageable "Historical English Grammar" for schools. Accordingly I have endeavoured to treat the development of modern English out of the older forms of the language with sufficient thoroughness to give the learner a clear comprehension of the way in which English has come to be what it is, as regards its elements, its forms, and its constructions, without distracting his attention and burdening his memory with details which are necessary only for the minute study of particular periods or individual authors. Much of the most difficult portion of what was necessary for this purpose has been thrown into the form of notes and appendices, the study of which may, if it be deemed desirable, be postponed until the learner has mastered the general text. The latter is quite within the comprehension of a pupil of ordinary intelligence. I have striven to set down what had to be said in short and clear sentences, every expression in which has been carefully weighed with the view of securing the utmost possible accuracy, and leading the pupil to *think*. There may be teachers to whom this last-named effort is unusual and unwelcome. It will be perfectly easy for such to find books called "English Grammars" which will exactly suit their requirements. It will be found that in several portions of the Syntax I have been able, by following constructions up to their source, to introduce important simplifications, especially with regard to the use of relatives, and the troublesome little words *as*, *that*, and *than*.

In one or two paragraphs the phraseology has been modified, with the view of bringing out still more clearly the cardinal distinction between the indicative and the subjunctive mood. (See §§ 193, 195, 466.) This distinction is carefully and philosophically developed by Mätzner.* It is substantially that of Becker (who, however, makes a needless separation between

---

* The student who desires to examine Mätzner's statements must consult the original text of his works. As presented in a recent translation his views are totally unintelligible.

conjunctive and *conditional*), and is expressed clearly enough by the best Latin* grammarians. Thus Madvig (§ 346) lays down that "in the conjunctive a thing is asserted simply as an idea conceived in the mind, so that the speaker does not at the same time declare it as actually existing." Dr. Kennedy (*Public School Latin Grammar*, § 37) says: "The indicative mood declares a fact or condition as real or absolute. The conjunctive mood states a fact or condition as conceived or contingent." So, again, Mr. Roby (*Latin Grammar* ii. p. 202) says: "The subjunctive mood, as distinguished from the indicative, expresses an action or event as thought or supposed, rather than as done or narrated;" a definition which would be improved by leaving out the words "or supposed" and "or narrated."

In discussing grammatical definitions, many writers seem to think they have done all that is requisite when they have explained the meaning of some grammatical term, as though the usages of human speech had been devised to comply with the requirements involved in certain names. The grammatical names in common use are of no authority whatever; they are only attempts, and usually very bungling ones to classify and describe the forms and usages of language. A philosophical grammarian uses them as mere *conventional* names; he gives his own account of that which they are used to stand for. A good many grammarians tell us that "mood means the *manner of the*

* Many of the older writers on English grammar made a grievous mistake in trying to dress out English constructions in a Latin garb, being misled by the notion that Latin grammar is a sort of universal test and touchstone in all grammatical questions. Some modern authors make an equally gross mistake of an opposite kind, when they refuse to take any account at all of Latin constructions, when dealing with those of the English language. In spite of all the differences of idiom that distinguish the two languages, there are numerous cases in which their constructions involve grammatical principles which are the same in both. As regards particular usages there are considerable differences between English and Latin in the use of the moods, but the fundamental ideas upon which the distinctions of mood are based (like those which relate to the functions of the parts of speech, of numbers, persons, cases, voices, tenses, &c.) are common to both languages.

action." It really means nothing of the kind. It denotes a certain *mental attitude of the speaker*, with relation to the predication that he is dealing with. (See §§ 195, 466.) *Subjunctive* is altogether a bad and misleading term; for the indicative may be used as freely as the (so-called) subjunctive in clauses which are *subjoined* to a principal clause, and the subjunctive is often used in clauses which are not subjoined to others. Many writers, however, are incapable of seeing this. They confound a subjunctive *mood* with a conditional *sentence*, and gravely tell us that when an action is stated conditionally we get the subjunctive mood. They seem to suppose that the subjunctive mood is the natural and indispensable mood for hypothesis or condition. One recent writer actually talks of "Indicative-Subjunctive forms." All this is utterly wrong. When I say "If he *is* at home, I will speak to him," the first sentence is *conditional;* but the verb is in the indicative mood, because the condition relates to an *actual* state of things, independent of my *thought* about the matter. If I say "If he *were* present, I would speak to him," we again get a conditional sentence, but the verb is in the subjunctive mood, because "his being present" is something that I only *think* of. But an indicative mood does not cease to be an indicative and become a subjunctive by having *if* or *though* put before it in English; and only very ignorant learners imagine that *si* must always be followed by the subjunctive in Latin. It is quite true that the subjunctive mood is more commonly found in conditional clauses than in others, but that is the natural result of its peculiar function. It is not an invariable phenomenon, nor does it determine the *definition* of the Mood.

C. P. MASON.

5, College Gardens, Dulwich,
   September, 1876.

PRELIMINARY NOTICE.

The various languages spoken by mankind admit of being grouped together in certain great *families*, the members of each of which have certain characteristics and elements in common, by which they are distinguished in a very marked manner from the members of other families. One of these families of languages has been called the Indo-European, or Aryan family. It includes the Sanscrit, Persian, Slavonian, Latin, Greek, Keltic, and Teutonic languages. The Teutonic branch of this family is divided into two principal stocks, the Scandinavian and the German; and the German stock is again subdivided into High German languages (spoken in the mountainous districts of the south of Germany) and Low German languages (spoken in the northern lowlands of Germany). English belongs to the Low German branch of the Teutonic stock, and is akin to Frisian, Dutch, Flemish, Platt-Deutsch, and Mœso-Gothic.

The inhabitants of Gaul and Britain, when those countries were invaded by the Romans, were of Keltic race, and spoke various dialects of the Keltic group of languages.

The conquered Gauls adopted the Latin language, and the Franks and Normans, who at a later time established themselves in the country, adopted the language of the people they conquered. Thus it has come about that French is for the most part a corrupted form of Latin, belonging to that group of languages which is called 'Romance.'

The Keltic inhabitants of Britain did not adopt the Latin language, but retained their own Keltic dialects. One of these is still spoken by the Keltic inhabitants of Wales.

English is the language brought into England by the Saxons and Angles, who in the fifth century conquered and dispossessed the British or Keltic inhabitants, and drove the remnants of them into the remote mountainous corners of the island, especially Wales and Cornwall. They were a Teutonic race, coming from the lowland region in the north-western part of Germany. The name *Angle* appears to have belonged at first only to one division of these Teutonic invaders; but in course of time, though long before the Norman Conquest, it was extended over the rest, and the entire body of the Teutonic inhabitants of our country called themselves and their language English,* and their country England (Anglo-land). In speaking of themselves they also, at least for a time, employed the compound term *Anglo-Saxon*. English thus became the predominant language in our island from the Firth of Forth† to the English Channel, and has continued so for more than thirteen centuries. During this time, it has, of course, undergone many changes. It has adopted many new words from other languages, and its forms have been altered to some extent; but it has lasted in unbroken continuity from its introduction until now.

Modern English is only a somewhat altered form of the language which was brought into England by the Saxons and Angles, and which in its early form, before the changes consequent upon the Norman Conquest, is commonly called *Anglo-Saxon*. The grammatical framework of modern English is still purely Anglo-Saxon.

As regards its form, Anglo-Saxon (or old English) differed from modern English in this respect, that it had a much greater number of grammatical inflections. Thus nouns had five cases, and there were different declensions (as in Latin); adjectives were declined, and had three genders; pronouns had more forms, and some had a dual number, as well as a singular and plural; the verbs had more variety in their personal terminations. The greater part of these inflections were dropped in the course of the three centuries following the Norman Conquest, the grammatical functions of several of them being now served by separate words, such as prepositions and auxiliary verbs. This change is what is meant when it is said that Anglo-Saxon (or ancient English) was an *inflectional* language, and that modern English is an *analytical* language.

The greater part of the foreign words that have been incorporated into English, and are now part and parcel of the language, may be divided into the following classes:—

1. *Words of Keltic origin.*—The Anglo-Saxons adopted a few Keltic words from such Britons as they kept among them as slaves or wives. These words consist chiefly of geographical

---

* It has been asserted that from the earliest times, Saxons, as well as Angles, called themselves ' English,' and nothing else. This is at variance with the fact that the names ' West Saxons,' ' South Saxons,' &c., were vernacular, and, as is abundantly evident from the laws and charters, were names by which the several divisions of the Saxons called themselves. The Saxon Chronicle, in dealing with the events of our history up to the time of Alfred the Great, discriminates between the Angles and Saxons, and notices the latter according to their local subdivisions. It would have been quite impossible that Alfred should style himself ' West Seaxna cyning,' if his subjects never called themselves anything but ' English.'

† Lowland Scotch is a genuine Anglian dialect, and has kept closer to the Teutonic type than modern English.

names, such as Avon, Don, Mendip, Wight, Kent, Durham, &c.; and words relating to common household matters, such as *basket, clout, gown, button, darn, gruel, mattock, mop, rug, wire*, &c. These are still in common use. Others are provincial words, or are found only in the older literature, and are now obsolete.

2. *Words of Scandinavian origin.*—Men of Scandinavian race (Picts, Norsemen, and Danes) made repeated incursions into this island during several centuries, and established themselves along the eastern coast. In consequence of this a good many Scandinavian words made their way into common use, and Danish or Scandinavian forms appear in many names of places in the districts occupied by the Scandinavian invaders, such as *by* ('town,' as in Grimsby); *Scaw* ('wood,' as in Scawfell); *force* ('waterfall,' as in Stockgill Force); *holm* ('island' as in Langholm); *ness* ('headland,' as in Furness); *ey* ('island,' as in Orkney), &c.

3. *Words of Latin origin, and Greek Words introduced through Latin.*—Of these we have now immense numbers in English, the words of classical origin being considerably more than twice as numerous as those of Teutonic origin, there being, according to some authorities, about 29,000 of the former to about 13,000 of the latter. These words came in at various periods, and under various circumstances.

a. A few¹ Latin words, connected with names of places, have come down to us from the time of the Roman occupation of Britain; as in Chester (*castra*), Gloucester, Stratford (*strata*), Lincoln (*colonia*), Fossbury (*fossa*).

b. A good many words of classical origin were introduced between the settlement of the Saxons and the Norman Conquest by the ecclesiastics who brought Christianity into England. These words are mostly ecclesiastical terms, and names of social institutions and natural objects previously unknown to the English. These words came direct from Latin, or from Greek through Latin.

c. A much larger number of words of Latin origin came to us through Norman-French, the acquired language of the Norman conquerors of England. After the Conquest this was of course the language of the Norman nobles and their retainers throughout England. To a more limited extent it had been introduced as the language of the court of Edward the Confessor. Most of the words in our language which relate to feudal institutions, to war, law, and the chase, were introduced in this way. English, however, never ceased to be the language of the mass of the native population, though an important change in it was at least accelerated, if not first commenced, by the influence of the Norman-French, which was established side by side with it. The numerous grammatical inflections of the older English began to be disused, and in the course of the three centuries that followed the Conquest were reduced to little more than their present number.

d. The revival of the study of the classical languages in the sixteenth century led to the introduction of an immense number of Latin and Greek words, which were taken direct from the original languages. Many of these importations have since been discarded. It often happens that the same classical word has given rise to two words in English, one coming to us through Norman-French, the other taken direct from Latin. In such cases, the former is the shorter and more corrupted form. Compare, for example, *minster* and *monastery*, *bishop* and *episcopal*, *hotel* and *hospital*, *reason* and *rational*.

4. *Words of Miscellaneous origin.*—The extensive intercourse maintained during the last three hundred years with all parts of the world naturally led to the introduction of words from most languages of importance, relating to natural productions, works of art, or social institutions, with which this intercourse first made us acquainted.

Thus it has come about that the two chief constituents of modern English are Anglo-Saxon and Latin, mixed with a small proportion of words of miscellaneous origin. Most of the Teutonic elements of English were introduced by the Saxons and Angles. But the Scandinavian races are also Teutonic, and a good many words of Teutonic origin were introduced into English by the Danes and Norsemen, who established themselves on the eastern coast of our island.

As a general rule (admitting, of course, of numerous exceptions) it will be found that words relating to common natural objects, to home life, to agriculture, and to common trades and processes, are usually of Teutonic origin. Words relating to the higher functions of social life—religion, law, government, and war, to the less obvious processes of the mind, and to matters connected with art, science, and philosophy, are commonly of classical and mostly of Latin origin. Most words of three or more syllables, and a large number of those of two, are of classical origin. The Teutonic element prevails (though very far from exclusively) in words of one or two syllables, and is by far the most forcible and expressive. Hence it predominates in all our finest poetry. It is impossible to write a single sentence without Teutonic elements, but sentence after sentence may be found in Shakspeare and the English Bible, which is pure English, in the strictest sense of that term.

One great advantage which English has derived from the mingling of the Teutonic and Romance elements is the great richness of its vocabulary, and its power of expressing delicate shades of difference in the signification of words by the use of pairs of words, of which one is Teutonic and the other French.[*]

The changes by which Anglo-Saxon (or the oldest English)

---

[*] Compare, for example, *feeling* and *sentiment*, *work* and *labour*, *bloom* and *flower*. The number of pairs of exactly synonymous words is small.

became modern English were gradual, and no exact date can be given for the introduction of this or that particular alteration. Still the process was influenced or accelerated at certain points by political events. The Norman Conquest, and the political relations between the conquering and the conquered race naturally made Norman-French the language of the court and the nobles, of the courts of justice, of the episcopal sees, and of garrisoned places. But the loss of Normandy in 1206, the enactments of Henry III. and Louis IX., that the subjects of the one crown should not hold lands in the territory of the other, and the political movements under John and Henry III., stopped the further influx of the Norman element. At the same time the absolutist tendencies of the kings drove the nobles into closer union with the Anglo-Saxon elements of the nation; and the French wars of Edward III. roused an anti-French feeling among all classes, which extended itself even to the language, insomuch that we learn from Chaucer that in his time French was spoken in England but rarely, and in a corrupted form. In 1362 appeared the edict of Edward III. that legal proceedings in the royal courts should be conducted in English.

Thus the course of the changes which English underwent was far from being equable. Koch divides the historical development of English into five periods, in the following manner:—

First Period, that of old Anglo-Saxon. This period extends from the time of the oldest literary monuments to about A.D. 1100. The language was divided into two groups of dialects, the Northern or *Anglian*, and the Southern or *Saxon*. In the latter the speech of the West Saxons, in consequence of the political supremacy acquired by that division of the nation, took precedence of the rest, and became the literary dialect of England.* (The chief grammatical inflections of this period will be found in Appendix A.)

Second Period, that of late Anglo-Saxon. This period extends over about 150 years, to the middle of the thirteenth century, and shows marks of the influence of the Danish and Norman settlements in disturbing the older system of inflections, obliterating many of its distinctions, and so preparing the way for the still greater simplification which followed.

Third Period, termed by Koch *Old English*. This period, which extends over some 100 years, from about 1250 till about 1350, exhibits a continued weakening of the old forms, spoken sounds and their written representatives being both in an unsettled state, and the influence of Norman French being distinctly traceable.

Fourth Period, called by Koch *Middle English*. This period, to

---

* As the main part of the Teutonic elements of modern literary English have come down to us from this *West-Saxon* speech, it is obviously allowable to speak of them in the gross as *Saxon*. There are critics, however, who wax wroth at the use of the term.

which belong Wiclif, Chaucer, and Maundeville, reaches nearly to the end of the fifteenth century. In it the Midland section of the Northern dialect becomes predominant.

Fifth Period, that of *Modern English*.—For further details respecting the characteristics of those periods,* the learner is referred to Appendix A.

Leaving the vocabulary of the language out of consideration, it may be stated summarily that English has preserved from its Anglo-Saxon stage the suffixes that it still possesses in nouns and pronouns; the conjugation of its verbs; the articles, pronouns, prepositions, conjunctions, and numerals; the comparative and superlative suffixes of adjectives, and the formation of adverbs; the flexibility and variety which it has in the formation of compounds; the most important part of the suffixes and prefixes by which derivatives are formed; the predominant principles of accentuation; and the compactness and straightforwardness of the syntactical arrangement of its periods. To French we owe a considerable modification of the sounds of the language, the suppression of the sound of *l* before other consonants, such as *f, v, k, m*, etc.; the partial suppression of the sounds of *h* and *gh*, and the use of *e* mute at the end of words; the introduction of the sibilant sounds of *j, g, ch* and *c;* the use of the letter *z*, and the consonantal sound of *v*. French influence assisted in the recognition of *s* as the general sign of the plural in nouns. To French we also owe a considerable number of the suffixes and prefixes by which derivatives are formed, and are probably indebted for our deliverance from that stiff and involved arrangement of sentences, under which modern German still labours. (*Mätzner*.)

---

* The details of the history of English Accidence and Syntax during these periods have been set forth by Koch with a fulness and minuteness which render it a difficult task to make further discoveries in the same field. Indeed, nothing of consequence has as yet been added to his results. His nomenclature is not unexceptionable, and in order to keep up the continuity of the name *English*, which certainly belonged to our language in the time of Alfred the Great, the best recent English authorities, while adopting Koch's subdivision, name the language at its successive stages, 'English of the First Period,' 'English of the Second Period,' and so on. The subdivision is, however, more elaborate than is necessary. There is no break of any consequence between the Third and Fourth Periods. No new principle of change begins to operate. We simply have in the Fourth Period a still further development, on exactly the same lines, of what was going on in the Third. There is no epoch at the dividing line of these two periods comparable to those formed by the Norman Conquest, which preceded the Third Period and the invention of printing and the revival of letters, which ushered in the latest period. It would be simpler and quite sufficient to divide English, in its historical aspect, into three periods—the first (Old English or Anglo-Saxon) embracing Koch's first two periods; the second (Middle or Transition English) comprising Koch's third and fourth periods; and the third (Modern English) coinciding with Koch's fifth period. Each of the two former has naturally an earlier and a later stage, between which, however, no exact boundary can be fixed. The names *First Period, Second Period*, &c., are very bald and unsuggestive, so that it requires considerable familiarity with them to be able to realize readily what particular stage of the language each represents.

ENGLISH GRAMMAR.

GENERAL REMARKS.

1 WHEN we wish to express what is passing in our minds, we talk, or else write down certain marks or signs, which people have agreed shall stand for the sounds which we utter when we talk.

2 That which we speak with our voice, or write down to represent what we speak, is called *speech* or *language*.

3 Grammar (from the Greek *gramma*, 'letter') is the science which treats about speech or language.

4 All people do not utter the same sounds, or write the same signs to express what they think. There are different languages or tongues made use of by different nations, as the English language, the French language, the Latin language, &c.; and since these differ widely from each other, it is necessary to have a separate grammar for each of them. These separate grammars, however, agree in many respects, and are all parts of the general science of grammar.

5 Speech or language is made up of words. A word is a significant combination of articulate sounds. A collection of words arranged so as to convey some complete sense, is called a sentence (Latin *sententia*, 'a thought or opinion'); as, "The boy learns his lesson;" "The cat has caught a mouse."

6 The words of which a sentence is made up are of different sorts. Thus in the sentence, "The bird flies swiftly," *bird* is the name of an animal; *the* points out which bird is meant; *flies* expresses an action, which it is asserted that the bird performs; *swiftly* denotes the manner in which that action is performed. The different sorts of words which a language contains are called Parts of Speech.

7 That part of grammar which treats of the letters of which words are composed, and of the proper mode of writing and spelling words, is called Orthography (from the Greek *orthos*, 'right,' and *grapho*, 'I write').

8   That part of grammar which treats of separate words, or of the parts of speech separately, showing the mode in which they are formed, and the changes which they undergo, is called Etymology (from the Greek *etymos*, 'true,' and *logos*, 'account.'

9   That part of grammar which treats of the mode in which words are combined so as to form sentences, and sentences combined with one another, is called Syntax (from the Greek *syn*, 'together,' and *taxis*, 'arrangement').

ORTHOGRAPHY.

10   Spoken words are made up of different sounds, and written words are made up of different signs, called *letters* (Lat. *litera*), which are used to represent the different sounds of which spoken words are composed.

11   The elementary sounds of the English language are represented by means of twenty-six letters, each of which is written in two forms, differing both in shape and in size; the large letters being called Capitals, or Capital Letters.* These letters are the following:—

A, a: B, b: C, c: D, d: E, e: F, f: G, g: H, h: I, i: J, j: K, k: L, l: M, m: N, n: O, o: P, p: Q, q: R, r: S, s: T, t: U, u: V, v: W, w: X, x: Y, y: Z, z.

12   The Anglo-Saxon alphabet had no *j, q, v*, or *z*, and *k* was very seldom used, *c* having a hard sound. On the other hand it had two symbols, which have since been discarded, namely ð *(eth)* and þ *(thorn)*, which both stood for *th*, ð occurring most frequently in the middle or at the end of words. In the thirteenth century we find ſ used, chiefly at the beginning of words. It had the sound of a somewhat guttural y. *W* was denoted by the symbol ƿ *(wen)*.

13   The whole collection of letters is called the Alphabet. Alpha and Beta are the names of the first two letters of the Greek alphabet. The English Alphabet, with the exception of the letter *w*, is taken from that used by the Romans, who, however, employed the letters k, y, and z only in writing foreign (especially Greek) words, and sounded *v* like our *w*. The Latin Alphabet, in its turn, was derived from the Greek, and that again from the Phœnician.

14   The letters *a, e, i, o,* and *u,* are called Vowels (Latin *vocalis*). They can be fully sounded by themselves.

---

* Capital letters are used at the beginning of proper names, for the nominative case singular of the personal pronoun of the first person, and for any noun, adjective, or pronoun, used in speaking of the Divine Being. They may also be used at the beginning of a common noun, when it is used in a special or technical sense, as *Mood, Voice, Person.* Adjectives derived from proper nouns are also written with capitals. We also write His Majesty, Her Majesty, &c.

Imperfections of English Alphabet –

proper alphabet must be based on two phonetic principles (a) every simple sound must be represented by a distinct syllable (b) no sound must be represented by more than by one sign. There are 43 sounds and 26 letters

(1) <u>Redundancy</u>. c. q. x are superfluous letters.

(2) <u>Imperfect</u>. the vowels a. e. i.. u represent 13 [?]... a...[?] the combinations – ough represent diff sounds in [?] [?]...

3) <u>Inconsistent</u> in the vowel sounds of a. e. o. u. and in c. x. y. w.

ORTHOGRAPHY.

The remaining letters are called Consonants (Latin *con*, ' together,' *sonans*, ' sounding '). They cannot be fully sounded without having a vowel either before or after them.

15. The extreme sounds of the vowel scale are those of *ee* (in *feet*) and *oo* (in *tool*). If the sounds of *ee*, *ā* (as in *fate*), *a* (as in *far*), *ō* (as in *pole*), and *oo* (as in *tool*) be pronounced in succession with a full and clear sound, the speaker will be sensible that the formation and position of the organs of speech change by successive steps, from the one extreme to the other. The primary vowel sounds are *ĭ* (as in *pin*), *a* (as in *far*), and *ŭ* (as in *full*). All others are lengthenings, combinations, or modifications of these.

In Italian or German the scale of vowel sounds will be represented by the letters *i, e, a, o, u*. Modern English has the peculiarity that in this scale the sounds of *ī* and *ē* (*ee* and *ay*) have been transferred or ' shoved on ' to *e* and *ā*. In Anglo-Saxon this was not the case. Short *i* and short *e* preserve their original force (as in *pin, tin, bid*, &c., *end, enter, set*, &c). The words *there, where*, and *ere* preserve the old sound of *e*.

16. There are thirteen simple vowel sounds in English; the sounds of *a* in *tall, father, fate, fat ;* the sounds of *e* in *met* and *mete ;* the sound of *i* in *pin ;* the sounds of *o* in *note* and *not ;* the sounds of *u* in *rule, pull, fur*, and *but*. These sounds are expressed in many various ways.

The letter *a* represents four simple vowel sounds, as in *fate, fall, far, fat*.

The letter *e* represents three simple vowel sounds, as in *mēte, pĕt, herd*.

The letter *i* represents one simple vowel sound, as in *pit ;* and one diphthongal sound, as in *bite*.

The letter *o* represents three simple vowel sounds, as in *poke, pot, for*.

The letter *u* represents four simple vowel sounds, as in *rūde, pŭll, fun, fur*.

The sound of *a* in *fate* is also represented by the written diphthongs *ai* (*braid*), *ay* (*say*), *ea* (*great*), *ei* (*neigh*), *ey* (*prey*), *ao* (*gaol*), *au* (*gauge*).

The sound of *a* in *fall* is the same as that of *o* in *for*, and is also represented by the written diphthongs *au* (*fraud*), *aw* (*claw*), *oa* (*broad*), *ou* (*ought*).

The sound of *a* in *far* is also represented by *e* (if followed by *r*) in such words as *clerk, Derby, Berkshire* (when pronounced *Darby, Barkshire*), and by the written diphthongs *au* (*aunt*), *ua* (*guard*), *ea* (*heart*).

The sound of *a* in *fat* is also represented by *ua* (*guarantee*), and *ai* (*plaid*).

The sound of *e* in *mete* is also represented by the written diphthongs *ea* (*seat*), *ee* (*feet*), *eo* (*people*), *ie* (*chief*), *ei* * (*receive*), *ey* (*key*), *ae* (*aether*), *oe* (*Phœnician*), *ay* (*quay*), *i* (*marine*).

The sound of *e* in *pet* is also represented by *a* (*many*), *ai* (*said*), *ay* (*says*), *u* (*bury*), *ea* (*tread*), *ue* (*guest*), *ie* (*friend*), *ei* (*heifer*), *eo* (*Leonard, Geoffrey*).

---

* It is convenient to bear in mind that with the exception of the words *seize* and *ceiling*, *ei* with the sound of *ee* is found only in words derived from the Latin *capio*, as *deceit* (decipio), *receipt* (recipio), *conceit* concipio). &c.

The sound of *e* in *herd* is also represented by *i* (*bird*), *u* (*curse*), *y* (*myrrh*), *ea* (*earth*).

The sound of *i* in *pit* is also represented by *y* (*syllable*), *u* (*busy*), *e* (*pretty*), *ui* (*build*), *ie* (*sieve*).

The sound of *i* in *bite* is also represented by *y* (*thy*), *ey* (*eye*), *ei* (*height*), *ie* (*dies*), *uy* (*buy*), *ui* (*guide*), and *ai* (*aisle*).

The sound of *o* in *poke* is also represented by *oa* (*coat*), *oe* (*toe*), *ou* (*soul*), *ow* (*tow*), *ew* (*sew*), *ow* (*owe*), *oo* (*door*).

The sound of *o* in *pot* is also represented by *a* (*what*).

The sound of *o* in *for* is also represented by *a* in *fall*, &c. (See above).

The sound of *u* in *rude*, is also represented by *o* (*move*), *oo* (*rood*), *ew* (*flew*), *ue* (*blue*), *ui* (*fruit*), *ou* (*through*), *oe* (*shoe*); *u* in *full* = *oo* in *good*.

The sound of *u* in *fun* is also represented by *o* (*love*), *oe* (*does*), *oo* (*flood*), *ou* (*rough*).

The sound of *u* in *fur* is also represented by *e*, *i*, *y*, *u*, *ea*. (See above).

17 When two vowel sounds are uttered without a break between them, we get what is called a vocal or sonant diphthong. There are four of them.

1. *i*, as in *bite*. (See above). This sound is made up of the *a* in father, and the *e* in *mete*.

2. *oi*, as in *hoist*. This dipthong is also written *oy* (*boy*), and *uoy* (*buoy*). It is made up of the sound of *a* in *fall*, and *e* in *mete*.

3. *eu* (as in *eulogy*). This diphthong is also expressed in writing by *u* (*mute*), *ew* or *ewe* (*few*, *ewer*), *eau* (*beauty*), *ui* (*suit*), *ue* (*hue*), *yu* (*yule*).

4. *ou* (as in *noun*). This is also expressed in writing by *ow* (*now*). When two of the letters called vowels are written together to represent either a sonant diphthong or a simple vowel sound, we get a written diphthong or *digraph*.

18 The letters *w* and *y* are commonly called *semi-vowels*. When they are followed by a vowel sound in the same syllable, their sound approaches that of a consonant, as in *win*, *twin*, *you*, *yonder*. When a vowel precedes them in the same syllable they combine with the preceding vowel to form either a diphthong or a simple vowel sound; as *awe*, *how*, *dray*, *bey*, *buy*. *Y* is a pure vowel whenever it is followed by a consonant (as in Yttria). In Anglo-Saxon *y* was a pure vowel. It was never followed by another vowel, but only by consonants. Afterwards it was used at the beginning of words to denote a *g* which had been softened, and supplanted the symbol ʓ.

19 The letters *l*, *m*, *n*, and *r*, are called Liquids. They can be partially sounded by themselves when pronounced with a vowel before them. The Liquids and Sibilants do not stop the breath sharply, but admit of a prolongation of the sound. *J*, *s*, *x*, *z*, soft *g* and soft *ch*, are called Sibilants (from the Latin *sibilare*, 'to hiss'). The other consonants are called Mutes.* When sounded after a vowel, they stop the passage of the breath more completely than the liquids and sibilants do. Of the mutes, *b*, *p*, *f*, and *v* are called *labials* or *lip-letters* (from the Latin *labium*, ' a lip '); *d*, *t*, *th* (for which in

---

* The *Mutes* must not be confounded with *mute letters*, *i.e.*, letters which are written but not sounded, like *k* in *knot*, or *e* in *awe*.

ORTHOGRAPHY.

Anglo-Saxon there were two symbols, ð and þ) are called *dentals* or *teeth-letters* (from the Latin *dens* 'tooth'); and *g, k,* hard *c,* and *ch,* (as in *loch*) are called *gutturals* or *throat-letters* (Latin *guttur,* 'throat').

20   The Mutes are also classified, not according to the organs by which they are pronounced, but according to certain differences in the mode in which the consonantal sound is pronounced. *P, t,* and *k* (or hard *c*), are called *thin* or *sharp* mutes; *b, d, g* are called *middle* or *flat* mutes; *f* and *v, th* in *thin,* and *th* in *thine, eh* in *loch,* and *gh* in *lough* are called *aspirated* mutes. The aspirates may themselves be divided into *sharp aspirates* (*f, th* in *thin, eh*), and *flat aspirates* (*v, th* in *thine, gh*). The sibilants *s* and *z* bear the same relation to each other as *p* and *b, s* being a sharp sibilant, *z* a flat sibilant.

21   A syllable (Greek *syllabe,* ' a taking together') is a single vowel, or a collection of letters pronounced together, and containing only one vowel sound.

A word which consists of a single syllable is called a Monosyllable (Greek *monos,* 'single'), such as *man, horse, hut.*

A word which consists of two syllables is called a Disyllable: as *folly, learning.*

A word that consists of three syllables is called a Trisyllable, as *vanity, loveliness.*

A word that consists of more than three syllables is called a Polysyllable (Greek *polys,* 'many'), as *singularity.*†

22   When a syllable beginning with a vowel is added to a monosyllable, or a word accented on the last syllable, ending in a single consonant preceded by a single vowel, the final consonant is doubled. As *sin, sinner; thin, thinner; rob, robber; sit, sitting; begin, beginning; expel, expelled; confer, conferred.* But if, in a word of more than one syllable, the accent does not fall on the last syllable, the final consonant is not doubled; as *offer, offered; differ, different; visit, visiting.* The letters *l* and *s,* however, are generally doubled, as *travel, traveller; revel, reveller; marvel, marvellous; hocus, hocussing.* There are also some other words in which the rule is violated, as *worshipper.* The reason for this doubling of the consonant is that the quantity or length of the preceding vowel may be preserved. A doubled consonant usually shows that the preceding vowel is short. Compare *running* and *tuning, sinning* and *dining, manning* and *waning.* Before *ll* and *ss, a* and *o* are often long, as in *roll, stroll, squall, fall, gross, grass,* &c.

23   When a syllable (not beginning with *i*) is added to a word ending in *y* preceded by a consonant, the *y* is changed into *i,* as *happy,*

---

* The *y* in the old-fashioned way of writing *the* (*y̆* or *ye*) is a corruption of þ.

† The proper way of dividing words into syllables is not yet quite settled. The methods adopted in most spelling-books are extremely arbitrary, not to say stupid. Two very absurd rules commonly laid down are, that "if two consonants come together between vowels, they should be divided," and that "each separate syllable should, as far as possible, begin with a consonant." In accordance with these rules, one of the commonest spelling-books gives us the following divisions: —*thirs-ty, trea-tise, righ-teous, poi-gnant, be-nign, e-clipse, a-noint, bur-gher, cou-rier, fron-tier, guar-dian.* Such divisions have neither reason nor convenience to justify them; they are simply ridiculous. It is impossible to lay down any rules of universal application, but the *principle* to be kept in view should be to divide words so that the *syllabic* division may, as far as possible, coincide with the *etymological* division, as in *right-eous, front-ier, an-oint, guard-ian, burgh-er.* So *cap-it-al* (not *ca-pi-tal*), *soft-en* (not *sof-ten*), &c.

happily, happier; pity, pitiless. When the final *y* is preceded by a vowel, it is not changed. Conversely when *ing* is added to a word ending in *ie*, the *i* is changed into *y*; as *die, dying; lie, lying.* In monosyllables *y* is not changed before a consonant; as *dryness, shyly.*

24   Mute *e* at the end of a word is generally omitted when a syllable that begins with a vowel is added; as *force, forcible; love, loving;* but the *e* is retained if it is required to preserve the pronunciation of the consonant, as *change, changeable,* and after *oe,* as *hoeing.*

Mute *e* preceded by a consonant at the end of a word is generally retained when a syllable that begins with a consonant is added, if the vowel sound of the last syllable of the word is long, as *pale, paleness;* but if the vowel sound of the last syllable is short, the *e* is commonly dropt, as in *judgment, lodgment.* It is retained, however, if necessary to preserve the pronunciation of the consonant that precedes it; as in *infringement.* Mute *e* is commonly employed to show that the preceding vowel is long, as may be seen on comparing *rob* and *robe, shin* and *shine, ban* and *bane, run* and *rune, men* and *scene.* It is always put after final *v,* whether the preceding vowel be long or short.

Mute *e* at the end of a word, and preceded by a vowel, is sometimes omitted when a syllable is added, as *true, truly; due, duly;* sometimes it is retained, as *eye, eyeless; true, trueness; blue, blueness.*

25.   The English orthographical system has many imperfections. Thus the same vowel sound is often represented in different ways, as in the modes indicated above for expressing the simple vowel sounds and diphthongs. On the other hand, the same letter or diphthong often represents very different vowel sounds. Compare *cat, pate, call, father; read, spread; broad, coach; goes, does, shoes, foetid, cull, full, yule.* Again, some consonants have not always the same sound. Compare *give, gin, gill* (a measure), *gill* (of a fish); *cent, can; dough, cough; arch, archangel; his, this; thin, thine.* The same sound is sometimes represented by different consonants. Compare *adds, adze; crutch, such; face, base; jury, gaol; know, no; plum, plumb; knowledge, privilege; fillip, Philip; picked, Pict.* Simple sounds are sometimes expressed by two letters, as by *ck* in *duck; ch* in *loch;* and most of the written digraphs. Complex sounds are sometimes expressed by single letters, as by *i* and *u* in *mine* and *muse; s* in *sure; j* in *just.* Hard *c, q, x,* and, perhaps, *w* and *y,* are superfluous letters; their sounds may be represented by other letters. If we include *w* and *y* as separate sounds, and the nasal *ng,* we shall have forty-one elementary sounds in English. *Wh* is pronounced like *hw,* and is not a separate sound. Consonants are often not pronounced, as in *through, plough, knell, know. L* after *a* or *o,* and before another consonant, is sometimes mute, as in *walk, folk,* sometimes sounded, as in *malt, fault. T* before *ch* is not radical, but is used simply to show that *ch* has the sibilant and not the guttural sound, as in *stitch* (from *stick*).

ACCENT.

26   When we speak we do not utter all words and syllables with the same degree of force. By a stress or forcing of the voice certain words and syllables have greater prominence and importance given to them. When the stress which

gives this prominence has reference to the idea which the word conveys, so that its function is *rhetorical*, it is usually called *emphasis*. When it has reference to the syntactical importance of a word, or the etymological importance of a syllable, so that its function is *grammatical*, it is usually called *accent*.

Words of two or three syllables have a stress laid upon one of these, as *ténder, mísery, indécent*. Words of more than two syllables have also sometimes a second accent upon the syllable next but one or next but two to that which has the chief accent, as *democrátical, còndescénd, èmbarcátion*. This secondary accent is sometimes scarcely perceptible, as in *wíldèrness, térrìfy*.

27   In English two systems of accentuation have been at work, the Teutonic or genuine English, and the French. The characteristic tendency of Teutonic accentuation is to throw the stress upon the root-syllable of a word, and leave the inflections and formative syllables unaccented,* as *lóve, lóver, lóveliness*. In French the accentuation naturally in the first instance followed that of Latin, which was not etymological but rhythmical, so that the accent often shifted its position with an alteration in the number of the syllables, falling on the penult (or last syllable but one) if it was long, or on the ante-penult (or last syllable but two) if the penult was short. Hence in old French *pastor* became *pàtre, pastórem* became *pasteúr*. The omission of final syllables of inflection in French often left the accent on the last syllable, even when that was not the root-syllable. Thus *virtútem* became *virtú ; civitátem cité*. When such words first passed from French into English they naturally had their French accent, as *distánce, contrée* (country), *manére*, (manner); *soláce*, &c. Even in Spenser we still find *progréss, succoúr, uságe, bondáge*, &c. Most of these adopted words however have been affected by the English accentuation, which tends to keep the accent away from the last syllable.† In words of French or Latin origin, and of more than two syllables, there is a tendency to throw the accent back on to the ante-penult, as in *monópoly, geógraphy*. Thus we now say *advértisement* (not *advertísement*), *théatre* (not *theátre*), *míracle, mirác̀ulous*, &c. French derivatives ending in *ade, -ier*, or *-eer, -ee, -oon, -ine* or *-in*, keep the accent on the last syllable. So also do adjectives which are seemingly taken from Latin with the simple rejection of the final syllable, as *benígn, robúst, humáne, políte*. The natural weight of the syllable has of course to be taken into account. Compare, for example, *cóncentrate* and *remónstrate ; cosmógony* and *declénsion, benéficent* and *benefáctor*. There is also a

---

* In compounds in which the component parts preserve a syntactical relation to each other, the accent falls as it would if the words were kept separate, as *íll-wíll, íll-foúrs, spít-fíre, indeéd, forsóoth*, &c. Nouns compounded with adverbial particles have the accent on the particle, as *óffshoot, úproar*. Verbs have it on the verbal root, as *out-dó, with-stánd*.

† Except in derivatives formed by prefixing an inseparable particle to a monosyllable, as *aslánt, betwíxt, mistrúst*. In verbs a final root-syllable tends to keep its accent, as *refér, consént*, &c., but with exceptions, as *óffer, prómise*, &c.

tendency to accentuate the root-syllable of the definitive word in a compound, as *allegory*, *mélancholy*. Words which have been adopted without alteration from foreign languages keep their original accent, as *torpédo*, *coróna*, *octávo*.

The influence of accent upon the etymological changes of words has been very important. When one syllable is made prominent, those adjacent to it, especially if short and unimportant in themselves, are pronounced carelessly, and frequently get dropped altogether. Thus we get *bishop* from *episcopus*, *reeve* from *gerefa*, *sample* from *example*. In this way English has lost nearly all its syllabic suffixes.

When this loss takes place at the beginning of a word, it is called by grammarians *aphaeresis* (taking away); when it occurs at the end of a word it is called *apocope* (cutting off); when two syllables are blent into one, the process is termed *syncope* (shortening by excision.)

Examples of *syncope* are seen in *lord*, from *Hlaford*; *lady*, from *Hlafweardige*; *sheriff*, from *Scirgerefa*. (*Koch*, i., p. 220.)

An accented syllable often gets lengthened. Thus from *hebban* we get *heave*, from *brecan*, *break*, &c.

An unaccented long syllable is apt to get shortened. Thus the adjective *minute* becomes the noun *minŭte*. Compare *cupboard*, *housewife*, &c.*

ETYMOLOGY.

[N.B. In conjunction with the section on Etymology it would be well for the learner to study the first few paragraphs of that on Syntax.]

PARTS OF SPEECH.

28 The words of which the English language is composed are distributed into eight parts of speech. These are: 1. Noun. 2. Adjective. 3. Pronoun. 4. Verb. 5. Adverb. 6. Preposition. 7. Conjunction. 8. Interjection.

NOUN.

29 The word *Noun* means *name* (Latin, *nomen*.)

A noun is a word used as the *name* of anything that we speak about.

The greater part of nouns may be divided into two classes—Common Nouns and Proper Nouns.

30 A Common Noun is a word that may be used as the name of each thing out of some class of things of the same sort, as *horse*, *man*, *stone*, *city*; or of any portion of a quantity of stuff of the same sort, as *iron*, *wheat*, *water*. A common noun distinguishes the things belonging to some class from

---

* The whole subject of accentuation has been treated by Koch with extraordinary care and fulness.

everything which does not belong to that class. Thus the word *horse* distinguishes the animal so called from all other sorts of things, but does not distinguish one horse from another.

31 A Proper Noun is a word used as the name of some particular person, animal, place, or thing, as John, London, Bucephalus, Excalibur. The word *proper* (Latin *proprius*) means *own*. A *proper name* is a person's or thing's *own name*.

Common nouns are *significant*. They not only *denote*, or mark out the objects to which they are applied, but also *connote*, or *note at the same time*, the whole combination of marks or attributes, through their possession of which the various individuals named by the common noun are grouped into one class.*

Proper nouns, as such, are not significant. Even if the name, considered merely as a word, has a meaning, it is not applied to the object which it denotes in consequence of that meaning. *Margaret* means *pearl*, but it is not implied that a person called *Margaret* has *pearly* qualities.

A proper noun serves to distinguish that for which it stands not only from things of a different sort, but also from other things of the same sort. Thus the name Cicero distinguishes the person who bore it, not only from a horse or a town but from other men who did not bear that name.

Proper nouns are written with a capital letter at the beginning.

32 Proper nouns are sometimes used like common nouns, when they denote classes or collections of persons; as the Howards, the Cæsars, the Alps; or when they represent the characteristics that marked some individual, as if we say of a poet, "He was the Homer of his age."

On the other hand, some common nouns are occasionally used as the name, not of each individual in a class, but of the class *as a whole*. When we say, "Man is mortal," we mean all mankind.

33 A noun which in the singular number stands for a collection or number of things, is called a Collective Noun: as *herd, parliament, council, multitude, mob*.

34 A noun which denotes a quality or attribute, is called an Abstract Noun; as *hardness, prudence, justice*. An abstract noun always pre-supposes the existence of an adjective from which it is derived.

Since verbs are attributive words (§ 294), nouns that denote the action indicated by a verb are properly classed among the abstract nouns, as *running, speaking, action, friction*. Such nouns, however, often pass out of their abstract sense, as when we talk of 'sweeping a *crossing*.'

---

* Sometimes the connotative power of a noun is so much in our thoughts, that the noun is used predicatively without an article, as " He was *secretary* to Mr. A. ;" " He became *king* of England;" " In this business he was both *knave* and *fool*."

ETYMOLOGY—NOUN.

35   There is a class of nouns which are sometimes confounded with abstract nouns. These are *General Names*, such as *colour, space, time, life, death,* &c. These, in the exact sense in which they are used, do not admit of plurals; they are significant or connotative general names.

Abstract nouns are sometimes used in the *concrete* sense, that is, standing for that which possesses the quality which they denote. Thus *nobility* frequently means the whole body of persons of noble birth; *youth*, the whole class of young people, and so on.

36   Nouns admit of the three variations of Gender, Number, and Case.

Gender.

37   Living beings are divided into two classes or *sexes*, the male sex and the female sex, the individuals in the one sex corresponding to those in the other. Things without life are not of either sex. Thus all things are arranged in three classes—things of the male sex, things of the female sex, and things of neither sex.

38   In like manner, nouns (and pronouns) are divided into three * classes or sorts (called Genders), which correspond to the three classes of things just mentioned. These are the Masculine Gender, the Feminine Gender, and the Neuter Gender. *Gender* comes from the Latin *genus,* ' a kind or sort.'

The name of anything of the male sex is called a masculine noun, or a noun of the masculine gender.

The name of anything of the female sex is called a feminine noun, or a noun of the feminine gender.

The name of anything of neither sex is called a neuter noun, or a noun of the neuter gender.

Man, king, father, horse, cock, bull, James, Henry, are masculine nouns.

Woman, queen, mother, mare, hen, cow, Mary, Jane, are feminine nouns.

Stone, tree, house, London, are neuter nouns.

In the case of animals and young children we often take no account of the sex, and hence they are frequently referred to by means of *neuter pronouns*.

---

* Nothing is gained either in convenience or in philosophy by the attempt to restrict the term *gender* to the *masculine* and the *feminine*. Those who run the term *neuter* so hard as this should be consistent, and translate it into *neither* when they use it. To talk of nouns being of *Neuter Gender* (especially with a capital N) is not good Latin, good English, or good sense. German grammarians, who have the terms *männlich, weiblich,* and *sächlich,* are spared the temptation to air this little crotchet.

39   *Genders* are classes of nouns (and pronouns) which correspond to the three classes of things of the male sex, things of the female sex, and things of neither sex.*

It is also customary to use the word *gender* in an abstract sense, and to speak of it as an *attribute* of nouns and pronouns. In this abstract sense *gender* may be defined to be a distinction in the form or use of nouns and pronouns, by virtue of which they stand respectively for things of the male sex, things of the female sex, and things of neither sex.

40   Things without life are often *personified*, or spoken of as if they were living beings, and therefore either of the male or of the female sex. Accordingly masculine and feminine pronouns are used in speaking of them. The simplicity and naturalness of the English system of genders gives peculiar force and vividness to this figure of speech.

Thus the Sun,† Time, Day, Death, rivers, winds, mountains, the ocean, the seasons, the stronger passions (as Fear, Anger, Despair), actions connected with strength or violence (as Murder, War, &c.), are looked upon as male persons, and their names are accordingly masculine.

The Moon, the Earth, Virtue, Night, a ship, countries and cities— such as Europe, England, Paris—Night, Darkness, the Arts and Sciences, most abstract conceptions, as Nature, Liberty, Charity, Victory, Mercy, Religion, &c., the Soul, the gentler emotions, and many other things, are spoken of as though they were female persons, and their names are accordingly of the feminine gender.‡

41   The names of animals sometimes do not indicate their sex, as *sheep*, *bird*, *hawk*, *bear*, *mouse*, *raven*, *swan*, *dove*.§ The words *duck* and *goose* are also employed in this way, especially in the plural and in compounds. Also various,

---

* It is only in English, however, that this simple classification is observed. In Latin, Greek, French, and other languages, the names of many things which do not belong either to the male or to the female sex, are either masculine or feminine. When this is the case, gender ceases to answer (except partially) to any *natural* distinction, and becomes merely *grammatical*, though originally, no doubt, based upon a real, or fancied, natural distinction. A noun is known to be masculine (or feminine), not by its denoting a thing of the male (or female) sex, but by its having associated with it adjectives and pronouns with masculine (or feminine) terminations. This arbitrary, or merely grammatical gender has disappeared from modern English. In French and Italian there is no neuter gender at all. In Anglo-Saxon, the genders were to a great extent merely grammatical or arbitrary, as in Latin.

† In Anglo-Saxon (as in German) *Sun* was feminine, *and Moon masc.*

‡ The gender employed in personification is, however, rather arbitrary. Usage is by no means uniform on this point. The feeling of appropriation has a curious influence in this matter. Cobbett remarks that the countryfolk in Hampshire call almost everything *he* or *she*. "The mower calls his scythe a *she*, the ploughman his plough; but a prong, a shovel, or a barrow, which passes promiscuously from hand to hand, and which is appropriated to no particular labourer, is called *he*.

§ In Anglo-Saxon such nouns had their *grammatical* gender, and were respectively either masculine or feminine, no matter which sex was spoken of.

names of persons, as *parent, spouse, servant*,* &c. Such nouns are said to be of common or undetermined gender.

42. In speaking of animals which have names of common gender, the neuter pronouns are employed when the animal is regarded simply as an object of natural history. But in poetry, fables, or narratives which imply a lively interest in the actions or feelings of the animal, the masculine or feminine gender is used, with a general tendency to employ the masculine for the larger and fiercer animals. Thus, *bear, hound, panther, eagle, hawk, camel, wolf, fox, hippopotamus, elephant, whale, rat, raven, bison, jackal,* &c., would commonly be treated as masculine, while *hare, ostrich, dove, plover, lapwing, swallow, partridge,* &c., are usually feminine. The larger domestic animals are often spoken of as if they were males.

43. *Sex* is a distinction between *things*, not between *names*. *Gender* is a distinction between *names*, not between *things*. It is therefore wrong to speak of the *masculine sex*, or the *male gender:* to speak of a man as a *masculine being*, or to talk of *things* being of the masculine or feminine gender. *Things* may be of the male or female *sex*, but only *words* can be of the masculine, feminine, or neuter *gender*.

44. The distinction of sex in living beings is marked in three ways in the nouns that stand for them.

First Mode.—Quite different words are used: as—

Masculine.	Feminine.	Masculine.	Feminine.
Bachelor	maid *or* spinster†	Horse *or* stallion	mare
Boar	sow		
Boy	girl	Husband	wife
Brother	sister	King	queen
Buck	doe	Lord	lady
Bull	cow	Man	woman
Bullock *or* steer	heifer	Milter	spawner
		Monk *or* friar	nun
Cock	hen	Nephew	niece
Colt *or* foal	filly	Papa	mamma
Dog	bitch	Ram *or* wether	ewe
Drake	duck	Sir	madam
Drone	bee	Sire	dame *or* dam‡
Earl	countess	Sloven	slut
Father	mother	Son	daughter
Gander	goose	Stag	hind
Gentleman	lady	Uncle	aunt
Hart	roe *or* hind	Wizard	witch

---

* These nouns are usually of Romance origin.

† The termination *-ster* was originally feminine. *Spinster* is the only word in which this feminine force of it survives. In *seamstress* and *songstress* we have two feminine endings combined, one Saxon (*-ster*), the other French (*-ess*). Many words in *-ster* now used as masculine, or as proper names, were originally feminine, and denoted occupations ordinarily carried on by women, as *sewster, maltster, tapster* (a bar-maid), *Baxter* (from *bake*), *Webster* (from *webban*, 'to weave'). &c.

‡ *Grandam* (*grannam* or *granny*) answers to *grandsire*. *Sire* and *dam*, in contrast with each other, are applied only to animals.

Man (like the German *Mensch*) was formerly used of the female as well as of the male. We see this in the compound *woman*, a modified form of *wimman*—i.e., *wifman*. The vowel sound of the first syllable is still preserved in the plural, *women*.

The male was distinguished as *wepned man*—i.e., *armed* or *weaponed man*. *Maid* had come to mean in Chaucer's time a grown-up person of either sex. Thus, 'I wot well that the apostle was a maid' (*Ch.* 5661). *Girl* (a diminutive of the low German *gör*) once denoted a young person of either sex. Chaucer (619, 666) still uses it in this manner. To distinguish the male, the compound *knavegirl* was used.

Father means 'one who feeds;' from the same root as *fee-d* and *fa-t* (compare *pa-ter* and *pa-sco*). *Mother* is from a root *ma*—'bring forth' (*Morris*). *Daughter* (Gr. θυγάτηρ) meant originally 'milkmaid.' The root is the same as in *dug*.

Husband (A.S. *húsbonda*) is the manager or *master of the house* (*Mätzner*). *Bonda* in A.S. means *tiller* or *manager*.

In *husbandman* and *husbandry* we have vestiges of the old meaning. In Anglo-Saxon *wif* was neuter (as *Weib* still is in German), and meant simply *a woman*.

Nephew and *niece* come to us (through French) from the Latin *nepos* (*nepot-is*) and *neptis*. The older Anglo-Saxon words were *nefa* and *nefe*. *Uncle* and *aunt* are from *avunculus* and *amita*. The provincial and colloquial appellations *gaffer* and *gammer* are corruptions of *godfather* and *godmother*.

Queen (or *quean*) meant simply *female* or *mother*. In Anglo Saxon *ewen-fugel* means *hen-bird*.

Lord is a shortened form of hláford (*i.e.*, hláfweard, 'loaf-warden, or 'bread-dispenser' (*Mätzner* and *Koch*). *Lady* is from the corresponding feminine, hlæfdige (hláfweardige). *Sir* or *sire* is from *senior*; *madam* from *mea-domina*; *monk* from *monachus*, 'one who leads a solitary life'; *nun* = *nonna*, 'grandmother.' *Friar* is from *frater* (Fr. *frère*).

Witch is now only feminine, but it might come indifferently from the Anglo-Saxon masculine *wicca*, or from the feminine *wicce*.* *Wizard* comes from the Scandinavian *viskr*, 'wise,' through the old French *guiseart*, and means 'a very wise man' (*Mätzner*). See § 311, 7.

Drake (old Norse *andriki*: root *and* = Lat. *anat*; *riki*, connected with German *reich*, and Latin *reg-em*) means 'king of the ducks.' *Duck* is connected with the verb *duck*, 'to dive.' In Anglo-Saxon we find a masculine *hana*, 'cock' (Germ. *Hahn*). *Goose* has lost the letter *n* (Germ. *Gans*). *Gander* is formed from the feminine, *d* being only an offgrowth of the *n*. *Goose* is often used as a masculine, especially as a descriptive epithet, as 'Tom is a goose.' *Geese* is of common gender.

Bee is now of common gender, but was originally exclusively feminine.

15 **Second Mode.**—The feminine is formed by adding certain suffixes to the masculine.

1. The commonest of these, and the only one by which

---

* "He is such a holy witch, that he enchants societies into him."—(Shaksp. *Cymb.* i. 6.)

fresh feminines can still be formed, is *ess*, as *count, countess ; host, hostess*.

This termination came to us through French, from the late Latin suffix *issa*. (Compare Gr. ισσα and εσσα.)

When this suffix is added, the masculine terminations *or* and *er* are usually either shortened by the omission of the vowel, as in *actor, actress; hunter, huntress;* or omitted altogether, as in *adulterer, adulteress;* so *Emperor, Empress; murderer, murderess; governor, governess; caterer, cateress; sorcerer, sorceress*. The masculines *author, mayor, prior,* and *tutor,* suffer no abbreviation The *o* of *negro* and the *y* of *votary* are dropped in forming *negress* and *votaress*.

Abbess (from *abbot*) is a shortened form of *abbadess. Lass* is probably shortened from *laddess. Duchess* follows the French form *duchesse. Marchioness* is formed from the mediæval Latin word *marchio*. In *mistress*, the *a* of *master* is modified.

Feminines in *ess* were formerly much more common than they are now. Such words as *cousiness, championess, suitress, creatress, &c.*, have quite disappeared.

2. Feminines in *trix* are direct importations from Latin, as *testatrix, administratrix*.

3. A few feminines have the Romance suffix *a*, as *sultana, signora, infanta*.

4. A few feminines have the Romance suffix *ine*, which came to us through Norman French, as *heroine* (from *hero*), *landgravine* (from *landgrave*). *Czarina* (from *czar*) has a combination of this and the last-mentioned suffix.

5. One word, *vixen*, the feminine of *fox*, preserves the old Teutonic feminine suffix *en* or *in* (compare German *inn*), the root vowel of the masculine being modified. (Compare German *Fuchs, Füchsinn*.)

In the oldest English we find such feminines as *gyden*, ' goddess; ' *municen*, ' nun ' (from *munec*); *elfen*, ' female elf,' &c. So in Scotch, we have *earlin*, ' old woman.'

6. *Bridegroom* is a masculine formed from a feminine (*bride*). *Groom* is a corruption of *goom* (A.S. *guma* = man). *Widower* is perhaps also a masculine formed from a feminine, or *er* may be only a modification of the Anglo-Saxon ending *a* (A.S. masc. *widuwa;** fem. *widuwe*). *Ruff* (the name of a kind of bird resembling a woodcock) has a feminine *reeve*.

16 **Third Mode.**—Masculine and feminine nouns or pronouns are prefixed or affixed to nouns of common gender.

---

* In Anglo-Saxon pairs of masculines and feminines were formed: 1, by the suffixes *-a* and *-e*, as *nefa*, "nephew," *nefe*, "niece;" *webba*, "male weaver," *webbe*, "female weaver;" 2, by the suffixes *-ere* and *-estre*, as *bæcere* (baker), *bæcestre*; *hoppere* (dancer), *hoppestre*; *fiðelere* (fiddler), *fiðelstere*, &c., of which the feminine suffix *-ster* has lost its force (see note on § 44); 3, by the feminine suffix *-e* added to the masculine, as *gát* (goat), *gáte* (she-goat); 4, by the suffix *-en* or *-in* (see above).

Masculine.	Feminine.	Masculine.	Feminine.
Man-servant	maid-servant	Cock-sparrow	hen-sparrow
Man-singer	woman-singer	Dog-fox	bitch-fox
He-devil	she-devil	He-goat	she-goat
Boar-pig	sow-pig		ewe-lamb
Buck-rabbit	doe-rabbit	Pea-cock	pea-hen
Bull-calf	cow-calf	Guinea-cock	guinea-hen
		Turkey-cock	turkey-hen

Sometimes proper names are used to answer this purpose, as in *jack-ass, jenny-ass ; tom-cat, tib-cat ; billy-goat, nanny-goat ; jackdaw*. In Anglo-Saxon, *carl* and *cwen* were used, as *carl-fugel* (*cock-fowl*), *cwen-fugel* (*hen-fowl*).

Number.

47 Number (Latin *numerus*) is a variation in the form of nouns (and pronouns), by means of which we show whether we are speaking of one of the things for which the noun (or pronoun) stands, or of more than one.

There are two* numbers, the Singular and the Plural.

That form of the noun which is used when we speak of one of the things for which the noun stands is called the *singular number*, as *ship, horse*.

That form which is used when we speak of more than one of the things for which the noun stands is called the *plural number*, as *ships, horses*.

As it is simpler to think and speak of one thing than to think and speak of several things at once, the singular is the original form of the noun. The plural form is derived from the singular by making some change in it. The process of making this change is called *inflection*.

48 The plural is derived from the singular in the following ways:—

First Mode.—By adding the syllable *es*, shortened to *s* whenever the pronunciation admits of it. The full syllable *es* is now added only when the singular ends in a sibilant (*s, sh*, soft *ch, x* or *z*) as *gas, gases ; lash, lashes ; witch, witches ; box, boxes ; topaz, topazes*. Words like *horse, horses* really come under this rule, the mute *e* not being regarded.

The letters *es* are also added (but without being sounded as a separate syllable) after several words ending in *o*, as *hero, heroes ; potato, potatoes ;* after *y* when it is preceded by a consonant, the *y* being changed to *i*, as *lady, ladies ;* †

---

* In Anglo-Saxon there was also a dual number in the personal pronouns.
† In words of this kind it is more accurate to say that *ie* has been changed in the singular into *y* ; as the old English way of spelling the words in the singular was *ladie, glorie*, &c. In proper names the *y* is usually retained in the plural.

and after Anglo-Saxon words ending in *lf* or *f* preceded by any long vowel sound except *oo*. In these cases the flat sound which *s* always has in *es* affects the preceding consonant, and *f* is changed to *v*, as *elf, elves; shelf, shelves; leaf, leaves; thief, thieves; loaf, loaves.* *Wife* and *knife* get *f* changed to *v* in a similar way—*wives, knives.* Nouns ending in *oof*, *ff*, and *rf*, and nouns in *f* of Norman-French origin, have only sharp *s* added to form the plural, and retain the sharp sound of the *f*, as *roof, roofs; cliff, cliffs; dwarf, dwarfs; chief, chiefs; relief, reliefs.* So also *reef, fife,* and *strife* (see *Mätzner* and *Koch*). *Beef, beeves;* and *staff, staves,* are exceptions in modern English, and other exceptions are found in the older writers, as *wharves, turves, scarves.*

49 All nouns except those above mentioned, and the few nouns which form their plurals in the second and third modes hereafter specified, have their plurals formed by the addition of *s* only, as *book, books; father, fathers;* the *s* having its sharp sound after a sharp mute (as in *books, cats, traps*), and the sound of the flat sibilant *z* after a flat mute, a liquid, or a vowel (as in *tubs, eggs, rods, pails, rams, nuns, bears, fleas*).

When *y* at the end of a word is preceded by a vowel, *s* only is added to form the plural, and the *y* is not changed, as *valley, valleys; boy, boys.* *Qu* counts as a consonant, hence the plural of *soliloquy* is *soliloquies.*

The usage in the case of words ending in *o* is arbitrary, and by no means uniform, *es* being commonly added. But *s* only is added to words ending in *io* and *oo*, and to the following words:—*domino, volcano, virtuoso, tyro, quarto, octavo, duodecimo, mosquito, canto, grotto, solo, rondo.*

50 The plural suffix *s* has arisen from dropping the vowel of the proper syllabic termination *es*, which is a modification of the Anglo-Saxon plural suffix *as*. The latter however was used only in masculine nouns. In Anglo-Saxon there were also other modes of forming the plural (see Appendix A), but the influence of Norman-French, in which *s* or *x* was the common plural suffix, led to their gradual disuse. When *as* was changed to *es* it long retained its syllabic force. Even in Spenser we find such forms as *woundes, cloudes, handes,* &c. (Koch.) In Middle English *ys* or *is* is often found for *es*.

51 Words which are not properly nouns, such as *aye, no, pro, con, extra, if,* &c., are sometimes used as substantives. Some writers form the plurals of these by adding *s* with the apostrophe before it (*'s*), as *aye's, no's, pro's,* &c.; others add *s* or *es* (*ayes, noes, ifs, buts, extras,* &c.). The latter mode is the more common, except perhaps in words ending in *o*. Some writers use an apostrophe in forming the plurals of proper names, as *the Percy's, the Smith's.*

52 **Second Mode.**—By adding *en*, as *ox*, *oxen*; *brother*, *brethren*; *child*, *children.**

The word *kine* (the plural of *cow*), also belongs to this class. There has been a change of the vowel sound besides the addition of the *en*. *Welkin*, the *cloud-covered sky*, is considered by some to be a plural of this class (German *die Wolken*, ' the clouds ').

53 **Third Mode.**—By changing the vowel sound of the word, as *tooth*, *teeth*; *mouse*, *mice*; *foot*, *feet*; *goose*, *geese*; *man*, *men.*†

54 Many Latin and Greek nouns are used in English without any change of form. The plurals of these words should be made in the same way as in the language from which they are taken. The following rules must be attended to in forming the plurals of such words :—

1. The termination *a* (in the singular) should be changed into *æ*, as *formula*, plural *formulæ*, [*minutia*] *minutiæ*.

2. The termination *us* should generally be changed into *i*, as *tumulus*, pl. *tumuli*; *radius*, pl. *radii*.

3. The termination *um* or *on* should be changed into *a*, as *animalculum*, pl. *animalcula*; *effluvium*, pl. *effluvia*; *phenomenon*, pl. *phenomena*; so *data*, *arcana*, *addenda*, *errata*, *strata*, *desiderata*.

4. The termination *sis* should generally be changed into *ses*; as *analysis*, pl. *anlyses*; *basis*, pl. *bases*; *axis*, pl. *axes*; *ellipsis*, pl *ellipses*.

5. The termination *ix* or *ex* should be changed into *ices*; as *radix*, pl. *radices*; *appendix*, pl. *appendices*.

6. The following forms should also be attended to :—

Sing.	Plur.	Sing.	Plur.
Genus	genera	Seraph (Heb.)	seraphim
Hiatus	hiatus	Bandit (Ital.)	banditti
Series	series	Beau (Fr.)	beaux
Species	species	Madame	mesdames
Superficies	superficies	Mister (*i.e.* Master)	messieurs
Cherub (Heb.)	cherubim	Miasma (Gr.)	miasmata

But if a foreign word has passed into common use, the plural may be formed in the usual English fashion. Thus we say *cherubs*, *seraphs*, *bandits*, *triumvirs*, *choruses*, *dogmas*.

Some Latin words have both a Latin and an English plural, as *appendices* and *appendixes*; *calices* and *calixes*; *vortices* and *vortexes*; *criteria* and *criterions*; *memoranda* and *memorandums*; *foci* and *focuses*; *fungi* and *funguses*. Occasionally these two plurals

---
* In *brethren* and *children* there is a modification of the vowel besides the addition of *en*. *Children* is a double plural, *childer* (A. S. *cildru*), being still used as a plural in Lancashire.

The second and third modes of forming the plural are restricted to a few nouns of Anglo-Saxon origin. Plurals in *-en* were more common in the older writers. Chaucer has *doughteren* and *sistren*. We find *shoon* (for *shoes*) in Shakspere (*Hamlet* iv. 5), *eyne* or *een* (for *eyes*) in Scott and Byron. *Assen*, *treen*, *been* occur in old writers. *Hosen* occurs in the Bible (*Dan.* iii. 21). *Kine* is possibly a double plural. The old plural of *cow* was *cy* or *cye*. *Kye* is still used in Scotch.

† The modified *o* in *women* happens to coincide with the original vowel sound of the word (§ 44).

differ in meaning, as *indexes* (of books) and *indices* (in algebra); *geniuses* (men of genius), *genii* (supernatural beings).

55   The word *die* has two plurals: *dies* (stamps for coining), and *dice* (small cubes used for gaming).

Penny has two plurals; *pennies* (a number of separate coins), and *pence* (used when we speak of a sum of money reckoned in that coin). The compounds *sixpence*, *ninepence*, &c., as the names of coins or of distinct sums, may have plurals made from them,—*sixpences*, &c.

The plural *brothers* is now used chiefly to express the ordinary family relationship. *Brethren* is used in a more metaphorical sense, to denote members of the same community.

Cloth has two plurals, *cloths* and *clothes* (garments). *Paths* drops the *e* of the suffix, but has the flat sound of the *s* and of the preceding consonant.

Shot takes a plural form only when it means the discharge of a missile.

56   Some nouns which were neuter and without plural suffix in Anglo-Saxon, are the same in the plural as the singular, as *sheep, deer, swine, neat* (*cattle*), *head,* (as in ten *head* of cattle), *yoke, year, pound;* also nouns expressing a quantity or number, or used in a collective sense, as *hundred-weight* ('the stone weighs ten *hundred-weight*'), *brace* ('he shot three *brace* of birds'), *pair, couple, dozen, gross* ('ten *gross* of buttons'), *couple, stone* ('he weighs eleven *stone*'), *fish** (meaning the race of fishes), *fowl,* sometimes *people* (meaning a number of persons), *sail* ('ten *sail* of the line'), and sometimes *fathom* and *mile* ('thirty *fathom*,' 'ten *mile*.' *Shaksp.*). With these may be compared the compound attributives in 'a three-foot rule;' 'a three-penny book'; 'a four-wheel chaise;' 'an engine of a hundred-horse power;' 'a five-pound note,' &c. *Horse* and *foot*, as abbreviations of *horse-soldiers*, and *foot-soldiers*, have become collective nouns, as have *shot* ('grape-shot') and *cannon*.

57   Names of materials or natural productions, such as *wheat, sugar, timber*, may be used in the plural number when different varieties of the articles are spoken of; as *raw sugars*, *French wines*.

The idea of repetition or succession is perhaps involved in such plurals as 'the *dews* of heaven,' 'the *rains* of winter,' 'the *waters* of the Nile.'

58   Names of sciences ending in *ics* (as *mechanics*) are plural as regards their form, but are frequently used as if they were singular.†

---

* Also the names of several sorts of fish, as *cod, salmon, plaice, trout, pike, perch, mackerel,* &c. On the other hand *shark, whale, sole, herring, eel, turbot, brill,* &c., form plurals in the ordinary way.

† Some have supposed that the different use of the singular *logic* and the plural *mathematics*, &c., has arisen from the fact that in the former we have adopted the Greek singular ἡ λογική (τέχνη), and in the latter the neuter plural τὰ μαθηματικά. This explanation of the use of the singular is, of course, correct, but as applied to the plural it is far-fetched and unnecessary. It is doubtful whether the first man who spoke of having the *rheumatics* thought he was representing the plural τὰ ῥευματικά. When adjectives are converted into substantives, it is the tendency of our language to use the plural form. A man talks of having *the rheumatics* just as in country districts, they talk of having *the dumps* or *the dismals* (Halliwell, *Dict.*) "Let them die that age and *sullens* have." (*Shakspere, R. II.* ii. 1). English freely allows the use of adjectives as substantives, provided the plural be employed, as *eatables, valuables, greens, sweets, news,* &c.

59 It is a mistake to use a plural of the word *folk*, as it is a noun of multitude, and means *several persons*. We should write, *folk say*, not *folks say*. "He laid his hands upon a few sick folk" (*Mark* vi. 5). Still, the plural use is very old. It is found in Chaucer and Maundeville.

60 The words *riches* (Fr. *richesse*), *eaves* (A. S. *efese*), and *alms* (A. S. *ælmesse*, from 'ελεημοσύνη), are not really plural nouns, but are generally used as if they were in the plural number. *News* is plural in form, but is used as if of the singular number. There is no sufficient reason why *means* should ever be treated as if it were of the singular number, though several good writers use such expressions as *a means*. We now use the singular *pea* and the plural *peas*; but *pease* (Lat. *pisum*, A. S. *pise*) has now a collective sense. *Summons* (old French *semonce*, or *semonse*), is properly singular. *Amends, gallows, sessions, shambles*, are plurals, but are commonly treated as singulars. *Small-pox* is plural (singular *pock*), but is used as a singular. *Odds* is used both ways, but usually as a plural. We always say *much* (not *many*) *pains*, but *pains* is usually followed by a plural verb; "your pains are registered" (*Shakspere*).

61 Abstract nouns, from the nature of the idea which they denote, do not generally admit of the plural number. But when they are used to denote *varieties* or *different instances* of the quality referred to, they may have plurals, as *affinities, negligences*. On the other hand, some nouns have no singular, as *scissors, bellows, breeches, tongs, annals, dregs, entrails, hustings, measles, billiards, oats*, &c. The things which they represent are double or multiform. The singular *wage* is a provincial form. The plural does not always involve exactly a repetition of the idea conveyed by the singular, as *compass, compasses; matin, matins; vesper, vespers; pain, pains; corn, corns; iron, irons*. Many plurals have a secondary signification which the singular has not, as *parings, hangings, leavings, sweepings*, &c., which denote the product of the action referred to; *effects* (property), *grounds* (dregs), *respects, parts* (capacity), *stocks, stays, spectacles, letters* (literature), *draughts, returns, gripes, grains, lists* (for tournaments), the *Furies, lights, returns, shrouds* (of a ship), &c.

62 In compound nouns like *father-in-law, hanger-on*, consisting of a noun followed by a definitive prepositional phrase, the mark of plurality is attached to the *noun* part of the compound,—*fathers-in-law, hangers-on*. In imperfectly fused compounds, where an adjective follows a noun, such as *court-martial, knight-errant*, the plural *s* is attached to the noun,—*courts-martial, knights-errant*. Nouns compounded of *full*, where the fusion is complete, have the *s* at the end, as *handfuls, mouthfuls*. All other compound nouns have the *s* at the end. (See § 300.) It is disputed whether the plural of Miss Smith should be "The Miss Smiths," or "The Misses Smith." The latter is correct, though now regarded as rather pedantic. The former is commonly used, and must now be regarded as a well-established form. It is perhaps right, on the supposition that "Miss-Smith" is to be regarded as a compound name. So "the two Doctor Thomsons" (*Goldsmith*). The words *twelvemonth* and *fortnight*, used as singulars, are relics of a usage which was once quite common, as "this seven year" (*Shakspere's Much Ado*, &c.) Even if the noun was

in the plural,* the compound was treated as a singular (as we still say, 'a sixpence,' or a 'twopence'); as "a twenty bokes"† (*Chaucer*); "a tedious twelve years" (*Fletcher*): "this fourteen years" (*Measure for Measure*).

Case.

63   Things of which we speak by means of nouns stand in various relations to other things, and to actions and attributes. Consequently, when these relations are expressed in language, nouns have various relations to other words in the sentences in which they are employed. In the sentence, "The horse eats the man's hay," *horse* stands for that which does the action described by the verb; *hay* stands for that upon which the action is performed; *man's* is used to indicate to whom the hay belongs. The words *horse* and *hay* have each a certain connexion with the verb *eats*, and *man's* has a certain connexion with the noun *hay*. Some languages have several different terminations which nouns are made to assume, to indicate the various relations in which they stand to other words. These different forms of the noun are called *cases*. The word *case* (Lat. *casus*) means *falling*. The ancient Greek grammarians took a fancy to represent that form of a noun in which it is used when it is the subject of a sentence, by an upright line, and compared the other forms to lines *falling* or *sloping off* from this upright line at different angles. Hence a collection of the various forms which a noun might assume was called the *declension* or *sloping down* of the noun. What we call the Nominative Case was called the *upright case*.

64   *Case* may be defined to be "the form in which a noun or pronoun is used, in order to show the relation in which it stands to some other word in the sentence."

---

* This usage still prevails in the case of multiples. We say 'twice five is ten,' because 'twice five' is treated as a single sum, though the full phrase of course is "twice five things are ten things." The *amount* is considered rather than the mode of its formation. When the latter idea is prominent, the plural is better, as 'twice five make ten!' The use of the plural *times* does not affect the question, because in 'three times ten is thirty,' *times* is not the subject of the sentence. *Three times* is an adverbial adjunct of the numeral *ten*, like *twice* or *thrice*.

† It must not be forgotten however that in Anglo-Saxon *twenty*, *thirty*, &c were substantives, (like *hundred* and *thousand*), and took a genitive case after them. 'Twenty men' was 'a twenty of men.' Also combinations like 'three and twenty,' 'nine and thirty,' were treated as compound substantives, and preceded by the indefinite article. The substantive use of the adjective numerals may have been introduced through a false analogy. In a similar way we may perhaps account for such genitives as, 'for forty's sake,' 'for ten's sake.'

The process of forming the different cases of a noun is called *inflection*.

In English there are now* three cases, the Nominative Case, the Possessive Case, and the Objective Case. †

In some of the pronouns these three cases are all different; in nouns the nominative and objective cases are alike. (See § 83.)

65 The **nominative case** is that form in which a noun (or pronoun) is used when it is the subject of a verb ; that is, when it stands for that about which something is said by means of a verb. In the sentence, "Men build houses," the noun *men* stands for that about which something is said by means of the verb *build*. The noun *men*, therefore, is in the nominative case, because it is the subject of the verb *build*. In the sentence, "The boy was struck by his brother," the noun *boy* stands for that about which something is said by means of the verb *was struck*, and therefore the noun *boy* is in the nominative case, because it is the subject of the verb *was struck*. If the verb of the sentence be in the active voice, the subject of the verb stands for the doer of the action described by the verb. If the verb be in the passive voice, the subject of the verb stands for the object of the action described by the verb. In either case the subject stands for that about which something is said by means of the verb.

---

* English was anciently a much more inflected language than it is now. When it was in its Anglo-Saxon stage, nouns and pronouns had five cases, answering to the Nominative, Genitive, Dative, Accusative, and Ablative of Latin, the dative and ablative being often alike in nouns. There were also various separate declensions of Nouns (see Appendix). In modern English (as in French) the use of case-endings has to a great extent been replaced by the use of prepositions. The function of a preposition was originally to give greater definiteness to the somewhat vague idea expressed by a case-ending. Thus, in Greek the genitive case denoted *from*, the dative *at*, the accusative, *to*. The preposition παρά conveyed the idea of *alongside of*, and so the genitive preceded by παρά meant *from the side of* something; the dative preceded by παρά meant *at the side of* something; the accusative with παρά meant *to the side of* something. Similarly in Latin the accusative case marked *motion to* some object. If motion *to the inside* of the thing was to be expressed, the vague notion expressed by the accusative was defined by prefixing the preposition *in* ; if motion *to the outside* only was implied, *ad* was prefixed. The use of all prepositions *originated* in this way. They did not *govern* cases, i.e., *require* certain cases to be used after them, but were prefixed to cases to give greater definiteness to the idea already expressed *by the case itself*. It will easily be seen how, in course of time, the case-ending in the word that followed a preposition would become superfluous, when prepositions were uniformly employed before the same cases. As an accusative always came after *ad*, and an ablative after *de*, it became needless to put any case-ending at all ; the preposition itself became all-important and sufficient. But though in modern English and French a preposition followed by a noun is the *substitute* for a case, it is wrong to call that combination itself *a case*. If a preposition and noun together make *a case*, it follows necessarily that there are as many cases as there are prepositions.

† *Nominative* comes from the Latin *nomino*, 'I name ;' *possessive*, from the Latin *possideo*, 'I possess ;' *objective*, from the Latin *objicio*, 'I throw towards.'

66 The noun in the nominative case is the answer to the question made by putting *who* or *what* before the verb. Thus in the preceding sentence: "*Who* build houses?" Ans. *Men*." "*Who* was struck?" Ans. *The boy*." *

67 The **possessive case** is that form of a noun (or pronoun) which shows that something belongs to the person or thing for which it stands. Thus in "I saw John's book," the possessive case *John's* shows that something (namely a book) *belongs to John*. "A *day's* journey" is a journey that *belongs to a day*, by taking place in it, or occupying the whole of it.

68 The noun in the possessive is in the attributive relation to the noun which stands for what is possessed. (§ 362, 3.)

69 As what is possessed must be a person or a thing of some kind, a noun in the possessive case can only be in the attributive relation to a *noun*.†

70 The possessive case in the singular number, and in those plurals which end in any other letter than *s*, is formed by adding the letter *s* with an apostrophe before it (thus, '*s*) to the nominative case; as, *John's*, *men's*, *geese's*. In those plurals which end in *s* the possessive case is indicated in writing by placing the apostrophe after the *s*, as, "the *birds'* feathers." Formerly the plural in *s* was used as a genitive or possessive without further mark, as 'Cristes lore and his *apostles* twelve He taught' (*Chaucer*, C. T. 529).

71 Sometimes the possessive case in the singular number of nouns that end in *s*, *x*, or *ce* is merely marked by placing an apostrophe after the word; as, *Æneas' son*; "Look, in this place ran Cassius' dagger through." But this practice is now nearly obsolete, except in a few common instances; as, "for conscience' sake," "for goodness' sake." It is found in Anglo-Saxon, as 'Urias wif;' 'Mattheus gerecydnys.'

72 In Anglo-Saxon the genitive termination *-es* (for which at a somewhat later period *-is* or *-ys* was often used) was restricted

---

* Such expressions as, "The noun boy is the *nominative case* to the verb," are incorrect. *Case* is equivalent to *form*. Now a *noun* is not a *form*, nor would there be any sense in talking of the *nominative form to a* verb. The case of a noun is not its relation to a verb, but the form which indicates that relation. Of course this fundamental distinction between a noun and the form of a noun is not affected by the accident that in English the nominative and accusative cases of nouns are alike. The incorrectness of the mode of speaking above referred to is rendered evident in an amusing manner by the mistake which beginners in Latin frequently make of explaining the accusative case which precedes an infinitive mood by saying that the noun in the accusative is the *nominative* to the verb.

† This noun is sometimes omitted. Thus we say, "He went to the baker's," i. e., to the baker's *shop*. "A picture of my father's" means "a picture of my father's pictures," or "one of my father's pictures." "A picture of my father," on the other hand, means "a painted representation of my father." See, however, § 168, *note*.

to the singular, and was not the only genitive suffix. (See Appendix A.) It formed a separate syllable.* The syllabic -*es* is often found in Spenser, and traces of it occur even in Shakspere, as in "To show his teeth as white as whales bone" (*Love's L.L.*, v. 2); "Swifter than the moones sphere" (*Mids. N. D.*, ii. 1); "You sent me for a ropes end as soon" (*Com. of E.*, xxiv. 1).

73   The apostrophe in the possessive case singular marks that the vowel of the syllabic suffix has been lost. We still see the vowel in *Wednesday*, *i.e.*, *Wodenesday*. It is therefore an unmeaning process to put the apostrophe after the plural *s* (as *birds'*), because no vowel has been dropped there.† In such possessives as *Thomas's* the vowel is sounded in speaking, but omitted in writing. This genitive or possessive termination *es* or *'s*, was not affixed to feminine nouns in Anglo-Saxon, except in adverbial genitives, as *nihtes* 'by night.' We still say *Lady-day* and not *Lady's-day*. (See Morris, *Spec.*, p. xix.)

74   The *general* use of the apostrophe is comparatively modern. Milton did not use it. We find it however already employed by Robert of Gloucester, who also uses -*es* or -*ys*.

75   In the case of a complex name, the termination of the possessive case is only affixed to the last of the names; as "Julius Cæsar's death;" "John Thomas Smith's father." It is even usual to carry out the same principle when *one thing* is possessed by several persons; as, "John, William, and Mary's uncle;" that is, the uncle of John, William, and Mary. This practice, however, cannot be defended on grammatical principles. In compound nouns like *father-in-law*, or when a noun is followed by determinative adjuncts of any kind, as 'Henry the Eighth,' 'The Queen of England,' 'Smith the baker, &c.' the possessive sign *'s* is placed at the end,‡ as 'My father-in-law's house,' 'the Queen of England's name,' &c. We no longer allow such constructions as "It is Othello's pleasure, our noble and valiant general." The Anglo-Saxon usage was to put both nouns in the genitive.

---

* It is almost incredible how many persons have been induced to adopt the silly notion that the *'s* of the possessive case is an abbreviation for *his*, so that *the king's crown* is *the king his crown*. The word *his* is itself the possessive case of *he*; so that, on this principle, his=he+his=he+he+his=he+he+he+his, and so on *ad infinitum*. Moreover, *Mary's bonnet* must be explained to mean *Mary his bonnet*. The mistake is so stupid, and shows such blank ignorance of the principles of grammatical forms, that one wonders how the notion could have originated. It is quite true, however, that the use of *his* after a noun, in place of a simple possessive suffix, is of very early origin and was widely prevalent. Some (as Ben Jonson) suppose that the alteration of the possessive termination -*es* into -*is*, and its pronunciation as a distinct syllable led to the usage. It is more probable that it arose from a pleonastic use of the pronoun, which is found also in the other cases, as "He Moyses and King Salomon" (*Chaucer*, 10564) " the sepulchre of him Darius" (*ib.* 6080); "The nobles they are fled" (*Shaksp. Rich. II.*, ii. 2).

† The plural *books* has just as good a right to an apostrophe as the possessive singular, a vowel having been omitted. The Anglo-Saxon termination was -*as*.

‡ This power of treating an inflected form or a complex phrase as though it were a single declinable word, and adding inflections to it, is very remarkable in English. Thus in Anglo-Saxon the genitives of the personal pronouns were treated as pronominal adjectives and declined; an inflected infinitive was used after *to* to form the gerund (see *Gerund* § 197), and even such a compound as *nâthwylc* (ne wat hwylc = I know not which), has suffixes like an ordinary adjective, as " in niŷsele nâthwylcum," ' in I-know-not-what dwelling.'

76. The possessive *'s* is the only case-suffix of nouns that has come down to us. The letter *s*, as the characteristic of the genitive suffix, is of general occurrence in the Aryan languages.

77. The meaning of the possessive case may be expressed by means of the preposition *of*, with the objective case after it. Thus, for "My father's *house*," we may say, "The house of my father." But the possessive case must not be substituted for the preposition *of*, unless the *of* implies 'belonging to,' in some one of the senses of that phrase.

78. In old English there is a use of the possessive case which has now disappeared, and which corresponds to what is called the *objective genitive* in Latin (as *amor pecuniæ*, "the love of money"). Thus in the English version of the Bible, *Thy fear* is used for *the fear of Thee*. In Shakspere *his taking off* means *the taking off of him*.

The possessive inflection *'s* may be added to nouns that denote persons, animals, or things that are personified, as "John's book;" "the cat's tail;" "reason's voice." Also when the noun is commonly preceded by the definite article, as "the sun's light;" "the earth's surface;" "the lightning's glare." Also in some idiomatical phrases, as with the word *sake*, "For his oath's sake;" "For thy name's sake;" "A day's journey." Poetry admits this possessive much more frequently than prose.

79. **The objective case** is that form in which a noun or pronoun is used when it stands for the object of the action spoken of in some verb, or when it comes after a preposition. In the sentence, "The stone struck the boy," the act of striking is spoken of as being directed to a certain object, namely, *boy*. The word *boy*, which stands for the object of the action, is called the *object of the verb*, and is in the objective case. It is in the Objective Relation to the verb (§ 366). In the sentence, "John was riding in a coach," the noun *coach*, which comes after the preposition *in*, is in the objective case.

80. The objective case is often used, like the Latin dative, to denote the *indirect object* of a verb, that is to say, it stands for some person or thing indirectly affected by the action, but not the direct object of it; as "Tell *me* a tale;" "Rob *me* the exchequer." In such cases the word in the objective case is in the Adverbial Relation to the verb (§ 372, 4).

81. When a noun in the objective case is the object of a verb, the noun in the objective case answers to the question formed by putting *whom* or *what* before the verb and its subject. As in the example given above, "Whom or what did the stone strike?" *Ans.* "The boy."

82. In nouns the objective case is the same in form as the nominative. The noun which is the subject of the verb, and therefore in the nominative case, is generally put before the verb (in assertions, not in questions): the noun which is the object of the verb is generally put

after the verb. These rules, however, are by no means invariable. The former is frequently disregarded in poetry, or when an adverb or adverbial phrase is used before the verb and its subject; as, "On rushed the foe;" "By the wayside sat an old man." The second rule is also sometimes neglected for the sake of emphasis: as in such a sentence as "The two brothers were equally guilty; John he punished, but William he forgave."

83 Strictly speaking, it ought to be said that *nouns* in English have only two cases or forms; one (such as *man*, *dog*) for which a new name would have to be invented, used indifferently for the subject and for the object of verbs; the other, the possessive case. But, as pronouns have three cases, and in other languages it is very common for the nominative and accusative cases to be alike, it does not seem worth while to alter the commonly received arrangement.*

84 The following are examples of the declension of nouns in English:—

	Singular.	Plural.
Nominative Case	Man	Men.
Possessive Case	Man's	Men's
Objective Case	Man	Men.
Nominative Case	Father	Fathers.
Possessive Case	Father's	Fathers'.
Objective Case	Father	Fathers.

ADJECTIVE.

85 When we think or speak of anything, we frequently have in mind not only the thing itself, but some quality or attribute that it possesses, or some fact or circumstance respecting it. We may think of a *rose*, and at the same time have in our minds the idea that it is *red*, and so speak of it as a *red rose*. We may be speaking about a *child*, and at the same time connect with it the idea that it is a child just spoken of or pointed to, and so speak of it as *this child*. We may speak of some birds, and at the same time

---

* The endeavour to distinguish a *dative* and an *accusative* case in modern English, is at variance with the genius and history of the language. We see from the pronouns (see Appendix A), that the form which maintained its ground was the dative, which first ousted the ablative, and usurped its functions, and then did the same with the accusative. It is unphilosophical to re-introduce grammatical distinctions which a language has ceased to recognise. One might as well attempt to restore the Locative Case to Latin, or the Ablative to Greek. As there is but one *form* (*him*, *her*, *them*, &c.) to denote both the direct and the indirect object, not only is nothing gained, but an important piece of linguistic history is obscured by having two names for it. It is much better to use the common name *objective*. It is true that there are two *uses* of the objective case, but that is another matter. A *case* is not the same thing as the *relation* that it expresses, any more than a *noun* is the same as the *thing* which it names.

indicate that there are *three* of them, and so speak of them, as *three birds*. The words that are used in this way with nouns are called Adjectives.*

86   *Definition.* An adjective is a word used with a noun to denote some quality, attribute, or fact, which we connect in thought with that for which the noun stands, so that the adjective and noun together form a compound description of that which we have in our thoughts.†

In the phrase *a white horse*, the word *white* is an adjective. It denotes a certain quality of the horse.

In the sentence, *I saw two men*, the word *two* is an adjective. It points out a fact respecting the men, that they were two in number.

In the sentence, *I love this child*, the word *this* is an adjective. It points out, with regard to the child spoken of, the fact that it answers to a certain designation made either by words or by pointing.

87   When it is attached directly to the noun to which it refers, an adjective is said to be used *attributively;* as "a *red ball;*" "a *bird flying* through the air;" "*which* hand will you have?" "*what* man said that?" When an adjective is connected with a noun by means of some part of the verb *be* (or some other verb of incomplete predication, such as *become*), it is said to be used *predicatively;* as, "the ball is *red*," "the bird was *flying*." All true adjectives can be used in both ways.

In combinations like *teaspoon, apple-tree, cannon ball*, the first word is not an adjective. It does not *express* an attributive idea, it merely *hints* at one, leaving the mind of the hearer to develop the idea for itself. The two nouns form a *compound name*. Hence those most commonly used have come to be written as one word.

88   As an adjective is not the *name* of a separate object of thought, an adjective can never be used as the subject of a sentence, or as the object of a verb, or be governed by a preposition.

89   Adjectives may be distributed into the following classes: —Qualitative Adjectives, Quantitative Adjectives, and Demonstrative or Determinative Adjectives.

90   1. **Qualitative Adjectives,** *i.e.*, adjectives which denote

---

* Latin *adjectivus*, "capable of being annexed or attached to something," from *adjectus*, "annexed or added to something."

† It is a mistake to call an adjective the *name* of a quality or attribute. Before we can name anything, it must be made a separate object of thought, and the *name* of anything that we can think or speak about is a *noun*. *Whiteness* is the *name* of a certain quality, and is a *noun*. *White* denotes the quality, but does not name it.

Beware of the absurdity of saying that "an adjective denotes the quality of a noun." A *noun* is a *name*. When we speak of a *red rose*, the adjective *red* does not denote a quality of the *name* rose, but of the *thing* for which the name stands. The blunder is very obvious, but is nevertheless committed in most English Grammars.

some *quality* or *attribute* (from the Latin *qualis*, ' of which sort'), as *virtuous, high, white, beautiful, such,* same, only.†* The verbal adjectives called Participles belong to this class.

91   2. **Quantitative Adjectives**, *i.e.* adjectives which denote *how much* or *how many* of that for which the noun stands we have in our thoughts (Latin *quantus* 'how great'). This class includes—

a. The Indefinite Article *an* (§ 121) and the Cardinal Numeral Adjectives, *one, two, three,* &c. (The words *hundred, thousand, million,* like *pair* and *dozen,* are nouns. They may be used with the indefinite article before them.‡)

b. The words *all,§ any, some, half, many, few, little, less, least, enough, much, more, most, both, several, whole, none* or *no* (=*not any*).

Examples. 'All men are mortal.' 'He rode all day long.' 'He sleeps all night.' 'He travelled all the next day.' 'Some men prefer this.' 'Give me some wine.' 'We had a half holiday.' 'Wait half an hour.' 'Few persons will believe that.' 'He has but little wealth, and less wisdom.' 'He has not given me the least trouble.' 'I have had enough wine.' 'Give him money enough.' 'I have much pleasure in doing this.' 'He has more sense than his neighbour.' 'Most persons admire valour.' 'He had both eyes put out.' 'They are both in fault' 'He has eaten a whole apple.' 'Make no noise.' 'Give none offence.' 'Give none occasion to the adversary.'

92   Some of these words are also used as substantives:—

All. 'All is lost.'

Few. 'I have a *few*‖ shillings.' The phrase *a many* is equally legitimate, but is obsolete. In A.S. *mænigeo,* 'multitude,' was a noun.

---

* When *such* is used with a noun which is preceded by the indefinite article, the article comes between the adjective and the noun; as, *such an event, such a sad story.*

† In such phrases as ' my only son,' *only* is always either an adjective used attributively, or an adverb. In "There are only four persons present;" "He only was saved;" "He is only pretending," *only* is an adverb. *Only* is never by any chance used *instead of a noun.* It is therefore absurd to call it a *pronoun. Only* (A.S. ænlic = one-like) is a derivative from *an* = *one*.

‡ In Anglo-Saxon they were followed by the genitive case, as though we said ' A hundred of sheep,' &c. (See App. A.)

§ The words *all, half, little, less, least, much, more, most, enough,* are also used as adverbs; as "*all round* the world;" "*half afraid*;" "I am but *little encouraged* by that;" "he is *less careful* than his brother;" "he is the *least* ambitious man that I know;" "he is *much more studious* than he used to be;" "he is *most anxious* to succeed;" "he is *tall enough.*"

‖ *Few* used as an adjective involves a negation of there being *many*. "He has few friends." *A few,* when *few* is used substantively, involves a negation that there are *none;* it implies *some, but not many. Little* is used in a similar way. In Anglo-Saxon *few* (feáwa, feá) was used in the singular for ' a small quantity.' Scotchmen still say ' a few porridge.'

D

84 ETYMOLOGY—ADJECTIVE.

Little, less, least; as, 'Little was said.' 'Less will not suffice.' 'Least said, soonest mended.' 'Give me a little of that.'
Enough. 'Enough is as good as a feast.'
Much, more, most. 'Much has been said, but more remains to be told.'
Whole. 'He spent the whole of the day in playing.'
None. 'None are altogether without hope.'

93 *Little, less,* and *least,* when they are used before a noun and are themselves preceded by an article, are qualitative adjectives; as, 'a little boy.' The comparative of *little,* in this sense, when it is used attributively, is often written *lesser;* as, 'the *lesser* evil of the two.'

Least, in the qualitative sense, is nearly obsolete, except in one or two phrases; as, 'Not in the *least* degree.'

Many may be used with a noun in the singular,* provided the indefinite article be placed before the noun; as, 'Many a man has lost his life by these means.'

94 *All, no, none, some, enough,* may denote either *number* or *quantity;* as, 'all men,' 'all the way,' 'some pens,' 'some beer,' 'no money,' 'no friends,' &c. When *all* denotes quantity, the definite article is commonly placed between it and the noun. 'All day' and 'all night' are exceptions.

The use of *none* before a noun is now old-fashioned. It differs from *no* as *mine* differs from *my;* i.e., *no* is used when the noun which it relates to is expressed, and *none* when the noun is not expressed; as, 'I have *no* horse, and my neighbour has *none.*'

95 In Anglo-Saxon *none* (nân = ne ân, 'not one') was used as a singular both adjectively and substantively with reference (not to *quantity,* but) to *number.* Its substantive use as a singular is becoming obsolete, but was formerly common, as in "None but the brave deserves the fair" (*Dryden*). *No* is a shortened form of *none* as *my* is of *mine.* The combination *no one* is pleonastic, for *no* by itself means *no one.*

96 The quantitative numeral *one* is often used substantively, meaning a single individual of some kind already mentioned. When thus used, it may even have a plural. 'Give me another pen, this is a bad *one;*' or, 'these are bad *ones.*'

97 *Both* is used when, in speaking of two things, attention is directed to the fact that *neither of them is excluded* from the predication (Gothic *baioths: A.S. begen, bá,* or *bu,* sometimes compounded with *twá,—bátwá.* In Old English we find *both two.* The origin of the *-th* is obscure).

98 **3. Demonstrative or Definitive Adjectives** (Latin *demonstro,* 'I point out') are adjectives which point out which thing or things we are speaking of, out of the class of things denoted by a common noun.—To this class belong
a. The Definite Article *the.*

---

* So *multus* and *plurimus* in Latin. "Plurimus in Junonis honorem aptum dicet equis Argos."—*Horace*

l. The so-called Adjective Pronouns, or Pronominal Adjectives, comprising the following classes:—
1. The Demonstrative Pronouns *this, these, that, those.*
2. The Interrogative and Relative Pronouns *which, what* and *whether.*
3. The Distributive Pronouns *each, every, either, neither.*
4. The Indefinite Pronouns *any, other, some.*
5. The Possessive Pronouns *my, thy, his,* &c.
6. The Reflective Pronoun *self.*

c. The Ordinal Numerals, *first, second, third,* &c.

In speaking we do not always express all that we have in our thoughts, when what is expressed shows clearly enough what is to be understood as *meant*, though not expressed. One result of this is, that adjectives are very often used without having the nouns to which they relate expressed. Thus, "The *good* are happy;" *i.e.*, good people. "Blessed are the *meek;*" *i.e.*, meek persons. Adjectives are then said to be used substantively. When speaking of *persons,* the singular is now avoided, though it used to be common, as "The poor is hated . . . but the rich hath many friends" (*Prov.* xiv. 20); "There will a worse come in his place" (*Shaksp.*) This use of Adjectives in the singular is now restricted to *general* or *abstract* ideas, as "The sublime," "The beautiful." In most cases adjectives used substantively must be preceded by a demonstrative (*the* or *these*) or a possessive, as 'our dearest;' but they may be used without the definite article when they are in pairs of opposites, as "I will follow you through *thick and thin*"; "For *better or worse*"; "*High and low, rich and poor* together." Also in a few phrases, as "He has this character *in common* with his neighbours"; "*In general* he avoids such mistakes"; "He recommended this *in particular*"; "*At least*"; "*At random*"; "*In future.*"

100 This use of adjectives is especially common with the quantitative and demonstrative adjectives. Thus, "*Many* (persons) are called, but *few* (persons) are chosen;" "*All* (men, or persons) heard, and *some* obeyed;" "I know *that;*" "I heard *what** you said." (See § 88.)

101 The preceding use of adjectives must be distinguished from the cases in which certain adjectives are used so completely as substan-

---

* When *what* and *which, that* and *this,* are used substantively, they are only of the neuter gender, unless they are connected by the verb *is* with a substantive, as "Which is the king?" "This is he," "That is the man." *These* and *those* may be of any gender.

tives, that they have the ordinary inflections of nouns. The adjectives which admit of this are—

1. National names, such as *German, Italian, Roman*. We say, "A Roman's rights"; "The Germans crossed the Rhine"; "The Italians' love of art." Those names which end in a sibilant sound (*Dutch, Chinese*, &c.) do not admit of inflection.

2. Names denoting the members of a sect or party; as Christian, Lutheran, Stoic, Jacobite, &c.

3. Various Latin comparatives, as *senior, junior, inferior*, &c., with the Anglo-Saxon *elder* and *better*.

4. Various adjectives denoting persons, and of French or Latin origin, as *native, mortal, noble, saint, criminal, ancient, modern*, &c., together with a very few of Anglo-Saxon origin, as *black, white, heathen*.

5. Adjectives used as substantives *in the plural only*, as *vitals, intestines, eatables, moveables, valuables, greens, the blues, sweets*, &c. (See § 58, note).

6. The adjective *other*. Some writers also use *either's* and *neither's* in the possessive singular.

102 Adjectives, in modern English, are not declinable words. With the exception of the words *this* and *that*, which have plural forms, *these* and *those*, and *self*, which has a plural *selves*, no adjective in English indicates gender, number, or case, by means of inflection.

103 The Anglo-Saxon adjectives were inflected to mark gender, number, and case. (See App. A.) By the time of Chaucer the various suffixes had been reduced to an inflectional *e* in the plural, especially of adjectives of one syllable, and of adjectives used substantively, and at the end of adjectives preceded by demonstratives and possessives.*

Comparison of Adjectives.

104 Adjectives admit of three varieties of form, called Degrees of Comparison. These are the Positive Degree, the Comparative Degree, and the Superlative Degree.

105 The Positive Degree of an adjective is the adjective in its simple form, used to point out some quality or attribute of that which we speak about, as "A *black* cat," "A *fine* day."

106 When we wish to indicate that one thing,† or one group of things, possesses the same quality or attribute as another, but in a greater degree, a change is made in the form of the

---

* Shakspere has preserved a solitary specimen of the old genitive plural suffix *er* (A.S.-*ra*) in the word *alderliefest* (for *allerliefest*, *d* being an offgrowth of *l* before *r*), meaning 'dearest of all' (*II. King H. VI.*, i. 1). Compare the German *allerliebst*. In Chaucer we find *alderlevest, alderfirst*, as well as *youre aller* = ' of you all.' In *olden, en* is perhaps a relic of the ancient inflection.

† The word *thing* means generally whatever we can *think* about, *i.e.*, make a distinct object of thought, including *persons*, as well as what we commonly denominate things.

simple adjective to mark this. The syllable *er** is added, before which a mute *e* is dropped, as "My knife is *sharper* than yours;" "John's book is pretty, but mine is *prettier* †;" "Your parents are *richer* than mine;" "This soldier is *taller* than those;" "These books are *larger* than that one." One thing may be compared either with *one* other, or with *a group of several;* and a group of things may be compared either with another group or with a single thing. Also a thing may be compared with *itself under other circumstances,* as "John is stouter than he was last year."

107 The Comparative Degree of an adjective is that form of it by means of which we show that one thing, or set of things, possesses a certain quality or attribute in a greater degree than another thing, or set of things.

108 It must not be imagined that the comparative degree expresses the existence of more of a certain quality in an object than the positive degree does. If we say, "William is a clever boy," and "John is cleverer than Thomas," we are not to infer that *cleverer* in the second case implies the existence of more cleverness in John than the adjective *clever* implies in the case of William. The fact may be that William is cleverer than John. The positive degree is used in the one case simply because William is not compared with any one else; and the comparative degree is used in the second case because John is compared with Thomas.

Even the use of an adjective in the positive degree often implies some standard of comparison; as when we use such words as *high, great,* &c. But this results only from the meaning of the words themselves, and does not affect the grammatical use of the words.

Some adjectives which are comparatives in origin are now used as positives, though they still involve the idea of *relation* in space or time. Such are *former, latter, elder, upper, inner,* &c.

109 When one *attribute* is compared with another in respect of degree, *than* must be used without an ellipsis of the verb following, as 'It is broader than it is long.' We cannot say 'It is broader than long.' But the ellipsis is allowable when *more* is used, as 'He is more witty than wise.' Such a sentence as 'Your company is fairer than honest' (*Shakspere, M. for M.,* iv. 3) is not correct. In Latin and Greek two comparatives were used, as *verior quam gratior,* 'More true than agreeable.' Also *magis* was used (like *more* in English) with two positives.

---

* In Anglo-Saxon the suffix was *-er* or *-or;* in declension dropping the vowel, and inflected according to the weak declension. The letter *r* is the softened form of a sibilant. In Gothic the suffix is *-iza*. With this we may compare the Latin comparative suffix *-ios* (Key *Lat. Gr.* § 241), the *s* of which is softened to *r* in declension. It is an ancient Aryan suffix. (Sansc. *tyas*). Another Aryan comparative suffix, *tar* or *ter,* which we get in the Greek -τερος, appears also in Latin and English, to indicate that one thing is viewed in its relation to some other, as *alter* 'one of two'; *uter* 'which of two'; *neuter:* other, either, neither, whether.

† When *-er* and *-est* are added to adjectives ending in *y,* the *y* is changed, or left unaltered, in the same way as when the plural *-es* is added. (See § 49).

110 The Superlative* Degree of an adjective is that form of it which shows that a certain thing, or group of things, possesses the attribute denoted by the adjective *in a greater degree than any other among several of which it is one*. It is formed by adding *st* or *est*† to the adjective in the positive degree; as, *greatest, largest*. Thus, of several boys in a group, we may say, " John is *the tallest*." Of the countries of Europe we may say, " England is *the wealthiest*."

111 If we say "John is *taller* than all the other boys in the class," we express the same relation as to height between John and the rest as if we say, " John is *the tallest* boy in the class." But in the former case, John is considered *apart from* the other boys of the class, so that the two objects which we have in mind are *John* and *the other boys in the class*. When the superlative degree is used, John is considered as *one of the group* of boys compared with each other.

note

112 When two things forming one group are compared, it is usual and proper to employ the comparative degree, as, " This line is *the longer* of the two." Nevertheless, as the two things do form one group, there is some excuse for saying "*the longest* of the two."

113 Many adjectives, from the nature of the ideas which they express, cannot have comparative and superlative degrees; as, *right, left, wrong, square, triangular*, together with most of the quantitative adjectives, and all the demonstrative adjectives. Sometimes, however, adjectives are used in a sense which falls short of their strict meaning, and then they admit of degrees of comparison which would not otherwise be tolerable. For example, *extreme, perfect, chief*. As when we say, " This specimen is *more perfect* than that"; " He died in the *extremest* misery "; " The *chiefest* among ten thousand."

114 In the case of some adjectives, the degrees of comparison are marked by what are commonly termed *irregular* forms. These are the following:

Positive.	Comparative.	Superlative.
Good	better‡	best
Little§	less	least

---

* Superlative (Lat. *superlativus*, from *superlatus*) means "lifting up above." The superlative degree *lifts* the thing that it is applied to *above* all the rest of the group.

† In Anglo-Saxon the termination was *-est* or *-ost*. In early English writers (as in Robert of Gloucester) we still find comparatives and superlatives in *-or* and *-ost*.

‡ In Anglo-Saxon *bet* is a comparative adverb, the comparative suffix being thrown off, as it was also in *leng* (longer), *ma* (more), *éþ* (more easily), *ær* (sooner). Best is a shortened form of *betst* or *betest*, like *last* from *latest*.

§ *Little* (A.S. *lytel*) is a derivative from the simpler form *lyt*. *Less* and *least* are not connected with this root, but are derived by Koch from a root *las*. From this root would be formed the comparative *læssa* or (with *s* softened to *r*) *læsra*, and the

ETYMOLOGY—ADJECTIVE. 39

Positive.	Comparative.	Superlative.
Much *	more	most
Many	more	most
Bad	worse†	worst
Late	later or latter	latest or last ‡
[Nigh]	nigher	nighest or next §
Fore	former	foremost or first
Old ‖	older or elder	oldest or eldest
Far	farther	farthest ¶
[Forth]	further	furthest.

115 Adjectives of more than two syllables, and most adjectives of two syllables, do not allow of the formation of comparative and superlative degrees by means of suffixes. But the same ideas are denoted by prefixing the adverbs *more* and *most* to the simple adjective, or adjective in the positive degree. Thus we say, *Virtuous, more virtuous, most virtuous; Learned, more learned, most learned*. The dissyllabic adjectives which do admit of suffixes of comparison are those ending in -y (*merry, merrier, merriest; holy, holier, holiest*); in -er (as *tender, tenderer, tenderest*); those in -ble

---

superlative *læsest*. If this be so, it is possible that *lesser* is not a double comparative (as is usually supposed), but simply the modern form of *læsra; less* being an abbreviated form of *læssa*, and *least* of *læsest*. *Lesser* is only used as an adjective in the sense of *smaller*. *Less* was also used thus by the older writers; as, "How to name the bigger light, and how the less" (*Shaksp., Temp.*). Shakspere (*Hamlet*, iii. 2) has the form *littlest*.

* *Much* is the modern form of the Anglo-Saxon *micel* 'great' (compare μέγας and *mag-nus*) softened into *michel* or *muchel*. *More* and *most* (A.S. *mara, mæst*) are from an old Aryan root *mah*. In old English they had the sense of *greater* and *greatest*; but the sense of *magnus* was gradually superseded by that of *multus*. In old English *moe* (A.S. *ma*) is found for *more* when referring to *number*.

† *Worse* (from A.S. *weor* 'bad') has the original *s* of the comparative suffix. (See note on § 106). The comparative *badder* is found in Chaucer. Shakspere uses the double comparative *worser*. *Worse* and *worst* are used as the comparative and superlative of *bad*, *evil*, and *ill*.

‡ *Later* and *latest* refer to time; *latter* and *last* refer (though not exclusively) to position in a series.

§ In Chaucer we find *hext* for *highest*. The modern positive *near* is in reality the comparative of the A.S. *neah* = *nigh*, which was both an adjective and an adverb. The three degrees should properly be *nigh, near, next* (*Mätzner*, i. p. 294). The comparative *near* is found more than once in Shakspere (*Abbott, Sh. Gr.* § 478), as "The *near* in blood, the nearer bloody" (*Macbeth*).

‖ There is an antiquated positive form *eld*, but *elder* and *eldest* are formed from *old* (A.S. *eald*), being the modern forms of *yldra* and *yldest*. We find this modification of the vowel in other cases, as *lang* 'long', *lengra*, *lengest*; *geong* 'young,' *gyngra, gyngest*. *Older* is an ordinary adjective of the comparative degree. *Elder*, though originally a simple comparative, has now lost that force, and is used to denote not so much greater age, as the relation of precedence which is a consequence of being *older*. *Elder* cannot now be followed by *than*.

¶ These forms are now established in the language, but they are formed upon a false analogy. From the adverb *forth* are derived *further* and *furthest*. But there being no adjective in the positive degree except *far*, *further* and *furthest* were corrupted into *farther* and *farthest*, and set down as derivatives from *far*. In Anglo-Saxon the comp. and sup. of *far* (feorr) were *fyrre* and *feorrest*. Shakspere uses *far* = *fyrre* as a comparative. (*W. T.* iv. 4, 442).

(as *able, abler, ablest*); those which have the accent on the last syllable, as *polite, politer, politest; severe, severer, severest;* and some others, as *pleasanter,** *pleasantest; narrower, narrowest.*

116 Combinations like *more learned, most virtuous,* may be called 'Degrees of Comparison' on the same principle as that on which 'I shall go' is called the 'Future Tense' of the verb *go*. The older writers use *more* and *most* with monosyllabic adjectives, as 'more strong' (*Shaksp*.); 'more sad' (*Pope*). This periphrastic mode of comparison is of Norman-French origin.

117 In Anglo-Saxon there were two superlative suffixes, *-ost* or *-est* and *-ema* (compare the Greek -ιστος in μέγιστος, and the Latin *-imus* in *simill-imus, intimus*, &c.). There are a few superlatives in English ending in *-most: hindmost, topmost, inmost, foremost, uttermost.*† Most of these are derived, not from adjectives in the positive degree, but from adverbs. They are not compounds of the adverb *most*, but double superlatives,‡ formed by the use of both terminations *-ema* and *-ost*. *Former* appears to be a comparative formed from the A.S. superlative *forma*.

118 Double comparatives and superlatives are common in the older writers, as "more kinder," "more braver," "the most unkindest cut of all" (*Shaksp*); "the most straitest sect," &c.

119 Some comparatives have become positive in meaning, as *near* (see § 114); *utter* or *outer* the comparative of *ût = out; inner* of *in; after* of *aft; nether* of *neath* (A.S. *niðe*). Superlatives are sometimes formed from comparatives, as *erst* from *ere* (A.S. *ær*). In old English we find *upperest, overest, utterest, hinderest*. (*Mätzner*).

ARTICLE.

120 The Articles§ are often classed as a separate part of speech, but they belong in reality to the class of Adjectives. There are two Articles, the Indefinite Article *an* or *a*, and the Definite Article *the*.

---

* Euphony is the guide in this matter. The suffixes *er* and *est* were more freely employed by the earlier writers. Thus *e.g.* we find *unhopefullest* in Shakspere, *honourablest* in Bacon, *virtuousest* in Fuller, &c. Several modern writers affect these old formations. In poetical diction comparatives and superlatives in *er* and *est* are allowed which are not usual in ordinary prose, such as *divinest, perfectest, properest*.

† The *r* in *uttermost, innermost*, &c., is merely phonetic, not formative. In Anglo-Saxon we find *hindemest, æftemost, innemest, formest*, &c.

‡ It is likely enough, however, that some of these words (as *hithermost, middlemost, undermost, topmost*) were really formed under the false conception that *-most* was the superlative adverb. We even find the comparative *more* in the double comparative *furthermore*.

§ Latin *articulus*, 'a joint;' a word used rather vaguely by the Latin grammarians.

121 The Indefinite Article *an* is a quantitative adjective. It is only another form of the numeral *one* (A.S. *án* ;* Scotch *ane*). When placed before a noun it indicates that we are speaking of *some one* of the things for each of which the noun is a name, as, '*A* dog bit me;' 'I saw *an* old man.'

122 The form *an* is used before words beginning with a vowel sound or mute *h*, as *an apple, an heir*.
An drops the *n*† and becomes *a* before words beginning with a consonant, the aspirate *h*, or the letter *u* when the sound of *y* is put before the *u* in pronunciation, as *A man, a horse, a yellow ball, a useful book*. But *an* is kept before the aspirate when the accent is not upon the first syllable of the word, as "an historical event."

123 In some expressions what is now commonly regarded as the indefinite article *a* was originally a weakened form of the preposition *on* (= in). Thus "Twice a week" was "tuwa on wucan" (*Luke* xviii. 12. See *Koch*, ii. p. 85; *Morris, Hist. Outl.*‡)

124 The definite article *the* is a Demonstrative Adjective. It is used before a noun, to define or mark the particular individual or individuals that we are speaking of out of the class named by the noun.

125 The definite article is used in English before significant nouns.
(A) It is used to mark out or individualise out of all the objects of thought that might be denoted by the significant name, that one to which attention is directed. It does this, *first*, by directing attention to some attributive adjunct by which the individual is distinguished from the rest of the class of which it is a member. Thus, when we say, *the black horse, the* points attention to the adjective *black*, by which the horse in question is distinguished from others of the group to which it belongs. When we say, *the Queen of England, the* points to the distinguishing adjunct *of England*. In *the man who stole my purse, the* points to the distinguishing adjective clause *who stole*, &c. The omission of the common name which is restricted by the adjective or attributive adjunct leads to such combinations as *the Thames* § (for *the river Thames*); *the Atlantic* (for

---
* *An* was sometimes employed in Anglo-Saxon as the indefinite article. Thus *e.g.* "Iob ascreep þone wyrms of his lice mid ánum croescearde" (Job scraped the corruption off his body with a potsherd. *Aelf. Hom.*). Its *regular* use in this manner was not established till after the Norman Conquest.

† In old English the form *a* or *o* is found for *an* (as *ae* in Scotch for *ane*) even when used as a numeral. We still say '*A* day or two'; 'They are both of *a* size,' *i.e.*, of *one* size. *None* (made up of *ne* and *án*) is commonly shortened to *no*.

‡ It is pretty clear, however, that after the use of the indefinite article had become general, people thought that in saying 'twice a year,' they were using the indefinite article, or they would not also have used such expressions as '*A* shilling *a pound*,' where *a* = *on* or *in* would be without meaning. When the article came to be employed in *a* was used, as 'sevene sithis (times) *in a* day' (*Matt.* xvii. 4), &c. Phrases like *on* or *in a year* might easily have been abbreviated by the omission of the preposition, just as we say, 'the cloth is a shilling *the* yard,' instead of 'for the yard.'

§ In Anglo-Saxon we find *Thames, Jordan*, &c. without the article.

the Atlantic ocean); *the Victory* (for *the ship Victory*). Secondly, by indicating that out of all the possible objects to which the significant name might be applied, we are speaking of that particular one with which we have some obvious connexion or concern, as when we say, *the sun, the moon, the Queen, the City, the street, the door, the army, the Church,* &c.

(B) The word *the* is used before significant nouns in the singular to show that one individual is taken as the representative of its class, as when we talk of *the lion, the eagle,* or when the name does not admit of more than one application in the sense in which it is used, as *the universe, the Deity, the ocean.*

(c) *The* is used before nouns in the plural to show that we are speaking of the whole of the class to which the name belongs, as when we speak of *the stars, the English, the good, the Alps.*

There is a corresponding use of *the* before an adjective when the two together form (not, as some say, an *abstract,* but) a *universal concrete name,* as *the sublime, the ridiculous.*

126 The definite article *the* is a weakened form of the old demonstrative *se, sco, that,* which in Anglo-Saxon, besides its ordinary force, had the weaker force of the article, though it was often omitted in cases where we now use *the*. In the later stage of Anglo-Saxon *se* and *seo* were supplanted by the collateral forms þe (*the*) and þeo (*theo*). Side by side with the inflected demonstrative there was an uninflected form *the*, but in early English writers (*Robert of Gloucester, Old English Hom.*) traces of the inflected article, such as Gen. *thas,* Dat. *tham,* Acc. *then,* are still found; also (especially in the Northern dialect) *that* was used as an article for all genders* (*Koch* and *Mätzner*); but ere long only the uninflected *the* was used for the article, and the inflected forms were used as demonstrative pronouns.

127 When a noun preceded by an article is qualified by an adjective, the adjective is generally placed between the article and the noun. But in the case of the adjective *such,* or an adjective qualified by the adverbs *so* and *too,* the indefinite article comes after the adjective, as "Such an event;" "So great a misfortune." The same is the case with the definite article and the adjective *all,* as "All the day."

PRONOUN.

128 A pronoun† is a word used instead of a noun, as when we say, "John has come in: *he* is very tired," instead of "John has come in: John is very tired."

---

* In early English are found the curious forms *the tone* and *the tother*. Mätzner considers these to have sprung out of the use of *that* or *thet* as an article, *thet one* and *thet other,*—forms which are actually found not infrequently.

† Latin *pronomen; pro* for, and *nomen* noun.

ETYMOLOGY—PRONOUN.

Pronouns are divided into two classes, Substantive Pronouns and Adjective Pronouns.

129 Strictly speaking, no word should be called a Pronoun unless it is a substantive. But it is usual to include under this head certain demonstrative adjectives which are very often used substantively. These bear the somewhat contradictory name of *Adjective Pronouns*. When they are attached to substantives which are expressed, as *this man, each time*, they should be called Demonstrative Adjectives.

Table of the Pronouns.

	SUBSTANTIVE.	ADJECTIVE.
130 I. Personal	I, thou, we, you or ye.	
II. Demonstrative	he, she, it, they.	this, these; that, those.
III. Relative—that.		
IV. Interrogative and Relative	who	which, what, whether.
V. Indefinite	one, aught, naught	any, other, some.
VI. Distributive		each, every, either, neither.
VII. Reflective		self.
VIII. Possessive		mine and my, thine and thy, his, her, and hers, its, our and ours, your and yours, their and theirs.

I.—Personal Pronouns.

131 Personal Pronouns are of two kinds. 1. Those of the First Person. 2. Those of the Second Person.

132 The Pronoun which is used when a person speaks of himself singly, or of himself in conjunction with one or more others, without mentioning any names, is called the Personal Pronoun of the First Person. It is declinable, and has the following forms:—

	Singular.	Plural.
Nominative Case	I	We
[Possessive Case]	[Mine *or* My]	[Our]
Objective Case	Me	Us

The Nominative Case *I* is always written with a Capital letter.

133 The Pronoun which is used when we speak of the person or persons spoken to, is called the Personal Pronoun of the Second Person. It is declinable, and has the following forms:—

ETYMOLOGY—PRONOUN.

	Singular.	Plural.
Nominative Case	Thou	Ye *or* You
[*Possessive Case*]	[Thine *or* Thy]	[Your]
Objective Case	Thee	You *or* Ye*

134. In Anglo-Saxon only the singular forms of this pronoun were used in addressing a single person. In Shakspere's time the singular was also used as the pronoun of affection towards children † or friends, of good-natured superiority to servants, and of contempt or anger to strangers. ‡ (*Abbott, Sh. Gr.* p. 153). At a very early period § the plural came to be used in speaking to a single person. It was at first employed as a mark of special respect (as when a subject speaks to a king, or a son to his father), as though the person addressed were as good as two or more ordinary people. ‖ In course of time the nominative *ye* (as thus employed) was superseded by *you*, and became exclusively plural in sense. It is now employed only in elevated or poetic style. *You* and *your* are now the ordinary pronouns of address, whether we are speaking to one person, or to more than one.

135. The Personal Pronouns have, properly speaking, no Possessive Case, that is to say, no Possessive Case with the force of a *substantive*. In Anglo-Saxon, when the genitives ¶ of these pronouns were used in the *possessive* sense, they were regarded as adjectives and inflected accordingly. As the possessive sense is the only one in which we have retained these forms, and as, when used in this sense, these forms were always regarded as adjectives, they should be regarded as such now; that is, *mine* and *my* are the equivalents not of *mei* but of *meus, thine* and *thy* of *tuus,* &c.

136. The plural forms of the pronouns of the first and second persons are not etymologically derived from the singular forms. In fact, the notion involved (for example) in *we* is not related to that expressed by *I* in the same way that the idea expressed by *men* is related to that expressed by *man. We* does not imply a simple repetition of *I.* The notion involved in the word *I* does not admit of plurality.**

---

* Several grammarians maintain that *ye is exclusively nominative*. It was so once, but the best writers in the language use *ye as an objective case*. As, " His wrath, which one day will destroy ye both" (*Milton*). "The more shame for *ye*, holy men I thought *ye*" (*Shakspere*). It is true, however, that *ye* is derived from the Anglo-Saxon nominative *ge*, and *you* from the accusative or dative *eow*. In the English Bible *ye is nominative and you* objective.

† In Shakspere fathers almost always address their sons with *thou*, sons their fathers with *you* (*Abbott*).

‡ "If thou thou'st him some thrice, it shall not be amiss" (*Twelfth N.* iii. 2). "Prithee don't thee and thou me; I believe I am as good a man as yourself" (*Miller of Mansfield*).

§ See Robert of Gloucester, &c.

‖ The use of the first person plural by royal personages may be accounted for in a similar manner.

¶ In Anglo-Saxon these genitives were also used as substantives, and were governed by verbs, &c., or used in the partitive sense, as *e.g. gemun þu min,* 'remember thou *me*' (*memineris mei*). The *substantive* use of *min* and *þin* did not last beyond the Anglo-Saxon stage of our language. The substantive use of *our* (*ure*) and *your* (*eower*) lasted till a later period. The abbreviated forms *my* and *thy* were not employed till the *substantive* use of *min* and *þin* had disappeared.

** It appears in fact that the earliest known form of the plural *we* (in Sanscrit) was equivalent to *I and these,* and that of *ye* to *thou and these* (*Koch,* i. p. 463).

137 The pronouns of the first and second persons do not mark distinctions of gender, because when a person speaks of himself or to another person, the sex, being evident, does not need to be marked in language by differences of gender, and the plural forms must of necessity be ambiguous, as *we* and *you* may include persons of different sexes.

II.—Demonstrative Pronouns.

138 The pronoun which is used when a person speaks of one or more other persons or things, without describing them by a noun, is often called the Personal Pronoun of the Third Person. It is, however, more correct to call it the Demonstrative Pronoun of the Third Person. It admits of the distinctions of number, case, and gender. It has the following forms:—

	SINGULAR.		
	Masculine.	Feminine.	Neuter.
Nominative Case	He	She	It
Possessive Case	His	Her	It's
Objective Case	Him*	Her	It

PLURAL.

Nominative Case	They
Possessive Case	Their } For all genders.
Objective Case	Them

139 The plural forms must be ambiguous as to gender, because they may be used when speaking of persons of different sexes, or of persons and things together. For the old forms of this pronoun see Appendix A.

140 *She* (*sche* or *scho*) was probably a collateral form of *heo* from very early times. It is connected with the feminine demonstrative *seo*.† *It* was in Anglo-Saxon *hit*. The *t* is a neuter suffix, like *d* in the Latin *i-d, quo-d*, &c. The regular genitive or possessive case of *hit* was *his*, as: "If the salt have lost *his* savour," &c. The possessive case *its* is of comparatively modern origin. It is found in Shakspere, but even there *his* is more common. There is only one example of it in the English Bible ‡ (*Lev.* xxv. 5).

141 The modern plural forms of this pronoun are borrowed from the demonstrative *se, seo, þæt*. (App. A). The genitive plural *her, hir* or *hire*, and the dative plural *him* or *hem* were in use for some

---

* *Him* was originally a *dative* case. It will be seen that the datives *him, her* and *them*, like *me, thee, us* and *you*, have supplanted the accusative forms (See § 83, note).
† The characteristic *s* appears in Gothic (*si*) and Old Saxon (*siu*), as well as in modern German (*sie*). *Ho* or *hoo* is still heard for *she* in Lancashire and Craven.
‡ Some old writers have an uninflected possessive *it* (for *his* or *its*); as "Go to *it* grandam, child, and *it* grandam will give it a plum" (*Shaksp., K. J.* ii. 1). See *Koch*, ii. p. 238.

time after *thai, thei,* or *they* was adopted for the nominative. They are found in Chaucer.*

142 The genitive cases of this pronoun were not declined as adjectives in Anglo-Saxon.† *Their* retained a substantive force after the other possessives had become pronominal adjectives. Traces of their substantive force still exist in their use as antecedents to relatives; as, "whose hatred is covered by deceit, *his* wickedness shall be showed before the whole congregation." "*Their* sorrows shall be multiplied that hasten after another God." They may now, however, be classed with the other possessives.

The Demonstrative Adjectives THIS and THAT.

143 *This* has a plural, viz., *these.* *That* has a plural, viz., *those.*‡ *This* refers to what is near the speaker (*near me*) in position; *that* refers to what is at a distance from the speaker. As "*This* apple is ripe, *that* is not." In this sense *this* and *that* are called *real* demonstratives, or words that point to *things* (Latin *res*).

144 *This* and *that* are also used to point, not to things themselves, but to some description of what we are speaking about, as, "The general was in command of a large force. *This* force consisted of infantry and artillery." "They remained one day at Rome. *That* day passed without any remarkable event." When thus used, *this* and *that* are called *logical* demonstratives. They often refer to *whole sentences* or to the *general idea* conveyed by a preceding phrase, as, "I know that he is innocent, and *this* is my chief consolation"; "Lend me a shilling, *that's* a good fellow." Here *that* = 'a person who will lend a shilling.'

When two things which have been already mentioned are referred to, *this* refers to what has been mentioned last, *that* refers to what was mentioned before it; as "Virtue and vice offer themselves for your choice: *this* leads to misery, *that* to happiness." *This* is also used to refer to something which is going to be mentioned, as, "*This* is my hope and prayer, that my children may grow up in the fear of the Lord."

---

* The colloquial abbreviation *a* for the pronoun of the third person occurs in old writers. "*A* brushes his hat o' mornings.... *A* rubs himself with civet" (*Shaksp., Much Ado,* iii. 2). It is still a provincial idiom (See Tennyson's *Northern Farmer.*) It is even used as a plural (*Koch,* i. 469).

† Traces of declension, however, appear at a somewhat later period (See *Koch,* ii. p. 234).

‡ Etymologically, however, *those* is not the plural of *that* (A.S. þæt). *These* and *those* are only various forms of þas, the plural of þes or þis (See Appendix A, 1, 2). In Middle English *that had a plural* tho, a variety of þá. Koch is probably in error when (ii. p. 242) he derives the plural *those* from *tho* by the addition of the plural suffix *s*. *This* was used as a plural even up to the sixteenth century. The proper plural of *that* was transferred to *it* or *hit*.

145 *This* and *that* (in the singular) are not used substantively to stand for persons, except as subjects of the verb *be* when the latter is followed by a noun as the predicate; as, "This is my brother;" "that is John." We cannot say, "This did the deed," meaning "this man;" or, "That shall be punished," meaning "that person." This restriction does not apply to the plural: "*These* are not drunken, as ye suppose;" "Upon *those* did Solomon levy a tribute." But this use of the plural is now almost obsolete.

146 *That* is properly the neuter of the Anglo-Saxon demonstrative pronoun (App. A), *t* being a neuter suffix (§ 140). Like *hit*, *that* was used substantively in Anglo-Saxon as a general demonstrative without regard to gender or number, as "is þæt min broðer"; "þæt were Brut and hys" *(Rob. Gl.)*. Ultimately it superseded the masculine and feminine. *This* is in like manner the neuter of the Anglo-Saxon þes, þeos, þis (App. A). Like *that* it was used substantively without regard to number or gender, as "þis sindon þa domas" (*this* are the decrees). Like *that*, *this* superseded the masculine and feminine forms.

147 The adverbs *there* and *here*, combined with another adverb (see § 271), form compounds which are often substituted for *that* and *this* preceded by prepositions; thus *therein*=*in that*; *hereby*=*by this*. The usage is getting antiquated; but *therefor* (*therefore*) is in common use.

147*b* The demonstrative adjective *yonder* or *yon* is sometimes classed among the pronouns, though it is now never used in place of a noun. The root *yon* is the same as in the German *jener*. In Anglo-Saxon *geond* was an adverb. *Yonder* is also an adverb in English.

III.—The Relative Pronoun THAT.

148 A Relative* Pronoun is a word which refers to some noun or pronoun which has been already used to mark the person or thing spoken about, and which is called the *antecedent* of the relative. Thus, in the sentence, "He is reading about the battle that was fought at Hastings," *that* refers to the noun *battle*, and *battle* is called the antecedent to the relative *that*.

The pronouns *who* and *which* are also used as relatives. In "I have found the sheep *which* I had lost," the pronoun *which* refers to *sheep*, and *sheep* is the antecedent to the relative *which*. In "This is the man *whose* house we saw," *whose* refers to *man*, and *man* is the antecedent to *whose*. The antecedent noun is often replaced by a pronoun, as:

---

* *Relative* is a bad term, because it is insufficient. *He, she, it, this, that, they* are also (literally) *relative* pronouns, because they refer to some preceding substantive or antecedent. The relative pronoun, however, differs from the definite article and the demonstrative adjectives *this* and *that* by having at the same time a grammatically connective force, and attaching subordinate adjective clauses to some word in the principal sentence.

"*He* to-day that sheds his blood with me, shall be my brother."

149   The relative pronoun **that** is the oldest* relative pronoun that we have in English. It is always used as a substantive, and may be used either of persons or of things. It is never placed *after* prepositions, and is governed by a preposition only when the preposition is placed at the end of the clause.† It has no variations in form to mark number, gender, or case. *Examples:* "The horse *that* I rode, fell." "This is the man *that* I spoke of."

150   *That* was originally the neuter of the Anglo-Saxon demonstrative‡ pronoun, *se, seo, þæt*, which was also used as a relative, just as *der, die, das*, still is in German. As in the case of the demonstrative *that*, the neuter superseded the masculine and feminine. This pronoun and the indeclinable *þe* were used as relatives before *who* was so used.§ In old-fashioned English *that* (like *what*) was used with its antecedent understood; as "We speak *that* we do know, and testify *that* we have seen" (*John* iii. 11); "*That* thou doest, do quickly" (*John* xiii. 27); "I am *that* I am."

151   *That* cannot be used in all cases where *who* can be used. It can now be used only when the relative clause is required to give to the antecedent its full signification. We cannot use *that* when the antecedent is a proper name, or when the antecedent noun has with it a demonstrative adjective which sufficiently defines the thing or person spoken of. We cannot say, "Thomas *that* died yester-

---

* Addison is quite wrong when in his "Humble Petition of *who* and *which*" he makes the petitioners say: "We are descended of ancient families, and kept up our dignity and honour many years, till the Jack Sprat *that* supplanted us."

† In such cases we should perhaps regard the preposition as an adverb forming a compound with the verb. Formerly the preposition (or adverb) was placed *before* the verb, as though we should say "the land which they in-lived"; "the settlement which they from were driven" (*Koch*, ii. p. 260). This idiom was first adopted for the uninflected *the* and *that*, and afterwards extended to the other relatives.

‡ The use of a *relative* pronoun marks an advanced stage of the language. Originally the principal clause and the accessory relative clause were co-ordinate, as: "Se hæfð brýd, se is býð-ruma" = "He has the bride, he is the bridegroom." The preponderating importance of the definitive clause was easily marked in speaking by emphasis. This emphasis at length received its grammatical expression by doubling the demonstrative, which was repeated in its indeclinable form *þe*, repetition of the inflection being needless. Hence arose the ordinary Anglo-Saxon form: "Se þe brýd hiefð, se is brýdguma" = "Who has the bride he is the bridegroom." As the relative force was given to the demonstrative by appending the indeclinable *þe*, the latter came to be regarded as specially containing the relative idea. Hence it came to be used sometimes by itself without the inflected demonstrative, as *vice versâ* the inflected demonstrative was often used as a relative without the appended *þe*, the accessory nature of the clause being commonly evident either from its meaning or from its position. The uninflected *that* was used as a relative by Orm and Layamon in the twelfth century (*Koch*, ii. p. 255). The indeclinable *þe* could even give a relative force to the personal pronouns, as "Fœder ûre, þu þe eart or heofenum" (Our Father *which* (= *thou that*) art in heaven); "Ic eom Gabrahel, ic þe stande beforan Gode" (I am Gabriel *who* stand before God). Compare *du, der du;* and *ich, der ich*, &c in German.

§ Before *who* came into use as a relative pronoun, the relative adverbs were *then, there, thither* (*þonne, þær, þyder*) instead of *when, where, whither*.

day, was my brother;" or "I have heard from my father, *that* is in America." The words *Thomas* and *my Father* explain perfectly by themselves who is meant. In other words, a clause beginning with *that* limits or defines the noun to which it refers, and is therefore improper when that noun does not admit of further limitation. This rule, however, holds good only in modern English. In the older writers *that* is used after proper names, or nouns limited by a definitive word. *That* never has the *continuative* force of *who* and *which* (See § 413), and is never used (like *which*) to refer to the general sense of an entire sentence.

IV.—The Interrogative and Relative Pronouns WHO, WHAT, WHICH, WHETHER.

152 The pronoun **who**, neuter **what** (A.S. *hwa*, neuter *hwæt*) was in Anglo-Saxon an Interrogative pronoun, and was used only substantively* (For the declension of *hwa*, see App. A). It had no feminine or plural. It is thus declined in modern English:—

Nominative Case	Who
Possessive Case	Whose
Objective Case	Whom

Even good writers often carelessly use *who* as the objective case, as "saw who?" (*Hamlet*, i.); "Yield thee, thief! To who? to thee?" (*Cymb.* iv. 2). This should be regarded as an error.
Whom is properly a dative, which, like *me, thee, him, her*, and *them* has supplanted the accusative.

153 **What** has the neuter suffix *t*. It is the neuter of *who*. It is now indeclinable, and is used not only as a substantive, but also as an adjective.† When used as a substantive it is neuter, like *that*.

154 **Which** (A.S. *hwylc* or *hwilc*), is a compound of *hwi* or *hwý* (the old instrumental case of *hwa*), and *lic* (*like*). In Scotch it is still *quhilk*. It is equivalent to the Latin *qualis*, 'of what sort?' and corresponds to the German *welcher*. It is properly an adjective, as "Which dress do you prefer?" but is also used **substantively**, as "Here are port and

---

* The word has the same root as the dialectic Greek interrogative κος and the Latin *quis*. The *hw* is a softened form of a guttural. In *what, when, &c.* we still pronounce the *h* before the *w*.

† Like the neuters *this* and *that* it was used in Anglo-Saxon as a substantive without regard to gender and number, as "Hwæt syndon ge?" (*what are ye?*). It was often followed by the genitive case, as "hwæt godes?" (*what of good?*); "hwæt weorces?" (*what of work?*). When the genitive suffix came to be dropped, except when it denoted possession, these combinations gave rise to an apparently adjective use of *what*, which was subsequently admitted before masculine and feminine as well as before neuter nouns. *What* is used adjectively with an intensive force, in exclamations, as "What a fool he was!"; "What knaves they are." In old English *which* was similarly used, as ' which a great honour it is' (*Chaucer*).

sherry, which will you take?" *Which* asks for one out of a definite number; *who* and *what* ask indefinitely.

155 **Whether** (A.S. *hwæðer*) is derived from *who* (*hwa*) by means of the comparative suffix *ther** (§ 106, note), and means 'which of the two?' As a pronoun it is now nearly obsolete. It was usually a substantive, as "Whether of them twain did the will of his father?" but was sometimes used adjectively, as "While thus the case in doubtful balance hung, unsure to whether side it would incline" (*Spenser*).

156 As *who*, *what*, and *which* (*hwa*, *hwæt*, *hwylc*) were used as *indefinite interrogatives*, by a natural transition they came to be used as *indefinite pronouns*, standing for some unknown or undetermined person or thing,† in the sense of *some one* or *any one*, *something* or *anything*, especially (though not always) after *if* (*gif*). This use of *who* is still found in Shakspere, "as *who* should say" (*Macb.* iii. 6) = "as one might say."

157 *What* is still commonly used thus in such phrases as "I'll tell you what," where *what* = *something*. The strengthened form *somewhat* is still more common. In the sense of *in some degree* or *partly*, *what* is used conjunctively, as, "What with the war, what with the sweat, what with the gallows, and what with poverty, I am custom-shrunk." (*Shaksp., M. for M.* ii. 1.) The interrogative adverbs *how*, *where*, *when*, *whether*, &c. had in like manner an *indefinite* sense. We still say some*how*, some*where*, some*whither*, &c.

158 A further step of great importance was made when the interrogative or indefinite pronouns **who, what, which** came to be used as **Indefinite Relative Pronouns**. This was effected by attaching to them the adverb *so*,‡ as

---

* *Uter* (once *quuter* or *cuter*, from *qui*) is precisely analogous to *whether*, from *who*, as is ποτερος from the interrogative and relative root πο.

† That is to say, in order to indicate a person or thing as yet unknown or undetermined, a word was employed that asked *who* or *what* it was. *Quis* was used in Latin in precisely the same way after *si*, *num*, *quum*, &c. Compare also the Greek τις. This use of the interrogative was quite common in Anglo-Saxon, as "gif *hwa* cow ænig þinge tô cwyð" (*Matt.* xxi. 3). 'If any one say anything to you'; "Gif eow *hwylc* secgð" (*Mark* xiii. 21), 'If any man say to you.'

‡ In Anglo-Saxon the demonstrative adverb *swâ* (so) was treated like the demonstrative pronoun. (See note on § 150.) In order to give it a relative force it was doubled. Thus *swâ* came to be regarded (like *þe*) as having in itself the power of attaching a relative sense to other words. It was placed both before and after the interrogative (or indefinite) pronouns, to give them the force of indefinite relatives; *swâ hwa swâ* (so *who* so = whoso); *swâ hwæt swâ* (so *what* so = whatsoever) &c. The words *that* and *as* (*als* = *also* = *all so*) were also employed to give relativity to the pronouns and adverbs beginning with *wh*, as "The highe God, on *whom that* we believe;" "Caton, *which that* was so wise" (*Chaucer*); "*When that* the poor have cried, Cæsar hath wept" (*Shaksp.*); "*When as* sacred light began to dawn," (*Milton, P. L.* ix. 192). *Whereas* still keeps its ground. In the Ormulum we find *summ* (*summ*) used for the same purpose (*whasumm* = whoso; *whatsumm* = whatsoever). This idiom is preserved in the now vulgar forms *whatsomever*, *howsomever*, &c. (sometimes pronounced *whatsomedever*, &c).

whoso. Thus, "Whoso sheddeth man's blood, by man shall his blood be shed" (*Gen.* ix. 6). These forms are commonly strengthened by the addition of *ever*, and the *so* is sometimes omitted. *Whoso* and *whoever* are not now declined. *Whosoever* is declined:—

    Nominative Case . . . Whosoever
    Possessive Case . . . Whosesoever
    Objective Case . . . Whomsoever.

Whatever, whatsoever, and *whichever* or *whichsoever,* are used both substantively and adjectively, as "*Whatever* (subst.) he undertook, prospered"; "*Whatsoever* (adj.) things are true, *whatsoever* things are pure," &c. (*Phil.* iv. 8). The antecedent of these indefinite relatives is usually omitted.

159 Lastly, the indefinite relatives *whoso,* &c., dropped the *so,* which was the sign of *relativity,* and **who, what,** and **which** became ordinary **relative pronouns.***

160 The pronoun **who** is used only when *persons* are spoken of. It does not mark the distinction of number, person, and gender. For its declension see § 152.

What was originally the neuter of *who,* and, as a substantive, refers only to *things.* It is also used adjectively, as "I gave him what help I could;" "What time I am afraid, I will trust in thee." The possessive case of it (*whose=hwæs* or *whas*), is still in use, though rarely employed except in poetry: as "The question *whose* solution I require" (*Dryden*); "I could a tale unfold, *whose* lightest word," &c. (*Shakspere*); "The roof, *whose* thickness was not vengeance proof" (*Byron*). The dative has disappeared. In the nominative and objective cases, *what* is never preceded by an antecedent,† but may be followed by *that,* as "*What* he hath won, *that* hath he fortified" (*Shak., K. J.,* iii. 4). Usually, however, the antecedent is not expressed.

160*b* It is, however, an utter mistake to treat *what* as though it were made up of, or were equivalent to, *that which.* It is simply a rela-

---

* *Who (wha),* as a relative, is first found in the Ormulum. *What* had been used as a relative somewhat earlier. "*That* came into use during the twelfth century to supply the place of the indeclinable relative *the*, and in the fourteenth century it is the ordinary relative. In the sixteenth century *which* often supplies its place; in the seventeenth century *who* replaces it. About Addison's time *that* had again come into fashion, and had almost driven *which* and *who* out of use" (*Morris*). Steele ridicules the too common use of *that* in the sentence: "My lords, with humble submission, that that I say is this; that that that that gentleman has advanced is not that that he should have proved to your lordships" (*Spect.* 80). *Whether,* as a relative, is obsolete, but is found in Chaucer.

† That is, not now. In the older writers *all what, nothing what, that what,* &c. are common.

tive with its antecedent *understood*, just as when we say, "Who steals my purse steals trash." It is like the German *was*, before which the antecedent *das* is commonly omitted, though it may be expressed. An adjective clause introduced by the relative *what* is therefore an adjective clause, *used substantively*. In the sentence, "I do not believe what has been said," *what* is in no sense the object of *believe*; it is the subject of *has been said*.

161. As *what* is no longer used as a *relative* when the antecedent is expressed, its place is supplied by the pronoun **which**. It is wrong, however, to call *which* the neuter of *who* (see § 154). It is an adjective pronoun, and not necessarily neuter. In old-fashioned English it is found instead of *who*, as "Our Father *which* art in heaven." At present, however, it is never used substantively as a relative, except with reference to animals and things. In such sentences as "The doctrine of the Nicolaitans, *which thing* I hate;" *which* is used adjectively.

162. In old-fashioned English, we often find *the* before *which*, as "To win time, in *the which* I have considered of a course" (*Cymbel.* iii. 4); "A chamberlaine, *the which that* dwelling was with Emilie" (*Chaucer*).* (Compare the French *le quel*, where *quel* is the equivalent of *which*, being derived from *qualis*).

163. The proper correlative of *which* is *such* (A. S. *swylc*, a compound of swŷ, the instrumental form of the root of *swá*, and *lic*, passing through the forms *swulc* and *sulche* to *such*)† as "Such which must go before" (*Bacon*). *Such—which = talis—qualis*.

164. *Which* preceded by a preposition is often replaced by *where*, as *wherein = in which; whereto = to which*, &c.

165. *Who* and *which* can always be used where *that*‡ can be used. They have also a *continuative* force, which *that* never has. (See § 413).

166. The relative pronoun is frequently understood, that is, implied, but not expressed; as, "He has not returned the book I lent him," for "the book *which* I lent him;" "That is the person I spoke of," "for the person *whom* I spoke of." But the relative is not now omitted in good

---

* *The whom* is found even in Shakspere (*Wint. T.* iv. 4.)

† *Hwylc*, in like manner, passed through the forms *whylc*, *whulch*, and *wuch* or *woch*. The pronunciation *which* has established itself, but *sich* is considered vulgar. In Anglo-Saxon *such* (*swylc*) was relative as well as demonstrative. In some dialects of English there still remains the demonstrative *thilk* or *thuck* (from *þy* and *lic = talis*).

‡ Some grammarians think that *who* and *which* are not properly used to introduce a *limiting* or *defining* clause, and that in such sentences as "That is the man *who* spoke to us yesterday," "The house *which* he built still remains," the word *that* is preferable. The best writers of English prose do not seem to entertain this view. When prepositions have to be employed, *whom* and *which* are preferred to *that*. In the English Bible it would be difficult to find a clause beginning with *that*, and having a preposition at the end; and when a defining or restrictive clause is wanted after the demonstrative *that*, it always begins with *which* in the English of the Bible.

English, unless, if expressed, it would be in the objective case.

167 The adverb *as* (A.S. *ealswa* = *also*, i.e., *all so*, German *als*) is often used as a substitute for a relative pronoun, especially after *same* and *such;* as, "This is not the same as that; " "His character is not such *as* I admire;" "I have not from your eyes that gentleness and show of love as I was wont to have;" (*Shakspere, Julius Cæsar,* i. 2, 45). In vulgar English *as* is commonly used as a simple relative. In old-fashioned German *so* is found doing duty as a relative pronoun. But see note on § 264.

V.—Indefinite Pronouns.

168 The Indefinite Pronoun <u>one</u> is the numeral adjective used substantively. *One* has a possessive case, as 'One's reputation is at stake.' The plural is used only with reference to a preceding noun, as "I saw three brown horses and two black ones." Its negative is *none*. (See § 95. A.S. *nân* = *ne ân*). In Anglo-Saxon *man* was used for *one** (Comp. Germ. *man.*).

169 Aught† (A.S. *âwiht*) is derived from the Anglo-Saxon substantive *wiht*, a 'thing,' which we still employ as a masculine in the noun *wight*, and *â* = *ever*. *Naught* is a compound of the negative *ne* and *aught*.

170 Any (*ǽnig*) is a derivative from *ân*, 'one,' just as *ullus* in Latin is a diminutive of *unus*. (Key, *Lat. Gr.*, § 334.) In negative and interrogative sentences when *any* refers to a singular noun, it implies *quantity;* when it refers to a plural noun, it implies *number:* as, "This food is bad, I will not eat *any*"; "There were some apples on that tree, did you pluck *any?*" Being used to express *indefiniteness*, it also serves to express *universality,* as "Any one can do that." The negative *nǽnig* (*n-any*) has vanished.

171 Other means *one of two* (like the Latin *alter*). It is formed from the root *an*, a variation of the *al* of ἄλλος and *alter*, by means of the comparative suffix *ther* (see § 106, note). When used as a substantive it has the ordinary inflections of a noun.‡

---

* Vestiges of this use of *man* still remain in such phrases as ' *men say* ' (*on dit*) ; 'That is all *a man* can desire.'
† The spelling *ought* and *nought* is old but incorrect. *Nought* was shortened into the adverb *not*.
‡ *Other* originally had the adjective plural suffix *-e*, the dropping of which left the old plural form *other*, as " When other are glad, than is he sad " (*Skelton* apud Mätzner).

ETYMOLOGY—PRONOUN.

	Singular.	Plural.
Nominative Case.	Other	Others.
Possessive Case	Other's	Others'.
Objective Case	Other	Others.

When *an* is used before *other* the two words are usually written together, *another*.

172 **Some** (A.S. *sum*) originally meant 'a certain' (Lat. *quidam*), as "Sum man hæfde twegen suna" (*a certain man had two sons*). It still has this force in *somebody*, *sometimes*, *something*. It very early came to mean an undetermined number or quantity forming part of a whole or class. It is used with numerals to give the sense of *about*, as "We four set upon some dozen" (*Shaksp., I. Henry IV.* ii. 4); "He will last you some eight year or nine year" (*Hamlet*).

VI.—The Distributive Pronouns EACH, EVERY, EITHER, NEITHER.

173 **Each** (A.S. *ælc* = *â-ge-hwylc*,* Scotch *ilka*) is used both adjectively and substantively.

173*b*. In such phrases as, "They loved each other," "They hated one another," the words *each* and *other*, and *one* and *another*, have a reciprocal relation to each other; but it is a mistake to call them compound pronouns (as though equivalent to the Greek *alleloi*). They are independent pronouns, having separate and different constructions in the sentences where they occur. In "They loved each other," *each* is in the nominative case, in the attributive relation to *they*, which it distributes in sense; *other* is in the objective case, governed by the verb *loved*.† In Spenser (*Faerie Queen*, i. 5, 6) we find—"With greedy force each other doth assail;" that is "each doth assail the other." In "They heard each other's voice," *each* is in the nominative case, agreeing with *they*; *other's* is in the possessive case, attached to the noun *voice*. Such phrases as *to each other*, *from one another*, &c., are corruptions, made upon a false analogy, though they are now thoroughly fixed in the language. In old-fashioned and *correct* English we find *each to other*, *one from another*. It seems anomalous at first sight, that a word like *each*, which is essentially singular, should be attached to a plural word, but we have exactly the same idiom in Latin. *Quisque* in the singular may be used to distribute a plural subject. *Each other* is now used when *two* are referred to, *one another* when more than two are meant; but this distinction is not a necessary one.

174 **Every** (old English *everælc* or *everilk*) is a compound of A.S. *aefre*, 'ever,' and *ælc*, and denotes all of a series taken

* The particle *ge* was prefixed to the indefinite pronouns in Anglo-Saxon to give the idea of universality, as *ge-hwa* = *every one*; *ge-hwylc* = *every one*; *ge-hwæðer* = *both*. (Compare the German *Gebrüder* and *Geschwister*.) These forms were strengthened by prefixing *â* = *ever*. Hence came *â-ge-hwylc* = *ælc* = *each*; *â-ge-hwæðer* = *ægðer* = *either*. (*Koch*. i. 483.)

† In Anglo-Saxon this difference is marked by the terminations.

one by one. *Each* and *every* both call attention to the individuals forming a collection. When *each* is used, the prominent idea is that of the subdivision of the collection into its component parts. When *every* is used, the prominent idea is that the individuals taken together make up some whole. In Chaucer, *every* (*everich*) is used substantively. This use is still found in legal phraseology.

175 **Either** (A.S. *ægðer* = *â-ye-hwæðer*) originally meant *both* or *each of two;* as "On *either* side one" (*John* xix. 18); "On *either* side of the river" (*Rev.* xxii. 2). *Neither* is a compound of *either* and the old negative *ne*. *Either* may have a possessive case, as : "Where either's fall determines both their fates" (*Rowe, Lucan* vi. 13).

Every, either, and *neither* are always singular.*

VII.—The Reflective Pronoun SELF.

176 **Self** was originally an adjective, meaning *same*.† It is now both an adjective and a substantive. *Self* (plural *selves*) is used with either the possessive or the objective case of the personal pronouns. It is preceded by what seems the possessive case of the personal pronouns of the first and second persons, and by the objective case of the pronouns of the third person, *myself, thyself, ourselves, yourself, yourselves, himself, herself, itself, themselves.*

The pronoun *self* may also be used substantively with the possessive case of a noun, especially along with the adjective *own;* as, "A man's own self." "Men's own selves." In such cases the pronoun is always in the possessive case, as "*his* own self," "*their* own selves."

The pronoun *one* is generally treated as being on a par with the pronouns of the third person; so that we write *oneself,* not *one's self.*

177 The constructions in which *self* appears to be used as a substantive are probably corruptions. In Anglo-Saxon *sylf* was always an adjective, and being declinable, was put in the same case and number as the personal pronoun to which it was attached. But this curious anomaly is found in Anglo-Saxon, that the nominative (or possibly *uninflected*) *sylf* might be preceded by the *dative* case of a pronoun, the compound being often attached to or followed by the nominative‡ pronoun (*Ic mesylf, þu þe sylf, he himsylf;* or

---

* The older writers were not clear upon this point. Shakspere frequently gives a plural sense to *every* and *neither*. Thus, "Every one to rest themselves betake" (*Rape of Lucrece*, 125) ; "When neither are alive" (*Cymb.* iv. 2, 252).

† "In that selve moment" (*Chaucer*) = 'in that *same* moment'; "That self mould" (*Shaksp., R. II.* i. 2) = 'that *same* mould.' Compare 'selfsame.'

‡ Modern grammarians are horrified at such expressions as "It is *me*." "Who

mesylf ic, &c ; so in Wiclif *we us silf, ye you silf*). This dative was perhaps originally rather the dative absolute, than a dative in apposition to a nominative. *Myself* and *thyself* were perhaps corruptions of *mesilf* and *thesilf*, the change being probably aided by the fact that *self* was beginning to be treated as a substantive. *Herself* is ambiguous. *Ourselves* and *yourselves* (which are comparatively late forms, *us selve, us silf, ourselven, yourselven*, &c., having preceded them) were probably formed on a false analogy to resemble *myself* and *thyself*. The dative form maintained its ground in *himself, herself, itself*, and *themselves*,* though this last form is a puzzle, because if *self* be used adjectively, it has no business with the plural suffix *s*, which does not belong to adjectives at any stage of the language. The variations and anomalies in the usage of different periods render it impossible to give any perfectly satisfactory explanation of the use of this pronoun.

In poetry the personal pronouns are used reflectively without being strengthened by *self*, as: "I do repent *me*"; "haste *thee*"; "Signor Antonio commends *him* to you."

VIII. – Pronominal Adjectives, or Possessive Pronouns.

178 Besides the possessive cases *mine* or *my, thine* or *thy, his, her, its, our, your, their*, which have now passed into the class of adjectives, we have the secondary adjective forms, *hers, ours, yours, theirs*, formed from the preceding by the possessive suffix *s*.† These forms, as well as *mine* and *thine*, are now used only when the noun to which they relate is not expressed. *His* is used in both ways. *Its* is seldom used without a noun. Formerly, *mine* and *thine* were used before words beginning with a vowel or mute

---

did that? *Me*, Sir," &c. Nevertheless, it is by no means clear that these forms are inconsistent with the idioms of our language. They are not more at variance with strict rules than *he himself, she herself*, &c.; and the French language tolerates the dative forms *moi, toi, lui*, &c., in constructions where grammatical purity would require the nominative, as " c'est moi."

Passing by instances of mere carelessness, examples of the objective pronoun in place of the nominative are found in writers of authority from early times onwards. Thus : "Lord, yworshiped be the" (*Piers Plowman*); "I would not be thee nuncle" (*King Lear* i. 4); "That's me" (*Twelfth N.* ii. 5); "Scotland and thee did in each other live" (*Dryden*). In some provincial dialects the two cases are used interchangeably.

* *His self* and *their selves* are found in the early writers. When *our* and *your* relate to a single person, *self* not *selves* is used, as " We will *ourself* in person to this war"; "You must do it *yourself*." In early English there is a very curious use of the numeral *one* in the sense of *self*, 'him one,' &c. The adjective *lane* (=*alone*) is similarly used in Scotch, ' my lane,' ' him lane,' &c. The pronoun appears to vary between the possessive and the objective, as it does with *self*.

† Compare the double superlatives (§ 117). It is now usual to omit the apostrophe in these words, but many writers still keep it (*our's, your's*, &c.) There is no valid reason for not retaining it. In old writers (as Maundeville and Chaucer) we find *oures, youres, hires*, so that *oures* should become *our's*, just as *kinges* became *king's*. In vulgar and provincial English we also find the double possessives, *ourn, yourn, hern, his'n, theirn*, which, though not recognised in polite English, are just as good as *ours, yours*, &c.

h, my and *thy* before the other letters. They are still sometimes used thus in poetry.

In the phrases *of mine, of yours* (as 'a book of mine') some grammarians* consider that we have a repetition of the idea of possession.

VERB.

179 A Verb† is that part of speech by means of which we are able to make an assertion about something.

180 The word which stands for what is spoken about is called the subject of the verb (or of the sentence). It is put in the nominative case. A verb expresses with regard to what is spoken about, that it *is something*, that it *does something*, or that it *is the object of some action*.

181 When an adjective is prefixed to a noun, the notion of some quality, attribute, or fact, is connected with our notion of that which is spoken about. If we say a *red apple*, the notion of *red* is connected with that of *apple*. The same end is attained by the use of a verb, with this difference, that when we prefix an adjective to a noun, the connexion between the two notions is spoken of as *already existing*; the use of a verb *effects* the union of the two notions. When we say *a blue coat*, the connexion between the object of thought and its attribute is pre-supposed. When we say, *The coat is blue*, the verb *is* effects the union of the two notions. [The different kinds of sentences that result from the use of verbs are treated of in the Syntax.]

182 Verbs are divided into two classes—Transitive‡ and Intransitive Verbs.

A Transitive Verb is one which denotes an action or feeling which is directed towards some object; as, *strike*, "He *strikes* the ball;" *love*, "He *loves* his father." The word which stands for the object of the action described by the verb is called the object of the verb. It is put in the objective case.

An Intransitive Verb is one which denotes a *state* or *con-*

---

* Dr. Adams takes this view of them. The general explanation is that "a book of *mine*" means "a book *of my books*" (*Latham, Eng. Lang.*, p. 443). If this were necessarily the case, such an expression as "this sweet wee wife of mine," in Burns's song, would suggest unpleasant ideas of bigamy. Koch (ii. p. 236) suggests the explanation that *of* is partitive, and *mine*, &c., universal in sense, so that *of mine* means ' of all that belongs to me.' Perhaps the true explanation is that the *of* does little more than mark identity, as in the expressions, ' The city *of* Rome,' 'A brute *of* a fellow.' In ' a book of yours,' we have a triple expression of the genitive or possessive idea, in *of, r,* and *s.*

† Latin *verbum*, "word;" the verb being emphatically the *word* of the sentence.

‡ Latin *transire*, "to go across;" the action passes over, as it were, from the doer of it to the object of it.

dition, or an action or feeling which is not directed towards, or exerted upon an object; as, *to be, to dwell, to stand, to sit, to rejoice, to run*. Verbs of this kind are sometimes called Neuter Verbs.

183. Many verbs which denote actions are used sometimes as transitive verbs, sometimes as intransitive verbs; as, " He *ran* away;" " He *ran* a thorn into his finger." " The child *speaks* already ", " He *speaks* several languages." In all such cases there is not only a difference of use, but a real difference of meaning. Thus, *speak*, " to utter articulate sounds " (intransitive); *speak*, " to use (a language) as the means of expressing ideas" (transitive). This intransitive use of a verb must not be confounded with the *reflective* use of a *transitive* verb, in cases where the reflective pronoun is understood,* as " The sea breaks (itself) on the rocks "; " The clouds spread (themselves) over the sky " ; " The boats drew (themselves) clear of one another "; " The earth moves (itself)"; " The needle turns (itself) towards the pole." Verbs properly intransitive may be used as transitive, as " He *swam* the Esk river " ; " He *fought* his adversaries " ; " The student *walks* the hospitals," &c. In old English intransitive verbs were often followed by a pronoun used reflectively, as " Hie thee home " ; " Fare thee well " ; " Sit thee down.'' Some compound verbs are used curiously in this way, as : " To over-sleep oneself "; " He over-ate himself "; " Vaulting ambition which o'erleaps itself."

Transitive verbs are sometimes used with a sort of passive signification, as: " The meat cuts tough," *i.e.*, ' is tough when it is cut ' ; " The cakes eat short and crisp," *i.e.*, ' are short and crisp when they are eaten ' ; " The book sold well " ; " The bait took "; " The bed feels hard," *i.e.*, ' is hard when it is felt ' ; " The rose smells sweet "; " The wine tastes sour."

184. Verbs admit of the following modifications:—Voice, Mood, Tense, Number, and Person.

Voice.

185. Voice is the form of a verb by means of which we show whether the subject of the sentence stands for the *doer*, or for the *object* of the action spoken of by the verb. There are two Voices, the Active Voice and the Passive Voice.

The Active Voice is made up of those forms of a verb which denote that the subject of the sentence stands for the

---

* It is only when thus used that a *verb* can properly be said to be used *reflectively*. Compare the difference between *lavat se* and *lavatur* in Latin, and between τύπτει ἑαυτόν and τύπτεται in Greek. The following verbs are some of those that may be used reflectively without having the reflective pronoun expressed:—*push, extend, stretch, drag, rest, lean, incline, keep, set, bend, feed, open, shut, harden, shorten, lengthen, melt, dissolve, recover, reform, prepare, wash, yield, change, dash, refrain, obtrude, intrude, pour, press, remove, settle, steal, stretch*, &c.

Several intransitive verbs were once reflective, as, *wend* (went), *abscond, venture, depart, consort, retire*, &c.

The following are a few of those which are both transitive and intransitive:— *act, talk, eat, drink, blow, fly, grow, abide, answer, boil, rain, shake, slip, stay, survive*, &c.

doer of the action described by the verb; as, "The boy *strikes* the ball." "The cat *killed* the mouse."

The Passive Voice is made up of those forms of a verb which denote that the subject of the sentence stands for the object of the action described by the verb; as, "The ball *is struck* by the boy." "The mouse *was killed* by the cat."

186 We may speak of one and the same action by means either of a verb in the active voice, or of a verb in the passive voice; but then the word that is the *object* of the active verb must be the *subject* of the passive verb, as in the above examples.

It is clear that only transitive verbs can properly be used in the passive voice. There are, however, some remarkable exceptions to this principle in English. When an intransitive verb is followed by a phrase made up of a preposition and noun, the intransitive verb may often be used passively with the preposition as an adverbial adjunct. Thus we may say, "I despair of success," "I hope for* reward," and also "Success is despaired of," "Reward is hoped for."* We can even say "He was taken care of"; "He was lost sight of," &c. The indirect object may also be the subject of a passive verb, as "The dead were refused burial"; "He was promised a new coat."

187 The Passive Voice of a verb is formed by prefixing the various parts of the verb *be* to the perfect participle of the verb. The perfect participle of a transitive verb is *passive* in meaning.

Some intransitive verbs have their perfect tenses formed by means of the verb *be*, followed by the past or perfect participle; † as, "I *am* come;" "He *is* arrived;" "He *is* fallen." Great care must be taken not to confound these with passive verbs. The sign of the passive voice is not the verb *be*, but the *passive participle* that follows it.

Mood.

188 Moods (that is, *modes*) are certain variations of form in verbs, by means of which we can show the *mode* or *manner*

---

* Respecting the view held by some grammarians that in such a phrase as, "I wonder at your folly," *at* has become an adverb, and *wonder at* a compound precisely equivalent to a transitive verb, and having *your folly* for its object, see the note on § 372. Those who maintain this view must be prepared to admit that "to promise a new coat to," and "to take good care of," are compound verbs governing the objective case.

† Some grammarians are pleased to order us to alter these forms into "I *have* come," "He *has* arrived," &c. They had better at the same time mend the French and German languages, which at present still tolerate the forms, *Je suis venu*, *Ich bin gekommen*.

in which the attribute or fact indicated by the verb is connected in thought with the thing that is spoken of.

In English there are four moods:—1. The Infinitive Mood. 2. The Indicative Mood. 3. The Imperative Mood. 4. The Subjunctive Mood.*

To these moods many grammarians add the *Potential Mood*, meaning by that mood certain combinations of the so-called auxiliary verbs *may, might, can, could, must*, with the infinitive mood. This is objectionable. *I can write*, and *I must go*, are no more *moods* of the verbs *write* and *go*, than *possum scribere* is a mood of *scribo* in Latin; or, *Je puis écrire*, *Ich kann schreiben* and *Ich muss gehen* moods of the verbs *écrire, schreiben*, and *gehen* in French and German. Moreover this potential mood would need to be itself subdivided into Indicative forms and Subjunctive forms. The sentences, "I *could* do this at one time, but I cannot now," and "I *could* not do this, if I were to try," do not contain the same parts of the verb *can*. In the first sentence, *could* is in the indicative mood; in the second, it is in the subjunctive mood.

1.—The Infinitive Mood.

189 The Infinitive Mood is that form of the verb which is used when the action or state that is denoted by the verb is spoken of without reference to person, number, or time. The verb is then not used predicatively, but the action or state that it denotes is treated as a separate object of thought, and consequently the infinitive mood has the force of a substantive, and may be used either as the subject or as the object of another verb, or after certain prepositions (namely *to* and *but*).

190 It is impossible to make an assertion by means of the Infinitive Mood.

191 The preposition *to* is not an essential part of the infinitive mood, nor an invariable sign of it. Many verbs (as *may*,† *can, shall, will, must, let, dare, do, bid, make, see, hear, feel, need*) are followed by the simple infinitive without *to*, as "You may *speak*"; "Bid me *discourse*"; "He made me *laugh*"; "I felt the shock *vibrate* through my nerves"; "I had rather not *tell* you." (See note on § 560). In "I cannot but *admire* his courage," *admire* is in the infinitive mood after the preposition *but*. (See § 505).

---

* *Mood* comes from the Latin *modus*, "*manner*"; *Indicative* from *indicare*, "*to point out*"; *Imperative* from *imperare*, "*to command*"; *Subjunctive* from *subjungere*, "*to join on to*"; *Infinitive* from *innnitus*, "*unlimited*," *i.e.*, as regards person, number, &c.

† The case is exactly analogous in German. The preposition *zu* precedes the infinitive mood after all verbs except such as answer to the English verbs after which *to* is not required. Becker (in his German Grammar) applies the term *supine* to this combination of *zu* with an infinitive mood. There would be advantages in the use of this name in English grammar, as the combination most nearly approaches the force of the Latin supine in *-um*, and the term gerund might then be restricted to the forms in *-ing*.

The simple infinitive (without *to*) used as the subject of another verb is legitimate, though somewhat archaic, as "Better *be* with the dead" (*Macbeth* iii. 2, 20); "Will't please your highness *walk*" (*Lear* iv. 7); "Mother, what does *marry* mean?" (*Longfellow*); "Better *dwell* in the midst of alarms than *reign* in this horrible place" (*Cowper*). So in Anglo-Saxon: "Leofre ys us *beon* beswungen for lare þænne hit ne cunnan" (*Ælf. Coll*); "*To be* flogged for learning is more welcome to us, than not *to know* it."

192. In Anglo-Saxon, the infinitive mood ended in* *-an*, and when used as such, had no *to* before it. A verb in the infinitive might be the subject or object of another verb, or even come after an adjective such as *worthy*, *ready*, &c. The infinitive was however treated as a declinable abstract noun, and a dative form (called the *gerund*), ending in *-anne*, or *-enne*, and preceded by the preposition *to*, was used to denote *purpose*. Thus in "He that hath ears to hear," *to hear* = *to gehyranne*; in "The sower went forth to sow," *to sow* = *to sáwenne*. This gerundive infinitive passed into modern English with the loss of the dative inflection, as in "I came *to tell* you"; "The water is good *to drink*," *i.e., for drinking*; "This house is *to let*";† "He is *to come* home to-morrow." Here the *to* has its full and proper force, and we have more than a mere infinitive mood. From denoting the *purpose* of an action, the *to* came to mark the ground of an action more generally, and so may indicate the *cause* or *condition* of an action, as "I am sorry *to hear* this;" "I am glad *to see* you," *i.e.*, 'at seeing you,' or 'in consequence of seeing you'; "*To* hear him talk (*i.e.*, on hearing him talk), one would suppose he was master here." But somehow or other this gerund with *to* came to be used in place of the simple infinitive, as the subject or object of another verb,‡ and so we say "*To err* is human, *to forgive* divine"; "I hope *to see* you." Here the *to* is utterly without meaning. We even find another preposition used before it, as "This is Elias which was *for to come*"; § "There is nothing left *but to submit*."

As this infinitive preceded by *to* has come to us from the Anglo-Saxon gerund, it is often called the *gerundial infinitive*, or the *gerund*. (The latter name is in this work applied to a different form.)

2.—The Indicative Mood.

193 The Indicative Mood comprises those forms of a verb which are used when a statement, question, or supposition is made respecting some event or state of things, past, present, or future, regarded as actual, and not as merely thought of: as, "He *struck* the ball;" "We *shall set* out to-morrow"; "If he *was* guilty, his punishment *was* too light."

---

* An infinitive suffix *-en* or *-e* is still found in Chaucer and Wiclif. As used by Spenser it is antiquated.

† The *active* infinitive in these phrases is the older and truer form. Chaucer uses "It is *to despise*" = "It is *to be despised*." In the North they still say "What is to do?" for "What is to be done?"

‡ Even in Anglo-Saxon we find such constructions as "hyt is alyfed wel to donne" (it is allowed to do good); "He ondréd þyder to faranne" (he dreaded to go thither).

§ This use of *for* occurs very early. We still say "I was *about* to observe." In the Northern dialect *at* was used for *to*, as "I have noght *at to with the*" (*Kock* ii. p. 61). *Til* (*till*) was also used.

3.—The Imperative Mood.

194 The Imperative Mood includes those forms of the verb by means of which we utter a command (requests and exhortations are only weaker kinds of commands); as, "*Give me that book*." "*Go away*."

A direct command must of course be addressed to the person who is to obey it. Hence a strictly imperative mood can only be used in the second person. When we express our will in connexion with the first or third person, we either employ the subjunctive mood (as "Cursed *be* he that first cries hold"; "Go *we* to the king"), or make use of the imperative *let*, followed by an infinitive complement (see § 395), as "Let us pray"; "Let him be heard." These are not imperative forms of *pray* and *hear*, but periphrastic expressions doing duty for them (see § 256).

4.—The Subjunctive Mood.

195 The Subjunctive Mood comprises those forms of a verb by means of which an event or state of things is spoken of not as *a matter of fact*, actual or assumed, but as merely *thought of*.

The primary distinction between the Indicative and the Subjunctive Mood is, that when the Indicative is used, the connexion between the subject and the predicate is regarded as answering to some *actual* event or state of things, past, present, or future; whereas, when the Subjunctive is used, this connexion is only made *in thought*, without being referred to anything actual outside the mind itself.* Hence the Subjunctive is employed to express a will or wish (as "Thy kingdom come"); in clauses denoting *purpose* (as "See that all *be* in readiness"; "Govern well thy appetite, lest sin *surprise* thee"); in clauses denoting the purport of a wish or command (as "The sentence is that the prisoner *be* imprisoned for life"); to express a supposition or wish contrary to the fact, or not regarded as brought to the test of actual fact (as "If he *were* here he would think differently"; "Oh! that it *were* possible"). (Look carefully at § 466.)

A verb in the Subjunctive Mood is generally (but not always) preceded by one of the conjunctions *if, that, lest, though, unless*, &c.; but the Subjunctive Mood is not always necessary after these conjunctions, nor is the conjunction a part of the mood itself.

196 In modern English the simple present or past tense of the subjunctive mood is often replaced by phrases compounded of the verbs *may, might,* and *should*, which for that reason are called *auxiliary* or *helping verbs*. Thus for "lest sin *surprise* thee," we now commonly say "Lest sin *should surprise* thee."

Participle.

197 Participles are verbal *adjectives*, differing from ordinary

---

* In modern English it is getting (unfortunately) more and more common to use the Indicative Mood in cases where the Subjunctive would be more correct. Thus for "See that all *be* in readiness," many people say "See that all *is* in readiness"; for "If that *were* to happen," they say, "If that *was* to happen." In Anglo-Saxon and early English the Subjunctive was (rightly) used in the dependent clause in which a person's speech or thought was reported. Even in Sidney's *Arcadia* we find: "And I think there she *do* dwell."

adjectives in this, that the active participle can take a substantive after it as its object.

There are two participles formed by inflection, the Imperfect Participle and the Perfect Participle. The imperfect participle always ends in *ing*.* The perfect participle in verbs of the Weak Conjugation ends in *d* or *ed*.† The Imperfect Participle is always *active*, the Perfect Participle is *passive*, provided the verb be a transitive verb; as, " I saw a boy *beating* a dog." " *Frightened* by the noise, he ran away."

198 Even in the perfect tenses, as, "I have *written* a letter," the origin of the construction is, " I have a letter written," where *written* is an adjective agreeing with *letter;* in Latin, *Habeo epistolam scriptam*. In French the participle agrees with the object in some constructions; as, " Les lettres que j'ai écrites." In Anglo-Saxon the perfect participle in the perfect tenses was originally indected, and made to agree with the object of the verb.‡

199 Besides the participles formed by inflection, there are the following compound participles:—
Active Perfect Participle—*Having struck*.
Active Perfect Participle of continued action—*Having been striking*.
Passive Indefinite Participle—*Being struck*.
Passive Perfect Participle—*Having been struck*.

Gerund.

200 Besides the participles (which are *adjectives*), most verbs in English have a substantive ending in -*ing* formed from them, called the *gerund*.§ A gerund is like an imperfect

---

* The termination of this participle in Anglo-Saxon was -*ende*, which was subsequently changed to -*inde*, and finally to -*inge*, -*ynge*, and -*ing*. In the Northern dialect the termination was -*ande* or -*and*, which long maintained its ground in the North of England and in Scotland, and sometimes occurs in Chaucer. The essential letters of the suffix are *nd*. This suffix is akin to the Latin -*ent* or -*nt* and the Greek οντ or εντ.

† The letter *y*, which is found as a prefix in one or two old forms (as *yclept* 'called'), and is affected by some writers in others, is derived from the Anglo-Saxon prefix *ge*.

‡ As " He hæfð man geweorhtne" (he has created man); " Hig hæfdon heora lofsang gesungenne" (they had sung their praise-song). But the accusative suffix began to be dropped even in Anglo-Saxon (*Koch*, ii. p. 36).

§ The true origin of the gerund is a point of some difficulty, owing to forms derived from more than one source having become almost inextricably blended together. There are two classes of verbal substantives in -*ing*. Of these one is merely a modification of the Anglo-Saxon verbal nouns in -*ung*, the continuous use of which can be traced. These have the ordinary construction of nouns, as " For earnunge ēcan lifes," '*for earning of eternal life*' (*Grein*, ii. p. 286); " Thei weren at robbinge," '*they were a robbing*' (*Layamon*); " On hunting ben they ridden," '*a hunting are they ridden*'; " I fare to gon a legging" (*Chaucer*); " I go a fishing" (*John* xxi. 3); " Forty and six years was this temple in building"; " While the ark was a preparing." (The *a* is a weakened form of *on* or *in*). Such phrases

participle in form, but is totally distinct from it in origin and construction. As the verbs *have* and *be* have gerunds, there are also certain compound forms, which may be called *compound gerunds*, made up of the gerunds of these verbs combined with participles; as, *having gone, being loved, having been writing, having been struck.*

201 Gerunds are followed by the same construction as the verbs from which they are derived. They are used either as the subjects or objects of verbs, or after prepositions,* as, "I like *reading*," "He is fond of *studying* mathematics," "He is desirous of *being distinguished*," "After *having been writing* all the morning, I am tired," "Through *having lost* his book, he could not learn his lesson."

202 Participles (being adjectives) are never used as the subjects or objects of verbs, or after prepositions. It must be observed, too, that in all such compounds as *a hiding-place, a walking-stick*, &c., it is the gerund, and not the participle, which is used. If the latter were the case, *a walking-stick* could only mean *a stick that walks*.

Tense.

203 Tense (Latin *tempus*, 'time') is a variation of form in verbs, or a compound verbal phrase, indicating partly the time to which an action or event is referred, and partly the com-

---

as "I am a doing of it," though now obsolete, are perfectly grammatical. The omission of the preposition led to what some have mistaken for a passive use of the participle in *-ing*, as "the house is building." We have here the direct descendants of the nouns in *-ung*. (Compare *e.g.* "ge beoð on hatunge," 'ye shall be hated.' (*Matt.* x. 22). Some maintain that there is no gerund in *-ing* distinct from these modernised nouns in *-ung*. To this view it may be objected that the nouns in *-ung* furnish no explanation of the origin of the compound gerunds, and that the verbals in *-ing* commonly called gerunds have a power of governing objects which never belonged to the nouns in *-ung*. When we say "he was hanged for killing a man," the objective relation of *man* to *killing* is (now at any rate) as distinctly in our thoughts as that of *man* to *killed* when we say "he killed a man." Consequently even if it could be shown that the formation in *-ung* was the parent of all the noun formations in *-ing*, a large class of these would still be entitled to a new classification and a new name, just as adverbs that have acquired the force of prepositions require to be classed and named as such. It is better to allow (with Koch) that, besides the descendants of the nouns in *-ung*, there is a class of verbal substantives in *-ing*, descended from the old Anglo-Saxon gerund, which Koch traces (ii. § 98) through such forms as *to bodianne, to bodiende, to fleonde, in tornand, to accusinge, for to brennyng*, &c. The weakening and final omission of the preposition would lead to the modern form, the development of which may have been assisted by the influence of the French *gerund* in *-ant*, which in most French grammars is confounded with the present participle. (In Italian the forms are distinct, and the extensive use of the gerund is remarkable). An *infinitive* in *-ing*, which is set down in some grammars as a modification of the *simple* infinitive in *-an* or *-en*, is a perfectly needless and unwarranted invention. The descendants of the *-ung* nouns are quite competent to discharge such special functions as are attributed to it.

* The grossness of the mistake which is made in confounding the participle with the gerund in English, becomes most palpable when beginners, who have been led astray by their English grammars, render such phrases as "He talks about fighting," by the Latin "Loquitur de pugnante." In such French expressions as *en attendant*, the word in *-ant* is a gerund, derived from a Latin form in *-ando-*. The adjective in *-ant* is derived from the participle in *-ans* (*-antis*).—*Max Müller*.

pleteness or incompleteness of the event at the time indicated.

204. If inflection alone were the criterion of tense, we should have to limit the tenses in English to two, the present and the past indefinite; but the theoretical precision of the arrangement would not be worth the inconvenience that it would entail.

205. There are three divisions of time to which an event or a state may be referred,—the Present, the Past, and the Future. Hence, if the *time* of an event were the only thing to be considered, there could not be more than three tenses. But, besides the time of an action, there are three ways in which an action or event may be viewed:—
1. It may be spoken of as incomplete, or still going on. A tense which indicates this is called an *imperfect* tense.
2. It may be spoken of as complete. A tense which indicates this is called a *perfect* tense.
3. It may be spoken of without distinct reference to other events, with regard to which it is complete or incomplete. A tense in which an action is thus spoken of is called an *indefinite* tense. The indefinite tenses are employed when an action or event is spoken of as one whole, without reference to its duration; as, "He *strikes* the ball." "He *fell* to the ground." "He *will break* his neck."

206. An action may be viewed in these three ways with reference to past, to present, or to future time. We thus get nine primary tenses.

A.
1. The Past Imperfect, showing that at a certain past time an action was going on; as, *I was writing; I was being taught.*
2. The Past Perfect, showing that at a certain past time an action was complete; as, *I had written; I had been taught.*
3. The Past Indefinite (or Preterite), speaking of the action as one whole referred to past time; as, *I wrote; I was taught.*

B.
1. The Present Imperfect, showing that an action is going on at the present time; as, *I am writing; I am being taught.*
2. The Present Perfect, showing that at the present time a certain action is complete; as, *I have written; I have been taught.*
3. The Present Indefinite, speaking of the action as one whole, referred to present time; as, *I write; I am taught.*

F

1. The <u>Future Imperfect</u>, showing that at a certain future time an action will be going on; as, *I shall be writing; I shall be being taught.*

2. The <u>Future Perfect</u>, showing that at a certain future time an action will be complete; as, *I shall have written: I shall have been taught.*

3. The <u>Future Indefinite</u>, speaking of an action as one whole, referred to future time; as, *I shall write; I shall be taught.*

207. From this table it appears at once that *perfect* and *past* are not the same. A tense is past, present, or future, according to the *time* with reference to which an action is spoken of, not according to the completeness or incompleteness of the action at that time. When we say, "*I have written*," although the act of writing took place in past time, yet the *completeness* of the action (which is what the tense indicates) is referred to *present time*. Hence the tense is a *present* tense, although it speaks of an action that is completed. To justify us in using this tense, it is necessary that the state of things brought about by the action should still exist at the present time. We may say, "England has founded a mighty empire in the East," because the empire still lasts: but we cannot say, "Cromwell has founded a dynasty," because the dynasty exists no longer.

208. The *indefinite* tenses are often *imperfect* in sense. Thus, "I stood during the whole of the performance." "While he *lived* at home he was happy." The verbs in such cases would have to be rendered into the past *imperfect* tense in French, Latin, or Greek (see § 216).

209 Besides the primary tenses given in § 206, we have the following:—

The Present Perfect of continued action — I *have been writing.*

The Past Perfect of continued action — I *had been writing.*

The Future Perfect of continued action — I *shall have been writing.**

210 The Present Indefinite Tense is used not only of what takes place now, but also of what frequently or habitually takes place; as, "John often *goes* to the theatre." "He *writes* beautiful poems." "It *rains* here almost every day." It is also used of what is universally true; as, "Virtue *is* its own reward." "Honesty *is* the best policy." It is also used with reference to what is future,† in cases in which in Latin a future or future perfect tense would be used; as, "When he *comes*, I will speak to him." "If

---

* Some grammars give combinations like "I am going to write," as *tenses (Present Intentional, Past Intentional,* &c.). This is quite unnecessary. "I am going to write," and "I am intending to write," are not tenses of the verb *write*, but of the verbs *go* and *intend*, followed by a gerundial infinitive, which constitutes either an object or an adverbial adjunct to it.

† Our language admits this idiom the more readily, as in Anglo-Saxon the same form served for both the present and the future tense.

he *hits* me, I will hit him again." In lively narrations also, the speaker or writer often imagines himself to be *present* at the events he is describing, and so uses the *present* tense in speaking of *past* events. When thus used, the tense is called the *Historic Present*.

211 A Substantive has no relation to any time in particular. The Infinitive Mood is virtually a substantive. Hence the Infinitive Mood does not indicate time.* It admits only of the distinctions in tense called Imperfect, Perfect, and Indefinite. "[To] *be writing*" is an Imperfect Tense, but it may refer either to present or to future time. In "I ought *to be writing* my letters now," it refers to present time; in "I shall *be travelling* to-morrow," it refers to future time.

212 The tenses of the English verb are made partly by inflection, partly by the use of auxiliary verbs.

The Present Indefinite and the Past Indefinite in the Active Voice are the only two tenses formed by inflection.

The Imperfect tenses are formed by the indefinite tenses of the verb *be*, followed by the imperfect participle. †

The Perfect tenses are formed by means of the indefinite tenses of the verb *have*, followed by the perfect participle.

The Future tenses are formed by means of the auxiliary verbs *shall* and *will*, followed by the infinitive mood: *shall* being used for the first person, *will* for the second and third in affirmative principal sentences; but in subordinate clauses, after a relative, or such words as *if*, *when*, *as*, *though*, *unless*, *until*, &c., the verb *shall* is used for all three persons; ‡ as, "If it *shall* be proved"; "When they *shall* turn unto the Lord"; "When He shall appear we shall be like Him."

213 When the verb *will* is used in the first person and the verb *shall* in the second and third, it is implied that the action spoken of depends upon the will of *the speaker*. *Shall* (like *sollen* in German) implies an *obligation* to do something. Hence *shall* is appropriately used in commands (as "Thou shalt not kill"), in promises or threats (as "You shall have a holiday"), and in the language of prophecy, which is an utterance of the Divine will or purpose. *Shall* is used in the first person as a simple

---

* The same is the case with the Participles in English. They express *imperfect* and *perfect*; but not *past* or *present*.

† It is pretty certain that the view adopted by Max Müller and others, that the compound imperfect tenses originated in the use of the verbal noun in -*ing* (*I am writing* having been originally *I am a writing*, &c.; see note on § 200) is incorrect. The *participle* in -*ende*, -*and*, -*yng*, or -*ing*, is found from the earliest period onwards, side by side with the use of the verbal noun in -*ung* or -*ing*, as: "Hig wieron etende and drincende," 'they were eating and drinking' (*Matt.* xxiv. 38); "Harold was *comand*" (*P. Langtoft*). The sense of the compound *imperfect* tenses was however commonly expressed by means of the uncompounded *indefinite* tenses. (See § 208.)

‡ In early English *shall* is the usual future auxiliary.

auxiliary of a future tense, on much the same principle as that on which a person subscribes himself at the end of a letter, "Your obedient humble servant." It implies a sort of polite acknowledgment of being bound by the will of others, or at least by the force of circumstances. By a converse application of the same principle, the verb *will* is used in the second and third persons to imply that the action referred to depends upon the *volition* of the person to or of whom we speak. In questions, however, and in reported speeches, the force of the verb *shall* is the same in the second and third persons as it would be in the answer, or as it was in the direct speech: "*Shall* you be present?" "I *shall*." "I *shall* not set out to-morrow;" "I said I *should* not set out to-morrow," or, "John said that he *should* not set out to-morrow." The verb to be used in a question depends upon the verb expected in the reply. We say, "Will you go?" if we expect the answer, "I will." *

214 All moods and tenses in the Passive Voice are made by means of auxiliary verbs; the Passive Voice of a verb consisting of its perfect participle, preceded by the various moods and tenses of the verb *be*.†

215 The Indefinite Tenses and the Indefinite Participles of the Passive Voice are a little ambiguous in meaning. They may refer either to the *action* indicated by the verb, or to the *results* of the action. In the latter case they are not strictly *tenses* of the passive voice, but the participle that follows the verb *be* is used as an adjective. In "He *was terrified* at the sight," *was terrified* is a past indefinite tense of the passive voice of the verb *terrify*. It represents an action exerted upon a certain person. In "He *was terrified*, so that he could not speak," the verb of the sentence is *was*, and *terrified* is a mere adjective.‡ In "Every house is built by some man," *is built* is a present indefinite tense passive of the verb *build*. In "This house is built of stone," *is* is the verb, and *built* is used as an adjective.

216 From the following table it will be seen that the English language admits of greater accuracy than any other in the expression of all the shades of meaning that are involved in *tense*. In other languages the same form often has to do double duty.

* In Anglo-Saxon the present often did duty for the future, as: "Aefter þrim dagon ic arise," '*After three days I shall rise again*' (*Matt.* xxvii. 63); "Aelc treow .... byð forcorfen," '*Every tree .... shall be cut down*' (*Matt.* iii. 10), but the compounds with *shall* and *will* were also used. The future perfect belongs only to modern English. The past indefinite often served for the modern past indefinite, present perfect, and past perfect, *e.g.* "mine eâgan gesâwon þine hǽle," '*mine eyes have seen thy salvation*' (*Luke* ii. 30).

† In Anglo-Saxon there were two auxiliary verbs for forming the passive, *beon* and *weorðan*, the latter (like *werden* in German) being employed to denote that something is the object of a *definite action*, and not merely that it is in the state resulting from an action. The participle being in the predicative relation to the subject, was made to agree with it.

‡ This distinction can be easily marked in Greek and in German. "The letter is written" may be rendered either "ἡ ἐπιστολὴ γράφεται," and "Der Brief wird geschrieben," or "ἡ ἐπιστολὴ γεγραμμένη ἐστι," and "Der Brief ist geschrieben." In Anglo-Saxon the present and past perfect passive were expressed by means of the present and past indefinite tenses.

Comparative Table of Tenses in English, Latin, French, German, and Greek.

ACTIVE VOICE.
INDICATIVE MOOD.

		English.	Latin.	Greek.	French.	German.
Present	Indefinite	He writes	scribit	γράφει	il écrit	er schreibt
	Imperfect	He is writing	scribit	γράφει	il écrit	er schreibt
	Perfect	He has written	scripsit	γέγραφε	il a écrit	er hat geschrieben
Past	Indefinite	He wrote	scripsit	ἔγραψε	il écrivit	er schrieb
	Imperfect	He was writing	scribebat	ἔγραφε	il écrivait	er schrieb
	Perfect	He had written	scripserat	ἐγεγράφει	{ il avait écrit il eut écrit }	er hatte geschrieben
Future	Indefinite	He will write	scribet	γράψει	il écrira	er wird schreiben
	Imperfect	He will be writing	scribet	γράψει	il écrira	er wird schreiben
	Perfect	He will have written	scripserit	..	il aura écrit	er wird geschrieben haben
	Perfect of continued action	He has been writing, &c.	..	..	..	..

PASSIVE VOICE.
INDICATIVE MOOD.

		English.	Latin.	Greek.	French.	German.
Present	*Indefinite*	It is written	scribitur	γράφεται	il est écrit	es wird geschrieben
	Imperfect	It is being written	scribitur	γράφεται		es wird geschrieben
	Perfect	It has been written	scriptum est / scriptum fuit	γέγραπται	il a été écrit	es ist geschrieben worden
Past	*Indefinite*	It was written	scriptum est / scriptum fuit	ἐγράφθη	il fut écrit	es wurde geschrieben / es wurde geschrieben
	Imperfect	It was being written	scribebatur	ἐγράφετο		
	Perfect	It had been written	scriptum erat / scriptum fuerat	ἐγέγραπτο	il avait été écrit / il eut été écrit	es war geschrieben worden
Future	*Indefinite*	It will be written	scribetur	γραφθήσεται	il sera écrit	es wird geschrieben werden
	Imperfect	It will be being written	scribetur	γράψεται		es wird geschrieben werden
	Perfect	It will have been written	scriptum erit	γεγράψεται	il aura été écrit	es wird geschrieben worden seyn

Number.

217 Number is a modification of the form of a verb, by means of which we show whether the verb is spoken of one person or thing, or of more than one. There are, therefore, two numbers in verbs, corresponding to the two numbers in substantives.

Person.

218 Person is a modification of the form of verbs, by which we indicate whether the speaker speaks of himself, or speaks of the person or persons addressed, or speaks of some other person or thing. There are three persons—the First Person, the Second Person, and the Third Person.*

The First Person includes those forms of the verb which are used when the speaker speaks of himself either singly or with others.

The Second Person includes those forms of the verb which are used when the subject of the verb stands for the person or persons spoken to.

The Third Person includes those forms of the verb which are used when the subject of the verb denotes neither the speaker nor the person spoken to.

CONJUGATION OF VERBS.

219 The conjugation of a verb is the formation of all the various inflections and combinations used to indicate the Voices, Moods, Tenses, Numbers, and Persons of which the verb is capable. The varieties in the conjugation of verbs depend upon the formation of the Infinitive, the Past Indefinite or Preterite Tense, and the Perfect Participle. All other parts of a verb are formed from these according to unvarying rules.

---

* Observe that the *subject* of the verb forms no part of the *person* of the verb. The first person of the present tense of the verb *be is am*, not *I am*. It is usual, however, to conjugate verbs with a subject expressed, for the sake of clearness.

The suffixes by which Person is marked were originally neither more nor less than the Personal Pronouns. These can be traced in various languages, but, as might be expected (see § 27), usually appear in very mutilated forms, or disappear altogether. The characteristic letter of the suffix for the first person was *m* (compare *mei*, *me*, &c.), for the second *s* (compare Greek συ, σε), for the third *t* (the root consonant of various demonstratives, as το in Greek, *tam*, *tum*, &c. in Latin, *the*, *this*, &c. in English). Combined with a mark of plurality, *s* or *n*, these are found in the plural. (Compare -*mus*, -*tis*, -*nt* in Latin; -*mes* in old High German). In English the suffix -*m* still appears in *am* (in A. S. also in *beom*). Compare the Latin *sum*, *inquam*, *amem*, &c. In -*st* or -*est* the *t* is a phonetic offgrowth of the *s*, which is the suffix in Gothic, and is found in the Northumbrian dialect (compare *amidst*, &c.). In the third person -*th* is now commonly softened to -*s*. The plural suffixes had in Anglo-Saxon become the same for all three persons (see Appendix A).

Verbs in English are divided into two well-defined and widely different classes, distinguished by the formation of the preterite. These are:
A. *Verbs of the Strong Conjugation.*
B. *Verbs of the Weak Conjugation.*

Verbs of the Strong Conjugation.

220 The Strong Conjugation is based upon a mode of forming the preterite which belongs to various members of the Aryan family of languages. In the Strong Conjugation the Preterite (or Past Indefinite Tense) was originally formed by *reduplication*, i.e. by repeating the root of the verb. This formation was weakened (1) by omitting the final consonant from the first member of the doubled root;* (2) by weakening the vowel sound of the initial syllable to one uniform letter, and frequently by weakening or modifying the vowel sound of the second root as well; † (3) by omitting the initial consonant of the second member of the doubled root, so that the vowel of reduplication and the vowel of the root came in contact with each other, and were commonly blended into one ‡ sound. Thus it has come to pass that in English (with two exceptions), the preterite of verbs of the Strong Conjugation is formed by modifying the vowel sound of the root.

Two preterites in English distinctly show reduplication, namely, *did* from *do*, and *hight* (was called) from the old verb *hátan*, where *gh* is a variety of the guttural *h* at the beginning.§

221 In English the perfect participle of all verbs of the strong conjugation was originally formed by the (adjective) suffix-

---

* In Sanscrit perfect tenses are formed thus, just as in Latin, from *tud* (the root of *tundo*) we get *tu-tud-i*; from *mord*, *mo-mord-i*; from *dic* (the root of *disco*) *di-dic-i*.

† In Greek the initial consonant is repeated, but with the vowel sound weakened to ε (as λε-λω κα). This formation occurs in several verbs in Latin, as *pe-pul-i* (from *pello*); *pe-pig-i* (from *pango*); *ce-cid-i* (from *cado*). In Gothic the reduplication consisted of the initial consonant followed by *ai*, as *haitan* (to call), *hai-hait*. In Anglo-Saxon the reduplication once consisted of the first consonant followed by *eo*. (*Koch*, i. p. 240).

‡ Thus in old Frisian the preterite from the root *hald* passed through the stages *ha-hald*, *ha-hild*, *ha-ild* to *held*. In Latin the root *lēg* (in *lego*) passed through the stages *le-leg-i*, *lĕ-ĕg-i* to *lēgi*; the root *vĕn* (in *venio*) through *vĕ-vĕn-i*, *vĕ-ĕn-i* to *vēni*; the root *fac* through *fĕ-fĭc-i*, *fĕ-ĭc-i*, to *fēci*.
It is obvious that the changes described tended to result in giving a fuller and broader sound to the vowel of the root.

§ In Gothic the preterite is *haihait*. A few other Anglo-Saxon preterites show reduplication, especially when compared with Gothic. Thus *rǽdan* (to advise), pret. *reord*, shortened from *reo-rǽd* (Gothic *rēdan*, *rairoth*); *lǽtan* (to let), pret *leort* (for *leolt*), shortened from *leolǽt* (Gothic *lētan*, *lailot*); *lǽcan* (to leap), pret. *leolc*, shortened from *leo-lǽc* (Gothic *laikan*, *lailaik*); *on-drǽdan* (to dread), pret *on-dreord*, shortened from *on-drǽ-drǽd*.

-en and the prefixed particle *ge*. The suffix *-en* has now disappeared from many verbs, and the prefix *ge* from all.

Verbs of the Weak Conjugation.

222 The characteristic of the Weak Conjugation is that the preterite tense was originally formed by annexing to the root the preterite of the verb *do* (root *da*). This suffix became abbreviated* in Anglo-Saxon to *-de* or *-te*,† and was attached to the root by a connecting vowel *o* or *e* (which disappeared after some consonants). In modern English the suffix *de* or *te* has become *d* or *t*, and the connecting vowel is always *e*. When a verb ends in *e*, that *e* is omitted before the connecting vowel of the suffix, as *love, lov-ed*. The suffix *-ed* is pronounced as a separate syllable only after a dental mute, as in *need-ed*, *pat-t-ed*, *mend-ed*. The vowel *y* after a consonant is changed into *i* before it, as *pity, pitied*. After a sharp guttural or labial mute *ed* has the sound of *t*, as in *tipped, knocked*.

It thus appears that in origin, as well as in meaning, *I loved* is equivalent to *I love did*, or *I did love*.

223 The perfect participle in the weak conjugation was formed by the suffix *d* or *t*,‡ joined to the root by *o* or *e* as a connecting vowel, and had the particle *ge* prefixed. The force of this particle was extremely feeble, and after a time it vanished (§ 221), so that now the perfect participle of most verbs of the weak conjugation is the same in form as the preterite.

224 Since the auxiliary suffix of the Weak Conjugation is a reduplicated or *strong* form, it follows that the Strong Conjugation is the older of the two. Whenever fresh verbs are formed or introduced, they are of the weak conjugation.§

225 **A.—Verbs of the Strong Conjugation‖.**

1. *Verbs in which the preterite is formed by vowel-change, and the perfect participle has the suffix* -en *or* -n.

---

* All suffixes were originally independent words, with a meaning of their own. Their frequent occurrence, and their position at the end of words, led to their being carelessly pronounced. Hence they became abbreviated and corrupted in form, till in many cases their original meaning can only be guessed at, or deduced from a comparison of several cognate languages.

† In Gothic the reduplicated auxiliary root (*ded*) appears in the dual and plural of the preterite indicative, and in all three numbers of the past subjunctive (Skeat, *Moeso-Gothic Glossary and Grammar*, p. 301).

‡ Probably an adjective formation, akin to the Greek τος and the Latin *tus*. (*Morris*, p. 168).

§ *String, strung, strung* is a solitary exception.

‖ Koch (followed by Morris) arranges these verbs according to their Anglo-Saxon forms, which is the most convenient plan when all the successive variations are to be traced. But as these forms are not original, but belong only to one stage in the process of change, and by no means explain all those that follow, an arrangement is here adopted, which is based upon the present usage of the language.

ETYMOLOGY—VERB.

	Pres.	Pret.	P. Part.	Pres.	Pret.	P. Part.
(a.)	blow	blew	blown	draw	drew	drawn
	crow	crew	[crowed]	fly	flew	flown
			once crown	lie	lay	lien *or* lain
	grow	grew	grown			
	know	knew	known	slay	slew	slain
	throw	threw	thrown	see	saw	seen
	show	[shew]* *or* showed	shown			
(b.)	drive	drove *or* drave	driven	stride	strode	stridden
				strike	struck	stricken
	give	gave	given	strive	strove	striven
	ride	rode	ridden	thrive	throve	thriven
	(a)rise	(a)rose	(a)risen	write	wrote	written
	smite	smote	smitten			
(c.)	forsake	forsook	forsaken	take	took	taken
	shake	shook	shaken			

2. *In most of the following verbs there is a tendency to assimilate the vowel-sound of the preterite to that of the perfect participle.*

Pres.	Pret.	P. Part.	Pres.	Pret.	P. Part.
bear	bare *or* bore	borne *or* born †	swear	sware *or* swore	sworn
beat	bent	beaten	tear	tare *or* tore	torn
break	brake *or* broke	broken	wear	wore	worn
cleave ‡	clave *or* clove	cloven *or* cleft	weave	wove	woven *or* wove
shear §	shore	shorn	choose ‖	chose	chosen
speak	spake *or* spoke	spoken	freeze	froze	frozen
steal	stole	stolen	tread	trode *or* trod	trodden *or* trod

3. *In the following verbs the preterite has a second form, which is only the perfect participle transformed into a preterite.*

Pres.	Pret.	P. Part.	Pres.	Pret.	P. Part.
begin	began *or* begun ¶	begun	get	gat *or* got	gotten *or* got
bid	bade *or* bid	bidden *or* bid	ring	rang *or* rung ¶	rung
drink	drank *or* drunk ¶	drunken ** *or* drunk	shrink	shrank *or* shrunk ¶	shrunken ** *or* shrunk

---

* A provincial form, found also in Spenser.
† *Born* is now used only with reference to *birth*. *Borne* means *carried*.
‡ Also weak, *cleave, cleft, cleft*.
§ Also of the weak conjugation.
‖ *Chese* was an old form of the present.
¶ These forms are now usually avoided by the best writers.
** These forms are now used only as adjectives.

ETYMOLOGY—VERB.

Pres.	Pret.	P. Part.	Pres.	Pret.	P. Part.
sing	sang or sung*	sung	spring	sprang or sprung*	sprung
sink	sank or sunk*	sunken † or sunk	stink	stank or stunk	stunk
spin	span or spun	spun	strike	strake or struck	stricken † or struck
spit	spat or spit	spit or spat	swim	swam or swum*	swum

4. *In the following verbs the preterite is the perfect participle ‡ used as a preterite.*

Pres.	Pret.	P. Part.	Pres.	Pret.	P. Part.
bind	bound	bound	shoot	shot	shotten or shot
bite	bit	bitten or bit	slide	slid ¶	slidden or slid
burst	burst	burst			
chide	chid §	chidden or chid	sling	slung	slung
			slink	slunk	slunk
climb	clomb	[clomben]	slit	slit	slit
cling	clung	clung	stick	stuck	stuck
fight	fought	fought	string	strung	strung
find	found	found	swing	swung	swung
fling	flung	flung	win	won	won
grind	ground	ground	wind	wound	wound
hang	hung	hung	wring	wrung	wrung
hide	hid	hidden or hid			

5. *In the following verbs the perfect participle has been borrowed from the preterite.*

Pres.	Pret.	P. Part.	Pres.	Pret.	P. Part.
abide	abode	abode	sit	sat	sat
awake ‖	awoke	awoke	stand	stood	stood
heave ‖	hove	[hoven]	strike	struck	stricken or struck
hold	held	holden or held	take	took	taken or took **
let	let	let			
shine	shone	shone or shined	spit	spat or spit	spat or spit
seethe ‖	sod	sodden or sod			

---

* These forms are now usually avoided by the best writers.
† These forms are now used only as adjectives.
‡ When there are two forms of the perfect participle, the short form is adopted for the preterite. Besides those given the short forms *driv, smit, rid, ris*, are used as preterites by some of the old writers. In vulgar English we often hear " I seen him "; " He done it "; " I give it him," &c.
§ *Chode* occurs in *Gen.* xxxi. 36, " Jacob chode with Laban." The weak form *chidde* is also found.
‖ Also of the weak conjugation.
¶ Formerly *slode*.
** *Took, mistook, forsook, shook, rode, strove, swam, drank*, &c., are used as perfect participles by Shakspere.

ETYMOLOGY—VERB.

6. *Unclassified forms.*

Pres.	*Pret.*	*P. Part.*	*Pres.*	*Pret.*	*P. Part*
eat	ate *or* eat	eaten	run	ran	run
dig	dug	dug	come	came	come
[bequeath]	quoth *				

B.—Verbs of the Weak Conjugation.

226 Besides the large class of what are frequently called Regular Verbs, because the preterite and perfect participle are uniformly made by the simple addition of *-ed*, which includes all verbs of French or Latin origin, the following verbs belong to the Weak Conjugation:—

1. *Verbs in which the addition of the suffix* d *or* t *is accompanied by a shortening of the vowel-sound of the root.*

Pres.	*Pret.*	*P. Part.*	*Pres.*	*Pret.*	*P. Part.*
bereave	bereft †	bereft	kneel	knelt	knelt
creep	crept ‡	crept	leave	left	left
deal	dealt	dealt	lose	lost	lost ‖
dream	dreamt §	dreamt	mean	meant	meant
feel	felt	felt	sleep	slept ‡	slept
flee	fled	fled	sweep	swept	swept
hear	heard	heard	weep	wept ‡	wept
keep	kept ‡	kept	shoe	shod	shod

2. *Verbs in which the suffix has been dropped after the shortening of the vowel.*

Pres.	*Pret.*	*P. Part.*	*Pres.*	*Pret.*	*P. Part.*
bleed	bled	bled	meet	met	met
breed	bred	bred	read	read	read
feed	fed	fed	speed	sped	sped
lead	led	led	light	lit	lit

3. *Verbs in which the addition of* d *or* t *is accompanied by a change in the vowel-sound of the root.*

Pres.	*Pret.*	*P. Part.*	*Pres.*	*Pret.*	*P. Part.*
beseech ¶	besought	besought	seek	sought	sought
buy	bought	bought	teach	taught	taught
catch **	caught	caught	think ††	thought	thought
bring ††	brought	brought	tell	told	told
sell	sold	sold			

---

* The simple queath (*cweðan*) is no longer used. To *bequeath* is to allot a thing by speaking. Compare the verb *bespeak*.
† Also *bereaved*.
‡ In early writers we find *crep* for *crepte*, *slep* for *slepte*, *wep* for *wepte*. *Kep* is a common vulgarism for *kept*.
§ Also *dreamed*.
‖ In Anglo-Saxon (*for*)*losen* was softened into (*for*)*loren*, which is still preserved in *lorn* and *forlorn*. In a similar way *frore* is found for *frozen*. "The parching air burns *frore*" (*Par. Lost*, ii. 595).
¶ *Beseech* is a compound of *seek*; *k*, *ch* and *gh* are only varieties of the guttural sound.
** The *t* is not radical. It is only used to indicate that *ch* has the sibilant sound.
†† The *n* in these verbs is not radical.

ETYMOLOGY—VERB.

4. *Verbs in which the suffix* te *has disappeared, but has changed a final flat mute into a sharp mute.*

Pres.	Pret.	P. Part.	Pres.	Pret.	P. Part.
bend	bent	bent	build	built	built *or* builded
blend	blended	blent			
gild	gilt *or* gilded	gilt *or* gilded	rend	rent	rent
			send	sent	sent
gird	girt *or* girded	girt *or* girded	spend	spent	spent
			wend	went *or* wended	wended
lend	lent	lent			

5. *Verbs in which the suffix has disappeared without further change.*

Pres.	Pret.	P. Part.	Pres.	Pret.	P. Part.
cast	cast	cast	set	set	set
cost	cost	cost	shed	shed	shed
cut	cut	cut	shred	shred	shred
hit	hit	hit	shut	shut	shut
hurt	hurt	hurt	slit	slit	slit
knit	knit	knit	split	split	split
put	put	put	spread	spread	spread
rid	rid	rid	thrust	thrust	thrust

6. *Verbs which have preserved the formation of the strong conjugation in the perfect participle.*

Pres.	Pret.	P. Part.	Pres.	Pret.	P. Part.
go	——	gone	shape	shaped	shapen *or* shaped
[en]grave	[en]graved	[en]graven *or* engraved	shave	shaved	shaven *or* shaved
help	helped	holpen *or* helped	shew	shewed	shewn *or* shewed
hew	hewed	hewn *or* hewed	sow	sowed	sown *or* sowed
load	loaded	laden *or* loaded	strew	strewed	strewn, strown, *or* strewed
melt	melted	molten *or* melted			
mow	mowed	mown *or* mowed	swell	swelled	swollen *or* swelled
rive	rived	riven *or* rived	wash	washed	washen *or* washed
saw	sawed	sawn *or* sawed	wax	waxed	waxen *or* waxed

7. *Verbs not included in the preceding classes.*

Pres.	Pret.	P. Part.	Pres.	Pret.	P. Part.
can	could	——	owe	ought	——
clothe	clad	clad	shall	should	——
freight	freighted	fraught *or* freighted	lay *	laid	laid
			say *	said	said
may	might	——	will	would	——

* The *y* in these verbs is a weakened form of the guttural *cg*.

ETYMOLOGY—VERB.

Pres.	Pret.	P. Part.	Pres.	Pret.	P. Part.
work	wrought or worked	wrought or worked	have	had (i.e. haved)	had
dare	durst	dared	make	made (i.e. maked)	made

8. *Tight* is a participle of *tie* (A.S. *tigan*). *Distraught* is an exceptional form from the verb *distract*. *Straight* is for *stretched*. *Dight* is from *deek* (= *bedecked*). *Yclept* is from the old verb *clypian* = to call. In *clad* the *a* is the original vowel (A.S. *claᵭ*). The *th* has disappeared before the *d*. *Go* borrows a preterite from the verb *wend* (properly *to wend* (or *turn*) *one's way*). *Be* has a participle of the strong form. *Am, was,* and *been* come from three different roots.

In Appendix A will be found a list of strong verbs that have become weak.

DEFECTIVE VERBS.

227. Several verbs in English are *defective*; that is, have not the full complement of moods and tenses. Those which are still in common use are *shall, will, may, must, can, ought, dare, wit.*

A peculiarity which all these verbs (except *will*) have in common, is, that the present tense is in reality a preterite of the strong conjugation,* which has replaced an older present, and has had its own place supplied by a secondary preterite of the weak conjugation. One consequence of this fact is, that they none of them take *s* as a suffix in the third person singular, as that suffix does not belong to the preterite tense.

228. **SHALL.**

No Infinitive Mood.† No Participles.

Indicative Mood.

Present Indefinite Tense.

Singular.
1. [I] shall
2. [Thou] shalt‡
3. [He] shall

Plural.
1. [We] shall
2. [You] shall
3. [They] shall.

Past Indefinite Tense.

Singular.
1. [I] should
2. [Thou] shouldst
3. [He] should

Plural.
1. [We] should
2. [You] should
3. [They] should

Subjunctive Mood.

Past Indefinite Tense.

Singular.
1. [I] should
2. [Thou] shouldest or shouldst ‖
3. [He] should

Plural.
1. [We] should
2. [You] should
3. [They] should

---

* This is evident from the tense suffixes in Anglo-Saxon, which are those of the preterite, not those of the present tense. These preterite presents may be compared with οἶδα, *novi*, &c., in Greek and Latin.

† In Anglo-Saxon *sculan* = *to owe*.

‡ The suffix *t* in the second person singular of the past indefinite in the strong conjugation is older than -*st*. It is found in Gothic.

‖ The termination -*st* in the second person singular in the subjunctive mood, is a deviation from the ancient principle of formation. In Anglo-Saxon, the three persons were alike in the subjunctive mood in both tenses.

229   *Shall* (A.S. *sceal*) is (in form) a preterite.* When it came to be used as a present tense, another preterite (*should*) of the weak conjugation was formed to supply its place. The *ou* of *should* comes from the *u* of *sculan*. In Anglo-Saxon, 'I shall' means 'I owe.' †
It then came to indicate some compulsion or obligation arising either from the will of some superior authority, or from some external source. Hence it is used in direct or reported commands, as "Thou shalt not steal"; "The general gave orders that he should be shot"; "Ye shall not surely die," *i.e.*, 'There is surely no edict that ye shall die'; "The tyrant shall perish," *i.e.*, 'Circumstances, or the will of others demands that the tyrant shall perish'; "He demanded where Christ should be born," *i.e.*. 'where it was fated or prophesied that he was to be born'; "You should always obey your parents," *i.e.*, 'It is your duty to obey your parents.' It often conveys this sense in the first person, as "What shall I do?" *i.e.*, "What ought I (*or* am I) to do?" and even when used as an auxiliary verb denoting simple futurity in the first person, the verb does not really lose this force (see § 213). It is now only a verb of incomplete predication, and is followed by the infinitive without *to*.
In exclamations it is often omitted, as "What, I love! I sue! I seek a wife!" "Thou wear a lion's hide!" (*Shakspere*).
In Scotch and in the Northern dialects *I shall* is often abbreviated to *I'se* or *Ish*.

230   **WILL.**

Infinitive Mood, [To] will.
Imperfect Participle, Willing.
Perfect Participle, Willed.

Compound Perfect Participle (active), Having willed.

The infinitive mood and the participles of this verb are only used when it has the stronger of its two senses.

Indicative Mood.

Present Indefinite Tense.   *Past Indefinite Tense.*

Singular.   Plural.   Singular.   Plural.
1. [I] will   1. [We] will   1. [I] would   1. [We] would
2. [Thou] wilt   2. [You] will   2. [Thou]   2. [You] would
                                                wouldest *or*
                                                wouldst
3. [He] will *or*   3. [They] will   3. [He] would   3. [They] would
   wills ‡

---
* According to Grimm *shall* or *skal* is the preterite or perfect of a verb meaning *to kill*. As killing involved the payment of the penalty or *wer-geld*, 'I have killed' came to mean 'I owe the fine,' and thence 'I owe' simply.
† "Hu micel scealt þu?" = "How much shalt thou?" = "How much owest thou"? (*Luke* xvi. 5). But the verb is also used in Anglo-Saxon as the auxiliary of the future tense.
‡ This form is used only when the verb is employed in its strong sense.

Subjunctive Mood.

Past Indefinite Tense.

Singular.
1. [I] would
2. [Thou] wouldest *or* wouldst
3. [He] would

Plural.
1. [We] would
2. [You] would
3. [They] would

231. The verb *will* is followed by the infinitive, without the preposition *to*; as, "I *will* strive"; "He *will* not obey." This verb, besides being used as a mere auxiliary for forming future tenses* in the second and third persons; is used to express determination or intention. It has this force in all its persons, as—"Not as I *will*, but as thou *wilt*"; "In spite of warning, he *will* continue his evil practices." When used in the strong sense of "having a determination" to do something, the verb *will* may be conjugated like an ordinary regular verb; but in this case the preposition *to* must be used with the infinitive that follows it.

232. This verb is also used to express the frequent repetition of an action; as, "When he was irritated, he *would* rave like a madman," "Sometimes a thousand twanging instruments will hum about my ears" (*Shaksp., Tempest*).

233. *Wilt* has been formed after the analogy of *shall*, although it is strictly a present tense (see note on § 228). In old English *shal* and *wil* are found for *shalt* and *wilt*.

234. An old form of the present was *I wol* or *I wole*, whence the negative *I won't*. In colloquial English the verb is often shortened by the omission of *wi* or *woul*, as *I'll*=*I will*, *I'd*=*I would*. In old English it was combined with the negative *ne*, *ic nille*=*I will not*, *ic nolde*=*I would not*. We still have the phrase *willy nilly*=*will he nill he*, or *will ye nill ye*.

235. ## MAY.

No Infinitive Mood. No Participles.†

Indicative Mood.

Present Indefinite Tense.

Singular.
1. [I] may
2. [Thou] mayest *or* mayst
3. [He] may

Plural.
1. [We] may
2. [You] may
3. [They] may

Past Indefinite Tense.

Singular.
1. [I] might
2. [Thou] might-est
3. [He] might

Plural.
1. [We] might
2. [You] might
3. [They] might

Subjunctive Mood.

The Present and Past Indefinite tenses of the Subjunctive in this verb are the same in form as the corresponding tenses in the Indicative Mood.

---

* See however § 213.
† That is, not now In Chaucer we find "If goodly had he might" (*Koch*, i p. 355)

236. The *g* in *may* is a softening of the *y* in the root *mag* (A.S. Inf. *magan*). The modern present, *I may*, &c., is in reality a preterite tense of an older verb,* and (like *memini*, *novi*, &c.) had originally a *perfect* meaning of its own, which passed into a secondary *present* sense, denoting the abiding result of some action. Instead of *thou mayest* we find in old English *thou miht* † or *myght* (compare *shalt*), afterwards *thou may* (compare *thou shal*, § 233).

237. A collateral variety of *may* was *mow* or *mowe*, of which the past tense *mought* is used by Spenser (*F. Q.* i. 1, 42), and is a common provincialism.

238. The verb *may* formerly denoted the possession of strength or power to do anything. ‡ It now indicates the absence of any physical or moral obstacle to an action, as "It may be so, though I scarcely believe it"; "A man may be rich and yet not happy"; "He might be seen any day walking on the pier," *i.e.*, 'there was nothing to hinder his being seen.' Hence it came to be used as an optative. "May you be happy," is as much as to say "I desire that you be free from hindrance to your happiness." The notion of *permission* also springs from this meaning, the hindrance which is absent being the prohibition of some authority.

The verb *may* is now often employed as a mere auxiliary (followed by an infinitive mood) to replace the simple subjunctive after *that* and *lest*. Instead of "Give me this water that I thirst not," we now say "that I may not thirst."

MUST.

239. *Must* (A.S. môste) is the preterite § of the verb môtan=*to be allowed*, or *to be in a position to do something*.‖ It still has this sense in such phrases as "You must not come in," *i.e.*, 'You are not permitted to come in.' The old present *mote* is still used by Spenser. ¶

240. When the preterite *must* came to be used as a present, it acquired a stronger sense, and was used to express (1) *being bound or compelled* to do something, as "He *must* do as he is bid": (2) being unable to control the desire or will, hence a *fixed determination* to do something; as "I *must* and will have my own way": "So you *must* always be meddling *must* you?": (3) *Certainty*, or the idea that a thing cannot but be as is stated; as "He surely *must* have arrived by this time"; "It must be so; Plato thou reasonest well."

241. The verb *must* is now used only in the indicative mood, sometimes as a present, sometimes as a past tense,** but there is no difference

---

* Compare note on § 227.
† Thus "Amende thee while thou myght."
‡ Thus "Gif þu wilt þu miht me geclænsian," 'If thou wilt thou canst make me clean' (*Matt.* viii. 2); "Bútan nettum huntian ic mæg," 'I can hunt without nets.'
§ The *s* of *must* is a softened form of the *t* of the root *mot* before the *t* of the suffix. Compare the form *wist* (? 245). See *Koch*, i. p. 356.
‖ *E.g.* "Josep bred Pilatus þret he môste niman þies Hælendes lichaman," 'Joseph begged Pilate that he might be allowed to (*must*) take the Saviour's body.' (*John* xix. 38).
¶ "Fraelissa was as faire as faire mote bee" (*F. Q.*, i. 2, 37). Byron, who sometimes affects archaisms without understanding them, uses *mote* as a *past* tense, "Whate'er this grief mote be, which he could not control."
** In "He must needs pass through Samaria" (*John*, iv. 4) *must* is in the past tense. When past time is referred to, however, *must* is usually followed by the perfect infinitive, as "It must *have been* a sad day, when the old man died."

ETYMOLOGY — VERB.

of form to mark tense, number, or person. It is a verb of incomplete predication followed by the infinitive without *to*.

242   CAN.
No Infinitive Mood.   No Participles.
Indicative Mood.

Present Indefinite Tense.   *Past Indefinite Tense.*
Singular.   Plural.   Singular.   Plural
1. [I] can   1. [We] can   1. [I] could *   1. [We] could
2. [Thou] canst   2. [You] can   2. [Thou]   2. [You] could
                                                  couldest *or*
                                                  couldst
3. [He] can   3. [They] can   3. [He] could   3. [They] could

Subjunctive Mood.
Past Indefinite Tense.

Singular.   Plural.
1. [I] could   1. [We] could
2. [Thou] couldest *or* couldst   2. [You] could
3. [He] could   3. [They] could

243   The present *can* is in reality the preterite tense of the verb *cunnan* = *to know*.† The infinitive *conne* is found in Chaucer (as "I shal not conne answer" = 'I shall not be able to answer'), and still subsists in the verb *to con* (as, "He was conning his lesson"). *Cunning* (now used as an adjective) is in reality the present participle of the verb. "He is a *cunning* fellow" means 'He is a *knowing* fellow.' The old perfect participle *cuð* (*known*), still survives in *uncouth*.‡ 'Thou *can*' for 'Thou *canst*' is found in old writers § (see § 233). *Can* is now a verb of incomplete predication, and is followed by the infinitive without *to*.

244   OUGHT.
Singular.   Plural.
1. [I] ought   1. [We] ought
2. [Thou] oughtest   2. [You] ought
3. [He] ought   3. [They] ought

Ought exhibits very clearly the substitution of a preterite for a present. It is the past tense of the verb *to owe*, and is used in its old sense by Shakspere (*I. King H. IV.*, iii. 3.), "He said you ought him a thousand pounds." It is now used as a past only in the reported form, as 'He said I *ought* to be satisfied.' In direct sentences the reference to past time is indicated by using a perfect infinitive after it, as "He ought *to have said* so," *i.e.*, 'It *was* his duty *to say*

---

* The *l* in *could* had no business to intrude itself. It is not found in the Anglo-Saxon verb. It was probably inserted to make *could* resemble *would* and *should*, where the *l* is radical. The Anglo-Saxon form is "Ic cuthe."

† "Ne cann ic eow" = 'I know you not' (*Matt.* xxv. 12); "They conne latyn out litylle" (*Maundeville*).

‡ In Milton (*Lycidas*, 186) the "uncouth swain" means the 'poet as yet *unknown* to fame.' So "his uncouth way" (*P. L.*) means 'his unknown way.'

§ As in Skelton.

so.' "He ought (*pres.*) to do it" means 'he owes the doing of it.'*

The original meaning of 'to owe' was 'to possess,' † *owe* and *own* being collateral forms.‡ "You *owe me* a thousand pounds" means "You *possess* (or have) *for me* a thousand pounds." Though the dative is really essential to the meaning, the verb came to have its modern sense independently of the dative. The adjective *own* is really a participle of *owe*.

There used to be a perfect participle *ought*.§ The verb *to owe*, in its modern sense, is conjugated regularly as a verb of the weak conjugation. In early writers there is a curious impersonal use of this verb, as "Wel *ought us* werche" (*Chaucer, C. T.* 15482), "*Us oughte* have pacience" (*Ch. Mel.*).

245 ## WIT.

To wit (A.S. *witan*) means 'to know.' "I do you to wit," means 'I make you to know.' The adverbial (gerundial) infinitive *to wit* is still common. The forms *I wot, God wot, you wot, they wot*, are found in old writers. *Wot* is a preterite of the strong form, which has supplanted the old present,‖ and has been replaced by a preterite *wist* of the weak conjugation.¶

Wots and *wotteth* (*Gen.* xxxix. 8) are false forms (see § 227), as is the participle *wotting* (*Winter's Tale*, iii. 2). The old form was *witende*. The correct form is retained in *unwittingly*.

Combination with the negative *ne* gave the old English forms *nat = know not, niste = knew not, &c.*

246 ## DARE.

Infinitive Mood [To] dare.
Participles, daring, dared, having dared.
Indicative Mood.

Present Indefinite Tense.		*Past Indefinite Tense.*	
Singular.	Plural.	Singular.	Plural.
1. [I] dare	1. [We] dare	1. [I] durst	1. [We] durst
2. [Thou] darest	2. [You] dare	2. [Thou]durstest(?)	2. [You] durst
3. [He] dare	3. [They] dare	3. [He] durst	3. [They] durst

* Compare the Latin 'Hoc facere debet.' *Debeo* is a compound of *de* and *habeo*: 'I have from' = 'I owe to.'

† So in Shakspere (*All's Well*, ii. 5), "I am not worthy of the wealth I owe." According to Grimm *I owe* (ic áh) is itself the perfect of a verb *eigan = to labour*, and means 'I have earned.' *Ought* is therefore a preterite or perfect of the second degree, being a preterite of a preterite.

‡ Thus in Chaucer (*Mel.*) we find "I own not to be conseiled by thee."

§ Phrases like "He hadn't ought to do it" are perfectly grammatical, though they are now vulgar.

‖ The root *wit* is the same as ϝιδ in the Greek ϝιδεῖν, and *vid* in the Latin *vid-eo*, and originally meant *see*. The preterite present *wot* may be compared with the Greek οἶδα. 'I have seen' = 'I know.'

¶ The *s* of *wist* is a softened form of the *t* of *wit* before the *t* of the suffix. This change occurs in various Teutonic languages. Compare *must* (§ 239, note), "I wist not that he was the high priest" = 'I *knew* not,' &c. (*Acts* xxiii. 5). *Wist* has nothing to do with an imaginary present *I wis*, which (when not a mere affectation) is simply a corruption of the word *ywis = certain* (A.S. *gewis*). The verb *to wiss = to show* or *teach* (A.S. *wisian* or *wissian*) is a different verb, though derived from the same root.

Subjunctive.

Past Indefinite [I] durst, &c.

I dare is a preterite (of the strong form) of the old verb *durran*, which has ousted the old present, and has itself been replaced by a preterite (*durst*) of the weak formation.* The use of *durst* as a present is quite incorrect.

As in the other verbs of this class (see § 227) the third person singular should be without the suffix *s; he dare,* not *he dares. Dare* (especially in the sense of *challenge*) is also conjugated like an ordinary verb of the weak conjugation, and some of these forms are occasionally borrowed for the defective verb; and so we find *he dares* and *he dared,* &c. The following infinitive must then have *to* before it, as '"He dared to refuse." The defective verb is followed by the infinitive without *to,* as " He durst not refuse."

247. The following defective verbs are now obsolete, or nearly so. *Quoth I* or *he (i.e., said I* or *he;* Anglo-Saxon, *ewethan, " to say"*). The impersonal *thinks* (= *seems,* from the Anglo-Saxon *thinean, " to appear,"* a different verb from *thenean, " to think"*), in *methinks* (*it seems to me*), *methought (it seemed to me.* Comp. the German verb *dünken, " to seem"*). *Me-lists==It pleases me; him listed==it pleased him.* Shakspere uses *list* as a *personal* verb.† *Worth (is* or *be),* as in the phrase " woe worth the day," that is, "*woe be to the day*"), a relic of the Anglo-Saxon *weorthan, " to become* " (German, *werden),* which was one of the auxiliaries by means of which the passive voice was formed. *Wont* is now used only as a participle. Formerly, *I wont, he wont,* &c., were used in the indicative mood. *Hight* ‡ *= was called* (§ 220).

From its resemblance in construction to the other verbs of incomplete predication, the verb *need* has the third person *he need* instead of *he needs.* When the inflected form is used, the following infinitive should have *to* before it.

248. ## The Notional and Auxiliary Verb HAVE.

Infinitive Mood.

Indefinite Tense, [To] have. *Imperfect Tense,* [To] be having.

Perfect Tense, [To] have had.

Participles.

Imperfect Participle, Having. *Perfect Participle* (passive), Had.

Compound Perfect Participle (active), Having had.

---

* The *s* of *durst* comes from the fuller form of the root *dars* or *daurs*, which appears in Gothic (*Koch*, i. p. 351). Compare the Greek θάρσ-ειν (*Morris*, p. 184).
† The intransitive verb þincan ' to appear' is related to the causative verb þencan ' to think,' just as *drincan* ' to drink ' is related to *drensan* ' to drench,' *i.e.* ' to make to drink or absorb.' To *think* is to *make* a thing *appear* to the mind.
‡ So the old impersonals *him hungrede,* &c., became *he hungered,* &c. (Compare §§ 514, 515, 523.)
§ As : "This grisly beast, which by name Lion hight, the trusty Thisbe . . . did scare away " (*Mids. N. D.,* v. 1). There is no particle *hight,* though Byron invents one. (Compare note on § 239.)

Indicative Mood.
Present Indefinite Tense.

Singular.
1. [I] have
2. [Thou] hast*
3. [He] hath or has

Plural.
1. [We] have
2. [You] have
3. [They] have

Present Perfect Tense.†

Singular.
1. [I] have had, &c.

Plural.
1. [We] have had, &c.

Past Indefinite Tense.

Singular.
1. [I] had
2. [Thou] hadst
3. [He] had

Plural.
1. [We] had
2. [You] had
3. [They] had

Past Perfect Tense.†

Singular.
1. [I] had had, &c.

Plural.
1. [We] had had, &c.

Future Indefinite Tense.

Singular.
1. [I] shall have
2. [Thou] wilt have
3. [He] will have

Plural.
1. [We] shall have
2. [You] will have
3. [They] will have

Future Perfect Tense.

Singular.
1. [I] shall have had, &c.

Plural.
1. [We] shall have had, &c.

Imperative Mood.

Singular.
Have [thou]

Plural.
Have [you or ye]

Subjunctive Mood.
Present Indefinite Tense.
(Used after *if, that, lest, unless*, &c.)

Singular.
1. [I] have
2. [Thou] have
3. [He] have

Plural.
1. [We] have
2. [You] have
3. [They] have

Present Perfect Tense.
(Used after *if, that, unless*, &c.)

Singular.
1. [I] have had
2. [Thou] have had
3. [He] have had

Plural.
1. [We] have had
2 [You] have had
3. [They] have had

---

* *Hast* is a contraction of *havest, had* of *haved, has* of *haves*.
† For the complete forms of these compound tenses, see the corresponding tenses of the verb *smite*.

a. Past Indefinite Tense.

Used mostly after *if*, *that*, *unless*, &c.

Singular.	Plural.
1. [I] had	1. [We] had
2. [Thou] hadst	2. [You] had
3. [He] had	3. [They] had

b. Secondary or Periphrastic* Form.

When not preceded by Conjunctions.†

Singular.	Plural.
1. [I] should have	1. [We] should have
2. [Thou] wouldst have	2. [You] would have
3. [He] would have	3. [They] would have

a. Past Perfect Tense.

Used mostly after *if*, *that*, *unless*, &c.

Singular.	Plural.
1. [I] had had	1. [We] had had
2. [Thou] hadst had	2. [You] had had
3. [He] had had	3. [They] had had

b. Secondary or Periphrastic Form.

When not preceded by Conjunctions.

Singular.	Plural.
1. [I] should have had	1. [We] should have had
2. [Thou] wouldst have had	2. [You] would have had
3. [He] would have had	3. [They] would have had

249   The verb *have* often has the sense of *to keep* or *to hold*. In this case it may have the *imperfect* tenses, and may be used in the passive voice like an ordinary verb.

For the formation of these tenses see the paradigm of the verb *smite*.

250   ## The Notional and Auxiliary Verb BE.

Infinitive Mood.

Indefinite Tense, [To] be.

Perfect Tense, [To] have been.

Imperfect Participle, Being.   *Perfect Participle*, Been.

Compound Perfect Participle, Having been.

---

* *Periphrastic* means 'expressing in a roundabout manner.' (Greek περί, *about*; φράζω, *I tell*.)

† After *if*, *though*, *unless*, *lest*, *except*, &c., the second and third persons are formed by *shouldst* and *should*, not *wouldst* and *would*.

ETYMOLOGY—VERB.

Indicative Mood.

Present Indefinite Tense.

Singular.
1. [I] am*
2. [Thou] art
3. [He] is

Plural.
1. [We] are
2. [You] are
3. [They] are

Present Perfect Tense.†

Singular.
1. [I] have been, &c.

Plural.
1. [We] have been, &c.

Past Indefinite Tense.

Singular.
1. [I] was
2. [Thou] wast *or* wert‡
3. [He] was

Plural.
1. [We] were
2. [You] were
3. [They] were

Past Perfect Tense.†

Singular.
1. [I] had been, &c.

Plural.
1. [We] had been, &c.

Future Indefinite Tense.

Singular.
1. [I] shall be
2. [Thou] wilt be
3. [He] will be

Plural.
1. [We] shall be
2. [You] will be
3. [They] will be

Future Perfect Tense.

Singular.
1. [I] shall have been, &c.

Plural.
1. [We] shall have been, &c.

Imperative Mood.

Singular.—Be [thou]   *Plural.*—Be [ye *or* you]

Subjunctive Mood.

Present Indefinite Tense.

After *if, that, though, lest,* &c.

Singular.
1. [I] be
2. [Thou] be
3. [He] be

Plural.
1. [We] be
2. [You] be
3. [They] be

---

* Another form of the present tense, indicative mood, still used in some parts of the country, and found in Shakspere and Milton, is [*I*] be, [*thou*] beest, [*he*] be, [*we*] be or ben, [*you*] be or ben, [*they*] be, ben, or bin. In " Everything that pretty bin " (*Shaksp.*), *bin* is probably *plural, everything* being treated as equivalent to *all things* (see ₰ 175). Byron's use of *bin* ("There bin another pious reason") is of no authority. See note on ₰ 239.

† For the full forms of these compound tenses see the paradigm of the verb *smite.*

‡ There is no necessity for regarding *wert* as exclusively a subjunctive form. In Anglo-Saxon the form was *wære. Thou were* is found in early English writers. *Wert* is formed after the analogy of *wilt* and *shalt.* The form *wast* did not appear in English before the fourteenth century, and was preceded by *was* (*thou was*). *Wert*, as a subjunctive form, belongs only to modern English. (*Koch*, i. p. 348.)

ETYMOLOGY—VERB.

Present Perfect Tense.
After *if, that, though, unless,* &c.

Singular.
1. [I] have been
2. [Thou] have been
3. [He] have been

Plural.
1. [We] have been
2. [You] have been
3. [They] have been

a. *Past Indefinite Tense.*
Used mostly after *if, that, though, unless,* &c.

Singular.
1. [I] were
2. [Thou] wert
3. [He] were

Plural.
1. [We] were
2. [You] were
3. [They] were

b. *Secondary or Periphrastic Form.*
When not preceded by Conjunctions.*

Singular.
1. [I] should be
2. [Thou] wouldst be
3. [He] would be

Plural.
1. [We] should be
2. [You] would be
3. [They] would be

a. *Past Perfect Tense.*
Used mostly after *if, that, though, unless,* &c.

Singular.
1. [I] had been
2. [Thou] hadst been
3. [He] had been

Plural.
1. [We] had been
2. [You] had been
3. [They] had been

b. *Secondary or Periphrastic Form.*
When not preceded by Conjunctions.*

Singular.
1. [I] should have been
2. [Thou] wouldst have been
3. [He] would have been

Plural.
1. [We] should have been
2. [You] would have been
3. [They] would have been

251   The conjugation of this verb is made up from three different roots. (1). The present tense of the indicative mood is formed from the old Aryan root *as*, which appears in Greek and Latin in the form *es*, in Gothic in the form *is*. The *s* of the root is softened to *r* in *am*† (= *arm*), *art* and *are*. *Are* is an abbreviation of the Anglo-Saxon *ar-on*, which has the personal suffix of a past tense. *Is* (a variety of the root *as*) has no suffix.

(2). The present subjunctive, the imperative, the infinitive, and the participles are formed from the root *be*. There was formerly also a present indicative from this root. (See note on § 250).

(3). The past indefinite tense of the indicative and subjunctive is formed from the root *wes* or *was* in the old verb *wesan* = [to] *be*, *s* being softened to *r* in the plural and in the subjunctive. *Wast* has the suffix *t* (like *shalt*, &c., see § 228). *Was* (like *is*) is without suffix.

---

* After the conjunctions *if, though, unless, lest, except*, &c., the second and third persons are formed by *shouldst* and *should*, not *wouldst* and *would*.

† See § 251 (3). The *t* in *ar-t* corresponds to the *t* in *shal-t*. (See § 228.)

In old English the forms *nam = am not; nart = art not,* &c., were made by prefixing the negative *ne*.

252 The verb *be* is a most important verb for the right understanding of the etymology and syntax of verbs in general, because it has distinct forms for the past indefinite in the indicative and subjunctive moods. In no other verb is there a corresponding difference of *form*, though there is a real difference of *mood*. This identity of form, concealing a real difference of construction, is a fact of very common occurrence in English; as in the nominative and objective cases of nouns, the three different persons in the plural of verbs, &c. The verb *be*, therefore, is a *test* verb. By substituting it in place of any other verb in a sentence where the construction is doubtful or difficult, we can see directly what part of the verb it is that is really used. In such sentences as, "He *would* not come when I called him;" "He *could* not lift the weight when he tried;" "Ye *would* not come unto me that ye might have life" (*i.e.*, Ye did not choose to come); "He told me that I might go" (*i.e.*, that it *was* permitted me to go); "You *should* not have done that" (*i.e.*, it *was your duty* not to have done that); the verbs *could, would, might,* are in the indicative mood: the sentences are simple assertions. On the other hand, in such sentences as these—"I *could* not do it if I *were* to try;" "I *should* not have said that, if you *had* not asked me;" "I *would* not tell you if I *could;*" "He *might* have done it if he *had* liked!"—the verbs which are in italics are in the subjunctive mood.

253 ## The Notional and Auxiliary Verb DO.

Infinitive Mood.

Indefinite Tense, [To] do.
Imperfect Tense, [To] be doing.
Perfect Tense, [To] have done.

Participles.

Imperfect, Doing.
Perfect (passive), Done.
Compound Perfect, Having done.

Do (when used as a notional verb) is not defective in Voice, Mood, or Tense. It is remarkable as being one of the only two remaining verbs in which the preterite is formed by reduplication (§ 220). It requires no *to* before the following infinitive (except in the phrase 'I do you *to wit*').

254 As a notional verb (or verb of complete predication) it is used both transitively* (as "He did the wrong"), and intransitively (as "I shall not *do* so," *i.e.*, 'I shall not *act* so'). It had also the sense of *put*. Thus *don = do on = put on; dup = do up = put up,* [German, *aufthun*] or *open; doff = do off = put off; dout (douse) = do out = put out.*

---

* The form *doest* is only used in this sense.

As a verb of complete predication *do* (when followed by the infinitive) had formerly the sense of *make* or *cause*. Thus "They have done her understonde" = 'They have made her understand' (*Gower*) ; "Here did she fall a tear," *i.e.*, ' Here she let a tear fall ' (*Richard II.*, iii. 4). "We do you to wit." When used as a mere auxiliary, it is employed—1, to give emphasis,* as "I do love you," "That does astonish me"; 2, to form interrogative sentences, as "Do you hear?" "Did you understand?"; 3, to form negative sentences, as "I do not hear you" "We did not speak." As an auxiliary *do* has none of the compound tenses.

255 Interrogative sentences are formed in two ways. 1st. By placing the verb before its subject, as, "Said he not so?" "Went they not this way?" With any of the compound tenses, active or passive, the subject of the verb is always placed after the auxiliary verb, as "Shall we begin?" "Have you dined?" "Were you hurt?"
2nd. By using the verb *do*, followed by the infinitive mood: "Do you hear?" "Did you learn your lesson?"
But the verb *do* is never employed when the *subject* of the sentence is an interrogative pronoun, or when an interrogative word qualifies either the subject or an adjective attached to the subject, as, "Who broke the window?" "Which boy did this?" "How many persons voted?"
In poetical language, a sentence is made negative by simply putting *not* after the verb; as, "I heard not his voice." In prose the verb *do*, with the infinitive mood, is employed; as, "I do not understand," "He did not reply." But *do* is never used in this way to replace a compound tense of the active voice, or any tense of the passive voice ; nor is it used, either in negations or in questions, with the verbs *have, be, may, can, must, shall, will, durst*.

256 The verb *let* is now employed (in the second person imperative) as a verb of incomplete predication, followed by an objective case and an infinitive mood, to form a substitute† for an imperative in the first or third person, as "Let me see"; "Let us pray"; "Let him go on," &c. (see § 572*d* for the analysis of these sentences). This use of *let* is based upon the same principle as that of *shall* in the future tense (see § 213). Formerly *let* had the stronger meaning of *make* or *cause*, as "He let her wit" (*Chaucer*, 785); "He lette two cofres make" (*Gower*).

Complete Conjugation of an English Verb.

257 The following table exhibits the personal *inflections* that are made use of in conjugating a verb. Let a single stroke

---

* Formerly this periphrasis conveyed no emphasis, unless stress was laid on the auxiliary. (See the English Bible and Shakspere *passim*.) With the elision of the dependent infinitive it still forms a weak repetition of a preceding verb; as, "I do not spend so much as he does [spend]." It is never followed by the infinitive *have* and *be*, except in the imperative mood, as "Do have patience"; "Do be quiet."

† It may be said that it is much easier to call 'Let us go' the first person plural imperative of the verb *go*, and so on. So it is. It is always easier to shirk a difficulty than to solve it. The objection to the easier course is that it is false. *Us* cannot be the subject of a *finite* verb, and *let* cannot be of the first person. (Compare the German ' Lasset uns beten.') A complex grammatical phrase has not been explained when its parts have been jumbled together into one lot, and ticketed with a wrong name.

ETYMOLOGY—VERB.   91

(————) stand for the infinitive mood (without *to*), and a double stroke (══════) for the first person singular of the past indefinite tense.

Imperfect Participle. ————ing.*

Indicative Mood.
Present Indefinite Tense.

Singular.		Plural.†
1. ————	1. ————
2. ———— est *or* st	2. ————
3. ———— eth,‡ es, *or* s.	3. ————

Past Indefinite Tense.

Singular.		Plural.
1. ══════	1. ══════
2. ══════ est *or* st§	2. ══════
3. ══════	3. ══════

Subjunctive Mood.
Present Indefinite Tense.

Singular.		Plural.
1. ————	1. ————
2. ————	2. ————
3. ————	3. ————

Past Indefinite Tense.
The same as in the Indicative Mood.

Verbs ending in a mute *e* drop the *e* before the suffixes *ing*, *est*, and *eth*.‖ *Do* takes *th*, not *eth* in the present tense (*doth*: *doeth* is obsolete). The suffix *eth* is now seldom used except in poetry. (See § 22.) The suffix *es* is added to verbs ending in a sibilant (as *pass-es*, *catch-es*); *o* (as

---

* Verbs in *ie* form the imperfect participle with *y* instead of *ie;* as *die, dying; tie, tying*. The verb *dye* retains the mute *e* (*dyeing*), to distinguish it from *dying*.
† It is curious that in early English the termination of the plural of this tense in all three persons was *-es* in the Northern, *-en* in the Midland, and *-eth* in the Southern districts: "They hopes" (N.); "They hopen" (M.); "They hopeth" (S.). —(*Morris, Spec.* p. xii.) The plural *-es* or *s* often occurs in Shakspere, as: "Words to the heat of deeds too cold breath gives" (*Oth.* ii. 1). In the modern editions these plurals have often been unwarrantably altered. (See *Abbott*, p. 235.)
‡ In old writers, when this suffix is added to verbs ending in a dental, we often find the vowel omitted, and the dental blended with the suffix into a *t*, as *bint* for *bindeth*; *fint* for *findeth*; *stant* for *standeth*; *holt* for *holdeth*. (*Mätzner.*) A solitary specimen of this is preserved in *list* ("When she list" Shaksp.).
§ This suffix originally belonged only to the weak conjugation. In the strong conjugation the suffix was *-e*, which long maintained its ground, *e.g., thou crewe, thou sawe* (*Skelton*). In the Northern dialect the *e* was thrown off, so that we find such forms as *thou gaf, thou saw*, &c. (See § 236.) In early English *est* or *st* was often thrown off in verbs of the weak conjugation, as "Why nad (= *ne had*) thou put" (*Chaucer, C. T.* 4086). This was especially the case in the Northern dialects.
‖ The pronunciation of *fle-eth, se-eth*, &c., shows that the suffix is *-eth* not *-th*. The *e* of *est* may be dropped whenever the pronunciation allows.

go-es, do-es); or *y* preceded by a consonant, as *fli-es, piti-es*. (See § 48.) If a verb ends in *ic*, *c* is changed to *ck* before *-ing, -ed,* or *-eth*, to preserve the hard sound of the *c*, as *trafficking, mimicked*. (See also § 22.) The letter *p* is usually doubled, even when the last syllable is not accented, as *kidnapped, worshipped*.

The formation of the compound tenses will be obvious on an examination of the following verb.* The learner must analyse it carefully, and it will then be unnecessary to set down the rules at full length.

SMITE.
ACTIVE VOICE.
Infinitive Mood.

Indefinite Tense, [To] smite.
Imperfect Tense, [To] be smiting.
Perfect Tense, [To] have smitten.
Perfect of continued action, [To] have been smiting.

Participles.

Imperfect, Smiting.
Perfect, Having smitten.
Perfect of continued action, Having been smiting.

Indicative Mood.
Present Indefinite Tense.

Singular.
1. [I] smite
2. [Thou] smitest
3. [He] smites *or* smiteth

Plural.
1. [We] smite
2. [You] smite
3. [They] smite

Present Imperfect Tense.

Singular.
1. [I] am smiting
2. [Thou] art smiting
3. [He] is smiting

Plural.
1. [We] are smiting
2. [You] are smiting
3. [They] are smiting

Present Perfect Tense.

Singular.
1. [I] have smitten
2. [Thou] hast smitten
3. [He] has smitten

Plural.
1. [We] have smitten
2. [You] have smitten
3. [They] have smitten

---

* It will not be easy to make mistakes in the verb which is here given. There is not a large choice of verbs which are transitive, denoting a single action which may be prolonged or repeated, having the past indefinite tense and the perfect participle different, and making some reasonable sense when conjugated through all varieties of voice, mood, and tense. Most grammars follow the very objectionable plan of giving as a model some verb in which the past indefinite tense and the perfect participle are the same in form. If a dozen beginners were set to analyse such a verb, three-fourths of them would probably pronounce the present perfect tense to be made up of *have* and the past indefinite tense.

Present Perfect of continued action.

Singular.
1. [I] have been smiting, &c.

Plural.
1. [We] have been smiting, &c.

Past Indefinite Tense.

Singular.
1. [I] smote
2. [Thou] smotest
3. [He] smote

Plural.
1. [We] smote
2. [You] smote
3. [They] smote

Past Imperfect Tense.

Singular.
1. [I] was smiting
2. [Thou] wast smiting
3. [He] was smiting

Plural.
1. [We] were smiting
2. [You] were smiting
3. [They] were smiting

Past Perfect Tense.

Singular.
1. [I] had smitten
2. [Thou] hadst smitten
3. [He] had smitten

Plural.
1. [We] had smitten
2. [You] had smitten
3. [They] had smitten

Past Perfect of continued action.

Singular.
1. [I] had been smiting, &c.

Plural.
1. [We] had been smiting, &c.

Future Indefinite Tense.

Singular.
1. [I] shall smite
2. [Thou] wilt smite
3. [He] will smite

Plural.
1. [We] shall smite
2. [You] will smite
3. [They] will smite

Future Imperfect Tense.

Singular.
1. [I] shall be smiting, &c.

Plural.
1. [We] shall be smiting, &c.

Future Perfect Tense.

Singular.
1. [I] shall have smitten, &c.

Plural.
1. [We] shall have smitten, &c.

Future Perfect of continued action.

[I] shall have been smiting, &c.

Imperative Mood.*

Singular.—Smite [thou].   *Plural.*—Smite [you or ye].

Subjunctive Mood.

Present Indefinite Tense.

(After *if, that, though, lest, unless,* &c.)

Singular.
1. [I] smite
2. [Thou] smite
3. [He] smite

Plural.
1. [We] smite
2. [You] smite
3. [They] smite

---

* A perfect imperative is now and then met with, as "Have done"; "Be gone."

Present Imperfect Tense.

After *if, that, though, lest,* &c.

Singular.
1. [I] be smiting
2. [Thou] be smiting
3. [He] be smiting

Plural.
1. [We] be smiting
2. [You] be smiting
3. [They] be smiting

Present Perfect Tense.

After *if, though, unless,* &c.

Singular.
1. [I] have smitten
2. [Thou] have smitten
3. [He] have smitten

Plural.
1. [We] have smitten
2. [You] have smitten
3. [They] have smitten

Present Perfect of continued action.

After *if, though, unless,* &c.

Singular.
1. [I] have been smiting, &c.

Plural.
1. [We] have been smiting, &c.

Past Indefinite Tense.

Used mostly after *if, though, unless,* &c.

Singular.
1. [I] smote
2. [Thou] smotest
3. [He] smote

Plural.
1. [We] smote
2. [You] smote
3. [They] smote

Secondary,* or Periphrastic Form.

When not preceded by Conjunctions.

Singular.
1. [I] should smite
2. [Thou] wouldst smite†
3. [He] would smite

Plural.
1. [We] should smite
2. [You] would smite
3. [They] would smite

Past Imperfect Tense.

Used mostly after *if, that, though, unless,* &c.

Singular.
1. [I] were smiting
2. [Thou] wert smiting
3. [He] were smiting

Plural.
1. [We] were smiting
2. [You] were smiting
3. [They] were smiting

---

* These secondary forms have almost replaced the older and simpler forms in conditional assertions. Instead of saying, "It *were* vain to tell thee all I feel," we should commonly say, "It *would be* vain," &c. Instead of "I *had fainted* unless I had believed to see the goodness of the Lord," we say now, "I *should have fainted*," &c. In German the corresponding forms keep their place side by side. *Ich wäre* = *Ich würde seyn*. After *that*, in clauses denoting *purpose*, the present indefinite and past indefinite subjunctive are usually replaced by *may* and *might*, followed by the infinitive of the verb.

† After the conjunctions *if, though, unless, lest, except,* &c., the second and third persons are formed by *shouldst* and *should*, not *wouldst* and *would*.

ETYMOLOGY—VERB.

Secondary or Conditional Form.
When not preceded by Conjunctions.

Singular.
1. [I] should be smiting
2. [Thou] wouldst be smiting *
3. [He] would be smiting

Plural.
1. [We] should be smiting
2. [You] would be smiting
3. [They] would be smiting

Past Perfect Tense.
Used mostly after *if, though, unless,* &c.

Singular.
1. [I] had smitten
2. [Thou] hadst smitten
3. [He] had smitten

Plural.
1. [We] had smitten
2. [You] had smitten
3. [They] had smitten

Secondary or Conditional Form.
When not preceded by Conjunctions.

Singular.
1. [I] should have   ⎫
2. [Thou] wouldst* have ⎬ smitten
3. [He] would have   ⎭

Plural.
1. [We] should have   ⎫
2. [You] would have   ⎬ smitten
3. [They] would have   ⎭

Past Perfect of continued action.
Used mostly after *if, that, though, unless,* &c.

Singular.
1. [I] had been smiting, &c.

Plural.
1. [We] had been smiting, &c.

Secondary or Periphrastic Form.
When not preceded by Conjunctions.

[I] should have been smiting; [Thou] wouldst* have been smiting, &c.

PASSIVE VOICE.

Infinitive Mood.
Indefinite Tense, [To] be smitten.
Imperfect Tense, [To] be being smitten.
Perfect Tense, [To] have been smitten.

Participles.
Indefinite Participle, Being smitten.
Perfect Participle, Smitten.
Compound Perfect Participle, Having been smitten.

Indicative Mood.
Present Indefinite Tense.†

Singular.
1. [I] am smitten
2. [Thou] art smitten
3. [He] is smitten

Plural.
1. [We] are smitten
2. [You] are smitten
3. [They] are smitten

---

* After *if, though, unless, lest, except,* &c., the second and third persons are formed by *shouldst* and *should,* not *wouldst* and *would.*

† In Anglo-Saxon and early English this tense had also the meaning now expressed by the present perfect tense.

ETYMOLOGY—VERB.

Present Imperfect Tense.

Singular.   Plural.
1. [I] am being smitten, &c.   1. [We] are being smitten, &c.

Present Perfect Tense.

Singular.   Plural.
1. [I] have been smitten   1. [We] have been smitten
2. [Thou] hast been smitten   2. [You] have been smitten
3. [He] has been smitten   3. [They] have been smitten

Present Perfect of continued action.
[I] have been being smitten, &c.

Past Indefinite Tense.

Singular.   Plural.
1. [I] was smitten   1. [We] were smitten
2. [Thou] wast smitten   2. [You] were smitten
3. [He] was smitten   3. [They] were smitten

Past Imperfect Tense.

Singular.   Plural.
1. [I] was being smitten, &c.   1. [We] were being smitten, &c.

Past Perfect Tense.

Singular.   Plural.
1. [I] had been smitten   1. [We] had been smitten
2. [Thou] hadst been smitten   2. [You] had been smitten
3. [He] had been smitten   3. [They] had been smitten

Past Perfect of continued action.
[I] had been being smitten, &c.

Future Indefinite Tense.

Singular.   Plural.
1. [I] shall be smitten   1. [We] shall be smitten
2. [Thou] wilt be smitten   2. [You] will be smitten
3. [He] will be smitten   3. [They] will be smitten

Future Imperfect Tense.
[I] shall be being smitten, &c.

*Future Perfect Tense.**

Singular.   Plural.
1. [I] shall have been   } smitten   1. [We] shall have been   } smitten
2. [Thou] wilt have been   2. [You] will have been
3. [He] will have been   3. [They] will have been

Future Perfect of continued action.†
[I] shall have been being smitten, &c.

Imperative Mood.

Singular.   Plural.
Be [thou] smitten   Be [ye] smitten

---

* This tense first makes its appearance in modern English.
† It may be doubted whether many examples of the passive perfects of continued action can be found in actual use.

Subjunctive Mood.

Present Indefinite Tense.*
After *if, that, though,* &c.

Singular.
1. [I] be smitten
2. [Thou] be smitten
3. [He] be smitten

Plural.
1. [We] be smitten
2. [You] be smitten
3. [They] be smitten

Present Imperfect Tense.
After *if, that, though,* &c.

Singular.
1. [I] be being smitten, &c.

Plural.
1. [We] be being smitten, &c.

Present Perfect Tense.
After *if, that, though,* &c.

Singular.
1. [I] have been smitten
2. [Thou] have been smitten
3. [He] have been smitten

Plural.
1. [We] have been smitten
2. [You] have been smitten
3. [They] have been smitten

Present Perfect of continued action.

[I] have been being smitten, &c.

Past Indefinite Tense.
After *if, that, though,* &c.

Singular.
1. [I] were smitten
2. [Thou] wert smitten
3. [He] were smitten

Plural.
1. [We] were smitten
2. [You] were smitten
3. [They] were smitten

Secondary or Conditional Form.
When not preceded by Conjunctions.

Singular.
1. [I] should be smitten
2. [Thou] wouldst be smitten †
3. [He] would be smitten

Plural.
1. [We] should be smitten
2. [You] would be smitten
3. [They] would be smitten

Past Imperfect Tense.
After *if, though,* &c.

Singular.
1. [I] were being smitten
2. [Thou] wert being smitten
3. [He] were being smitten

Plural.
1. [We] were being smitten
2. [You] were being smitten
3. [They] were being smitten

Secondary or Periphrastic Form.
When not preceded by Conjunctions.

[I] should‡ be being smitten, &c.

---

* See note * on p. 94.   † See note * on p. 95.   ‡ See note * on p. 96.

Past Perfect Tense.

The same in form as the Past Perfect Indicative.

Secondary, or Periphrastic Form.

When not preceded by Conjunctions.

(j) should have been smitten; [Thou] wouldst* have been smitten, &c.

Past Perfect of continued action.

The same in form as the Past Perfect of continued action in the Indicative Mood.

Secondary or Conditional Form.

When not preceded by Conjunctions.

I should* have been being smitten, &c.

258 In some of the regular verbs of the weak form the *d* at the end of the past indefinite and perfect participle is sounded like *t* (especially after a sibilant, as in *published, passed, incensed, pushed;* after *p*, as in *stepped;* and after *ck*, as in *picked*), and is sometimes replaced by *t*, as *spilt* for *spilled*, *dwelt* for *dwelled*, *learnt* for *learned*, *leapt* for *leaped*, *pent* for *pen ed*.

Some modern writers follow the older practice of writing *t* in all cases where the suffix has a sharp sound,† and write *pusht, past*, &c.

In the verbs *lay, say*, and *pay, laid* is written for *layed, said* for *sayed*, and *paid* for *payed*.

ADVERB.

259 When we think of a thing and connect with it the notion of some action or attribute, we often take account of the conditions or circumstances which modify or define the action or attribute, such as *place* ("He lives *here*"), *time* ("The man died *yesterday*"), *manner* ("The bird flies *swiftly*"), *degree* ("The house is *very* large," "The distance is *too* great"). The words by which these conditions or circumstances are denoted are called *adverbs*. ‡

---

* See note * on page 95.

† This, in reality, is not an innovation, and has much to recommend it. See an essay on "English Orthography," by the late Archdeacon Hare, in the "Philological Museum," vol. i.

‡ *Adverbium*, from *ad* (to) and *verbum* (verb), the name *adverb* implying a word attached to a verb.

260 *Definition.*—An **adverb** is a word which shows the conditions of place, time, manner, degree, cause, effect, &c., which modify or limit an action or attribute.* Adverbs are most commonly attached to verbs, adjectives, or other adverbs; but they may also be used with abstract nouns (gerunds) denoting an action or state, as " He succeeded by working diligently." Adverbs are usually said to modify the words to which they are attached.

261 Adverbs may be classified in two ways, (1) according to their syntactical force, (2) according to their meaning.

262 As regards their syntactical force adverbs are of two kinds :—1. Simple Adverbs; 2. Conjunctive or relative Adverbs.

A *simple* adverb is one which does nothing more than modify the word with which it is used as, *yesterday* (" We arrived yesterday "); *now* (" I hear him now "); *hither* (" He is coming hither ").

A *conjunctive* or *relative* adverb is one which not only modifies some verb, adjective, or other adverb in its own clause, but connects the clause in which it occurs with the rest of the sentence; as *when* (" Come when you are ready "); *whither* (" I know not whither he has gone ").

263 A relative adverb always refers to some demonstrative word, expressed or understood, which stands to it in the same sort of relation that the *antecedent* stands in to a *relative pronoun*, as, "Come (*then*) *when* you are ready;" " *There, where* a few torn shrubs the place disclose."

Care is necessary to distinguish connective *adverbs* from connective words which are not adverbs. Many conjunctions refer to time, place, cause, &c.; but *they do not refer to these conditions in connexion with any verb or adjective of the clause which they introduce;* but the whole of the subordinate clause has the force of an adverb attached to some word in the principal clause of the sentence, as, " He said that *because* he believed it." Here *because* does not, by itself, modify either the verb *believed* or the verb *said*, but the clause *because he believed it* is an adverbial clause modifying the verb *said*.

264 The following words are *conjunctive* or *relative* adverbs : *When, where, whither, whence, why, wherein, whereby, wherefore, whereon, whereat, whereout, whereafter, wherever, as*†

---

* It is self-evident that any word which fulfils the functions of an adverb must be an adverb. It may discharge other functions as well, but an *adverb* it is and must be. *When, where*, &c., do not cease to be adverbs because they also connect a subordinate clause with a principal clause, any more than *who* and *which* cease to be pronouns because they also do the same. If *when, where*, &c. are to be called *conjunctions* because they join sentences, *who* and *which* must be called conjunctions also, for the same reason.

† *As* is a difficult word to deal with. It is both a simple or demonstrative adverb and a relative or connective adverb. It is, in fact, a compound of *all* and

(when it answers to *so*, *such*, or the demonstrative *as*), *than*.*

265 With reference to their signification both simple and

so (like the German *als*), which has been shortened into *as*. The *demonstrative* sense of the word is therefore the original one, but like other demonstratives it was also used as a relative. The transition from the demonstrative to the relative sense, especially in the case of the strengthened form *al-so* (*all-so*), is easily understood. " Thou art me leof also mi fader" (*Layamon*), ' Thou art dear to me as my father,' is only a step removed from " Thou art dear to me. All so (dear), *i.e.*, just so (dear) is my father." (See note on § 158). So "He wolde crie as he were wod" (' He would cry as if he were mad') is, " He would cry. All so (*i.e.*, ' in this state of things,' ' crying so ') " he would be mad." As a demonstrative adverb it only qualifies adjectives or adverbs, and is followed by *as* used *relatively*. In practice it is often difficult to distinguish *as* from a relative pronoun (see § 167). However, let it be borne in mind that the *mode* or *manner* in which a thing *is*, may represent some *quality* which it possesses (as in *Terence, Phormio* iii. 2, 42. *Sic sum. Ego hunc esse aliter credidi. Ego isti nihilo sum aliter ac fui*). So in answer to the question,"Is that boy a dunce?" we may reply, "He is *so*." "Is that true?" " It is *so*." On a similar principle we may say, "He talked like a fool, *as* he was." "He seemed to be a foreigner, *as* in fact he was." (*Peregrinus, ut erat, visus est.* "He looked like a foreigner, and *so* be was.") If the force of these examples is well understood, there will not be much difficulty in the *as* which follows *such* and *same*. As, " His health is not such as it was " Demonstratively, " His health was *so* and *so*, it is not *such* now." "'This is not the same *as* that [is]." "This is *so* and *so*, that is not the same ; " the *manner* in which a thing *exists* being used to denote either a quality of the thing, or even the thing itself, since no two things can possibly exist *in the same way*. In old English *so* (*swa*) was used relatively. Its use as a *connective* adverb is still found in Shakspere, as : " So I were out of prison and kept sheep, I should be as merry as the day is long " (*K. J.*, iv. 1). A great number of clauses beginning with *as* are elliptical. The construction of these will be discussed in the section on Analysis (§ 545, &c.). Writers who make *as* a pronoun would have to do the same with *wie* and *als* in German. (*Ein solcher wie er.*) It need hardly be added that sentences like, " He is the man as did this," " That is the horse as I saw yesterday," are utter abominations. From denoting the *mode* or *manner* of an action, *as* came to be used to mark the *time* of an action (*e.g.*, ' He arrived as I was setting out '), or even (in old writers), to denote *place* (*e.g.*, ' as ys bones lyggeth ' = ' where his bones lie.' (*Rob. of Gl.*) In " He grows wiser *as* he grows older," *as* is a relative adverb of *degree*. In this sense it may also give a concessive force to a clause, as " Rich *as* he is, one would hardly envy him."

. * *Than* is often set down as a mere conjunction. This is a mistake. *Than* and *then* are only various forms of the same word (A.S. ponne or panne). In Skelton (i. 79) we find, " *Whan* other are glad, *Than* is he sad." In later English the spelling *than* has been restricted to the adverb as it is used after comparatives. In Anglo-Saxon *than* (ponne) means ' when,' having the common relative force of *se, seo,* pæt and its derivatives. In this sense it was used after comparatives to introduce the *standard of comparison*. " He came sooner than I expected," meant in fact, " When I expected [him to come soon] he came sooner." " John is taller than Charles," meant, " When Charles is tall (*i.e.*, when the tallness of Charles is regarded) John is taller." " I have no other home than this," is, " When I have this, I have no other home." In course of time *than* ousted the dative case, which in Anglo-Saxon was used (like the ablative in Latin) to denote the standard of comparison. In Scotch *be* (= *by*) is used for a similar purpose, as, " Hey's yunger be onie o thaim," = " He's younger by (*i.e.*, ' by the side of,' ' compared with ') any of them." The curious provincial and Scotch use of *nor* after comparatives is quite different. " He is older nor John," possibly means " He is older, and not John." Clauses beginning with *than* are usually elliptical, and require a verb, either expressed or understood. From what has been said above, it appears that *than* is a connective adverb, qualifying (adverbially) this verb. *Quam*, in Latin, does not strictly answer to *than*, but is an adverb of *degree* (like the demonstrative *tam*), qualifying the adjective or adverb (expressed or understood) which follows it.

relative adverbs admit of being classified according to the ideas of time, place, &c., which they indicate.

1. *Adverbs of Time.* Now, then, after, before, presently, immediately, when, as (in such sentences as "*As I was returning, I met him*"), &c.

2. *Adverbs of Place and Arrangement.* Here, there, where, whither, wherever, whithersoever, thence, whence, wherein, whereat, whereupon, in, out, up, down, under, within, inside, without, backwards, firstly, secondly, &c.

3. *Adverbs of Repetition.* Once, twice, &c.

4. *Adverbs of Manner.* Well, ill, badly, how, however, so, as.

To this class belong the numerous abverbs formed from adjectives by the suffix *ly*, as *rightly, virtuously, badly,* &c.

5. *Adverbs of Quantity or Degree.* Very, nearly, almost, quite, eke (A.S. *eâc* = Germ. *auch*), much, more, most, little, less, least, all, half, any, only, as, the. These are only a particular kind of Adverbs of Manner.

6. *Adverbs of Affirmation and Negation.* Not, no, nay, aye, yea.

7. *Adverbs of Cause and Effect.* Therefore, wherefore, why.

266 As regards their origin, adverbs are for the most part formed by inflection, derivation, or composition, from nouns, adjectives, and pronouns.

267 **Adverbs derived from Nouns.**—Adverbial genitives* still remain in *needs* (= *of necessity*), *straightways*† (comp. *straightway*), *noways* (comp. *noway*), *always* (comp. *alway* = ' all the way '; A.S. *ealne weg*).

Some adverbial phrases, as 'Day and night,' 'Summer and winter,' 'One day,' were once genitives.

We have one adverbial dative left in *whilom* (A.S., *hwilum*), a dative plural, meaning 'at whiles' ('formerly,' 'on a time'). *Ever* and *never*‡ were once datives singular. The adverbs in -*meal* were compounds of the dative plural *maelum*, 'by portions'; as *piecemeal*, *inchmeal* (Shaks., *Temp.* ii. 2), *limbmeal* (*Cymb.* ii. 4).

In § 372, 3, it is noticed that many adverbial adjuncts consist of a noun (which was originally in the accusative), qualified by an adjective. Several of these have hardened into compound adverbs,

---

* Adverbial genitives were common in Anglo-Saxon, as '*sóðes*' (*of a truth*); '*nihtes*' (*by night*); '*dæges*' (*by day*, compare ' of an evening,' ' of mornings '); '*sylfwilles*' (*of free will*), &c. Many of them have been replaced by *of* followed by the noun.

† Some of these are mixed up with the compounds of *wise*. Thus we have *lengthways* and *lengthwise*, *noway* and *nowise*.

‡ *Ev-r* is sometimes wrongly substituted for *never* in such expressions as "He told never so many lies," "Be they never so many," i.e., 'be they many, so that they were never so many.' In like manner people commonly say, 'Don't do more than you can help,' instead of 'Don't do more than you can't help' (*De Morgan*).

as *sometimes, always, otherwise, likewise* (= in like manner) *meantime, midway, yesterday* (A.S., *gestran dæy*), *straightway.* The adverbs *north, south, east, west, home,* were formerly accusative cases.

A large class of adverbial adjuncts consist of a noun preceded by a preposition (see § 372, 2). Some of these adverbial expressions have been welded together into adverbs. Thus, with the preposition *on* (weakened to *a*), we get *abed, asleep, afoot, ahead, astern, adrift, afloat, agape, amiss, away, aback, aboard,** &c.

In a similar way we get *indeed, betimes* (i.e., *by-times*), *besides, beforehand, forsooth, to-day, to-morrow, to-night, overboard,* &c.

A few adverbs are derived from nouns by the suffix *-long* (formerly *linge,* answering to *-lings* in German), as *headlong* (formerly *heedlynge*), *sidelong,* or *sidling*† (*sidelinges*). *Darkling* comes from an adjective.

268   **Adverbs derived from Adjectives.**—Specimens of the genitive suffix *s* appear in *else* (formerly *elles,* the genitive of a root *el* or *al,* meaning *other*), *once* (for *ones,* from *one*), *twice* (formerly *twyes*), *thrice* (formerly *thryes* or *thries*), *unawares, inwards,*‡ *outwards,* &c. (by the side of the forms *inward, outward,* &c.). *Much* (as in *much greater* = *greater by much*) and *little* were datives (*miclum* and *lytlum*). Other adverbs were formerly accusative adjectives, as *all, enough, right, far, near, ere.* By prefixing a preposition to an adjective, and then dropping the old case suffix, we get such adverbs as *amid* (A.S., *on-middum*), *abroad, withal, aloud, awry, along, together.*§ We still say *in general, in vain,* &c.

269   The common adverbial suffix in Anglo-Saxon was *-e,*∥ the omission of which reduced many adverbs to the same form as the adjectives from which they were derived.¶ Thus, "He smot him harde" became "He smote him hard." "His spere sticode faeste" = "His spear stuck fast." "He weop biterlice" = "He wept bitterly." It was thus that we got such adverbs as those in the phrases, 'to run *fast*'; '*right* reverend'; '*sore* displeased'; 'to talk *like* a fool'; 'to speak *loud*'; 'to sleep *sound*'; 'to live *godly*'; 'to come *early*'; 'you are very *likely* aware,' &c. In Anglo-Saxon there was a numerous class of secondary adjectives ending in *-lic,* the adverbs from which ended in *lice* (= *like* = *ly*), as *biterlice*

---

* These must not be confounded with French compounds of *à* (= *ad*), such as *apart, apace, afront, apiece, agog.* (See *Mätzner,* i. 441.)

† In *Morte d'Arthur,* ii. 286, we read "Felle downe *noseling,*" i.e., 'on to his nose.' (*Halliwell, s. v.*)

‡ *Ward* (A.S. *weard*), is in reality an adjective (used only in compounds), and equivalent to the Latin *vergens,* 'inclining *or* stretching.'

§ Thus also were formed *anon* (= ou âne, 'at one [time],' 'without interval.' The *nonce* is a corruption of *then once* (= *than ane*(*s*), 'that one purpose or time' *Koch,* ii. p. 309.)

∥ Adverbs in *-e* are still found in Spenser.

¶ In old French there was an adverbial use of adjectives, which found its way into English. Hence we say, "You play me *false*;" "That is *very* good;" "*Sure* that cannot be true;" "I *scarce* touched him," "That is *quite* true." It is often a question whether we are dealing with an adverb, or with an adjective used as the complement of the predicate, *e.g.*, "Hope springs *eternal* in the human breast" (*Pope*); "*Slow* and *sure* comes up the golden year" (*Tennyson*).

(*bitterlike* = ' of a bitter sort '), *biterlice* = ' in a bitter sort of way.' As the adverbial suffix *-e* fell into disuse, the suffix *lice* (= *ly*) came to be treated as an ordinary adverbial suffix, the intervening *adjective* in *-lie* (*-ly*) being either suppressed or not formed.* Thus we now have ' bitter ' (*adj.*) and ' bitterly ' (*adv.*), but not ' bitterlike'; and the suffix is appended to Romance as well as to Anglo-Saxon words, as *perfectly, divinely.*†

270 **Pronominal Adverbs.**—These are formed from the pronominal roots (*a*) by the suffix *-re,* marking *place:—here, there, where;*‡ (*b*) by the suffix *-ther:—hither, thither, whither;* (*c*) by the suffix *-n* (A.S., *ne*, the accusative masculine suffix §):—*then* or *than* (A.S., *þanne* or *þonne*), *when;* (*d*) by the compound suffix *-nce,* of which *ce* (= *es*) is the genitive suffix‖:—*hence, thence, whence;* ¶ (*e*) from the Anglo-Saxon instrumental case we get *the* (= *þy*), used before comparatives, as in ' *The* sooner *the* better'; *why* (= *hwi* or *hwy*) and *how* (= *hwu*). The neuter relative pronoun *that* is often used as a connective adverb. *What* has in old writers the sense of *why ?* or in what degree ? *Thus* is probably only a variety of *theos,* the instrumental case of the neuter *this.*

271 Many adverbs are identical in form with prepositions, as *by* (' he rode by '), *on* (' come on '), *off* (' be off '), *to* (' he came to '), *out* (' go out '), &c. *From,* as an adverb, survives in *to and fro.* The adverbial use of the words is in fact the older of the two (see farther on, under ' Preposition '). These adverbs combine with the pronominal adverbs, and form the compound adverbs *herein, thereby, herewith, hitherto, whereat, thereout, thenceforth,* &c.

272 **Adverbs of Negation.** The old English negation was *ne,* put before the verb, while *not* is put after it, when the verb is finite. *Not*

---

* We often have pairs of adverbs (commonly with a slight difference of meaning) formed with or without the intervention of the adjective in *lic,* as *light, lightly ; right, rightly ; hard, hardly,* &c.
   Like was itself an adverb, as in "Like as a father pitieth his children, so the Lord pitieth them that fear Him." Here *like* is repeated in *so*. In " He talks like a fool," *like* is an adverb, and is itself qualified adverbially (§ 372, 4) by '[to] a fool.' (Compare the dative after *similiter* in Latin.)
   † When adverbs are formed from adjectives in *-le* preceded by a consonant, *e* is cut off and *y* only is added, as *able, ably.* *Y* is changed to *i* before *ly,* as in *bodily, merrily, daily*. Before *-ly ll* is reduced to *l,* as *full, ful-ly*. The *e* of *ue* is elided, as in *truly. Ly* is not added to adjectives ending in *ly*. The adverbial suffix *-ly* was sometimes omitted, so that we get such phrases as ' grievous sick ' (*Shaksp. R. II.* i. 4); ' exceeding great ' ; ' Thou didst it excellent' (*Taming of Shrew,* i. 1, 89); ' Does easy ' (*Macb.* ii. 3, 143); ' Less winning soft, less amiably mild ' (*Par. Lost,* ii. 478).
   ‡ These adverbs are often used for those in *-ther* by the best writers, as "There I throw my gage" (*Shaksp.*); " Your horse will carry you there" (*Scott*), &c.
   § Compare the Latin *tum* and *quum*.
   ‖ *Hence,* &c., are secondary forms. The older forms are *heonan, heonne, hethen, henne,* and then *hennis, hennes, hens, hence; hwanon, wanne, whethen, whennes ; thanon, thanne, thennes.* The *-n* or *-ne* appears to mark *motion from*. (Compare the Latin *i-n-de, u-n-de,* and German *hi-n.*)
   ¶ These adverbs followed the course of the corresponding pronouns. Those derived from *who* were at first interrogative and indefinite, and are still so used. They have the indefinite sense in *somewhere, anywhere, elsewhere, nowhere, somehow, anyhow. Seldom* is possibly a corruption of *seld-hwonne* = *rarely-when* (*Koch,* ii. p. 313). *The* is both relative and demonstrative. Before *who* (*hwa*) and its derivatives were used as relatives, *there, then, than,* &c., had this sense.

is a shortened form of *nought* or *naught*[*] (*i.e.*, *ne-á-wiht* = *n-ever a thing*), and consequently is a strengthened negative,[†] meaning ' in no degree,' or ' in no respect.' It was at first used to strengthen a previous negative,[‡] just as Chaucer and other writers use *nothing* (" Nothing ne knew he that it was Arcite," *C. T.* 1521).

No and *nay* are only varieties of *ná* = *never*, which was used before comparative adverbs, as ' nû þý læs ' = *nevertheless*. *No* is now used before comparative adverbs and adjectives, as *no further, no bigger*. The form *No* is now employed as the absolute negative, as " Did you speak ? No." The older form for this was *nay*. The affirmative particle *ay* or *aye* is the same as the Anglo-Saxon *á* = *ever*. (*For aye* = *for ever*.) *Yea* (A.S. *geá*) is of the same origin as the German *ja*. *Yes* (A.S. *gese*) is a compound of *yea* or *ye* and the old subjunctive *si* or *sie* ' be it.' (*Mätzner*, i. 446.) *Ay* or *aye* and *nay* (= *ever* and *never*), as adverbs, once formed part of a phrase containing a verb which they qualified.[§] In *yes* the traces of such a verb are still left.

273 Adverbs are sometimes used after prepositions, so as to serve as compendious expressions for a qualified substantive, as " I have heard that before *now;*" " He has changed since *then*." *Now* is equivalent to " the time *now* being;" *then* to " the time *then* being," &c. Adverbial phrases are also used thus, as " From *beyond the sea*."

Comparison of Adverbs.

274 Some adverbs (like adjectives) admit of degrees of comparison.

The comparative degree of an adverb is that form of it which indicates that of two actions or qualities which are compared together, one surpasses the other with respect to

---

[*] In Anglo-Saxon the elements are found separate, as " He *ne* mehte *wiht* gefeohtan" 'He could not fight.' (*Beowulf.*) *Ne-ne* was equivalent to *neither -nor*. Byron now and then uses this double negative.

[†] We have the negative doubly strengthened in such phrases as ' not a bit,' ' not a jot,' ' not a whit ' (where *whit* or *wiht* in fact occurs twice). *A bit, a jot, a straw,* &c., are accusatives of measure.

[‡] In old English negatives were strengthened, not neutralized, by repetition : *e.g.*, ' Ne geseah næfre nán man God" (*John* i. 18) ' No man hath not never seen God.' The use and position of *not* arose from the omission of the negative *ne*. Thus " Heo nefden noht ane moder (*Layamon* i. 10) = " They *ne* had *not*, &c." became " They had not," &c.

[§] In fact we must repeat with them the previous subject and predicate. Thus " Is not this true ?—Ay, Sir," is at full length :—" Ay (*i.e.*, ever) this is true." " Did you speak ?—No ; " is :—' No *or* nay (*i.e.*, never) did I speak.' Judged by the present usage of *not* and *no*, *not* should be used in all such contracted sentences as " Do you believe this or not ?" But *or no* has also the sanction of the best writers, as " If you be maid or no " (*Shaksp. Temp.* I. 2) ; " Thou knowest alone whether this was or no " (*Tennyson*). The phrase ' whether or no ' has established itself in common use. *Ná* and *nay* were similarly used in Anglo-Saxon and early English. (*Mätzner*, ii. p. 131) Also *never* (= *ná* or *no*) is found for *not*, as " we witen never " = ' we know not ' (*Wiclif; John* ix. 21).

ETYMOLOGY—COMPARISON OF ADVERBS. 105

some circumstance of manner or degree by which they are both marked, but in different degrees. Thus, "John reads *ill*, but Thomas reads *worse*;" "I was but *little* prepared for that event, for he was *less* prepared." The superlative degree of an adverb is that form of it which indicates that out of several actions or qualities which are compared together one surpasses all the rest with respect to some circumstance of manner or degree by which they are all marked, but in different degrees; as, "Of all these boys, William writes the *worst*;" "John was less cautious than I, but Thomas was the *least* cautious of the three."

It is only some adverbs of *time*, *distance*, *manner*, and *degree* which admit of degrees of comparison.

275   The suffixes for comparison are now -*er* and -*est*. In Anglo-Saxon they were -*or* and -*ost*, which were appended to adverbs in -*e* and -*lice*, the final *e* of which was struck off. In modern English adverbs in -*er* and -*est* are usually formed from those adverbs which are the same in form as the corresponding adjectives, as *hard, harder, hardest; long, longer, longest; fast, faster, fastest*, &c. These suffixes are not now appended to adverbs in -*ly* (except *early*). Shakspere uses *proudlier, truer, easier*, &c. *Oftener* and *oftenest* are still common. The usual mode of indicating comparative and superlative is to prefix the adverbs *more* and *most*, as *wisely, more wisely, most wisely*. There are some instances in which the adverbial suffix -*ly* is appended to comparative and superlative adverbs, as *nearly, mostly, formerly, firstly, lastly*.

276   The following forms should be noticed.*

Positive.	Comparative.	Superlative.
well	better	best
evil (*contr.* ill)	worse	worst
much	more	most
nigh *or* near	nearer	next
forth	further	furthest
far	farther	furthest
	ere †	erst
late	later	last
[*adj.* rathe ‡]	rather	

The comparatives *nether* (from *be-neath*,) *upper, inner, outer,* or *utter, hinder* (*be-hind*), are used only as adjectives. Respecting the superlative forms, see § 117.

---

* Compare § 114 and the notes.
† In early English *ere* was sometimes spelt *or*, as: "We, or ever he come near, are ready to kill him" (*Acts* xxiii. 15), "or ever the silver cord be loosed" (*Eccles.* xii. 6).
‡ "The rathe (early) primrose." (*Milton, Lyc.*)

PREPOSITION.

277 Prepositions* are words placed before substantives, by means of which we show the relation in which things, and their actions and attributes, stand to other things. In the sentence, "I saw a cloud in the sky," *in* is a preposition, and marks the relation (of place) in which the *cloud* stands to the *sky*. In the sentence, "Tuesday comes after Monday," *after* is a preposition, and shows the relation (of time) in which the *coming* of Tuesday stands with respect to Monday. In "He struck the dog on the head," *on* is a preposition, and denotes the relation of the act of *striking* to the *head*. In "Tom peeped through the keyhole" *through* denotes the relation (of movement from one side to the other) of the *act of peeping* to the *keyhole*.† In "He is fond of music," *of* denotes the relation of *music* to the attribute *fond*. The substantive which follows a preposition is in the objective case, and is said to be governed by the preposition.

278 Things and their actions and attributes can only bear these relations to other *things*. Therefore a preposition can only be placed before a word that stands for a *thing*, that is, a *substantive*, or a substantive clause, which is equivalent to a substantive (comp. § 273), and can connect the substantive which follows it only with a substantive, a verb, or an adjective, since these alone stand for things and their actions and attributes.

Origin of Prepositions.

279 It has been already pointed out (see note on p. 27) that the original function of prepositions was to give precision and definiteness to the somewhat vague ideas of the relations of actions to things, which were expressed by the case-ending of nouns.‡ They exhibit three

---

* The word *preposition* gives a very imperfect description of this part of speech, as it merely implies 'placed before' (Latin *prae* = *before*, *positus* = *placed*), and is self-contradictory when (as is sometimes the case) a preposition comes *after* the word that it governs, as in ' the pen *which* I wrote *with*.'

† Some grammarians maintain the crotchet that a preposition invariably denotes the relation of a *thing* to a *thing*. If the above sentence is consistent with this definition, the difficulty of a camel's going through the eye of a needle is reduced to very manageable proportions. The *original* function of a preposition (as will be seen from what follows) was to define the relation of an *action* to a *thing* (§ 280). In a recent grammar a preposition is said to be "a word which shows the relation of one *noun* to another." Does "Jack in the box" imply that the *noun* Jack is in the *noun* box?

‡ I find that this view of the matter has the weighty sanction of Matzner (i. p. 447).

stages of construction. (1) They were prefixed to the verb, which they qualified adverbially, forming in fact a compound with it. (2) They were detached from the verb, but not prefixed to the noun. At this stage it is often difficult to tell whether we are dealing with a preposition or an adverb. (3) They acquired the force of prepositions, and were prefixed to the nouns.* The first stage is represented by such a sentence as "Bigstandað me strange gencatas" (*Caedmon*) = 'Stout vassals bystand me'; the second stage by "He heom stod wið" (*Layamon*) = 'Ho them stood against,' or "Again the false paiens the Christen stode he by" (*P. Langtoft*) = 'Against the false pagans the Christians he stood by'; the third by "He stood by the Christians."

280 From this it is obvious that the primary function of prepositions is to show the relation between an action or attribute and a thing. It is only through the intervention of an attributive word, which was afterwards dropped, that they came to show the relation of one *thing* to another. "The book on the table" = "The book lying (or being) on the table," and so on.

281 As regards their etymology, prepositions may be arranged in the following classes :—

(1.) *Simple Prepositions.*

at	forth †	of *or* off	till
by	from ‡	on	to
for	in	through	up
			with

(2.) *Prepositions derived from Adverbs.* §

　　a. By a comparative suffix.

　　　　　after　　　　over　　　　under

The dative which followed these comparatives was the dative marking the standard of comparison (*Koch*, ii. p. 321).

　　b. By prefixing a preposition to an adverb. ‖

---

* The student of Greek will have no difficulty in tracing these three stages. The originally adverbial force of prepositions is unmistakably evident from the formation of the greater part of them, and is clearly seen in such words as *between, among*, &c.

† *Forth* is found as a preposition in Shakspere: "They issue forth their city" (*Cor.* i. 4). It is sometimes strengthened by another preposition, 'from forth.' It is now commonly used only as an adverb.

‡ In Chaucer and Wiclif we find *fro*.

§ All these prepositions were originally adverbs.

‖ Compare § 273. In these prepositions the steps of formation are perfectly clear. (1) From a simple adverbial or prepositional particle, such as *út* (*out*), or *æft* (*behind*) is formed an adverb (*útan, æftan*, &c.) by means of the old adverbial suffix -*an*, denoting locality. These adverbial forms sometimes acquire the force of prepositions in Anglo-Saxon, sometimes not. (2) This adverb is preceded by a preposition (*be* = *bi* or *by*, *with*, and *on*, weakened to *a*, being those most frequently used), and a secondary compound is sometimes formed by prefixing *a* (= *on*). The resulting compounds are adverbs, and are used as such, but also acquire the force of prepositions.

108   ETYMOLOGY — PREPOSITION.

abaft (A.S. â-be-æftan)
above (A.S. â-be-ûfan)
about (A.S. â-be-ûtan)
afore (A.S. on-foran) or æt-foran)
before (A.S. bi-foran or be-foran)
behind (A.S. be-hindan)

beneath (A.S. be-neoðan)
beyond (A.S. be-geondan)
but* A.S. be-ûtan)
throughout (late A.S. þurh-ut)
underneath (A.S. under-neo-ðan)
within (A.S. wið-innan)
without (A.S. wið-ûtan)

(3.) *Prepositions formed by prefixing a preposition to a noun or an adjective used substantively.*

aboard (= on board)
across (from Fr. *croix*)
adown † or down (A.S. of dûne)
against‡ (A.S. on-gegn, on geán)
along (A.S. andlang §)
amid or amidst (A.S. on middum).
among or amongst (A.S. on-gemang ‖)
anent (A.S. on-efen or on-emn = ' on a level,' ' over-against ')
around or round
aslant

astride
athwart (A.S. on þweorh *crooked*)
atween (*see* between)
below
beside ¶ or besides (A.S. be-sídan)
between** (A.S. betweonum = 'by two ')
betwixt (A.S. betwih, betwix, or betwux)
since ††
inside
outside
withal ‡‡

Aloft (on lyfte = in the air) and *abreast* are used now and then as prepositions.

---

* This old preposition is often wrongly taken for the conjunction *but*. It means literally ' on the outside of,' and thence ' without' or 'except.' Thus " Bûtan nettum huntian ic mæg" = ' I can hunt without nets' (*Coll.*) "Ealle bûtan ânum " (*Beow*, 705) = ' all but one.' This is the regular construction in Anglo-Saxon after *all* (*eal*). Phrases like ' all or none but he' are ungrammatical. In Chaucer we find " But meat or drinke she dressed her to lie in a dark corner of the house alone." The motto of the Duke of Sutherland is, "Touch not the cat but the glove" (*Koch*, ii. p. 366). *But* may be followed by the infinitive without *to*, as "He did nothing but laugh." Respecting the cases in which *but* appears to mean *only*, see § 505.
† Literally, ' off the hill.' Dûn = hill.
‡ In *against. amidst*, und *amongst* the *s* is the adverbial genitive suffix (§ 268). The *t* is an offgrowth of the *s*. *Again* is the older form.
§ From the old Anglo-Saxon preposition *and* = *opposite*, or *in presence of*, which we have in *an-swer*.
‖ *Gemang* in A.S. means an assemblage or multitude.
¶ *Beside* has now reference to place, as ' A house beside a river.' *Besides* means ' in addition to,' as " Besides the profit there is the honour." This distinction is modern, and is purely arbitrary. *On-this-side* is used as a preposition, like *beside*, *inside*, and *outside*.
** *Between* comes from the numeral adjective *tween* (= Lat. *binus*), a derivative from *twa* or *twi* (= *two*). *Betwih* was formed from the root *twi*. To this was added the adverbial genitive suffix *s* (*betwix*), and subsequently the offgrowth *t* (§ 218). The parts of the compound *betweonum* might be separated. ' Be sǽm tweonum ' (*by the lakes twain*) = ' between the lakes.'
†† *Since* or *sinnes* is formed by the suffix -*es* from *sin* (" Sin thilke day," = since that day – *Chaucer*), a shortened form of the adverb *siðan* (*sithen*), derived from *við* = *later*.
‡‡ Always placed at the end of the clause.

(4.) *Prepositions formed by prefixing an adverbial particle to a preposition:—*

  into until* upon without
  onto unto within

(5.) From the adjective *weard* (= Lat., *vergens*), preceded by the *T* adverb *to*,† we get in Anglo-Saxon the adjective *toweard*, meaning 'approaching, future.'‡
Toweard and *toweardes* (formed by the genitive inflection, (*see* § 268), were used as adverbs, and then acquired the force of prepositions. *Nigh* (*neah*), *near, nearer,* and *next,* are adjectives used first as adverbs and then as prepositions. (See § 114.) When used as adverbs they are followed by *to*. *Ere* (A.S., *œr*) is a comparative adjective, used first adverbially and then as a preposition. *Past,* once an attributive participle, is now a preposition, as " He went past the house."

282 In Anglo-Saxon passive and other impersonal verbs might be used without a subject of any kind expressed (§ 382), simply to affirm that *an action takes place,* without referring it to any agent. Participles are often employed impersonally in exactly the same manner. As we may have a nominative absolute consisting of a participle qualifying a substantive (see § 372, 5), so we may have a participle used absolutely without any substantive for it to qualify, as: " Speaking generally, this will be found true"; " Barring accidents, we shall arrive to-morrow." Participles thus used are sometimes wrongly set down as prepositions, as *concerning, considering, respecting,*§ &c. In some cases these active participles have supplanted passive participles which qualified the noun. Thus, " *considering* his conduct" was " *his conduct* considered," just as we still say, "All things considered." *Notwithstanding, pending,* and *during* are participles qualifying the noun that follows in the nominative absolute. *Notwithstanding* is sometimes placed *after* the noun, especially in legal phraseology. *Save.* (Fr. *sauf*) and *except* are of French origin, and are remnants of Latin ablatives absolute in which *salvo-* and *excepto-* were used. In old English, *out-taken* is found for *except.* In Shakspere we still find *excepted:* " Always excepted my dear Claudio." As both the nominative and the objective case are used in the absolute construction (§ 372, 5), *save he* and *save him* are both allowable.

283 The principal relations which prepositions indicate are those of *place, time,* and *causality.*‖

---

* The old Gothic preposition *und* (= German *bis*) appeared in Anglo-Saxon as *ŏð* (just as the Gothic *tunthus* became *toth* or *tooth*). The older form maintained its ground in *und-til* (*until*) and *und-to* (*unto*) = 'all the way to.'
† The adjective (or adverb) *ward* (*weard*) forms various compound adverbs, as *northward, heavenward, Godward.* These are sometimes preceded by the preposition *to* as *to Godward* (2 Cor. iii. 4).
‡ Hence ' inclining to,' ' favourable.' The opposite of this is ' froward ' (= *from-ward*), and the negative of it ' untoward.' In old English *fromward* is used as a preposition, meaning ' away from.'
§ Sometimes these participles (as, *e.g., respecting*) have retained or acquired a shade of meaning peculiar to themselves
‖ By *causality* is meant the *cause, reason,* or *purpose* of any action or event. When we say, *full of water, of* marks the *cause* of the *fulness.*

Prepositions were first used to express relation in *space*, then they were applied to relation in *time*, and lastly were used metaphorically to mark relations of *causality* or *modality*. The following examples will show the course of these changes.

284. **By** means—(1) 'Alongside of,' or 'close to,' in connexion either with rest or with motion, as 'Sit *by* me'; 'The path runs *by* the river'; 'We went *by* your house'; 'He lives *by* himself,' *i.e.*, 'with himself as his only neighbour'; 'To put a thing *by*' is to put it somewhere *near*, or *by our side*, not *in front*; hence, *out of the way*, just as we say 'to put *aside*.' If a man swears *by* an altar or a relic, it is natural that he should place his hand on it, or at least go close up to it. (2) If I arrive *by* ten o'clock, the time of my arrival is *close to*, or *just before*, ten o'clock. *By* and *by* properly denotes a time *close to* the present.* 'Day *by* day,' implies that one day is *next to* the other without interval. (3) It is natural to seek the doer or instrument of an act in close neighbourhood to the locality of the action. Hence *by* came to denote the agent † or instrument. "Abel was killed by Cain," means literally 'Abel was killed beside Cain.' "He is older *by* two years," implies that the excess of age is caused by two years.

For in Anglo-Saxon means '*in front of*,' '*before*,' with reference both to place and to time (compare the Latin *pro*). From the idea of *standing in front of* came first that of *defending*, as when we say 'To fight *for* one's king; and then that of *representing*, or *taking the place of* (compare ἀντί and *pro*). Thus an advocate appears *for* his client, or one person is 'taken *for* another'; or is 'responsible *for* another.' This idea of *substitution* or *exchange* often occurs, as in 'To die *for*'; 'To exchange, barter, or sell *for*'; 'Eye *for* eye.' *Exchange* passes into the sense of *requital*, as 'He was punished *for* the crime.' The idea of 'in return or exchange for' underlies such phrases as 'grateful *for*,' 'sorry *for*,' 'to work *for*,' 'to seek *for*,' 'to wait *for*,' (*work*, &c. being the *price* in exchange for which the object is secured). Hence *for* comes to signify '*purpose*' in general. 'He did this *for* love of me' means 'in *presence of* his love of me as a *stimulating motive*.' 'In presence of' may pass into the meaning 'in spite of' (just as when we say " He persevered *in the face* of all obstacles "), as in " For all his wealth, he is unhappy." The idea of *interest* or *benefit* may spring out of that in which *for* denotes *in place of*, and thence *on behalf of*, *to the advantage of*.

Of and **off** are only various modes of writing and pronouncing the same word. It is only in later English that *off* has been restricted to particular shades of the general meaning. The word indicates *movement* or *separation from* something, or the starting-point from which some action proceeds, as in 'Get *off* that chair'; 'A long way *off* the mark'; 'he went out *of* the room'; 'He comes *of* a good stock'; 'To buy *of* a person'; 'To expect something *of* a person'; '*Of* a child,' *i.e.* '*from* the time when he was a child.' A vessel is *off* the coast when it is at a short distance *from* it. The idea of *separation* underlies all such phrases as 'to cure *of*'; 'to clear *of*';

---

* Chaucer speaks of " two yonge knightes ligging *by and by*," *i.e.*, " lying side by side."

† Compare the provincialism "That's all *along of* you."

'to cleanse *of*'; 'to deprive *of*'; 'to acquit *of*'; 'free *of*'; 'destitute *of*.' 'To beware *of*' implies 'keeping aloof from.' If a thing' smells *of* musk,' or 'tastes *of* onions,' the smell or taste comes *from* the musk or onions.

That which comes from, or is taken from a thing, was a part of it, or belonged to it in some way. Hence spring two meanings. 1. *Of* is used in the *partitive* sense, as in 'A piece *of* cheese'; 'One *of* the men'; 'To partake *of*,' &c. 2. *Of* denotes *possession*, as in 'The house of my father,' or marks that an attribute *pertains to* something, as in 'The brightness of the sun.' It thus becomes the general equivalent of the genitive or possessive case.

A thing is made *from* the material of which it is composed. Hence we say, 'A bar *of* iron'; 'A book *of* poetry'; 'A stack *of* corn'; 'A pint *of* beer.' From denoting the *material* of a thing, *of* passes on to denote the constitution or characteristic of a thing in general, as in 'A man *of* high rank'; 'A person *of* great wealth.'

A man's works or productions come *from* him. Hence we speak of 'a play *of* Shakspere'; 'a symphony *of* Beethoven,' &c. *Of* also marks generally the *source from which* an action proceeds. Hence it denotes the agent or means, as 'He was led *of* the Spirit'; 'Tempted *of* the devil'; 'The observed *of* all observers,' *i.e.*, 'The person observed *by* all observers.' 'Full *of* water,' *i.e.*, 'Filled *with* water.'

A result springs *from* a cause. Hence *of* marks the *cause* or *ground* of an action or feeling, that which excites it; as in 'To die *of* a broken heart'; 'To do a thing *of* one's free will,' '*of* right,' or '*of* necessity'; 'To be sick *of* a fever.' 'The love *of* money' is 'the love excited by money,' and so 'directed towards it.' So 'Fond *of*'; 'weary *of*'; 'guilty *of*'; 'proud *of*'; 'conscious *of*'; 'sensible *of*,' &c., denote emotions *caused by*, or *springing from* something.

'I heard *of* his death' marks that 'his death' was the starting-point of the news that came to me. Hence *of* comes to mean *concerning* or *respecting* in a variety of phrases. If we 'speak of Cicero,' Cicero is the starting-point of our speech. 'A copy *of* a thing' is 'a copy taken *from* it.' A man is 'strong *of* arm' when his strength proceeds *from* his arm. 'He lived there upwards *of* a year,' means 'during a certain period reckoned *from* the end of the year.'

To (spelt **too** in some of its adverbial uses) denotes the point to which a movement is directed (as in 'go *to* '), or the proximity which is the result of the movement (as in 'close *to* '), or (metaphorically) the object or purpose of some action (as in 'He came *to see* me'; 'They came *to* dinner '), or that *to which* the influence of some action or attribute *extends*, and which is therefore affected by it (as in 'That is a pleasure *to* me'; 'This is painful *to* me '). 'Give him a shilling and a loaf too,' means 'Give him a loaf *in addition to* the shilling.' 'That is too bad' means 'something *in addition to* bad, something more than merely bad.'

With is a shortened form of the Anglo-Saxon adverb *wiðer*, formed by the comparative suffix *ther* (§ 106, note), from an ancient root *wi* or *vi*, denoting *separation*. The ancient meaning of *with* (*wið*) is *from,** which we still preserve in *withhold* and *withdraw*. The notion of *separation* passed into that of *opposition*, from which *with* derived its ordinary Anglo-Saxon meaning of 'against,' still maintained in '*withstand*,' '*to be angry with*'; "weigh oath *with* oath" (*Shakspere*), i.e., 'weigh oath against oath,' &c. *Opposition* implies *proximity*, and *proximity* suggests *association*, and so *with* came by its modern sense, as in 'Come with us.' In this sense it denotes *attendant circumstances* (as in 'I will come with pleasure'). Among the attendant circumstances of an action is the instrument with which it is performed. Hence another of the common meanings of *with*. All its other senses are only modifications of these two. In the case of the other prepositions, their various metaphorical meanings are easily deduced from the primary *relation in space* which they denote. *With* has supplanted the old preposition *mid* (= German *mit*).

Most of the above words are adverbs as well as prepositions. The mode in which they are used will always determine which part of speech they are. When they are prepositions there is always a substantive, expressed or understood, which they govern. (But compare § 273.) In, "He laid one book above the other," *above* is a preposition. In, "One was below, the others above," *below* and *above* are adverbs.

CONJUNCTION.

285 **Conjunctions** are so called because they join words and sentences together (Lat. *con* = 'together,' *jungo* = 'I join'); but a word is not necessarily a conjunction because it does this. *Who, which,* and *that* are connective words which are pronouns. (See § 408.) *When, where, whither, as, than,* &c., are connective words which are adverbs (§§ 262, 263).

286 *Definition.*—Conjunctions are connective words, which have neither a pronominal nor an adverbial signification.

287 Prepositions show the relation of one *notion* to another. Conjunctions show the relation of one *thought* to another. (see § 294). Hence conjunctions for the most part† join one sentence to another.

---

* "He gedælde lif wið lice," "He separated life from [the] body' (*Beowulf*, 733).

† The single exception is the conjunction *and*, which, besides uniting one sentence to another, may unite words which stand in the same relation to some other word in the sentence, as in "Two and three make five," where *two* and *three* stand in the same relation to the verb *make;* "Tom sat between John and James," where *John* and *James* are in the same relation to *sat between*. It is easy to see that in such cases *and* does not show a connexion between the *notions* expressed by 'two' and 'three,' or 'John' and 'James,' but in each case shows the connexion between two *thoughts*, namely, that *two* has to do with the making of *five*, and that *three* has to do with the making of *five;* that *Tom* has a relation of position to *John*, and that *Tom* has a relation of position to *James*. Some grammarians will have it that in all such cases two co-ordinate sentences are contracted (§ 443) into one, but it is

288. As regards their syntactical use conjunctions may be divided into two classes:—1. Co-ordinative Conjunctions; 2. Subordinative Conjunctions.*

As regards their *signification*, conjunctions may be thus classified:—
1. *Simple:*—and, both, that.
2. *Adversative* or *exceptive:*—but.
3. *Alternative:*—either—or; neither—nor.
4. *Causal:*—because, since, as, for, lest.
5. *Hypothetical:*—if, an, unless, without, except.
6. *Concessive:*—though, although, albeit.
7. *Temporal:*—after, before, ere, till, until, now, while, since.

283b. 1. Co-ordinative conjunctions are those which unite either co-ordinate clauses (§ 402), or words which stand in the same relation to some other word in the sentence.

The co-ordinative conjunctions are *and, but, either, or, neither, nor, whether, both.*

Either—or, neither—nor, whether—or, both—and, are used in pairs as correlatives. In old English *ne—ne* were used for *neither—nor.*

Both (in A.S. *bá*, the neuter plural form of *begen,* as *twá* of *twegen;* see § 97) is simply a numeral adjective (as in "They were both killed"), which has come to be used as a conjunction. The pronoun *whether* (see § 155) in like manner is now used as a conjunction to introduce two alternative indirect interrogatives (as "I will tell you whether it is true or not"), or one of two alternative hypotheses (as "I will do it, whether (= either if) you like it or not").

Or is a contracted form of the old pronoun *other*† (A.S., awðer, âðor *or* âðer), which was used as an *alternative* conjunction.

---

quite futile to attempt to cut the preceding into separate sentences. To say 'Two make five and three make five,' or 'Tom sat between John and Tom sat between James,' is sheer nonsense, and it is quite inadmissible to substitute some other verb for *make,* or some other preposition for *between.* Grammatical analysis has to deal with the expressions before us, not with something else that we are told to substitute in their place. Some grammarians adopt the eccentric idea that in cases like the above "*and* does the work of a preposition" (= *with*). They should at least be prepared to maintain that "Tom *and me* took a walk" is good English. To say that 'Prepositions connect words and conjunctions connect sentences,' is neat and terse in form, but imperfect, inexact, and misleading in sense. The statement in § 287 contains all that is true in it, and excludes what is inexact and erroneous.

* Most grammarians distribute conjunctions into *copulative* and *disjunctive* conjunctions. A *copulative conjunction* is a *joining word which couples together.* A *disjunctive conjunction* is a *joining word which disjoins.* A person need be very keen-sighted to see the sense or utility of this classification.

† This word is not the same as *other* = the Gothic *anthar.* There were two compounds of 'hwæðer' in Anglo-Saxon, 'á-ge-hweðer,' from which we get *either* [which properly means *both,* see §§ 173, 175], and 'á-hweðer,' from which came the pronoun *awther* or *other,* and its negative *náðer, nother,* or *nouther,* which have still a provincial existence. This (formed without the particle *ge,* which gives the idea of combination) is the proper *alternative* pronoun, but has been supplanted by *either.*

The co-ordinative use of *but* sprang out of its subordinative use (note on § 289), in which it introduced an exception to a general statement. From that it came to denote *contrast*, and so acquired the force of a co-ordinative and adversative conjunction, and supplanted the old word ' ac.'

288c 2. Subordinative conjunctions are those which unite *subordinate* clauses (see § 412) to the *principal* clause of a sentence. They never couple *words* only.

The subordinative conjunctions are *that, as, if, an, lest, unless, though, although, but, after, ere,* before, for, till, until, without, because, now, while, albeit, since, except.*

289 *That* was originally the neuter demonstrative pronoun, used to point to the fact stated in an independent sentence, as "It was good; he saw *that*." By an inversion of the order this became "He saw *that*, (namely) it was good," and so passed into the form, "He saw that it was good," where *that* has been transferred to the accessory clause, and become a mere sign of grammatical subordination. A subordinate clause of this kind becomes the equivalent of a substantive (see § 403). It may be used as the subject of a verb (*e.g.*, "That he has gone away is certain"), as the object of a verb (*e.g.*, "I know that he said so"), or in apposition to a substantive or a demonstrative pronoun.†

290 One function of the adverb **as** was to give a relative force to the

---

* *Ere* is often written *or* in old writers (§ 276).
† *E.g.*, "Is þæt sægd þæt hi cômon," ' *That* is said, *that* they came' (*Bed.* i. 1). It was through the intervention of this second *that*, that substantive clauses were at first used after prepositions, as "Ic cwime fer þam þæt he gað," ' I will come ere *that*, that he goes'; " Sc apostol hine swang for þan þæt he wolde Godes hyrde forlétan," ' The apostle chastised him *for that*, that he wished to abandon God's flock.' "Ealle þa þing sindon on þinre handa bûton þam ânum, þæt þu þine hand on him ne âstrecce," ' All those things are in thine hand but that one, that thou stretch not thine hand upon him' (*Job* i. 12). Here the accessory clause is in apposition to the demonstrative governed by the preposition. Next the conjunctive ' þæt' was weakened to ' þe,' and attached to the preceding demonstrative, which was thus made relative or connective in its force (see note on § 150), and so in its turn passed over to the accessory clause; as "Ærþam þe se cocc cráwe," ' ere that the cock crow.' The dropping of ' þe' gave rise to such forms as "For þam heora ys heofena ríce" = ' for that yours is the kingdom of heaven.' The use of the indeclinable *that* in place of the inflected forms of the pronoun, or the omission of the inflected form and the retention of the conjunction ' þæt' (as in " Hit ne mæg tó náhte bûton þæt hit sy ût-aworpen," ' It is good for naught but that it should be cast out,' *Matt.* v. 13), gave rise to such constructions as " In that He Himself hath suffered, being tempted," &c. (*Heb.* ii. 18); " I would have come, but that I was unwell"; " Before that certain came from James he did eat with the Gentiles" (*Gal.* ii. 12), &c. In these cases *in, but, before,* &c., are still prepositions which are followed by a substantive clause. Lastly, the conjunction *that* disappeared, leaving such constructions as " ǽr he biscop wǽre," ' ere he was bishop'; " Nǽbbe ge lif on eow bûtan ge etan min flǽsc," ' Ye have not life in you but (= except) ye eat My flesh' (*John* vi. 53); " He went away before I came," &c., in which the prepositions *ere, but, before,* &c., have absorbed the conjunctive particle, and so may at last be regarded as being themselves conjunctions. (Compare what is said respecting *because, while,* &c.) Some grammarians prefer to regard them as being still prepositions followed by a substantive clause, which has dropped the *that* (§ 406). In the case of *bûtan*, an ellipse of the verb gave such constructions as: " Nân man nât bûton fræder âna" (= ' No man knoweth but my father only'), for "bûton þæm þæt fæder âna wât." This may justify (but does not necessitate) such constructions as " Nobody knows it but *I*."

indefinite and demonstrative adverbs *when, where, then, there* (see note on § 158). Thus were formed *when-as* and *whereas*.* Not only, however, were *when* and *where* used without the *as ;* as might be used without the *when* or *where,* as " I met James *as* I was coming hither "; " þe quer *as ys bones lyggeð* " (= *where his bones lie*). From denoting *place,* ' whereas' came to indicate *attendant circumstances.* Thus " I held my tongue *whereas* the rest kept talking," = ' I held my tongue [in circumstances] *in which* the rest kept talking.' The adverbial sense of *whereas* has now become so weakened, that it is commonly regarded as a mere conjunction. It is sometimes in this character replaced by *as.* Thus " *As* you say so, I must believe it." *As* is also used in the sense of *as if,* or *as though* (" His heart throbbed as it would have burst," *Scott*).

291 **If** (A.S. *gif*) is connected by the best authorities with the Gothic *iba* or *jabai*.† It is sometimes strengthened by *and*, which once (like *et* and καὶ) had the sense of *also* or *even. And if = even if.* In Anglo-Saxon there was also a particle *ono,* which had a conditional force. This probably is the source of *an*, meaning *if*, as in " He shall an it please him " (*Hamlet,* iv. 6) *An* and *and* are sometimes confounded.

291*b* **Lest** is the same as the superlative adverb *least*. In Anglo-Saxon we find ' læs ' (*less*) preceded by ' þy ' (the ablative of þæt), and sometimes followed by ' þe ', which gave a relative or subordinative force to the phrase, ' þy læs,' or ' þy læs þe,' being the equivalent of the Latin *quominus* = ' that by so much the less." ‡ The superlative was used in like manner, ' þe laeste þe ' is found (*Sax. Chr.* 694, F.) = *quo minime.* " Flee lest he slay thee," means " Flee, *that so least* he may slay thee." We sometimes find *lest that,* where *that* (like þe) gives a subordinating force to *lest* (§ 158, *note*).

291*c* **Unless** is a compound of *on* and the comparative *less,* and means much the same as *minus* in arithmetic. " He will be ruined unless you help him ", means ' Subtract [from all the circumstances of the case] your helping him, and he will be ruined.'

291*d* **Though** was originally an adversative adverb, meaning ' nevertheless.' It is still so used, as : " You are still in time ; make haste though." To give it a subordinative power þe or *that* was originally appended, but afterwards dropped.

291*e* The mode in which the prepositions *but, after, ere, before, for, till,*§ *until*, and *without* became conjunctions has been already explained (§ 289, note), and is illustrated by the use of *because, now,* and *while.*

Because was originally ' by the cause that, ' *while* was ' the while that ' (*while = hwil =* ' *time*'), *that* introducing a substantive clause in appos tion to the noun *cause* or *while.* When *that* was dropped, its subordinative power passed to the preceding phrase, which hardened into a conjunction. ‖ *Now that* became the conjunction *now* in a similar way. **Since** is formed by the adverbial genitive suffix

---

* "There, whereas all the plagues and harms abound " (*Spenser, F.Q.* IV. i. 20)
† Not with the verb *give*, though at first it seems natural to regard it as the imperative of that verb, of which the Scotch *gin* (= *gi'en = given, i.e.,* granted) is the participle.
‡ *E.g.,* " Wariað eow, þy-læs eower heortan gehefigode syn," ' Beware, *that by so much the less* (= *lest*) your hearts be over-charged (*Luke* xxi. 34.)
§ *Till* and *until* were used in the Northern dialect for *to* and *unto.* When they passed into general use they became restricted to rotations of *time*.
‖ *Whilst* was formed by the adverbial genitive s ..ix *s* and its offgrowth *t*.

(*ce* = *s* or *es*) from *sin*, a shortened form of *sithen*, from *sið þam* = 'after that.'* **Albeit** (*all-be-it*) is a short concessive or imperative sentence. **Except** at first formed a nominative (or objective) absolute with the following clause. When *that* was dropped, *except* became a conjunction.

291 ƒ Many words which are frequently set down as conjunctions are really simple adverbs, not having even a connective force, except in so far as every demonstrative word, which refers to something that has already been said, causes a connexion in thought,† though a mere demonstrative is not, *grammatically speaking*, a connective word. Such words as *therefore, still, yet, nevertheless, notwithstanding, consequently, however, hence, accordingly, likewise, also*, are *adverbs*, inasmuch as they indicate some of the conditions or circumstances under which the predicate of the clause to which they belong is asserted of the subject. (See further in the Syntax, under the head of *Collateral Sentences*, § 408.)

INTERJECTION.

293 Interjections are words which are used to express some emotion of the mind, but do not enter into the construction of sentences; as, *Oh! O! Ah! Ha! Alas! Fie! Pshaw! Hurrah!*

In written language interjections are usually followed by what is called a mark of admiration (!). The word *interjection* comes from the Latin *inter*, 'between,' and *jacio*, 'I cast.'

---

* The derivation of the conjunction is slightly different from that of the preposition (§ 281).

† As "He suddenly lost all his fortune. *This* was a great blow to him." No one would treat *this* as a relative or connective pronoun in such a sentence. The same is obviously true of such a sentence as, "He was idle. For that reason he did not succeed." But put, instead of *for that reason*, its exact grammatical equivalent *therefore*, and half the writers of grammars will tell us that *therefore* is a conjunction.

A proper attention to the nature and use of adverbs will enable us to correct mistakes on the subject which are to be found in the grammars of most languages. Even the best Latin and Greek grammars are not free from them. Thus, *quum* in Latin is an adverb, not a conjunction, even when, for the sake of convenience, we translate it by *since*. The explanation is not that *quum* is sometimes an adverb and sometimes a conjunction, but that the Romans used a word meaning *when* in cases where we use the word *since*. *Quum* is in form and meaning the correlative of *tum*, and, like it, refers both to *time* and to *attendant circumstances*. So *ut = as, ut = how, ut = that, ut = when*, is the same part of speech in all these uses, and to a Roman ear conveyed in all cases the same fundamental meaning. The adverbial force of *ut* may be indicated by treating it as other relatives are often treated in translation, namely, by substituting for it a demonstrative with a conjunction. As *qui = and he*, so *ut = and so*. Thus, *tam validus est ut nemo eum superare possit*, "He has such and such a degree of strength, *and so* no one can overcome him." The *ut* refers to the *circumstances under which* the verb *possit* is affirmed of the subject. To set down phrases like *howbeit, in as far as*, &c., as *compound conjunctions*, is quite inadmissible. Each word in such phrases admits of being parsed separately.

GENERAL CLASSIFICATION OF WORDS AND FORMS.

294 The pupil who has carefully studied the definitions of the Parts of Speech already given, will be prepared to comprehend the classification of the constituent parts of language contained in the annexed table.

Language is made up of words and forms. By these we express all the conceptions that the mind is capable of forming. All thought—and, consequently, all speech—is about something. The basis of every thought, therefore, is the notion of a *thing*, that is to say, of whatever we can make an object of thought. The words that stand for things are *nouns* and *pronouns*.

Besides things themselves, we form conceptions of the actions and attributes of things. The words that express these are *adjectives* and *verbs*. Both these classes of words express attributive notions, the difference between them being that the verb expresses an attribute together with the idea of assertion or predication; the adjective does not *assert* the connection between the thing and its attribute, but *assumes* it; or (to borrow a metaphor from mechanics) the adjective is a *static attributive*, the verb is a *dynamic attributive*. The adjective is a sort of weakened verb.

Further, besides things and their attributes, we form conceptions of the limitations of these attributes—the mode, manner, time, place, or other *conditions* under which the attribute is regarded as attached to the thing. These conditions are expressed by *adverbs*.

These are all the simple notions that we can form. But when we think, we combine notions together, and this combination is represented in language partly by words called relational words, that is, words that denote the relation between notions and thoughts, and partly by grammatical forms and inflexions. There are two sorts of relational words, prepositions and conjunctions. Prepositions only denote the relation of one *notion* to another. (*See* Definition of Preposition, § 277.) Conjunctions denote the relation of one *thought* to another, a *thought* being already the combination of at least two notions. The relation of a verb to its subject; of an adjective to a noun; of an object to the word that governs it; and of an adverbial adjunct to an attributive word, is indicated by grammatical forms and inflexions.

TABLE OF THE CONSTITUENT ELEMENTS OF THOUGHT AND SPEECH.

Conceptions.

A. Simple Notions
- 1. Notions of Things .... *expressed by* — **Notional Words:**
  - 1. **Nouns.**
  - 2. **Pronouns.**
- 2. Notions of Attributes of Things ... *expressed by*
  - 1. **Verbs.** (Assertive or Dynamic Attributives.)
  - 2. **Adjectives.** (Assumptive or Static Attributives.)
- 3. Notions of the Modes or Conditions of Attributes .... *expressed by* **Adverbs.**

B. Conceptions of Relation
- 1. Of Notions to Notions .... *expressed by* — **Relational Words:**
  - 1. Inflexions.
  - 2. **Prepositions.**
- 2. Of Thoughts to Thoughts .... *expressed by* **Conjunctions.**

COMPOSITION AND DERIVATION.

295 The words of which the English language is composed may be divided into two classes, *primary* words, and *secondary* or *derivative* words.

A word is a *primary* word when it does not admit of being resolved into simpler elements; as *man, horse, run*.

A word is a *secondary* word when it is made up of significant parts, which exist either separately or in other combinations.

296 Secondary words are formed partly by *Composition*, partly by *Derivation*.

COMPOSITION.

297 A word is a *compound* word when it is made up of two or more parts, each of which is a significant word by itself; as *apple-tree, tea-spoon, spend-thrift*.

298 All compounds admit of being divided primarily into two words; but one of these may itself be a compound word, so that the entire word may be separated into three or four words; as *handicraftsman* (made up of *man* and *handicraft*, *handicraft* being itself made up of *hand* and *craft**); *midshipman* (made up of *man* and *midship*, *midship* being itself made up of *mid* and *ship*). In such cases the subordinate compound is usually the first of the two words into which the whole is divisible.

299 In most compound words it is the first word which modifies the meaning of the second. (The second denotes the *genus*, the first distinguishes the *species*.) *Rosebush* means a particular kind of *bush*, namely, one that bears roses. A *haycart* is a certain kind of *cart*, namely one for carrying hay. The accent is placed upon the modifying word when the amalgamation is complete. When the two elements of the compound are only partially blended, a hyphen is put between them, and the accent falls equally on both parts of the compound, as in *knee-deep*. We do not get a true compound so long as the separate elements both retain their natural and full significance, and their ordinary syntactical relation. *Composition* is accompanied by *limitation* of significance. Compare *blue bell* and *bluebell, red breast* and *redbreast, monk's hood* and *monkshood*.

A.—Compound Nouns.

300 Compound Nouns exhibit the following combinations:—

1. A noun preceded by a noun, of which the first (1) denotes what the second consists of, is characterized by, or attached to, as *haystack, cornfield, oaktree, wineshop, churchyard*; (2) denotes

---

* The *i* in *handicraft* and *handiwork* is a relic of the syllable *ye* in the A.S. *handgeræft* and *handgeweorc*.

the purpose for which the thing denoted by the second is used,* as *teaspoon*, *milking-stool*, (see § 202), *inkstand;* or with which its activity is connected, as *man-killer*, *bush-ranger*, *sun-shade;* (3) is a defining genitive, or the equivalent of one, as *swordsman*, *kinsman*, *Wednesday* (*Woden's day*), *sun-beam*, *noon-tide*, *day-star*.

2. A noun preceded and modified by an adjective, as *roundhead*, *blackbird*, *halfpenny*, *quicksilver*, *Northampton*, *Eastham*, *midday*, *midriff* (A.S. hrif = bowels.) *Twilight (twi = two)*, *fortnight* (i.e., *fourteen-nights*), *sennight* (i.e., *seven nights*) are from numerals.

3. A noun preceded by a verb of which it is the object, as *stopgap*, *pickpocket*, *makeweight*, *turncock*, *wagtail*, *spitfire*.†

4. A noun denoting an agent preceded by what would be the object of the corresponding verb, as *man-slayer*, *peace-maker*.

5. A gerund preceded by a governed noun (§ 200, note §), as *wire-pulling*, *blood-letting*.

6. A verb preceded by a noun, as *godsend* (very rare).

7. A noun preceded by an adverb, which modifies (adverbially) the noun, when that denotes an action, or else is in the quasi-attributive relation to the noun (§ 362, 4), as *forethought*, *foresight*, *neighbour* (A.S. *neah-búr* = 'one who dwells near'), *offal* (i.e., *off-fall*), *off-shoot*, *aftertaste*, *by-play*, *by-path*, *inroad*, *anvil* (A.S. *anfilt* or *onfilt*, from *fillian* ' to strike ').

8. A noun preceded and governed by a preposition, as *forenoon*, *afternoon*.

9. A verb preceded or followed by an adverb which modifies it, as *inlet*, *welfare*, *onset*, *go-between*, *standstill*, *income*.

301 The following compound nouns, in which one or both of the elements have been changed or become obsolete, are given by Koch (iii. *p.* 98 *f.*).

hangnail	= ang-naegele	(*a sore under the nail*)
bandog	= bond-dog	(*a dog chained up*)
barn	= bere-ern	(*barley house*)
brimstone	= bryn-stân	(*burning-stone*)
bridal	= brýd-ealu	(*bride-ale*)
distaff	= disc-stæf	(*flax-staff*. 'To dise' (prov.) is 'to supply with flax')
garlic, hemlock	from leác	(*leek*)
gospel	= god-spell	(*good news*, or *God's message*)
grunsel	= grund-syl	(*ground-sill*, *threshold*)
huzzy	= hûs-wîf	(*house-wife*)
icicle	= îs-gicel	(provincial, *ice-shoggle*)
lammas	= hláf-messe	(*loaf-mass*)
moldwarp or *mole*	= molde-weorp	(*mould-thrower*)
midwife	= mêd-wîf	(*hired woman*)

* The modifying word may be a verb used substantively, as in *washtub*, *grindstone*, *stewpan;* or the pronoun *self*, as *self-will*, *self-murder*.
† These words are peculiar. See § 299.

ETYMOLOGY—COMPOSITION. 121

nostril	= nas-þyrl	(*nose-hole.* Comp. *drill*)
orchard	= ort-geard	(*wort-* or *root-garden*)
stirrup	= stîg-râp	(*mounting-rope*)
steward	= stige-weard	(*sty-* or *stall-warden*)
shelter	= scyld-truma	(*troop-shield*)
tadpole	= toad-in-pool	
wedlock	= wedlâc	(*pledge-gift*)
world	= wer-eld	(*man-age*, *a generation*)
leman	= leof-man	(*loved* or *dear person*)

B. Compound Adjectives.

302 Compound Adjectives exhibit the following combinations:—
  1. An adjective preceded by a noun, which qualifies it adverbially (comp. § 267), as *sky-blue, fire-new, pitch-dark, blood-red, ankle-deep, breast-high, head-strong, childlike, warlike, sinful, hopeful* (and other compounds of *full*, written with one *l*, once formed with the noun in the genitive, as *willesful = wilful*), *shamefaced* (originally *shamefast*, A.S. *sceamfæst*), *steadfast*.
  2. The adjective in these compounds is often a participle, as in *seafaring, bed-ridden, heart-broken, tempest-tossed, sea-girt*, &c.
  3. An imperfect participle preceded by its object, as *tale-bearing, heart-rending, time-serving*, &c.
  4. An adjective or participle preceded by a simple adverb, as *upright, downright, under-done, out-spoken, inborn, almighty, alone* (i.e., *all-one*).
  5. A noun preceded by an adjective, as *barefoot;* in modern English mostly restricted to those compounded with numerals, as *two-fold, manifold*, a *three-bottle* man, a *twopenny* cake, a *three-foot* rule. In A.S. more common, as *mild-heart* (mild-hearted), *ân-êâge* (one-eyed), *twi-fingere* (two-fingered). (Compare the nick-names *Hotspur, Longshanks, Roundhead, Blue-noses*, &c.) In modern English these compounds have taken the participial ending, *bare-legged, one-eyed, pigeon-breasted*, &c.

C.—Compound Pronouns.

303 See §§ 154, 158, 169, 173, 174, 175.

B.—Compound Verbs.

304 These present the following combinations:—
  1. A verb preceded by a separable adverb, as *overdo, understand, fulfil, undergo, cross-question. Twit* is a corruption of *æt-witan.*
  2. A verb preceded by its object, as *back-bite, brow-beat.* (See § 301, 3.)
  3. A verb preceded by its adjectival (objective) complement (§§ 391, 395), as *white-wash, rough-hew.*
  4. A verb followed by an adverb, as *don* (= *do* or *put on*), *doff* (= *do* or *put off*), *dout* or *douse* = *do out*, *dup* = *do up*. (Comp. Germ. *aufthun.*)

305 For compound adverbs, prepositions, and conjunctions, see §§ 267, 269, 271, 281, 291, &c.

DERIVATION.

306   Most words in all languages have been built up by the combination of simpler elements. Words generally admit of being arranged in groups, all the words belonging to one of which have a certain portion which is common to all, and which represents a certain fundamental notion, which in its various aspects, or in combination with other notions, gives rise to the different conceptions which are represented by the several words of the group. Thus, *love* is common to all the words [*he*] *loves*, *loving*, *lover*, *loveable*, *lovely*, *loveless*, &c. So in Latin, *fac* is common to *facio*, *feci*, *factum*, *factor*, *efficio*, *factio*, *facies*, &c. This common fundamental part of a group of words is called a *root*.

307   In languages of kindred origin many roots are found in all or several of such languages, as the bases of groups of words. All *roots* are monosyllabic, and the most primitive roots consist of a single vowel, or a vowel and a consonant.* Roots are subdivided into *predicative roots*, representing *notions*, and *demonstrative* or *relational roots*, indicating the relations of notions to each other or to the speaker. Primitive roots are not *words*, but elements from which words are formed, either by combination or by making some change in the form of the root; which latter process was certainly in many cases, and possibly in all, the result of the blending of some earlier combination of different roots, or of the weakening of existing sounds in anticipation of such as were added.†

308   In the course of time a large number of the formative elements by which words have been formed from roots, or from other words, have lost their independent existence and significance, and have been reduced to mere prefixes and suffixes; and in English, through the decay and disuse of suffixes, many words have been reduced to mere roots.

309   *Derivation*, in the wider sense of the term, includes all processes by which words are formed from roots, or from other words. In practice, however, *derivation* excludes *composition*, which is the putting together of words both or all of which retain an independent existence, and *inflexion*, which is the name given to those changes in certain classes of words by which the varieties of their *grammatical* relations are indicated, *inflexion* being subdivided into the inflexion of nouns, adjectives, and pronouns, which is termed *declension*, and the inflexion of verbs, which is termed *conjugation*.

---

* See Max Müller, *Lectures, &c.*, i. 273, &c.
† Compare, for example, the first syllable in *nation* with that in *national;* the sound of *cat* with the *kit* in *kitten*, *brother* with *brethren*, *child* with *children*. The change of *goose* into *geese*, *foot* into *feet*, &c., is a relic of a similar process, the added syllable having disappeared. (See Helfenstein, Comp. Gr. p. 2).

310. That part of an inflexional word upon which the inflexions are based is called the *stem** or *crude form* of the word. In English the formative elements by which *stems* were once formed from *roots* have often disappeared. Thus the root *love* answers for both the verb *love* and the noun *love*. In Latin the root *am-* becomes *ama-* as the stem of the verb, and *amor-* as the stem of the noun.

311. When two words are related to each other, it is sometimes evident from the form alone which is the primary and which the derived word. We see at once that *bestir* is derived from *stir* and *bondage* from *bond*, derivation being a process of addition, not of subtraction. In less obvious cases we must be guided partly by analogy, partly by a consideration of the relation of the ideas represented. That will be named first in language which exists first in thought. As a *stitch* is the result of *stick-ing* and a *ditch* of *digging*, the verb will be earlier than the noun.

A.—DERIVATION BY MEANS OF TEUTONIC PREFIXES AND SUFFIXES.

Derived Nouns.

312.   Noun Prefixes of Teutonic Origin.

1. *un ;* as in *unrest, undress.*
2. *mis ;* as in *misdeed, mishap, mistrust, misconduct.* This prefix (connected with the verb *miss*, and the Old English *mys = evil*) implies error or fault in the action referred to. In many words of Romance origin, as *mischance, mis =* Old French *mes*, from Lat. *minus.*

313.   Noun Suffixes of Teutonic Origin.

1. *-dom* (connected with *deem* and *doom*, implying *jurisdiction, sway, sphere of action or existence, condition*), as in *kingdom, Christendom, earldom, thraldom, martyrdom.* (Compare Germ. *thum.*) *Freedom* and *wisdom* are from adjectives.
2. *-hood* (A.S. *hâd = person, condition, state, calling*), as in *manhood, priesthood, wifehood, childhood.* (Comp. Germ. *heit.*) *Head* in *maidenhead, godhead,* is the same. *Likelihood* and *hardihood* are from adjectives; *brotherhood* and *sisterhood* have become *collective* nouns, like *youth, nobility,* &c.
3. *-red* (A.S. *ræd = counsel, power, state, mode*), *hatred, kin-d-red.* In O.E. *freondrede (friendship), sibrede (relationship),* &c.
4. *-ship, skip, scape* (denoting *shape, condition, fashion*, from *seapan = to shape*), as in *landskip* or *landscape, friendship, worship,* i.e., *worthship*. (Compare Germ. *schaft* from *schaffen.*) Added

---

* The analogy implied in the words *root* and *stem* must not be pressed too far. A grammatical *stem* is the *root* + something else. The *root* of a tree forms no part of its *stem*.

also to Romance words, as *relationship*. *Hardship* is from an adjective.

5. *-en* (forming diminutives from nouns); *maiden, kitten, chicken** (from *cock*).

6. *-kin* (forming diminutives from nouns), as in *lambkin, pipkin* (comp. "a *pipe* of wine"), *mannikin, bumpkin, thumbkin*. In proper names, as *Perkin* (= *Peterkin*), *Tomkin, Wilkin, Hawkin* (from *Hal*), *Watkin* (from *Walter*), *Simkin* (from *Simon*), *Hodgkin* (from *Roger*). Compare Germ. *chen*.

7. *-ling* (forming diminutives from nouns), as in *duckling, gosling,* kidling, stripling* (a little *strip* or *stripe*). *Darling* (*dear*), *fatling, firstling* are from adjectives. *Suckling, starveling, hireling, witling* are from verbs. Comp. Germ. *lein*.

The diminutive sense easily passes into that of *depreciation*, as in *worldling, groundling*.

8. *-rel* (diminutive and depreciative) occurs in a few words of Teutonic root, as to which it is difficult to believe that the very unusual suffix is of Romance origin: as *pickerel* (a little pike), *cockerel* (a young cock), *gangrel* (a vagabond), *mongrel* (from the root *mong* = *mix ;* comp. *mingle, among*), *wastrel* (a spendthrift).

9. *-y, -ie, -cy* (diminutival), as in *daddy, Sally, Charlie* or *Charley, Annie*.

10. *-ock* (forming diminutives from nouns), as in *bullock, hillock, ruddock* (robin-redbreast), *pinnock* (tom-tit). In Scotch we get *wifock, laddock, lassock*, &c., and with *ie*, *wifukie* (wee little woman), *drappukie* (wee little drop). In proper names, as *Pollock* (*Paul*), *Baldock* (*Baldwin*), *Mattock* (*Matthew*).

11. *-ing* (= A.S. *-ung*) forming abstract nouns from verbs, as *hunting, blessing ;* or denoting the result of a process, as in *building, dripping, gelding ;* or giving a collective sense, as in *paling, flooring, shirting, clothing*. These from nouns. *Tidings* is a later form of the participial *tidende* (see § 197 note).

12. *-ing* (in A.S. = 'son of,' as "Cerdie wæs Elesing," i.e., 'son of Elesa') appears as a tribal or communal name in *Tooting, Hardingham, Sherington*, &c. With the force of 'belonging to,' or 'connected with' it appears in *whiting, herring* (the shoal or army fish, A.S. *here* = army), *tithing, farthing*.

13. *-en, -on*, or *-n*, as in *garden, kitchen* (from *cook ;* see note on § 307), *token, beacon, rain, loan, brain*.

14. *-er* (A.S. *-ere*) denoting the agent, as in *digger, baker, seeker, singer*.

15. *-er* (not the same as the preceding), as in *hammer, hunger, summer, winter, bower, water, heather*.

16. *-el, -l, -le* (in A.S. also *-ol* and *-ul*), as in *navel, kernel, angle, apple, girdle, shuttle, bundle, sickle, spittle*. Many of these are from verbs, and denote the instrument. In A.S. they often end in *-ls*, as *byrgels* = *burial*-place, *bridels, gyrdels*.

---

* See note on § 307.

ETYMOLOGY—DERIVATION. 125

17. *-ter*, *-ther*, *-der*, denoting the agent or instrument; as in *father*, *mother*, *daughter* (see § 44), *laughter*, *rudder* (row), *weather* (Gothic *waian* = to blow), *ladder* (Germ. *Leiter*, root *hli* = mount), *bladder* (*blow*, in Scotch *blaw*), *spider* (= *spinder* or *spinner*).

18. *-ster* (in A.S. denoting a *female* agent, § 44, note †); *spinster*, *gamester*, *trickster*, *punster*, *Brewster* (brew), *Webster* (weave), *Baxter* (bake), *bolster*, *holster*.

19. *-om* or *-m*; *bloom*, *blossom*, *bosom*, *doom*, *qualm* (intrans. *quail* and trans. *quell*), *dream*, *stream*, *slime* (comp. Lat. *saliva*).

20. *-ow* (= A.S. *-u*); *shadow*, *meadow*, *shallow* (*shoal*).

21. *-ness*, forming abstract nouns from adjectives — *dearness*, *redness*, *goodness*, &c. Formerly added to nouns, as in *wilderness* (= wild-deer-ness). A.S. *rumnes*, *nydnes*, &c., have been replaced by *roominess*, *neediness*, &c. *Witness* is from the verb *wit*.

22. *-th*, *-t*, *-(s)t*, *-d* (varieties of the same suffix), originally forming passive participles or adjectives, as *couth* (in *un-couth*), from *cunnan* 'to know' (Goth. *kunths*,* Germ. *kund*), *brought*, *loved*, *dead* (from *die*). Many of these became nouns, of which a large proportion are abstract. The suffix appears in *gift*, *might* (*may*), *theft*,† *weft*, *sight*, *wrist* (*writhe*), *shrift*, *rift* (*rive*), *flight*, *length*,† *strength*,† *breadth*,† *height* (properly *highth*), *mirth* (*merry*), *sloth* (*slow*), *growth*, *stealth*, *ruth* (to *rue*), *flood* (*flow*), *health* (A.S. *hál* = whole), *truth* and *trust* from *true* or *trow*, *death* (*die*).

23. *-nd*, *-n* (old suffix of the imperfect participle). *Fiend* (Goth. *fijan* 'to hate'), *friend* (Goth. *frijon* 'to love'), *wind* (Goth. *waian* 'to blow'). *Youth* in reality belongs to this class, *th* having replaced *d* and *n* having disappeared. (Comp. Germ. *Jugend*, and see note * on 22.)

24. *-est*: *harvest* (comp. Gr. καρπ-ος), *earnest*.

Adjective Prefixes of Teutonic Origin.

314   1. *a*, *alive*, *aweary*. *Athirst* is in A.S. *of-þyrst*, *an-hungered* is *of-hyngred*.

2. *a*, a corruption of *ge*; *alike* = *gelic*.

3. *un* (negative, not the same as the *un* in verbs): *unwise*, *untrue*, and before Romance words, as *uncourteous*. An *umpire* is one who makes the two sides *uneven* (*in* or *un*, *par*) by joining one of them.

Adjective Suffixes (Teutonic).

315   1. *-ed*; the common participial suffix; see 311, 22. Also added to nouns, as in *ragged*, *wretched*, *wicked* (probably = *witched*), *left-handed*, &c. See § 302, 5.

2. *-en* or *-n* (used also as a participial suffix); *wooden*, *golden*, *linen* (from *lin* = *flax*), *heathen* (a dweller on the *heath*), *green*, *fain*, *brown*, &c.

3. *-er* or *-r*; *bitter*, *lither*, *fair*.

---

* Compare *tooth* with Goth. *tunthus*.   † See note on § 307.

4. *-ern* (a compound of the two last); *northern, southern,* c.
5. *-el* or *-le* (A.S. *-ol*), *fickle, little, brittle, idle.*
6. *-ard* or *-art* (= *hard*, A.S. *heard*, as *irenheard* = 'hard as iron'; gives an intensive force), added to adjectives and verbs, as *dullard, drunkard;* from verbs *laggard, dotard, braggart, blinkard, stinkard.* Most of these are now used as nouns. This suffix made its way into the Romance languages, out of which some derivatives have come into English, as *bastard, standard* (O.F. *estendre* = *extendere*), *coward* (*codardo* from Lat. *cauda;* properly a dog that runs away with his *tail* between his legs). *Dastard* is a corruption of *dastrod* or *adastrod*, the pass. part. of A.S. *adastrian* 'to frighten.'
7. *-ish, -sh, -ch* added to nouns to denote 'belonging to,' 'having the qualities of,' as *swinish, slavish, foolish, Romish, Turkish, Welsh, French.* Comp. Germ. *-sch.* Added to adjectives it naturally gives a diminutive force, as *blackish, dullish.*
8. *-less* (A.S. *leas* = *loose, free from, without*). *Heedless, senseless, lawless, houseless,* &c. Very common.
9. *-ly* (a corruption of *like*), added (of course) to nouns. *Godly, heavenly, ghastly* (from *ghost*), *manly.* Very common.
10. *-some*, added to verbs and adjectives to denote the presence of the quality that they indicate. *Winsome, buxom,* (from *bugan* = to yield), *tiresome, quarrelsome, wholesome, blithesome, fulsome.*
11. *-th* or *d* (originally a superlative suffix : see *Koch* iii. p. 24), in numerals. *Third, fourth,* &c.
12. *-y* = A.S. *-ig*, added usually to nouns to indicate the presence of that for which the noun stands. *Greedy, bloody, needy, thirsty, moody, sorry,* (*sore*), *dirty,* &c. Added to Romance words in *savoury,* &c. From verbs,—*sticky, sundry* (*sunder*), *weary.* The same suffix appears in the nouns, *body, honey.* In A.S. *dysig* (= *dizzy*) is a noun, meaning 'an act of folly,' as well as an adjective.
13. *-ward*, denoting 'becoming' or 'inclining to' from A.S. *weorðan. Northward, froward* (*from*), *toward* (*to*). *Awkward* (from *auk* or *auke*, noun and adjective, meaning 'left hand,' 'left-handed,' 'perverse').
14. *-ow* (in *narrow, callow,* &c.) has replaced A.S. *-u.* See 314, 20.

316 For **Derived Pronouns** see §§ 154—175.

Derived Verbs.

Teutonic Prefixes to Verbs.

317 1. *a-* (a weakened form of Gothic *us* or *as*), meaning formerly *out, away, off* (A.S. áceorfan 'to cut off'), afterwards *back* or *again*, now merely an *intensive* particle, prefixed to verbs :—*arise, abide, awake.*
2. *be* (= *by*) denotes the application of an action, or of an attributive idea, to an object, and so (*a*) makes intransitive verbs transitive, as *bemoan, bespeak, bestride, befall,* or (*b*) forms transi-

tive verbs out of adjectives or nouns, as *bedim, begrime (grim), benumb, becloud, befriend, bedew,* or (e) strengthens the meaning of transitive verbs as *betake, bestow, bedazzle.* Used also before Romance words, as *becalm, belabour, besiege, betray.*
Believe is probably a corruption of A.S. *gelyfan.*

3. *for* (= German *rer*) usually implies that the action indicated by the simple verb is negatived, or done in a bad sense, as *forbid, forsake, forget. Forgive* meant originally 'to make a present of.' (Compare Lat. *condonare.*)

4. *mis,* denoting *error* or *defect* (see § 312, 2), as in *misspell, misbelieve, misgive, misbecome, misbehave.* Before Romance words, *misadvise, misdirect.*

5. *un* (Gothic *and* = *against, back,* German *ent*), implies the reversal of the action indicated by the simple verb :—*unbind, undo, untie. Answer* (A.S. *andswarian*) has the same prefix; also *ambassador* (Gothic *andbahts* = *servant*). *Unbosom, unkennel, unsex,* &c., are formed directly from nouns, without the intervention of the uncompounded verb.

6. *gain* (root of *against,* German *gegen*); *gainsay, gainstrive.*

7. *with* (see § 284 ' with'); *withdraw, withstand, withhold.*

8. *to* (= Germ. *zer ;* not the preposition *to*); *to brake* (' broke to pieces' is still found in *Judges* ix. 53. Compounds of this particle were once very numerous.

Verbal Suffixes (Teutonic).

318 1. *-el* or *-le,* added to the roots of verbs and nouns gives a combined frequentative and diminutive force: *dazzle (daze), straddle (stride), shovel (shove), swaddle (swathe), dribble (drop), gamble (game), draggle (drag), waddle (wade), snivel (sniff), grapple (grab), dwindle* (A.S. *dwinan* = to *fade*), *wrestle, dabble;* from nouns—*kneel (knee), nestle (nest), sparkle (spark) throttle (throat) nibble* (nib or *neb*), *curdle, scribble (scribe).*

2. *-er* (giving much the same force as the last), *glimmer (gleam), wander (wend), sputter (spit), patter (pat), fritter (fret), flitter* and *flutter (flit), batter (beat).*

3. *-k* (frequentative) ; *hark (hear), talk (tell).*

4. *-en* forming causative or factitive verbs from nouns and adjectives; as *strengthen, lengthen, frighten, fatten, sweeten, slacken.*

5. *se,* forming verbs from adjectives ; *cleanse, rinse* (comp. Germ. *rein*).

319 Verbs are often formed from nouns by a modification or weakening of the vowel sound, or of the final consonant, or of both. Thus *bind* (from *bond*), *sing* (from *song*), *breed (brood), feed (food), knit (knot), drip (drop), heal (whole), calve (calf), halve (half), breathe (breath), bathe (bath), shelve (shelf), graze (grass), glaze (glass), hitch (hook).* The same process is seen in Romance words, as *prize* from *price, advise (advice),* &c. The weakening was occasioned by verbal suffixes (see note on § 307), which have since disappeared.

320 Transitive (causative) verbs are often formed by a slight modification or weakening of the root vowel from intransitive verbs denoting the act or state which the former produce. Thus *fell* (from *fall*), *set* (from *sit*), *raise* (from *rise*), *lay* (*lie*), *drench* (*drink*), *wend* (*wind*), *quell* (*quail*, A.S. *ewêlan* 'to die').

321 Almost any noun may be turned into a verb; as, *to iron* a shirt; *to deck* a ship; *to ham-string* an animal; *to black-ball* a candidate; *to paper* a room; *to ship* goods, &c. *Vice-versâ*, many nouns are only verb-roots used substantively, as *work, print, walk*, &c.

322 A *k* or *g* sound at the end of words in old English tends to become softened in modern English. Sometimes this variation may constitute derivation, sometimes it is mere divergence. Compare *dike* and *ditch, stink* and *stench, wring* and *wrench, mark* and *march* (= *boundary*), *lurk* and *lurch, bank* and *bench, stark* and *starch, seek* and *beseech, bark* and *barge, bake* and *batch, stick* and *stitch, wake* and *watch, tweak* and *twitch*. Also *sc* tends to become *sh*, as A S. *scacan* = *shake*, A.S. *scâdu* = *shadow*, A.S. *sceal* = *shall*, A.S. *seeâp* = *sheep*, A.S. *scapan* = *shape*, A.S. *scip* = *ship*, &c., *scuffle* = *shuffle, screech* = *shriek, scabby* = *shabby, skirt* = *shirt*, &c.

323 Other collateral forms involve the retention or omission of an initial *s*. Compare *smash mash, splash plash, smelt melt, squash quash, squench quench, swag way*.

324 For Derived Adverbs, Prepositions and Conjunctions see §§ 267—291.

DERIVED WORDS* CONTAINING PREFIXES AND SUFFIXES OF LATIN ORIGIN.

325   **Prefixes of Latin Origin.**

1. *a, ab, abs* (from or away). *Avert, abduction, abstract* The *d* in *advance* is an error; Fr. *avancer* from *ab* and *ante*.

2. *ad* (to) found also in the forms *ac, al, an, ap, as, at, a*, according to the consonant that follows it. *Adore, accede, allude, announce, appear, assent, attend, aspire*.

3. *amb-* or *am-* (round). *Amputate, ambiguous*.

4. *ante* or *anti* (before). *Antediluvian, antecessor* (or *ancestor*), *anticipate*.

5. *circum* or *circu* (round). *Circumlocution, circuit*.

6. *con* (with), also *com-, col-, cor-, co-*, according to the following consonant. *Conduct, compact, collision, correct, coheir*.

7. *contra, contro* (against), often Anglicized into *counter*. *Contravene, controvert, counteract, country-dance* = *contre-danse*.

8. *de* (down, from). *Denote, describe, descend*.

---

* The greater part of these words of Latin origin were adopted ready-made into English, either directly, or indirectly (through French); they were not formed by the internal development of our language. In some cases, however, the formation has been imitated.

ETYMOLOGY—DERIVATION. 129

9. *dis* (in two, apart), also *dif-, di-, de-*. *Dissent, differ, dilute, deluge* (= *diluvium*), *depart, demi-* = *dimidium*. Naturalized and used as a negative before Teutonic words; *disband, disbelieve, distrust*.

10. *ex* (out of), *ec-, ef-, e-*. *Extrude, efface, educe*. Disguised in *astonish*, (*étonner* = *extonare*), *afraid* (*effrayer*), *scourge* (*ex-corrigere*), *scorch* (*ex-corticare*), *sample* (= *example*), *issue* (*exire*).

11. *extra* (beyond). *Extravagant, extraneous, stranger*.

12. *in* (in, into), modified to *il-, im-, ir-, en-, em-*. *Induce, illusion, impel, irruption, endure, embrace*. Naturalized and used before Teutonic words, *embody, embolden, endear*. Disguised in *anoint* (*in-unctus*).

13. *in* (negative). *Insecure, improper, illegitimate, irrational*.

14. *inter, intro* (among, within). *Interdict, introduce*.

15. *mis-* (Old Fr. *mes* = Lat. *minus*); *mischance* (comp. Fr. *méchant*), *mischief*.

16. *ob, obs* (against), *oc-, of-, op-*. *Oblige, obey, occur, offend, oppose*.

17. *per* (through), *pel-*. *Permit, pellucid*. Disguised in *pardon* (*per-donare*), *pilgrim* (Ital. *pellegrino* = *peregrinus*), *appurtenance*.

18. *post* (after). *Postpone*.

19. *prae* or *pre* (before). *Praelection, preface*. Disguised in *provost* (= *prae-positus*).

20. *praeter, preter* (past). *Preterite, preturnatural*.

21. *pro* (forth, before), *pol, por-, pur-*. *Promote, pollute, portray, purchase* (*pro-captiare*), *purpose, purveyor*.

22. *re* or *red* (back, again). *Redaction, redound, reduce*. (*Rally* = *re-alligare*, O.E. *relie*, Fr. *relier*.) Used before Teutonic words in *reset, reopen*, &c.

23. *retro* (backwards). *Retrograde*. *Rear* in *rearward*.

24. *se* or *sed* (apart). *Seduce, sed-ition*.

25. *sub* or *subs* (under), *suc-, suf-, sur-, sus-*. *Subdue, succeed, suffuse, surrogate, suspend*. Disguised in *sojourn* (*sub diurno*). Prefixed to Teutonic words in *sublet*, &c.

26. *subter* (beneath). *Subterfuge*.

27. *super* (above), *sur*. *Superscribe, surface* (= *superficies*), *surfeit, surcharge*.

28. *trans* or *tra* (beyond). *Translate, tradition*. Disguised in *be-tray, treason, tres-pass*.

29. *ultra* (beyond). *Ultramontane*. *Outrage* = late Latin *ultragium*.

326   Suffixes of Latin Origin.

1. *-e* (1) = Lat. *ea* in *line, lance*; (2) = Lat. *ies, face*; (3) = Lat. *ium* in *exile, homicide*, &c.

2. *-ee, -ey, -y* (= Lat.-*atus* or *ata*); *nominee, attorney* (late Latin *attornatus*), *deputy, army* (*armata*), *country* (*con-terrata*), *jur-*

K

(*jurata*), *journey* (*diurnata*); *decree* from *decretum*; *d -gree* from *gradus*; *party* from *partita*.

3. *-y* (1) = Lat. *-ia*, in *memory*, *infamy*; (2) = Lat. *-ium* in *remedy*, *study*; (3) = Lat. *-aeus* in *pigmy*; (4) = *-eus* in *ivory*; *-ee* = *aeus* in *Pharisee*, &c. Also in abstract nouns of late formation, as *bastardy*, *gluttony*, *beggary*, *simony*.

4. *-te, -t, -ate, -ete, -eet, -ite, -ute*, in adjectives, nouns and verbs derived from adjectives or participles in *-tus, -atus, -etus, -itus, -utus*, as *chaste, honest, perfect, advocate, concrete, discreet, erudite, statute, appetite, joint, point, fact, habit, assault, conduct, relate*, &c.

5. *-ade*, from *-atus* through Spanish and Italian; *brigade, cascade, lemonade*, &c.

6. *-se, -ce, -s* (= Lat. *-sus*), in *case, process, decease, oppress, sauce* (*salsus*), *advice, spouse*.

7. *-ice, -ess* (= Lat. *-itia*), in *avarice, justice, duress* (*duritia*), *largess* (*largitia*); *-ice, -ise* = Lat. *-itium* in *service, solstice, exercise*; *-ace* = *-atium* in *palace, solace*; *-ice* = *ex* in *pumice*. Latin *-ia*, or Greek *-εια* preceded by *t* or *s* gave rise to *-cy* or *-sy* in *aristocracy, abbacy, fancy* or *phantasy* (φαντασία), *grace*. Imitated in *intimacy, obstinacy, bankruptcy*, &c. Mostly abstract nouns.

8. *-ace, -ass* (= Lat. *-accus, -a*): *populace, cutlass* (*cultellacea*). From *-ax* in *furnace*.

9. *-age* (late Latin *-agium*, a modification of *-aticum*); *age, voyage* (*viaticum*), *savage* (*silvaticus*), *personage, homage, marriage* (*maritagium*). Naturalized and added to Teutonic words, as in *tillage, windage, wharfage, bondage*. This suffix denotes (1) the condition or occupation of the person indicated by the primary noun, as *vassalage, pilotage*; (2) a collection, quantity, or summing-up, as *poundage, mileage, herbage*; (3) a state or process in which something is concerned, as *wharfage, bondage, windage*; (4) when added to verbs, the result of an act, or the sum total of separate acts indicated by the verb, as *breakage, leakage, pillage* (*pil* or *peel* = strip), *coinage*, &c.

10. *-al*, (Lat. *-alis*, added to nouns, and denoting 'possessing the qualities of,' 'belonging to'); *legal, regal, general, annual*; freely used in modern formations, as *comical, whimsical*. Neuter adjectives of this formation often gave rise to substantives in *-al* and *-el*, as *canal* or *channel, hospital* or *hotel, jewel* (*jocale*), *chattels* or *cattle* (*capitalia*). Modern formations, *trial, denial, proposal*, &c.

11. *-el* (= *-elis*), *cruel*.

12. *-ile, -il, -cel, -le, -cl* (= Lat. *-ilis*), *servile, civil, genteel, gentle, kennel* (*canile*).

13. *-ile, -il, -le* (= Lat. *-ilis*, denoting 'capable of' or 'adapted for' the action indicated by a verb-root): *fragile, frail, subtle, able* (*habilis*), *agile*.

14. *-able, -ible, -ble*, (= Lat. *-abilis, -ibilis*, the same in sense as the preceding): *culpable, probable, flexible, feeble* (from *flebilis*, O. Fr. *floible*, compare the German *wenig*, formerly *weinic* or *weinig*, from *wein-en*). Naturalized and added to Teutonic roots, as *teachable, eatable*, &c.

15. *-ne* or *-n* (= *-na*, *-num*); *plane, plan, fane, reign, sign.*

16. *-an, -ain, -ane, -en, -on* (= -anus, a, um, and denoting 'connected with'): *pagan, publican, captain, chaplain, certain, mundane, humane, mizzen (medianus), scriven-er, surgeon (chirurgianus), sexton* (=*sacristan*), *parishion-er* (*parochianus*); *-en* from *-enus* in *alien.*

17. *-ine, -in, -im* (= Lat. *-inus, a, um,* same meaning as the preceding): *divine, saline, equine, marine, canine,* &c.: Nouns, *doctri, e, rapine, pilgrim, matins.*

18. *-ain, -aign, -eign, -ange* (= Lat. *-aneus*), *mountain, champaign, campaign, foreign* (*foraneus*), *strange* (*extraneus*).

19. *-ar* (= Lat. *-aris*); *regular, singular,* &c.

20. *-ary,* with the secondary formations *-arious, -arian* (= Lat. *-arius*); *necessary, adversary :* Nouns, *granary, salary. Gregarious, nefarious, antiquarian, librarian,* &c.

21. *-er, -ier, -eer, -or* (= Lat. *-arius,* denoting usually 'one whose functions are connected with' that for which the primitive noun stands); *archer* (*arcuarius*), *carpenter, mariner, butler, officer, usher* (*ostiarius*), *farrier* (*ferrarius*), *brigadier, cannoneer, chancellor, councillor. Engineer* (Fr. *ingénieur*) from *ingeniator.*

22. *-ery, -ry, -er* (from nouns in *-aria* or *-eria,* denoting a 'condition' or a 'collection,' or forming a generic name for acts of a certain kind); *slavery, cavalry, pantry* (*panter* = *panetarius*), *nunnery, carpentry, river* (*riparia*), *gutter* (that in which *guttae* i.e., *drops* collect).

-ry was naturalized (with the same force) as an independent formation, as in *jewry, fairy, jewelry, poetry, poultry* (*poult*), *spicery, peasantry, thievery, knavery, cookery.*

23. *-ess, -ese* (= Lat. *ensis*), *burgess, Chinese.*

24. *-ess,* feminine suffix: see § 45.

25. *-el, -le, -l* (= Lat. *-ulus, -a, -um,* and the secondary forms, *-allus, -ellus, -illus*); *angle, people, buckle* (*buccula,* from the *face* with which it was commonly adorned), *table, sample, metal, chancel* (*cancelli*), *castle, chapel, libel, veal* (*vitulus*). *Participle* (*participium*), *principle* (*principium*), and *chronicle* (*chronica*) are anomalous.

26. *-el, -le,* (= Lat. *-ela*); *quarrel* (*querela*), *candle.*

27. *-ble, -bule* (= Lat. *bulus, -a, -um*), *fable, stable, vestibule.*

28. *-cle, -cel, -sel* (= Lat. *culus, a, um* or *cellus, -a, -um,* with diminutive force), *uncle, carbuncle, article, particle, parcel* (*particella*), *damsel* (*dominicella*).

29. *-cle, -cre* (= Lat. *culum* or *crum,* denoting usually the instrument of some action); *receptacle, obstacle, tabernacle, sepulchre, lucre.*

30. *-ive, -tive, -tiff, -sive* (= Lat. *-ivus,* or when added to the stem of the perfect participle, *-tivus, -sivus,* denoting 'inclined to' or 'apt for' the action denoted by the verb); *adoptive, restive pensive, fugitive, active, native, plaintive, plaintiff, caitiff* (*captivus*) *indicative, abusive, bailiff* (*bajulivus*), &c. Naturalized in *talkative Hasty, jolly, testy* have lost an *f :* in old French they are *hastif jolif, testif* (= *heady*). See Koch iii. 2. *p.* 48.

31. *-ose, -ous* (= Lat. *-osus*, Fr. *-eux*, denoting 'full of,' or 'abounding in'); *jocose, verbose, curious, famous, glorious*. Imitated in *marvellous, chivalrous,* &c.

32. *-ous,* (= Lat. *-us*) in *assiduous, anxious, omnivorous*. Naturalized and added to Teutonic stems in *murderous, wondrous*. Adjectives in *-acious,* and *-ocious,* are enlarged from the Latin *-ax* and *-ox,* as *mendacious, loquacious, ferocious*. *Piteous* for the older *pitous* (*pietosus*). *Righteous* a corruption of *rihtwis*.

33. *-estrial, -estrian,* enlarged from Lat. *-estris*. *Equestrian terrestrial*.

34. *-ant, -ent* (= Lat. *ans, ens,* termination of imperfect participle); *distant, current,* &c. These forms are often used as nouns, as *accident, tenant,* &c.

35. *-ance, -ancy, -ence, -ency* (= Lat. *-antia, -entia,* forming abstract nouns from the preceding); *distance, infancy, continence, decency, chance* (*cadentia*). Imitated in *grievance,* &c. *Province* (*provincia* = *providentia*); = *nd.* from Lat. *-ndus* : *legend, deodand*.

36. *-ion, -tion, -sion, -son, -som* (= Lat. *-ion,* giving *-tion, -sion,* when added to the stem of the perfect participle); *opinion, nation, tension, mission,* &c. *Poison* (*potion-*), *treason* (*tradition-*), *ransom* (*redemption-*), *reason, venison, season* (*sation-,* sowing time).

37. *-ure, -ture, -sure* (= Lat. *-ura,* and with *p. p.* suffix, *-tura, -sura*); *figure, venture, scripture, measure*.

38. *-ter ; master* (*magister* from *magis*), *minister* (from *minus*).

39. *-tor, -sor, -er, -or, -our* (= Lat. *-tor, -sor, -ator*): *doctor, successor, censor, founder* (*fundator*), *juror* (*jurator*), *enchanter, emperor, saviour*. The abbreviated *-er* got mixed up with the A.S. *-ere*.

40. *-our* (= Lat. *-or*), *labour, ardour, honour*. Through French *-eur*. Imitated in *behaviour,* &c.

41. *-tory, -sory, -ser, -or, -our, -er* (= Lat. *-torium, -sorium*), *auditory, accessory, censer, mirror* (*miratorium*), *parlour* (*parlatorium*), *manger* (*manducatoria*).

42. *-ter, tre* (= Lat. *-trum*) : *cloister, theatre*.

43. *-me, -m, -n* (= Lat. *-men*) : *volume, charm, leaven* (*levamen*), *noun*.

44. *-ment* (= Lat. *-mentum,* denoting the *means* or *instrument,* or the *act* itself) : *ornament, pigment*. Naturalized in *payment, bewitchment, fulfilment,* &c.

45. *-ty* (= Lat. *-tat*) : *vanity, cruelty, city* (*civitat-*), &c.

46. *-et, -let* (compare *-ing* and *-ling*), having a diminutive force; of obscure origin, but naturalized in English. *Owlet, cygnet, bullet, circlet, pocket, coronet, bracelet, armlet, cutlet, streamlet, tartlet*.

47. *-on, -one, -oon* (denoting a *large* specimen of the thing in question, as in the Latin nick-names *Naso* = Big-nose, *Capito* = Bighead). *Balloon, trombone, cartoon, million, flagon, pennon, glutton*.

48. *-ish* (from Lat. *-esco,* through the French inchoative conjugation in *-ir, -issant*: see Brachet's *Hist. Fr. Gr.* p. 131) : *flourish, banish, punish,* &c.

ETYMOLOGY—DERIVATION. 133

49. Words in *-ave, -tic, -atic, -aceous, -id, -lent, -lence, -mony, -esque (-iscus* from *icus), -tude, -bund* or *-bond, -und, -umn*, &c., will be readily recognized as of Latin origin.

327 There are two principal modes in which verbs are formed in English from Latin verbs. One mode is by taking simply the crude form of the infinitive mood or present tense, without any suffix; as *intend, defend, manumit*. Sometimes mute *e* makes its appearance after a long vowel, as in *incline, opine, revise*. The second mode is to adopt as a suffix the termination of the perfect participle passive (slightly modified), *t, s, ate,* or *ite* (Lat. *tus, sus, atus, itus*); as *create* (from *creatus*), *conduct* (from *conductus*), *credit* (from *creditus*), *expedite* (*expeditus*), *incense* (from *incensus*). When derivatives are formed by both methods, one generally retains one of the meanings of the original verb, the other another. Compare *deduce* and *deduct; conduce* and *conduct; construe* and *construct; revert* and *reverse; convert* and *converse*.

328 Nouns (or adjectives) and verbs of Latin origin are often the same in form, but are distinguished by the accent, the noun or adjective having the accent on the first syllable, the verb on the second.

Noun.	Verb.	Noun or Adjective.	Verb.
áccent	accént	óbject	objéct
áffix	affíx	próduce	prodúce
cóllect	colléct	fréquent	frequént
cóncert	concért	ábsent	absént
cónvert	convért	cómpound	compóund
éxtract	extráct	présent	presént
ínsult	insúlt	rébel	rebél

GREEK PREFIXES.

329 The following prefixes are found in words of Greek origin:—
1. *a* or *an* (not). Anarchy.
2. *amphi* (on both sides, or round). Amphibious, amphitheatre
3. *ana* (up). Anabasis, anatomy, analogy.
4. *anti* (against). Antithesis, antipathy.
5. *apo* (from). Apogee, apology.
6. *cata* (down). Catalepsy, catastrophe.
7. *di* (two, or in two). Disyllable, diphthong.
8. *dia* (through, among). Diameter, diaphanous.
9. *en* or *em* (in or on). Emphasis, enema.
10. *endo* (within). Endosmose.
11. *epi* (upon). Epilogue, epitaph.
12. *ec* or *ex* (out of). Exodus, ecstatic.
13. *exo* (outside). Exosmose.
14. *hyper* (over). Hyperbolical

15. *hypo* (under). Hypotenuse, hypothesis.
16. *meta* (implying change). Metamorphosis.
17. *para* (beside). Parabola, paraphrase.
18. *peri* (round). Peristyle, perimeter.
19. *pro* (before). Program.
20. *pros* (to). Prosody.
21. *syn* (with, together), modified into *sym* or *syl*. Syndic, syntax, symbol, syllogism, syllable.
22. *eu* (well). Euphony, eulogy.

GREEK SUFFIXES.

330 The following suffixes mark words of Greek origin:—
 1. *-e : catastrophe.*
 2. *-y* (= ια): *anatomy, monarchy.*
 3. *-ad* or *-id. Iliad, Æneid, Troad.*
 4. *-ic, -tic. Logic, cynic, ethics, arithmetic.*
 5. *-ac, maniac, Syriac.*
 6. *-sis, -sy, -se* (= -σις) : *crisis, emphasis, palsy* (*paralysis*), *hypocrisy, phrensy, eclipse.*
 7. *-ma : diorama, enema.*
 8. *-tre, -ter* (-τρον) : *centre, meter.*
 9. *-st, iconoclast, sophist, baptist.*
 10. *-te, -t* (= της) : *apostate, comet, patriot.*
 11. *-sm : sophism, spasm, aneurism.*
 12. *-isk : asterisk, obelisk.*
 13. *-ize* (in verbs): *baptize, criticize.* This termination and its derivatives have been imitated in modern formations, as *minimize, theorize, deism, egotism, egotist, annalist, papist.*

331 When a compound or derived word is made up of elements derived from different languages, it is called a *hybrid* (*hybrida* = *mongrel*, from Greek ὕβρις), as *falsehood, politely.* Some writers speak as if all such formations were faulty, and lay down as a rule that "in derived words all the parts must belong to one and the same language." This is quite a mistake. When a word of foreign origin has been thoroughly naturalized in English, it is capable of receiving all the inflections, prefixes, and affixes which are employed in English. If this were not the case we could not decline such words when they are nouns or conjugate them when they are verbs. Such words as *falsehood, grateful, unjust, rudeness, doubtless, useless, artful, accuser, seducer, politeness, grandfather, conceited, readable, martyrdom, wondrous,* are all hybrids, the stem and the prefix or suffix being the one of English, the other of classical origin ; but any rule which would condemn such formations should be rejected as arbitrary and groundless. The following principle, however, is observed in the formation of derivatives:—If a

derived word has been formed by means of an English suffix, and a secondary derivative has to be formed by means of a prefix, the prefix should be English. If the suffix of the first derivative is of classical origin, the prefix should be classical. Thus we say *undecided* and *indecisive*, *un-* and *-ed* being both English, *in-* and *-ive* both Latin. So *ungrateful, ingratitude; unjustly, injustice*. But one or two suffixes of Latin origin (like *-able*) are treated as if of English origin, as in *unspeakable*.

332 Words compounded of Latin elements have often undergone considerable mutilation, so that they are not easy to recognize. Thus *ostrich* = *avis struthio*; *constable* = *comes stabuli*; *parsley* = *petroselinum*; *bittern* comes from *mugi-taurus*, corrupted into *bugi-taurus*; *migrim* (Fr. *migraine*) = *hemi-cranium*, 'a pain affecting half the head'; *bustard* = *avis tardus*; *jeopardy* = *jocus partitus* (a sportive venture, consisting in a choice between two alternatives); *copperas* = *cupri rosa*; *porpoise* = *porcus piscis*; *porcupine* = *porcus spinosus*; *vinegar* = *vinum acre* (*alegar* is 'eager' or *sour ale*); *verdict* = *vere dictum*; *verjuice* = *viridum jus*; *viscount* = *vice-comes*; *grandam, granny* (through French *grande dame*) = *grandis domina*; *gramercy* = *grand merci*; *rosemary* = *ros marinus*; *maugre* = *male gratum*; *van* (*avant*) = *ab ante*; *rear, arrear* = *ad retro*; *chanticleer* = *chante clair*; *summons* = *submoneas*; *kerchief** = *couvre chef*; *curfew* = *couvre-feu*; *tennis* = *tenez* 'catch'; *lamprey* = *lambe petram*, 'lick-stone,' from its habit of adhering to rocks by suction; *agree* (originally an abverb *a gré*) = *ad gratum*; *dandelion* = *dent de lion*; *alert* = Ital. *all'erta* (*erta* from *erectus*); *alarm* = Ital. *all'arme* 'to arms' (from *arma*). Verbs in *-fy* usually represent compounds of *-ficare*, as *edify, mortify, deify*. *Defy* is from *fidere*.

333 An attentive examination of § 326 and section IV. of Appendix B will show the usual changes that are to be looked for when a Latin word has passed through French into English. The following (amongst others of less difficulty) should be borne in mind:—

1. *b* often vanishes from between vowels. Compare *sudden* and *subitaneus*.

2. *c* or *g* often vanishes when it occurs before a dental or between vowels. Compare *feat* and *factum*, *sure* and *securus*, *pay* and *pacare*, *deny* and *denegare*, *display* and *displicare*, *rule* and *regula*, *seal* and *sigillum*, *allow* and *allocare*.

3. *d* or *t* vanishes. Compare *prey* and *praeda*, *ray* and *radius*, *chair* and *cathedra*, *cue* and *cauda*, *roll* and *rotulus*, *round* and *rotundus*, *treason* and *tradition-*, and look at *chance, obey, recreant, defy, chain, fay*, &c., and see § 326, 2.

---

* The sense of *head* (*chef*) so completely disappeared, that the secondary compound *handkerchief* was formed; in which again the meaning of *hand* was disregarded, so that the word *neckhandkerchief* was made, which literally ought to mean 'a *head*-covering used for the *hands* tied round the *neck*.'

4. Initial *c* becomes *ch*, as in *chief, chance, chandler, chant, change*, &c.
5. The consonantal force of *ll* disappears; as in *couch* from *collocare, beauty* from *bellitas*, &c.
6. *b* or *p* becomes *v* or *f*, as in *chief (caput), ravin (rapio), river (riparius), cover (co-operire), van (ab-ante)*.
7. *di* before a vowel becomes soft *g* or *ch* or *j*, as in *siege (assedium), journey (diurnata), preach (praedicare), Jane (Diana)*.
8. *ti* undergoes a similar change, as in *voyage (viaticum), age (aetaticum)*.
9. *bi, pi, vi* before a vowel becomes *ge* or *dge*, as in *abridge (abbreviare), change (cambiare), plunge (plumbicare), rage (rabies), deluge (diluvium), assuage (ad-suavis), sage (sapio)*.

334 A Latin word adopted in old English or brought in through French has sometimes been re-introduced at a later period directly from the Latin. In that case the older word shows a more mutilated form than the later. Compare *bishop* and *episcopal; minster* and *monastery; priest* and *presbyter; pistol* and *epistle; balm* and *balsam; sure* and *secure*.

335 Sometimes the older form has kept its ground with a different shade of meaning. Compare *penance* and *penitence; blame* and *blasphemy; chalice* and *calix; forge* and *fabric; countenance* and *continence; feat* and *fact; defeat* and *defect; poor* and *pauper; ray* and *radius; treason* and *tradition; frail* and *fragile; loyal* and *legal; couch* and *collocate; rule* and *regulate*.

336 There has also been a tendency to reject French modifications and other corruptions, and bring words back again to their original form. Compare *aferme* and *affirm; auter* and *altar; coler* and *collar; scoler* and *scholar; noterer* and *notary; dotyr* and *doctor; parfyt* and *perfect; sotil* and *subtile; dortoure* and *dormitory; caitiff* and *captive; aunterous* and *adventurous*.

337. Proper names are often curiously disguised in common words. Thus *dunce* is merely the name of the celebrated schoolman *Duns Scotus; tawdry* is a corruption of *St. Audrey (Etheldreda)*, a fair at which gaudy wares were sold having been held on her feast-day; *grog* is so called after Admiral Vernon, who first served out to his sailors rum mixed with water, and was nicknamed *Old Grog* from a cloak of *grogram* which he was in the habit of wearing; *tram-ways* are named after their inventor *Outram*; *cordwainers* dealt in *Cordovan* leather; a *lumber-room* was a room in which *Lombard* pawnbrokers kept the goods pledged with them; *sarcenet* was made by the *Saracens; cambric* was made at *Cambray; cherries* came from *Cerasus; damsons* from *Damascus; shalloon* was made at *Chalons; copper* was named from *Cyprus; muslin* came from *Mossul* on the Tigris.

For fuller lists of similar words the student must consult some of the various glossaries that deal with them.

SYNTAX.

342 THE word *syntax* means *arrangement* (Greek *syn*, together *taxis*, arrangement). The rules of syntax are statements of the various ways in which the words of a sentence are related to each other.

343 A sentence is a collection of words of such kinds, and arranged in such a manner, as to make some complete sense.

By "making some complete sense" is meant, that *something is said about something*.

344 It is plain, therefore, that every ordinary* sentence must consist of two essential parts: 1st, that which stands for what we speak about; 2nd, that which is said about that of which we speak.

345 The word which stands for that about which we speak is called the *subject* of the sentence. The *subject* of a sentence, which is a *word*, must not be confounded with the *thing* that is spoken about.

346 That part of a sentence which consists of what is said about the thing spoken of consists of two portions or elements. One part represents some idea which we attach in thought to what is spoken about; this is called the *predicate*. The other part consists of the means by which the predicate is connected with the subject; this part is called the copula (or *link*). That act of the mind by which the notion expressed by the predicate is joined to the notion expressed by the subject, is called a *judgment*. The result of a judgment is a *thought*. The expression of a thought is a *sentence*.

347 The grammatical copula in every sentence consists of the *personal inflections*† of the verb. In the sentence, "Time flies," the subject is *Time;* that which is predicated or asserted of *time* is *flying;* the personal termination of the verb *flies* unites this idea to the subject. In the sentence, "The rose is red," the subject is *rose;* that which is predicated of the rose is, *being red;* the personal inflection by which *is* becomes a third person singular, is the copula.

---

* In Latin we have sentences in which there is absolutely no subject, as *pluit* (it rains), *tonat* (it thunders), *concurritur* (a rush together takes place). The word *it*, that we use in such cases, is the mere ghost of a subject. There is really nothing definite to which it relates. (See further ₴ 383.)

† That is, the inflections by which number and person are marked, and by which the verb is made a *finite* verb.

If we say, "The journey was pleasant," what we assert of the journey is its *having been pleasant*, it being clear that the notion of *time* belongs to the predicate.

Inasmuch as the personal terminations of a verb have no existence apart from the verb itself, it is usual (and convenient) in grammar to treat the copula as a part of the predicate. Thus in the sentence, "Time flies," *time* is called the subject, and *flies* the predicate. This mode of speaking is slightly different from the use of the word *predicate* in *Logic;* but it must be understood that in using the word *predicate*, we mean *the predicate and copula combined.**

348 In grammar it is usual to employ the terms *subject* and *predicate* in a more restricted sense than in Logic. In Logic, the *subject* of a proposition is *the entire description* of that which is spoken of: the *predicate* is *all that is employed* to represent the idea which is connected with the subject. Thus, in "This boy's father gave him a book," the subject is "this boy's father;" the predicate is "gave him a book." But in grammar, the single noun *father* is called the subject, and *gave* the predicate, the words connected with *father* and *gave* being treated as enlargements or adjuncts of the subject and predicate.

349 Whenever we speak of anything, we make it a separate object of thought. A word that can stand for anything which we make a separate object of thought is called a *substantive*.

350 It follows, therefore, that the *subject* of a sentence must be a *substantive*, or what is equivalent to a substantive.

351 An adjective denotes an attribute which is attached to some thing, but is not the *name* of a separate object of thought. An adjective, therefore, can never be the subject of a sentence.

352 Substantives may be arranged in the following classes:—
  1. Nouns.
  2. The Substantive Pronouns (see § 130).

---

* In Logic every proposition is thrown into a shape in which a part of the verb *be* is the copula. This is simply for the purpose of *conversion*, i.e., of altering the proposition so that the subject becomes predicate and the predicate subject. In grammatical analysis this is perfectly needless. The business of grammar is to analyse the forms and combinations which language actually gives us, not other barbarous expressions which are asserted to be their equivalents. "Time flies," or "Tempus fugit" is a perfect sentence *as it stands*, and yet involves no part of the verb *be*, either expressed or understood. If we put together the facts, that there may be a perfect proposition without the use of the verb *be*, that when that or any other verb is used, there is no proposition unless the verb is in a finite form, and that when the verb is put into its appropriate finite form, we get a proposition, perfect both in grammar and in sense, it follows that the *link* or *copula* by which the predicative idea is attached to the subject is the personal inflections of the verb.

SYNTAX. 139

3. The Infinitive Mood (see § 189).
4. Gerunds, or Verbal Nouns (see § 200).
5. Any word which is itself made the subject of discourse, every word being *a name for itself*.
6. A phrase or quotation; a phrase being, to all intents and purposes, *a name for itself*.
7. A Substantive Clause, that is, a clause which, in its relation to the rest of the sentence, has the force of a single substantive (§ 402).

353 The only part of speech by means of which we can make an assertion is the verb (see § 179). The essential part of every affirmation respecting an object of thought is a finite verb (*i.e.*, a verb in some one of its *personal* forms, not the infinitive mood or participle).

354 The subject and the verb are the cardinal points of every sentence. All other words in a sentence are attached directly or indirectly to one or other of these two.

355 When a sentence contains only one subject and one finite verb, it is said to be a *simple* sentence.

When a sentence contains not only a principal subject and its verb, but also other dependent or subordinate clauses which have subjects and verbs of their own, the sentence is said to be *complex*.

The subject of a complex sentence may be an entire clause.

When a sentence consists of two or more principal and independent sentences connected by co-ordinative conjunctions, it is said to be *compound*.

356 The subject of a sentence stands for some object of thought: the predicate denotes some fact or idea which we connect with that object, and the union between the two is effected by the copula. But this union may be viewed in more ways than one.

1. When it is our intention to declare that the connexion which is indicated between the subject of discourse and the idea denoted by the predicate does exist, the sentence is *affirmative*; * as, "Thomas left the room."

2. When it is our wish to know whether the connexion referred to subsists, the sentence is *interrogative*; as, "Did Thomas leave the room?"

3. When we express our *will* that the connexion between the object of thought denoted by the subject, and that

---

* A *negative* sentence is only a particular variety of affirmative sentence. If we deny that John is here by saying, "John is not here," we *affirm* that John *is no here*.

which is expressed by the predicate, should subsist, the sentence that results is called an *imperative* sentence; as, "Thomas, leave [thou] the room." *

4. When we express a *wish* that the connexion may subsist, the sentence that results is called an *optative* sentence; as, "May you speedily recover."

In some imperative sentences the *will* is so weakened as to become simply a *wish;* as, "Defend us, O Lord." "Sing, heavenly muse." The *grammatical* force of the sentence, however, is not altered by this.

357 In all the above-named kinds of sentences, the *grammatical* connexion between the subject and the verb is the same. It is sufficient, therefore, to take one as a type of all. The affirmative sentence is the most convenient for this purpose.

RELATION OF WORDS TO ONE ANOTHER.

358 The starting point in a sentence is the subject. To this the other words of the sentence are attached directly or indirectly. The modes in which the various words and groups of words in a sentence are related to each other may be classed as follows:—1. The Predicative Relation. 2. The Attributive Relation. 3. The Objective Relation. 4. The Adverbial Relation.

The Predicative Relation.

359 The Predicative Relation is that in which the predicate of

---

* It is amusing to see how some writers puzzle themselves about the *grammatical* equivalence of all these forms, owing to the fact that grammar has borrowed from logic (which does not take account of questions or commands) the term *predicate*, to denote the notion of action or attribute which, by means of a verb, we *connect in thought* with something that we think about. Of course *predicate*, if taken literally, implies *assertion*, and commands and questions are not assertions. But, till we get a better term, it is quite easy to use *predicate* in a *technical* sense, with a limitation of its literal meaning, just as a mathematician puts up with the terms *addition* and *multiplication* in algebra, although the operations so designated may be (arithmetically) *subtraction* or *division*. No one scruples to call *so* an adverb, even though in *so many* it qualifies not a verb, but an adjective. One writer propounds the curious statement that in imperative sentences the nominative becomes vocative, and a noun in the vocative case cannot be the *subject* of a verb in the imperative mood; and therefore imperative verbs have no subject. Of course in 'Thomas, leave the room,' the noun 'Thomas' is reduced to a vocative, because nouns are always of the *third* person, and therefore a noun cannot be the subject of either an assertive or an imperative sentence in which the verb is in the *second* person. The introduction of the personal pronoun is indispensable when Thomas *is addressed*, as in 'Thomas, you left the room,' or 'Thomas, leave [you] the room.' The *pronoun*, expressed or understood, is then the *subject*. It is often expressed even with imperative verbs, as 'Hear ye, Israel.' Sentences like 'Audi tu, populus Albanus' are common enough in Latin, and show that the *nominative* force of *tu* is sufficient to lead to the substitution of a *nominative* in apposition to it, in lieu of the vocative that might have been expected.

a sentence stands to its subject.* The predicative relation to the subject may be sustained by a verb, or by a verb of incomplete predication and its complement (see § 392). In the sentence, " The boy ran away," the verb *ran* is in the predicative relation to the subject *boy*. In the sentence, " The ball is round," not only the verb *is*, but the adjective *round*, which belongs to the predicate, is said to be in the predicative relation to the subject *ball*.

The Attributive Relation.

360 When we speak of anything, and connect with it the idea of some attribute that it possesses, or some circumstance respecting it, *assuming* the connexion, but not *asserting* it, the word or phrase by means of which the attribute is indicated, is said to stand in the *attributive* relation to the word which denotes the thing spoken of. Thus, in " Wise men sometimes act foolishly," the adjective *wise* stands in the attributive relation to the noun *men*. The attribute which it denotes is *assumed* to belong to the men, but it is not *asserted* of them. If we say, " The men are wise," then *wise* is in the predicative relation to *men* ; the attribute is *asserted* of them. If we say, " Socrates was wise," *wise* is in the predicative relation to *Socrates*. If we say, "Socrates was a wise man," then *wise* stands in the attributive relation to the word *man*, and *wise man* stands in the predicative relation to *Socrates*.

361 As an attribute can only belong to a thing, it is only to substantives that words can stand in the attributive relation. Words or combinations of words, which stand in this attributive relation to a substantive, may be called *attributive adjuncts*.

362 Attributive adjuncts may be of the following kinds :—

1. An adjective or participle, either used simply, or accompanied by adjuncts of its own ; as, " *A large apple, many men* " ; " the soldier, *covered with wounds*, still kept his ground."

2. A noun in apposition to the substantive ; as, " *John Smith, the baker*, said so," or a substantive clause in apposition to some substantive, as, " the report *that he was killed*

---

* A relation of this sort is, of course, reciprocal. In the sentence, " The boy ran away," while *ran* is in the predicative relation to *boy*, *boy* is in its turn in the *subjective* relation to *ran*. But as these are only two different modes of viewing the *same* grammatical combination, a separate classification is unnecessary.

is untrue," where the clause *that he was killed* is in apposition to *report*.

3. A substantive in the possessive case; as, "My *father's* house"; "*John's* book"; "The man *whose* house was burnt down," &c. Or a substantive preceded by *of*, used as the equivalent of the genitive case in any of its meanings when it was attached to a noun; as, "One *of us*"; "The leader *of the party*"; "The love *of money*."*

4. A substantive preceded by a proposition, forming what would naturally be an adverbial adjunct of an attributive word, but which through the omission of some participle or adjective has become attached directly to the noun,† as: "A horse *for riding* (*i.e.*, 'A horse *kept*, or *being*, or *suitable for riding*'); "A mistake *to be avoided*" (*i.e.*, 'A mistake *which is* to be avoided'); "Water *to drink*" (*i.e.*, 'Water *that is* for drinking'); "The trees *in the garden*"; "A time *to weep*" (§ 192); "A man *on horseback*," &c. A simple adverb may be used in the same way, as: "The house *here*"; "An *outside* passenger"; "The *then* state of affairs." These may be called *quasi-attributive adjuncts* of the noun.

Under this head we may class those instances in which an adverb or adverbial prepositional phrase is attached to a noun by virtue of the idea of *action* which the noun involves,‡ as: "Our return *home*" (compare 'We returned home'); "His journey *to Paris*" ('he journeyed to Paris'); "The revolt of the Netherlands *from Spain*" ('The Netherlands revolted from Spain'), &c.

5 An Adjective Clause. (See § 408.)

363 Adjectives (including participles) must always be either in the attributive, or in the predicative relation to some substantive expressed or understood. But one noun in the plural may be used distributively with two or more adjectives, provided no obvious

---

* One curious use of *of* is that in which it replaces the relation of apposition, as in "The month of June"; "The island of Sardinia"; "A brute of a fellow"; "A milksop of a boy." The genitive is similarly employed sometimes in Latin. On the other hand, apposition has sometimes replaced the use of *of*, as in 'A hundred sheep'; 'A dozen yards.' *Of* reappears when the numeral is used *with the plural suffix*; as "Hundreds of pounds;" "Dozens of persons."

† Similarly in Greek οἱ νῦν ἄνθρωποι is οἱ νῦν ὄντες ἄνθρωποι. As the mention of a thing presupposes its *being* (at lea t *notionally*, which is all that is necessary) the omission of that which indicates *being* is very easy. When a noun is used *attributively* (§ 362, 2) it may be qualified by an adverb just like any other attributive word, as "This man, *once the possessor* of a large fortune."

‡ It is the *notional signification* of a verb, not its predicative function, which is qualified by an adverb, or defined by an objective case. Hence participles and gerunds, which are not *predicative*, have objects and adverbs attached to them, and some nouns admit of at least an approach to the same construction.

ambiguity be produced, and the article *the* be not repeated. Thus: "He is master of the English, French, and German languages," meaning 'The English language, the French language, and the German language;' "The European and African races," meaning 'The European race and the African race,' 'The third and fourth regiments,' &c. If we say "The European and the African races," we mean 'The European races and the African races,' but 'The European and the African race' means the same as 'The European race and the African race.' But when the adjectives denote attributes that may *co-exist in the same thing*, such phrases are ambiguous. "The black and white balls" might mean 'The balls which are black and white' (parti-coloured), 'The black ball and the white ball,' or 'The black balls and the white balls.' If the first meaning is not intended, we should say, 'The black and the white ball,' or 'The black and the white balls,' according to circumstances.

361 When a word (not being a substantive in the possessive case) is in the attributive relation to a substantive, it must agree with it in number, gender, and case, if it is capable of expressing those distinctions by its form; as, "*This man*"; "*These men.*"

365 Words which stand in the attributive relation to a substantive should (in English) be placed next it, except when the attributive is qualified by an adverb or adverbial phrase.*

Attributive adjectives (or participles), when used singly or accompanied by not more than a single adverb, should precede the nouns that they qualify; as, 'A black hat'; 'A very large dog'; 'A quickly passing shower': but if they are modified by a complex adverbial adjunct, or are followed by an object, they should be placed after the noun; as, "They were implicated in the plot so fatal to their party"; "I saw a man stealing the apples."

365*b* One attributive adjunct may often be replaced by another. Thus, for "The king's palace," we may say, 'The palace of the king,' or 'The palace which belongs to the king,' or 'The palace belonging to the king,' &c. An attributive adjunct sometimes (especially in poetry) expresses a *condition*, and may be replaced by an adverbial clause. Thus, in "Foreknowledge had no influence on their fault, which had no less proved certain unforeknown" (*Milton*), *unforeknown* is equivalent to 'if it had been unforeknown.'

365*c* Attributive adjuncts may be used in two ways. (1) They may be *distinguishing* or *definitive*, as when we say, 'A *black* horse,' or '*Four* men.' Here *black* and *four* distinguish the thing or things referred to from others comprehended under the same common name. (2) They may be *descriptive*, *i.e.*, adding some additional description to a thing already defined by its name. or by some definitive word, as in "Louis Napoleon, *Emperor of the French*"; "Next came the king, *mounted on a white horse.*" (Compare

---

* The following sentence, therefore, is faulty:—"The country—beyond which the arts cannot be traced of civil society or domestic life." (*Johnson, Rasselas.*) Such sentences as: "The death is announced of Mr. John Brown," are getting frequent in the newspapers, but are quite indefensible.

the definitive and continuative uses of the relative pronoun. *See* § 413.)

The Objective Relation.

366 When a verb, participle, or gerund denotes an action which is directed towards some object, the word denoting that object stands in the *objective relation* to the verb, participle, or gerund. Thus, in "The dog bites the boy," *boy* is in the objective relation to *bites*. In, "Seeing the tumult, I went out," *tumult* is in the objective relation to *seeing*. In, "Hating one's neighbour is forbidden by the Gospel," *neighbour* is in the objective relation to the gerund *hating*. The object of a verb is the word, phrase, or clause which stands for the object of the action described by the verb.* .

367 As an action can be exerted only upon a *thing*,† it is only a *substantive*, or a phrase or clause which is equivalent to a substantive, that can stand in the objective relation to a verb, participle, or gerund. An adjective can never be the object of a verb.

368 When an infinitive mood is used after another verb, it always stands to the latter in the objective relation when not preceded by *to*, and very often when it has *to* before it.

369 The objective relation is not indicated by prepositions.‡ In declinable words the objective relation is indicated by the use of the objective case.

---

* This use of the term *object* is perfectly simple, intelligible, and unobjectionable. It would be better if it were the only use of it allowed in grammar. Many writers, however (following Becker), apply the term to any sort of grammatical adjunct which serves to determine or restrict the *general* application of a verb. Thus not only the direct object of a transitive verb, but the *place*, the *manner*, nay, even the *cause* of an action, are included under the name *object*. This is altogether unnatural and arbitrary, and there is not the slightest necessity for it. To say that in the sentence, "He severed the head from the body," *head* and *from the body* are both *objects* of *severed*, will confuse the learner rather than help him. Grammatical ideas are not simplified or arranged by being jumbled together under one title, any more than papers are sorted or classified by being bundled together into one pigeon-hole. The term *completing object* which is applied by Becker to what in this work is called the *object*, is also objectionable. If we compare such sentences as "He strikes the ball," and "He runs across the meadow," it seems obvious enough that *strikes* expresses the action in the first, quite as completely as *runs* does in the second. The description of the action *as such* is completely expressed by the verb in each case. At any rate, if *ball* is to be called the completion of the predicate in the one case, *across the meadow* should be so also in the second.

† That is, what we can make a separate object of thought.

‡ A substantive preceded by a preposition always constitutes either an attributive adjunct (§ 362, 4), or an adverbial adjunct (§ 372, 2). When the preposition is used to denote the relation of a thing to a thing (§ 277), we get an attributive adjunct; when it denotes the relation of an attribute or action of a thing to some other thing, we get an adverbial adjunct.

370 The objective relation is expressed by the rule, that "transitive verbs, with their imperfect participles and gerunds, govern nouns and pronouns in the objective case."

In compound sentences an entire clause may be in the objective relation to a verb, participle, or gerund.

The Adverbial Relation.

371 The functions of an adverb are defined in § 259. Any word, phrase, or clause which is attached to a verb or adjective to show the conditions or limitations of place, time, manner, degree, cause, effect, &c., which modify or limit an action or attribute, stands in the *adverbial relation* to the verb or adjective, and may be called an *adverbial adjunct* to it.

372 Adverbial adjuncts may be of the following kinds:—

1. An adverb (see § 259); as, "He fought *bravely.*" "I set out *yesterday.*" "He is *very* industrious."
2. A substantive preceded by a preposition; as, "He hopes *for success.*" "I heard *of his arrival.*"* "He is sitting *on a stool.*" "He killed the bird *with a stone.*" "I love him *for his virtues.*" "He is fond *of reading.*" "He is guilty *of murder.*" "All but one † were present."

The gerundial infinitive (§ 192) often forms an adverbial adjunct of a verb or adjective; e.g., "He toils *to earn a living.*" "He strives *to succeed.*" "We eat *to live.*" "He has gone *to fetch his hat.*" "This food is not fit *to eat.*" "This coat is too good *to give away.*" "This house is *to let* ‡ (= *for letting*)." "He is a foolish man *to throw away such a chance.*" Here *to throw away,* &c., is in the adverbial

---

* Some grammarians hold that in these cases the verb and preposition should be taken together as forming a sort of compound transitive verb, of which the noun that follows is the object. This is inadmissible. It contradicts all analogy. It is absurd to attempt to isolate English from cognate languages, and to explain constructions common to English and several other languages by methods which, even if valid at all, would be applicable only to English. "I am speaking of you" is precisely analogous to the French, "Je parle de vous," the German "Ich spreche von dir," and the Latin "Loquor de te." Nobody would for a moment admit that *loquor de* makes a *compound transitive verb*, and that *de* has ceased to be a preposition and become an adverb united to the verb. It is true we can say in English, "This was spoken of;" but so can we also say, "He was taken care of," "He was promised a new coat." It will be amusing to find "to-promise-a-new-coat," "to-take-care-of," &c., set down as compound transitive verbs governing the objective case. (See § 186.)

† In Anglo-Saxon '*bútan ánum.*'

‡ In Anglo-Saxon the *active voice* is always used in phrases of this sort ; *e.g.*, "Mannes sunu ys tó syllanne on manna handa," 'the Son of Man is to be given (to give) into the hands of men' (*Matt.* xvii. 22).

relation to *foolish*. An adverbial adjunct may also consist of a *substantive clause* governed by a preposition (see §§ 289, 418). *But*, followed by an infinitive mood or a clause, often forms an adverbial adjunct; as, "I would buy it but that I have no money," where '*but that—money*' forms an adverbial adjunct to *would buy*.

In many adverbial adjuncts of this class the noun preceded by the preposition *of* or *to* was formerly in the genitive or dative case, as, for example, after *full, clean, mindful, guilty, weary*, &c. Prepositional phrases have sometimes replaced direct objects, as in '*to admit of*'; '*to accept of*'; '*to dispose of*'; '*to approve of*,' &c.

3. A noun qualified by some attributive adjunct, and so forming a phrase denoting *time when*, the *measure* of space or time, *direction*, &c., or marking some attendant circumstance of an action; as, "He arrived *last night*." "We see him *every day*." "We stayed there *all the summer*." "He walked *ten miles*." "He lives *three miles* away." "*A hundred times* better." "*Three furlongs* * broad." "Go *that way*." "They advanced *sword in hand*." "They went over *dry foot*."† "The ship drove *full sail*."† "*Day by day*." "*Night after night*." "*Step by step*," &c., are adjuncts of this class. In all such expressions the noun is in the objective case, representing either a dative or an accusative case.

4. A substantive in the objective case, before which some such preposition as *to* or *for* might have been put, and which in Latin, Greek, or German would be in the dative case; as, "Give *me* (*i.e., to me*) the book." "I will sing *you* (*i.e., for you*) a song." "Do *me* (*i.e., for me*) the favour." "Teach *me* Thy statutes." "You are like† *him* (*i.e.*, like to *him*)." This use of the objective may be called the *adverbial objective*. A noun thus used with a verb is often called the *indirect object* of the verb.§

It is perhaps under the head of the *adverbial relation* that we should class such anomalous passive constructions as, "He was taught *his lesson*." "He was paid *his bill*." "He was promised *a*

---

* In cases like this the genitive was used in Anglo-Saxon, as "þreora furlanga brād" (three furlongs broad). This genitive is represented in old English by *of*, as "Let a gallows be made *of fifty cubits* high" (*Esther* v. 14); "He was of eyghte and thrytty yer old" (*Rob. of Gl.*). The *dative* was used in defining a comparative. *Much* (as in *much better*) or *little* (as in *little more*) were datives, '*miclum*' and '*lytlum*.' '*A foot* taller' means 'taller *by a foot*.'

† In Anglo-Saxon these expressions would have been in the dative case.

‡ The adverb *like* may also be modified by an adverbial objective, as "He talks *like* a fool." *Similiter* in Latin may be accompanied by a dative.

§ See Shakspere (*Taming of the Shrew*, i. 2) for a humorous illustration of the difference between the dative and the accusative sense of the English objective.

new coat," &c., where an objective case seems to be governed by a passive verb. The accusative case in Latin is often used adverbially to define or limit the range within which the meaning of the verb is applicable.

Generally speaking, when two objective cases are used with a verb (except in the case of verbs of incomplete predication), one of them is the *direct object*, the other an *adverbial adjunct*.*

What is often termed the *cognate accusative* (or objective) (as in 'to run *a race*,' 'to die *a happy death*') should more properly be classed among the adverbial adjuncts.† In Anglo-Saxon the dative was used in some cases, as, "Men libban þam life" (Men live *that life*); "He feaht miclum feohtum" (He fought *great fights*). See *Koch*, ii. p. 94.

5. A substantive (accompanied by some attributive adjunct) in the nominative or objective ‡ absolute; as, "*The sun having risen*, we commenced our journey." "*He being absent*, nothing could be done." A substantive clause may be used absolutely, like a simple substantive, as, "*Granted this is true*, you are still in the wrong."

Participles may be used absolutely in this manner without having any noun to be attached to (see § 282). In such a sentence as "Speaking generally, this is the case," the phrase 'speaking generally' is an adverbial adjunct of the predicate.

6. An adverbial clause.

373 Adverbs themselves admit of limitation or qualification as regards *degree*; as, "He writes *very badly*." "He will be here *almost immediately*."

374 When a noun stands in either the predicative or the attributive relation to another substantive, it may have words standing to it in the adverbial relation; as, "Napoleon, *lately Emperor of the French*."

375 The greater part of adverbial adjuncts are included in the following classification:—

---

* Care is necessary in distinguishing these, as the construction after a verb is not always uniform. Thus in 'He taught me Latin,' *me* answers to the dative case. In 'He taught me thoroughly,' *me* answers to the accusative.

† The cognate objective sometimes appears in a metaphorical shape, as in "to look *daggers* at a person"; "To rain fire and brimstone." The vague pronoun *it* is freely used in this construction, as, "We shall have to rough *it*"; "Go *it*, boys," &c.

‡ Some grammarians insist that in these constructions the objective (as the representative of the old dative) is the only proper case, and that the use of the nominative is the result of a mistake. Milton uses both constructions. Thus, "Him destroyed for whom all this was made, all this will soon follow" (*P. L.*, ix. 130); "Us dispossessed" (*P. L.*, vii. 140). On the other hand, we find, "Adam, wedded to another Eve, shall live with her enjoying, I extinct" (*P. L.*, ix. 944); "Which who knows but might as ill have happened, thou being by" (*P. L.*, ix.). Shakspere also uses the nominative: "Thou away, the very birds are mute." When the forms admit of a choice, the nominative is preferred by modern writers. When the abbreviated participle *except* (§ 283) is used, we always find the objective case, as *all except me*. The dative was used in Anglo-Saxon.

1. *Adverbial adjuncts of Time.*—" I arrived *before his departure*"; "Come *when I bid you*"; "He slept *all day.*"
2. *Adverbial adjuncts of Place.*—" He lives *over the way*"; " He still lay *where he had fallen* "; " He lives *a long way off.*"
3. *Adverbial adjuncts of Manner or Circumstance.*—" You must do it *in this way*"; " You must act *as I tell you*"; " *There being nothing to see*, we came away "; " His statements are *for the most part* untrue."
4. *Adverbial adjuncts of Condition.*—" *If this is so,* the case is hopeless " ; " *Though He slay me,* yet will I trust in Him " ; " *This being granted,* the proof is easy."
5. *Adverbial adjuncts of Cause.*—" He left me *on that account*"; " He sold the horse *because he could not manage it.*"
6. *Adverbial adjuncts of Consequence.*—" He that sweareth *to his own hurt,*" &c. ; " He was so exhausted, *that he could not stand.*"

SUBJECT AND PREDICATE.

376 As both the subject and the verb of a sentence are spoken of the same thing (the subject naming or denoting it, and the verb making some assertion respecting it), they must agree with each other in those points which they have in common, otherwise there would be a mutual contradiction.

The points which they have in common are *number* and *person.*

377 Hence the rule that " A verb must agree with its subject * in number and person."

378 The subject of a finite verb is put in the nominative case.

379 Thus, the predicative relation is indicated partly by the subject of the verb being in the nominative case, and partly by the verb indicating by its inflection the same number and person as the substantive which is its subject.

There is, however, an exception to this rule. The relation of the verb to the subject is often modified to suit the *sense* of the words rather than their *form.* Hence a noun in the singular number which denotes a *multitude* (as *crowd, senate, army, flock*) may have its verb in the plural number, when the idea to be kept in view is

---

* It is common to say that a verb must agree with its *nominative case* in number and person. This mode of speaking is incorrect. It confounds a *substantive* with a *case*. A *case* of a substantive is a certain *form* of it ; but it is obviously nonsense to talk of a verb agreeing with a *form* of a substantive. In the sentence, "I wrote the letter," *I* is not a *nominative case*, but a *pronoun in the nominative case.* Through this mischievous habit of treating *nominative case* as synonymous with *subject*, beginners in Latin, when parsing dependent sentences, are constantly betrayed into the absurdity of speaking of the subject of the dependent verb as being in the *accusative* case, because it is the *nominative* to the verb in the infinitive mood.

SYNTAX.   149

not the *multitude viewed as one whole*, but the *individuals* of which the multitude is composed. As, "The multitude were of one heart and one mind." But we should say, "The army *was led* into the defile," because we then speak of the army *as a whole*.

381 The verb is put in the plural number when it has for its subject two or more nouns in the singular coupled by the conjunction *and ;** as, "John and Thomas were walking together." But when the compound subject is considered as forming one whole, the verb is kept in the singular ; as, "The mind and spirit remains invincible"; "Hill and valley rings" (*Par. L.* ii., 495).

382 In English every finite verb must have a subject in the nominative case expressed or understood.† Such a sentence as, "That is the man whom I heard was ill," is faulty, because the verb *was* is left without a subject ; the relative pronoun, which ought to be the subject, being wrongly put in the objective case. It should be, "That is the man who, I heard, was ill." ‡ "I will give this to whomsoever wants it" is faulty in a similar way. *Wants* must have *whosoever* for its subject. Besides, the preposition *to* marks a relation not to the relative pronoun, but to the antecedent *him* (understood) which is qualified by the adjective clause. Moreover, a verb must only have one subject, and one subject can only belong to one verb. §

383 The subject of a verb is sometimes understood as, "I have a mind presages me such thrift," for '*which* presages,' &c. ; "So far as [it] in him lies"; "*Do* [he] what

---

* When nouns are connected by the preposition *with*, the verb is sometimes put in the plural, in accordance with the general sense, but in violation of the strict rule of syntax. Thus: "Gedaliah, who with his brethren and son were twelve" (1 *Chron.* xxv. 9).

† In Anglo-Saxon we find passive and other impersonal verbs used absolutely without any subject expressed or understood. Thus : " þam ylcan dôme þe ge démaþ cow byð gedémed" (with the same judgment that ye judge to you [it] shall be judged); " him hungrede" (him hungered). Compare *tonat, pluit, pugnatum est,* &c., in Latin. The word *it*, that we now use in such cases, is the mere ghost of a subject. See §§ 344, 387, note.

‡ The construction of a relative or interrogative pronoun may always be tested by that of a demonstrative pronoun used in its stead. The construction of "Whom I heard was ill," would be the same as that of "I heard him was ill."

§ An exception to this rule has the sanction of some of the best writers. Since a subordinative particle (such as *if, though,* &c.) cannot *precede a relative pronoun,* and yet must stand (if used) *before the subject* of its clause, *who* cannot be the subject of a hypothetical clause unless it is repeated in the shape of *he, she, it,* or *they*. Hence we find in Milton, " A right noble and pious lord, *who* had *he* not sacrificed his life and fortunes to the commonwealth," &c. " Lend it rather to thine enemy, *who* if *he* break, thou mayst with better face exact the penalty" (*M. of Ven.*, i. 3). This difficulty does not present itself in Latin. In *qui si dedisset, qui* is the subject of *dedisset*.

he will, he cannot make matters worse." The subject of a verb in the imperative mood is usually omitted.

Subject.

384 The subject of a sentence may be simple, compound, or complex.

385 The subject of a sentence is *simple* when it consists of a single substantive, or a simple infinitive mood; as, " *I* love truth "; " *Men* are mortal "; " To err is human." (See § 352.)

386 The subject of a sentence is *compound* when it consists of two or more substantives coupled together by the conjunction *and*; as, "Cæsar and Pompey were rivals." " You and I will travel together." * The conjunctions *either, or, neither, nor*, do not couple substantives together so as to form a compound subject. They imply that *one* of two alternatives is to be taken. not that the assertion can be made of both subjects *simultaneously*. The sentence is not simple, but compound and contracted (§ 445). Hence the verb is put in the plural only when the subject which is the nearer to it is in the plural; as, " Neither John nor Thomas has arrived"; " Either he or his brothers were in fault."

387 The subject of a sentence is *complex* when it consists of an infinitive phrase,† of a substantive clause, or of a quotation; as, " To love our enemies is a Christian duty "; " How to do it is the question "; " That he said so is certain "; " ' England expects every man to do his duty,' was Nelson's watchword." A complex subject is very often anticipated ‡ by means of the neuter pronoun *it*, as,

---

* Many grammarians insist that in cases of this kind we are to regard the sentence as a contraction of two co-ordinate sentences joined by *and*. This explanation might do very well for such a sentence as, " John and William are eleven years old "; that is, " John is eleven years old, and William is eleven years old "; but it is simply absurd when applied to such a sentence as, " Two and three make five," or, " He and I are of the same age"; " Blue and yellow make green," &c. Be it observed, *we have no right to alter the phraseology of the predicate*. It is obvious, on the face of the thing, that what we have to deal with is not two verbs in the singular, but *one verb in the plural*. Similar remarks apply to the case of two *objects of a verb*, or two nouns after a preposition, when they are coupled by the conjunction *and*; as, "He drank a glass of brandy and water." (See § 287.)

† In old English the infinitive in such phrases is often without the *to*, as, "Me channced of a knight encountered be" (*Spenser*, i. 2); " To know my deed 'twere best not know myself" (*Macb.*, ii. 2); " Better be with the dead."

‡ This is especially the case with the impersonal verbs, such as, *it repents me, it becomes you*, &c. These verbs were formerly much more numerous, as, *it glads me, it pities me*, &c. They were often used without *it* (or *hit*), as, ' *me forthinketh* ' (it repents me); ' *me shameth that*, &c.'; ' me remembreth of the day of dome' (*Chaucer*); ' me douteth of the truth' (*Wiclif*). See § 382, note 1.

"It is certain that he said so"; "It is wicked to tell lies." In such cases the complex subject is in apposition to the word *it* (§ 398). A pronoun is often used pleonastically to repeat a simple subject, as "The Lord, He is God"; "The green boughs, they wither." The word *there* in such sentences as, "There was a man of the Pharisees," cannot be taken as being anything else than an adverb. It is not the subject of the verb. It answers to the adverb *y* in the French phrase "*Il y a.*" Its force, however, has almost evaporated.*

388 The subject of a sentence may have any attributive adjunct attached to it † (see §§ 360, 362); as, "*This tree* is dead." "*The man* told a lie." "*Good men* love virtue." "*Edward the Black Prince* did not succeed his father." "*John's coat* is torn." "*The defenders of the city* were slain." "*The brave old man* died maintaining his innocence." "*The general, having reviewed his troops,* advanced to meet the enemy." If the subject is a verb in the infinitive mood, or a gerund, it may be accompanied by objective or adverbial adjuncts; as, "To rise early is healthful"; "To love one's enemies is a Christian duty"; "Playing with fire is dangerous."

Predicate.

389 The predicate of a sentence is either simple or complex.
390 The predicate of a sentence is simple when the notion to be conveyed is expressed by a single finite verb; as, "Virtue *flourishes.*" "Time *flies.*" "I *love.*"
391 Many verbs do not make complete sense by themselves, but require some other word to be used with them to make the sense complete. Of this kind are the intransitive verbs *be, become, grow, seem, can, do, shall, will,* &c., and such transitive verbs as *make, call, deem, think*. To say, "The horse is," "The light becomes," "I can," or "I think the man," makes no sense. It is requisite to use some other word or phrase (a substantive, an adjective, or a verb in the infinitive) with the verb; as, "The horse *is black.*" "The light *becomes dim,*" "I *can write.*" "William the Norman *became King of England.*" "I *think* the man *insane.*" "It *made* the man *mad.*" "He *was made king.*"

---

* In German the neuter pronoun *es* is used in such phrases. In old English *hit* (*i.e., it*) was sometimes used instead of *there*.

† In such cases the subject is sometimes said to be *enlarged*. The term is a bad one, because the grammatical subject is not enlarged, but *restricted*, by the use of adjuncts, at least as regards its comprehension. *Men* includes more than *wise men*.

Verbs of this kind are called *Verbs of incomplete Predication*, and the words used with them to make the predication complete may be called the *complement of the predicate.*[*] The complement may consist of any attributive adjunct (§ 362), as *e.g.*, 'The earth is *the Lord's*,' 'The coat was *of many colours.*'

Verbs which are capable of forming simple predicates are often followed by complements, being verbs of incomplete predication *so far as the matter in hand is concerned.* Thus *live* is not always and necessarily a verb of incomplete predication, but in the sentence, "He lived happy ever afterwards," the predicate is *lived happy*, and *happy* forms a (subjective) complement to *lived*, which, therefore, is, *so far*, a verb of incomplete predication. So in "They went along singing," *singing* is the complement of *went*; in "He stood gazing on the scene," *gazing* is the (subjective) complement of *stood*. In "He made a mistake," *made* is a verb of complete predication; in "He made his father angry," *made* is a verb of incomplete predication, and requires the (objective) complement *angry* to make the sense complete.

392 The predicate of a sentence is complex when it consists of a verb of incomplete predication accompanied by its complement.

393 When a verb of incomplete predication is passive or intransitive, the complement of the predicate (if it be an adjective or substantive) stands in the predicative relation to the subject of the sentence; as, "He is called John." "The wine tastes sour." "He feels sick." This kind of complement may be termed the *Subjective Complement*, inasmuch as it is closely connected with the *subject* of the sentence.

In such sentences as 'It is I,' we must regard *it* as the subject, and *I* as the complement of the predicate; '*it* (*i.e.*, 'the person you have in mind,' &c.) is *I*.' In Anglo-Saxon this was reversed. We find "gyf þu hyt eart," *if thou art it* (*Matt.* xiv. 28); "Ic hyt com," *I it am* (*Matt.* xiv. 27). Afterwards we find the *it* omitted, as, "gif thou art" (*Matt.* xiv. 28); "I my silf am" (*Luke* xxiv. 39).

A verb is an *attributive* word (§ 294), and an infinitive mood or infinitive phrase is often used instead of an adjective as a subjective complement, as, "He seems to have

---

[*] I find that this use of the term *complement* is adopted by Koch. The complement follows a verb, not in its *predicative*, but in its *attributive* character (§ 294). Hence participles and infinitive moods may have complements attached to them, as, "*Feeling sick*"; "He strove *to become rich.*"

forgotten me." If the infinitive thus used is itself a verb of incomplete predication, it may be followed by a complement, which may be called the *secondary complement*. Thus, in " He appears to be honest," *to be* is the complement of *appears*, and *honest* the complement of *to be*.

The complement of the predicate in these cases is spoken of the subject, and must therefore agree with the subject in all that they can have in common. Hence the rule that the verbs *be, become, feel, be called*, &c., take the same case after them as before them. The objective complement with an active verb becomes the subjective complement of the passive, as, " He cut the matter short," "The matter was cut short."

394 An adverb or adverbial phrase never forms the complement of a predicate. A substantive clause may be used as a complement, just like a simple substantive, as, " My advice is *that you do not meddle with the matter*."

395 When the verb is transitive, and in the active voice, the complement of the predicate stands in the attributive relation to the object of the verb; as, " He dyed the cloth red." "She called the man a liar." This kind of complement may be termed the *Objective Complement*, inasmuch as it is closely connected with the *object* of the verb.

In such sentences as "He dyed the cloth red"; "He found the man dead," the adjective distinguishes the thing referred to not from other things of the same class, but *from itself under other circumstances*. The mode in which the complement attaches itself to the verb may be illustrated by the way in which the perfect participle is used in the perfect tense, as 'I have written' (where the participle used to agree with the *object*; see § 198), and by the passive form, " The cloth *was dyed red*." &c.

In 'I made him run,' the verb *run*, though in the infinitive mood, is still an *attributive* word, and has the same relation to *him*, as the adjectives in the preceding examples. In old English the participle was often used in these cases, as, " To mak the Inglis *fleand*," *to make the English fly* (P. Langtoft, in *Koch*, ii. p. 101).

The third kind of complement is that which follows such verbs as *can, will, must*, &c., as " I can write," " He must go." This may be termed the *infinitive complement*, or *complementary infinitive*. The *object* of the sentence is often attached to the dependent infinitive.*

* The *complementary* infinitive must be carefully distinguished from the *objective* and the *adverbial* infinitive. In " He seems *to know* me," *to know* is the complement of *seems*. In " I rejoice *to know*" (*i.e.*, *at knowing*), *to know* is an *adverbial* infinitive. In " Permit me *to say*," *to say* is the *object* of *permit*, *me* being the *indirect object* of the verb.

396 A predicative verb may have any objective or adverbial adjuncts attached to it. In such cases it is sometimes said to be *enlarged* (see note on § 388).

Object.

397 The object of a verb may be either simple, compound, or complex. These distinctions are the same as in the case of the subject (see §§ 386—388). There is also a peculiar kind of complex object, in which a substantive clause is replaced by a substantive followed by a verb in the infinitive mood. Thus, for "I wish *that you may succeed*," we may have "I wish *you to succeed*"; for "I believe *that the man is guilty*," we may have "I believe *the man to be guilty*." In such sentences as "I saw him fall," "I heard the dog bark," the construction is of the same kind.* It is analogous to that of the accusative with the infinitive in Latin.

398 When the object of a verb is complex, it is often preceded by the word *it*, to which it then stands in apposition, as, "I think it foolish to act so," "I think it is a pity that he should waste so much time." In such cases the predicate is complex. Compare § 387.

399 The object of a verb, and the complement of a predicate, may have objective, attributive, or adverbial adjuncts attached to them (see note on § 388).

Complex Sentences.

400 A Complex Sentence is one which, besides a principal subject and predicate, contains one or more subordinate clauses, which have subjects and predicates of their own.

401 Subordinate Clauses are of three kinds:—Substantive Clauses, Adjective Clauses, and Adverbial Clauses.

A Substantive Clause is one which, in its relation to the rest of the sentence, is equivalent to a substantive.

An Adjective Clause is one which, in its relation to the rest of the sentence, is equivalent to an adjective or an attributive adjunct.

An Adverbial Clause is one which, in its relation to the rest of the sentence, is equivalent to an adverb, or an adverbial adjunct.

402 A complex sentence is produced whenever the place of a

---

* This construction is closely analogous to that of the objective complement. The verb in the infinitive is *attributive* with respect to its subject, as we see from the passive construction, 'He was believed to be guilty'; 'It was made stand upon the feet' (*Dan.* iii. 4), &c.

substantive, an attributive adjunct, or an adverbial adjunct is supplied by a substantive clause, an adjective clause, or an adverbial clause.

If we say, "He announced the arrival of Cæsar," we get a simple sentence, containing only one subject and one predicate. If we say, "He announced that Cæsar had arrived," we get a complex sentence, the substantive clause *that Cæsar had arrived* being substituted for the substantive (with its attributive adjunct) *the arrival of Cæsar*.

If we say, "He has lost the book given to him by me," we have a simple sentence. If we say, "He has lost the book which I had given to him," we get a complex sentence, the adjective clause *which I had given to him* being substituted for the attributive adjunct *given to him by me*.

If we say, "The boy went out to play on the completion of his task," we get a simple sentence, containing one subject and one finite verb. If we say, "The boy went out to play when he had completed his task," we get a complex sentence, the adverbial clause *when he had completed his task*, which contains a subject and predicate of its own, being substituted for the adverbial adjunct *on the completion of his task*.

It must never be forgotten that a dependent or subordinate clause is *an integral part* of the principal sentence to which it belongs, just as though it were an ordinary substantive, adjective, or adverb.* Subordinate clauses are attached to the principal clause by means of connective or relative pronouns (§ 145), connective or relative adverbs (§ 204), and subordinative conjunctions (§ 288).

Substantive Clauses.

403 A Substantive Clause is one which, in its relation to the rest of the sentence, is equivalent to a substantive. It may be either the subject or the object of the verb in the principal clause, or it may be in apposition to some other substantive, or be governed by a preposition. Thus, in the sentence, "I know that he did this," the clause, "*that he did this*," is the object of the verb *know*. In "He asked how old I was," the clause "*how old I was*" is the object of the verb *asked*.† In "When I set out is uncertain," the clause, "*when I set out*" is the subject of the verb *is*. In "The idea that he would be reduced to poverty rendered him miserable," the clause "*that he would be reduced to*

---

* Many books on the analysis of sentences quite ignore this most important point, to the great bewilderment of their young readers. The subordinate clause must have its construction in the entire sentence as strictly and precisely indicated, as if it were a single word. Phrases like 'Noun sentence to I.,' 'Adjective sentence to II.,' &c., are quite unmeaning. An adjective clause cannot bear the relation of an adjective to a *sentence*. It is attached to some definite substantive in the sentence.

† In cases of this sort we get what is termed an *indirect question*. In Anglo-Saxon the verb in an indirect question was in the subjunctive mood.

poverty" is in apposition to the noun *idea*. In " We should have arrived sooner, but that we met with an accident," the clause "*that we met with an accident*" is governed by the preposition *but*. In " In that He himself hath suffered, being tempted, He is able also to succour them that are tempted" (*Heb.* ii. 18), the preposition *in* governs * a substantive clause. (Look carefully at § 289, note †.)

A substantive clause may also follow a phrase which, *taken as a whole*, is equivalent to a transitive verb. Thus: " He other means doth make, How he may work unto her further smart," where 'make means' = *endeavour*, or *try*. So '*I am afraid* that he will not succeed' is equivalent to '*I fear* that he will not succeed.'†

404 When a substantive clause is the subject of the verb of the principal clause, the sentence is commonly formed by using the word *it* as the *grammatical* subject of the principal verb, and putting the substantive clause after the main clause. In this case the substantive clause is *in apposition* to the subject of the main verb. As, " *It* is not true *that he died yesterday.*" (See § 387.)

405 It is to verbs that substantives and substantive clauses most commonly stand in the objective relation. This has nothing to do with the *predicative* force of the verb, but depends upon the fact that the verb denotes an action or feeling directed towards an object. Participles and gerunds take objects after them, and even some nouns which denote a transitive action or feeling may have a substantive clause as an object. Thus, 'There is no *proof* that he did this'; We have no hope that he will recover'; 'He did this on *purpose* that he might ruin me.'

406 Substantive clauses usually begin either with the conjunction *that*, or with an interrogative word.‡ The conjunction *that*, however, is frequently understood; as " I saw *he was tired.*"

Adjective Clauses.

408 An Adjective Clause is one which, in its relation to the rest of the sentence, is equivalent to an adjective. It stands

---

* In such cases the preposition and the substantive clause governed by it constitute together an adverbial adjunct of the predicate, just like a preposition and noun (§ 372, 2). *What* is sometimes improperly substituted for *that*, as, 'I had no idea but *what* the story was true'; and *that* is sometimes omitted, as, 'It never rains but it pours' (*i.e.*, 'leaving out the times when it pours, it never rains'); 'But I be deceived, our fine musician groweth amorous' (*Shaksp., Tam.*, iii. 1). In these cases the *but* acquires the function of a conjunction (§ 289, note †). See further §§ 515–517, 522.

† It is also possible to treat the substantive cla se in such cases as being analogous to the adverbial accusative, or accusative of closer definition in Latin. Thus, "I am sorry that you are not well" is 'I am sorry *as regards the fact* that you are not well.'

‡ Interrogatives are also used with verbs in the infinitive mood to constitute a *substantive phrase*, as 'I do not know *where to go*' (§ 387).

in the attributive relation to a substantive, and is attached to the word which it qualifies, by means of a relative pronoun, or a relative adverb which is equivalent to a relative pronoun preceded by a preposition. Thus, in the sentence, "Look at the exercise which I have written," the clause "*which I have written*" qualifies the noun *exercise*. In "The man with whom you dined yesterday is dead," the clause "*with whom you dined yesterday*" qualifies the noun *man*. In the sentence, "That is the house where I dwell," the clause "*where I dwell*" qualifies the noun *house*, *where* being equivalent to *in which*. In the sentence, "Autumn is the time when fruits ripen," the clause "*when fruits ripen*" qualifies the noun *time*, *when* being equivalent to *in which*.* "I return to view where once the cottage stood" = 'to view [the place] *in which*,' &c.

409   The relative is sometimes omitted, as, "Where is the book *I gave you?*" for *which I gave you;* "I have a mind *presages me such thrift*," &c., for *which presages*, &c.; "They are envious *term thee parasite*," for *who term*, &c. In modern English this omission of the relative is hardly permissible unless the relative, if expressed, would be in the objective case, except after a simple assertion or denial of the existence or identity of something (as in 'There is nothing vexes him more'; 'It was John told me'), or when the relative would be the complement of the predicate (as, 'He is no longer the man he was').
Sometimes adjective clauses are used substantively, *i.e.*, with no antecedent expressed, as, "Who steals my purse, steals trash." This omission of the antecedent is usual when the relative *what* is used, as, "I heard what he said," "There is no truth in what he said."

410   Care must be used to distinguish those clauses in which an indirect question is involved in the use of *who, what, when, where*, &c., from clauses in which these words are mere *relatives*. In such sentences as, "Tell me what I ought to do," "I asked him who said so," "I know why he did it," "He asked me when I had arrived," the dependent clauses are indirect questions, and are substantive clauses, having no antecedent expressed or understood to which they relate. In "That is what I said," "This is where I live," the dependent clauses are adjective clauses. The distinction is analogous to that between clauses beginning with *quis* or *quid*, in Latin, and clauses beginning with *qui* or *quod*.

411   Adjective clauses are very often co-ordinate with the demonstrative adjectives *this, that,*† &c. In such cases the demonstrative word is

---

* So in Latin *unde* often means *from whom*, or *from which; ubi* is *at which*, &c.
† In the same way, in Latin, adjective clauses beginning with *qui, qualis, quantus*, and *quot*, qualify the same substantive as a preceding *is, talis, tantus*, or *tot*, and are co-ordinate with them. In "Non tales miror libros quales scribit," the clause *quales scribit* is an attributive adjunct to *libros* equally with *tales*. Compare the author's *Analysis of Sentences applied to Latin*, § 110, &c. Abbott's *Shaksperian Grammar.* D 64.

simply preparatory to the adjective clause by which its own import is more fully explained. Thus in the sentence, "I never received those books which you sent," the adjective *those* and the adjective clause *which you sent* are both in the attributive relation to *books*, and are co-ordinate * with each other.

412 Clauses beginning with *as* must be regarded as adjective clauses, when they follow *such* and *same*. The *as* must be considered not exactly as a relative *pronoun*, but as doing duty for a relative (see note on § 264). Thus, in "I do not admire such books as he writes," the clause *as he writes* is an adjective clause qualifying *books*, and co-ordinate with *such*. In old English we find *which* or *that*, instead of *as ;* as, "Such which must go before" (*Bacon*); "Thou speakst to such a man that is no fleering tell-tale" (*Shakspere, J. C.*).

413 An adjective clause (like an ordinary adjective) has usually a determinative or restrictive force. But it often happens that clauses introduced by relatives, although in *form* they are adjective, are, as regards their *force* and *meaning*, co-ordinate † with the principal clause. Such a clause is *continuative* rather than *determinative*. Thus, in "I wrote to your brother, who replied that you had not arrived," the sense of the sentence would be the same if *and he were* substituted for *who*. Sentences beginning with *which* must often be treated as co-ordinate with the preceding clause, when *which* relates not to any one substantive, but to the general import of the clause, as, "He heard that the bank had failed, which was a sad blow to him'; "He was not at home; for which reason I could not give him your message."

The continuative relative may even belong in reality to an adverbial clause ‡ contained *within the entire clause* which it introduces. Thus :—"Which when Beelzebub perceived . . . . he rose" (*Par. L.*, ii. 299), equivalent to "And when Beelzebub perceived this, —— he rose." "Which though I be not wise enough to frame, Yet as I well it meane, vouchsafe it without blame" (*Spenser*, vi. 4, 34), *i.e.*, 'And though I be not wise enough to frame this,' &c. Modern writers rather eschew these constructions.

When the relative is in the objective case, it is not always (in English) the object of the first finite verb that follows it. Phrases like 'A promise which he would have given worlds to recall'; 'The game which he spent the morning in shooting,' are admissible, but must be used with caution.§

Adverbial Clauses.

414 An Adverbial Clause is one which, in its relation to the

---

* This point is of importance, as it indicates the correct mode of dealing with correlative adverbs.

† The anticipative or provisional subject *it* (see § 387) often has an adjective clause as an adjunct. Thus, "It was John who did that" = "It (the person) who did that was John." In such cases, when the relative is the subject of the following verb, that verb usually agrees in number and person with the predicative noun or pronoun instead of the subject *it;* as, "It is my parents who forbid that;" "It is I who say so."

‡ Many writers, who ought to know better, blunder terribly in the attempt to turn an adjective clause into the reported form. 'That is the man who was so ill' is often modified into 'That is the man whom I heard was so ill.' This is altogether wrong. (See § 382.) The only way of meeting the difficulty is to turn 'I heard' into a parenthesis, ' who (I heard) was ill.'

rest of the sentence, is equivalent to an adverb. It stands in the adverbial relation to a verb, an adjective, or another adverb. Thus, in the sentence "He was writing a letter when I arrived," the clause "*when I arrived*" indicates the time at which the action expressed by the verb *was writing* took place. The clause "*when I arrived*" is therefore in the adverbial relation to the verb *was writing*. The sense and construction may be represented by a single adverb: "He was writing a letter; I arrived *then*." So, "He still lay *where he had fallen*;" *i.e.*, "He had fallen [somewhere]: he still lay *there*." "I give you this *because I love you*;" *i.e.*, "I love you; *therefore* I give you this."

415 Adverbial clauses admit of the same classification as ordinary adverbial adjuncts. (See § 375.)

1.—Adverbial Clauses relating to Time.

416 Clauses of this kind begin either with the relative adverbs which denote time (see § 265), or with the conjunctions *before, after, while, since, ere, until,* &c. (see §§ 288c, 289). As, "Every one listens *when he speaks.*" "I was glad *when he had finished.*" "He read *while I wrote.*" "He punished the boy *whenever he did wrong.*" "He never spoke *after he fell.*" It must be observed that when relative adverbs introduce adverbial clauses, they not only connect the adverbial clause with the principal clause, but themselves qualify the verb of the clause which they introduce.

2.—Adverbial Clauses relating to Place.

419 Clauses of this kind are introduced by the relative adverbs *where, whither, whence,* &c. As, "He is still standing *where I left him.*" "*Whither I go* ye cannot come." "*Whithersoever I went* he followed me." "Let me alone, that I may take comfort a little before I go *whence I shall not return.*" The relative adverbs connect the dependent clauses with the main clause, and at the same time qualify the verbs of the dependent clauses themselves.

3.—Adverbial Clauses relating to Manner.

420 Adverbial clauses relating to manner are commonly introduced by the relative or connective adverb *as*. *E.g.*, "He did *as he was told.*" "It turned out *as I expected.*" Here the dependent clauses qualify the verbs of the main sentences, while the adverb *as* refers to the manner of the action spoken of in the dependent clauses themselves. Clauses beginning with *as* are generally elliptical. At full length the above would be, "He did as he was told *to do.*"

4.—Adverbial Clauses relating to Degree.

421 Clauses of this kind are introduced by the adverbs *than, the* (§ 270), and *as*.

As *degree* is an idea which attaches not to actions (*per se*), but to attributes of things, and to the mode or manner of actions, adverbial clauses denoting *degree* are always attached to adjectives or adverbs. They are almost always elliptical. (See note, § 261.)

422. *E.g.*, "He is not so (or as) tall as I thought" (*i.e.*, as I thought he was tall). Here the clause "as I thought [he was tall]" qualifies (or is in the adverbial relation to) the adjective *tall*, and is co-ordinate * with the demonstrative adverb *so*; and the relative adverb *as* at the beginning of the adverbial clause qualifies the adjective *tall* understood.

"He is taller than his brother;" *i.e.*, "He is taller than his brother [is tall]."† "I love study more than ever [I loved it much]." The real force of clauses beginning with *than* has been already explained (See note † on § 264). *Than* originally meant *when*. The clause beginning with *than* is in the adverbial relation to the predicate of the main clause, and *than* is in the adverbial relation to the predicate of its own clause.‡

"The more I learn, the more I wish to learn." Here the adverbial sentence "*the more I learn*" qualifies the comparative *more* in the main clause, and is co-ordinate with the demonstrative adverb *the* which precedes it; the word *more* in the adverbial clause being itself qualified by the relative adverb *the*. (See § 270.) The first *the* is relative or subordinative, the second *the* is demonstrative.

5.—Adverbial Clauses relating to Cause.

423 Clauses of this kind usually begin with the conjunctions *because* and *for*.

E.g., "I love him because he is good." Here "*because he is good*" is an adverbial clause qualifying the verb *love*.

"He could not have seen me, for I was not there." Here "*for I was not there*" is an adverbial clause qualifying the verb *could*.

6.—Adverbial Clauses relating to Purpose and Consequence.

424 Clauses of this kind are commonly co-ordinate with the adverb *so* expressed or understood.

E.g., "He ran so fast *that he was out of breath*." Here the adverbial clause "*that he was out of breath*" stands in the adverbial relation to *fast*, and is co-ordinate with *so*, the indefinite meaning of which it amplifies and defines.

425 Adverbial clauses relating to *purpose* come also under this head. *E.g.*, "He labours *that he may become rich*." Here the adverbial clause qualifies the verb *labours*. "I will not make a noise, *lest I should disturb you*." Here the adverbial clause qualifies the verb *make*.

---

* In like manner adjective clauses are often used as *co-ordinate* with a demonstrative adjective, the vague meaning of which they indicate more precisely (§ 411), and adverbial clauses of other kinds are often co-ordinate with some preceding demonstrative adverb, the vague signification of which they determine, as when *then* is accompanied by a clause beginning with *when*, *there*, by a clause beginning with *where*, &c.

† That we must understand the adjective *tall* as well as the verb *is*, will easily be seen if it be considered that every clause or subordinate sentence must have a predicate as well as a subject. If then we ask what is predicated of *his brother*, the answer obviously is, *being tall*.

‡ The subordinate clause is attached *grammatically* to the *verb* of the main clause; but *logically* it modifies that verb only *after the comparative adjective or adverb with all belonging to it has been attached to the predicate*. In other words, the subordinate clause qualifies, not the *grammatical*, but the *logical* predicate of the main clause. The Latin *quam* means (not 'when,' but) 'in what degree,' 'by how much.' *Ditior est quam ego* means 'in what degree I [am rich], he is richer.'

426 These adverbial clauses beginning with *that* were originally substantive clauses in apposition to a preceding demonstrative *that*.* Consequently the *that* at the beginning is not an *adverb*, but the conjunction—the sign of grammatical subordination (§ 289).

7.—Adverbial Clauses relating to Condition.

427 Clauses of this kind begin with the conjunctions *if, unless, except, though, although,* and the compounds of *ever (however, whoever, whatever,* &c.).†

428 In adverbial clauses of *condition,* the principal sentence is called the *consequent clause (i.e.,* the clause which expresses the *consequence);* the subordinate sentence is called the *hypothetical clause (i.e.,* the clause which expresses the *hypothesis, supposition,* or *concession*).

429 Suppositions may be of two kinds. (**A.**) Suppositions of the first kind relate to some *actual* event or state of things, which was, is, or will be *real,* independently of our thought respecting it. (It makes no grammatical difference whether the actual fact agrees with, or contradicts our supposition.) In such suppositions the indicative mood is employed. (Read here the remarks made in the Preface to this work.)

430 *Examples.*—" If the prisoner committed the crime, he deserves death. If he did not commit it, all the witnesses have sworn falsely." " If he is at home, I shall see him." " If your exercise is finished, bring it to me." " He has arrived by this time, unless he has met with some accident." " He deserves our pity, unless his tale is a false one."

431 In like manner *concessive clauses (i.e.,* clauses in which something is *granted*) beginning with *though* or *although,* which relate to what *actually is or was the case,* have the indicative mood; as, " Though he was there, I did not see him." " Although he is rich, he is not contented." " Bad as the accommodation is, we must put up with it."

432 In a hypothesis relating to some definite event still future, the future tense of the indicative mood was formerly sometimes used in the hypothetical clause. *E.g.,* " If we *shall say* 'from heaven,' he will say, ' Why then did ye not believe him?' " (*Mark* xi. 31). " If they *shall enter* into my rest" (*Heb.* v. 5). This construction is now obsolete, and in such cases we now use the present tense. *E.g.,* " If it *rains* tomorrow, we shall not be able to go out." " If he does not arrive before next week, he will be too late."

433 (**B.**) Suppositions of the second kind treat an event or a state of things *as a mere conception of the mind,* and do not involve (though they do not always preclude) the idea that what is supposed may possibly correspond to what was, is, or will be the fact. In suppositions of this class, the subjunctive mood is employed (*see* §§ 195, 466).

---

* *E.g.,* " þæs lang þæt" = *that long that,* &c. ; " to þæs heard þæt" = *to that* [*degree*] *hard, that;* " to þam fæst þæt," ' to that [degree] strong, that,' &c. ; " hig namon stānas tó þam þæt hig woldon hine torfian," 'they took up stones to that [intent] that they might stone him' (*John* viii. 59). As the adverb *so* means much the same as ' to that [degree],' these substantive clauses came to be used in apposition to *so,* and to *such,* which is a compound of *so.*

† Sentences of this kind present considerable difficulty, because the practice of the best writers is not quite uniform or consistent, and common usage tolerates in some cases a departure from what is required by the principles of grammatical construction. (See note on § 195.)

M

434 A supposition which is contrary to some fact, present or past, is necessarily a mere conception of the mind, and therefore the subjunctive mood is used both in the hypothetical and in the consequent clause, the past indefinite tense* of the subjunctive being used in the hypothetical clause with reference to present time, and the past perfect with reference to past time. In the consequent clause the secondary past indefinite subjunctive (or *conditional*) is used after a supposition referring to present time, and the secondary form of the past perfect subjunctive (or *conditional perfect*) after a supposition relating to past time.

Examples.—" If he were present (which he *is* not), I would speak to him." " If he had confessed his fault (which he *did* not *do*), I should have forgiven him." " If he were not idle (which he is), he would make rapid progress." " If our horse had not fallen down (which he did), we should not have missed the train."

435 In old-fashioned English and in poetry we also find the past perfect subjunctive used in the consequent clause, instead of the secondary form (or conditional perfect); as, " I *had fainted* unless I had believed to see the goodness of the Lord."

436 Clauses expressing a *wish* contrary to the fact have also the subjunctive mood. Thus, " I wish that he *were* here (which he is not)." " Would that this had never happened (but it did happen)."

437 When we make a supposition with regard to the future as a mere conception of the mind, and state its consequence, without connecting with it the idea that the matter will be decided one way or the other, the subjunctive mood must be used in both clauses.

Examples.—" If he were rewarded, he would be encouraged to persevere." " If he went (*or* should go *or* were to go) away without speaking to me, I should be grieved." " If he lost (*or* should lose, *or* were to lose) his money, he would never be happy again." " He could not (*or* would not be able to) do it if he tried (*or* were to try)." " I would not believe it unless I saw (*or* should see) it." " If he were to fail, it would be a great disgrace." The use of the indicative in such suppositions (as " If he *was* to fail," &c.,) is a common vulgarism.

438 When a hypothesis is made respecting the future (especially if the case be put *generally*, and not with reference to some *definite* event), there is a natural tendency to treat the event supposed as a mere conception of the mind, and accordingly to use the subjunctive mood in it, even though the consequent clause, by the use of the indicative or imperative, show that we do not exclude the idea of the supposed event being brought to the test of reality. *E.g.*, " If this *be* granted, the proof will be easy." " If thy right eye *offend* thee, pluck it out." So in concessive clauses: " Though he *slay* me, yet will I trust in him." " Though hand *join* in hand, the wicked shall not be unpunished."

439 The older writers also use the subjunctive in suppositions relating to present fact, especially to indicate reluctance to entertain the supposition, or doubt of its possibility. *E.g.*, " If there *be* iniquity in my

* It seems anomalous to have a *past* tense in any mood referring to *present* time; but the idiom is found in French, German, Latin, and Greek. In French and Greek we even have a past tense of the indicative mood used in sentences of this kind (The verb *be* is of great value as a criterion for the *mood* in English.) It seems to have been felt that the past tense used with reference to present time marked better the want of congruity between the supposition and the fact.

hands" (*Ps.* vii. 3); "If it *be* thou, bid me come to thee" (*Matt.* xiv. 28); "If thou *have* power to raise him, bring him hither" (*Shakspere*); "If it *be* so, our God is able to deliver us" (*Daniel* iii. 17). If the case put be *general*, and not *particular* or *definite*, the use of the subjunctive is quite natural.

440 In suppositions the conjunction *if* is often omitted. *E.g.*, "Had I known this (i.e., If I had known this), I would not have come." "Were it not so (i.e., if it were not so), I would have told you."

441 An interrogative or imperative sentence is sometimes used in such a way as to be equivalent to a hypothetical clause. *E.g.*, "Is any afflicted (i.e., if any one is afflicted), let him pray." "Take any form but that, and my firm nerves shall never tremble."

442 Conditional clauses (in the older writers) often begin with *so.** *E g.*, "I am content *so* (i.e., on this condition, namely, that) thou wilt have it so" (*Rom. and J.*, iii. 5). Just as the demonstrative *that* became the relative or connective *that* (*see* note on § 150), the *so* in conditional clauses became *as*. *E.g.*, "As I were a *shepherdess*, I should be piped and sung to; *as a dairy-wench*, I would dance at maypoles" (*Ben Jons.* Cynth. Rev. iv. 1). This *elliptical* use of *as* (in the second clause) is still quite common.

Compound Sentences.

443 A compound sentence is one which consists of two or more co-ordinate principal sentences, joined together by co-ordinative conjunctions, as "He is happy, but I am not"; "John is clever, and Richard is industrious"; "They toil not, neither do they spin"; "Either you are mad or you are drunk." Co-ordinate clauses are grammatically independent of each other, whereas every subordinate clause is a *component part* of some other clause or sentence. They are either simply *coupled* together (as, "You are rich and your brother is poor"), or coupled and at the same time *opposed* to each other (as, "He is not clever, but he studies hard").

444 The co-ordinate members of a compound sentence may themselves be complex sentences, as (*a*), "I will tell your brother when I see him, but (*b*) I do not think that he will arrive this week."

N.B.—The conjunction itself does not enter into the construction of the clause which it introduces.

Contracted Sentences.

445 When co-ordinate sentences contain either the same subject, the same predicate, the same object, the same complement, or the same adverbial adjunct to the predicate, it often happens that the portion which they have in common is ex-

---
* *Si* in Latin is apparently only another form of *sic*.

pressed only once. In this case the compound sentence is said to be *contracted*.

Examples.—" Neither I nor you have seen that"; *i.e.*, "Neither I [have seen that,] nor you have seen that." "He loved not wisely, but too well"; *i.e.*, "He loved not wisely, but [he loved] too well." In these contracted sentences the predicate is expressed only once.*

"He stole a purse, and was convicted of the theft", *i.e.*, "He stole a purse, and [he] was convicted of the theft." "Religion purifies and ennobles the soul"; *i.e.*, "Religion purifies and [religion] ennobles the soul." In these contracted sentences the subject is expressed only once.

"He is either drunk or mad"; *i.e.*, "Either he is drunk or [he is] mad." Here the subject and the verb of incomplete predication *is* are expressed only once.

"He advances slowly but surely"; *i.e.*, "He advances slowly, but [he advances] surely." Here the common subject and predicate are expressed only once.

"He reads and writes well"; *i.e.*, "He reads [well] and [he] writes well." Here the common subject and the common adverbial adjunct are expressed only once.

446   Contracted sentences ought always to be so constructed, that when arranged without conjunctions, so that what is common to both or all is placed before or after what is not common, the common and separate portions, when read off continuously, make complete sense. Thus, "Religion purifies and ennobles the soul," may be written—

Religion { purifies / ennobles } the soul;

and complete sentences are obtained when the parts that are common, and written once, are read with each of the separate portions in succession. So, "He gave me not only some good advice, but also a sovereign," may be arranged thus—

He gave me { not only his blessing / also a sovereign.

"He possesses greater talents, but is less esteemed than his brother,"—

He { possesses greater talents / is less esteemed } than his brother.

If we take such a sentence as, "Man never is but always to be blest," and subject it to this test, we see in a moment that it is faulty—

Man { never is / always to be } blest,

cannot be read off both ways.

447   It has been already remarked (§ 387, note) that a sentence is not necessarily a contracted sentence because we find co-ordinative con-

---

* The predicate which is expressed must, of course, agree with the nearer of the two subjects. The predicate which is not expressed may have to be modified when supplied to suit its own subject. Thus, "Neither you nor I am right"; "Neither you nor your brother is in fault."

junctions used in it. "John and Charles are brothers," is as much one sentence as "These two boys are brothers." One predication may be made of two things taken together. "The child has a red and white ball," does not mean " The child has a red ball, and the child has a white ball." The attributes *coexist* in the same object. So when the same act is directed *simultaneously* to two or more objects, the verb may have two or more objects after it; but the sentence need not, on that account, be split up into two or more sentences. A similar principle applies to the case of adverbial adjuncts. But every verb makes a distinct predication, consequently every verb requires a separate sentence for itself. The conjunction *or* always involves a complete sentence for each of the words or phrases that it introduces, because the word implies some *alternative*, so that the idea of simultaneousness is excluded.

448 It follows, from the principle on which co-ordinate and contracted sentences are constructed, that the co-ordinative conjunctions must always join words and clauses which *stand in the same relation* to the other parts of the sentence. It would make nonsense if we attempted to join an adjective to a noun (unless the latter be used *attributively* or *predicatively*), or a subject to an adverb, or a verb in the indicative mood to a verb in the imperative mood.*

Collateral Sentences.

449 We frequently find sentences side by side, which have a connexion with each other as regards their sense and use, but have no *grammatical* link of connexion between them (that is, no conjunction, relative pronoun, or relative adverb). The complex idea that such sentences suggest to the mind is the same as if they were co-ordinate clauses coupled by conjunctions. For example—" I came. I saw. I conquered." " Fear God. Honour the king."

" The way was long, the wind was cold ;
The minstrel was infirm and old."

" So he spoke, so I replied." "This is foolish, that is wise." " I was robbed of all my money; for that reason I was unable to proceed." "I believed, therefore have I spoken." " He is virtuous ; consequently he is happy."

Such sentences as those placed side by side in the above examples may be called *collateral* sentences.

450 A proper consideration of the nature of collateral sentences will enable us materially to thin the usual list of conjunctions. A word is not a conjunction because it *refers* us to something that precedes. Simple demonstratives do this. (See § 291, *f.*) Such words as *therefore, consequently, likewise, also* (*i.e., all so = just in that manner*),

---

* Young letter-writers constantly forget this rule at the close of their epistles, where such combinations as, " I have no more to say, and believe me yours truly," are very frequent.

nevertheless, notwithstanding, are not conjunctions, but demonstrative adverbs.

451 We frequently have a series of sentences which are partly collateral and partly co-ordinate.

Example:—
" He stay'd not for brake, and he stopp'd not for stone;
He swam the Esk river, where ford there was none."

452 Collateral sentences may be *contracted* in the same way as co-ordinate sentences; as, "A true friend advises justly, [a true friend] assists readily, [a true friend] adventures boldly, and [a true friend] continues a friend unchangeably."

Elliptical Sentences.

453 Elliptical sentences differ from contracted sentences in the following respect :—In contracted sentences a certain portion which is common to the sentences is expressed only once in one of them, and has to be repeated in the others. In elliptical sentences, the part to be supplied in one clause, although suggested by what is expressed in the other, is not necessarily exactly the same in form. Moreover, contracted sentences or clauses are always co-ordinate; an elliptical clause is usually a subordinate clause, the portion to be supplied being suggested by the principal clause; as, "He is taller than I," *i.e.,* "than I am tall"; "This does not cost so much as that," *i.e.,* "as that costs much."

GENERAL RULES OF SYNTAX.

454 The following is a brief summary of the laws of the structure of sentences, and of the functions of the different parts of speech.

455 The primary elements of every sentence are the substantive, which forms the subject of the sentence (see § 345), and the verb, by means of which an assertion is made about that for which the subject stands (see §§ 347, 348, 353, 359).

456 The subject of a sentence is in the nominative case (§§ 380, 381).

457 The nominative case is also used for the subjective complement of a verb of incomplete predication, which is intransitive or passive, such as *be, become, seem, be called, be made,* &c. (§ 393).

A noun or pronoun in the nominative may also be used absolutely (§ 372, 5).

458 For an account of the function and use of the possessive case, see §§ 67, 68, 69, 78, 178 note.

459 The objective case is used when a noun or pronoun is the direct object of a transitive verb, participle, or gerund (§ 366). It is also used for the objective complement of various transitive verbs of incomplete predication (§§ 391, 395). It is used to mark the indirect object of a verb, that is, to indicate the person or thing affected by, or concerned in, the result of the action, without being the direct

object of it (§ 372, 4), and is employed in various kinds of adverbial adjuncts (§ 372, 3). It may be used absolutely (§ 372, 5). Nouns or pronouns governed by prepositions are in the objective case (§§ 79, 372). It is sometimes employed (especially in colloquial language, and in connexion with the word *self*) when the strict laws of grammar would require the nominative, as, ' That's *him* ' ; ' Who is there ? Me, sir ' (§ 177). In this way it is often used after *than*, even by good writers.* The relative pronoun is always put in the objective after *than*.†

The objective case is used in exclamations, as, ' Ah me ! ' ; ' Oh me, unhappy ! '

460   A noun or pronoun may have another noun attached to it attributively, giving a further description or definition of the person or thing spoken of. This second noun is said to be *in apposition* to the former (§ 362). It is, of course, in the same case. But the sign of possession is not appended to the first of two nouns in apposition (§ 75).

461   Sometimes the idea expressed by an entire sentence is repeated (pleonastically) by means of a noun, for the purpose of appending some complex attributive phrase, as, " He rashly ventured to ascend the mountain without a guide, *an act* which cost him his life."

462   The general rule respecting the concord of verbs is, that a verb agrees with its subject in number and person (§ 376). See 380—382.

463   Words that are plural in form (as *mathematics, politics*) are sometimes treated as singular in construction (§ 58), and some singular nouns have been mistaken for plurals (§ 60). A plural used as the title of a book, &c., must be treated as a singular, as, " Johnson's ' Lives of the Poets ' is a work of great interest." For the usage when the subject is a collective noun, see § 380, and for the case of a compound subject, § 381.‡

464   When subjects differing in number, or person, or both are connected by *and*, the verb must always be in the plural; and in the first person if one of the subjects is of that person ; in the second person if one of the subjects is of that person, and none of the first, as, ' I and he are of the same age ' ; ' You and I shall be too late.'

465   Subjects connected by *or* and *nor* imply an alternative. Hence a plural verb cannot be attached to two such subjects, if they are in the singular. The sentence is in fact contracted (§ 386), as, " Either John [is mistaken] or Thomas is mistaken" ; "Neither John [is mistaken] nor Thomas is mistaken." §

---

* *E.g.*, " A stone is heavy, and the sand weighty; but a fool's wrath is heavier than them both " (*Prov.* xxvii. 3).

† "Beelzebub . . . . than whom, Satan except, none higher sat" (*Par. L.*, ii.). There is no grammatical justification for this. The case of an interrogative or relative pronoun ought to be the same as that of the demonstrative pronoun which would answer to it. But " None sat higher than *him*" would be bad grammar.

‡ Sometimes nouns joined by *and* are regarded not as a compound subject, but as the independent subjects of a contracted sentence (§ 445). Thus: "To rive what Goth and Turk and Time hath spared " (*Ch. Harold*), implies a contraction of ' what Goth [hath spared], and [what] Turk [hath spared], and [what] Time hath spared.'

§ This sort of contraction is not legitimate unless the subjects are in the same number and person, for it is only then that *the same* verb is *common* to the two sentences (§ 445). But many grammarians tolerate contraction in other cases, and lay down the rule that if the alternative subjects differ in number, or person, or both, the verb should agree with the subject that is nearest to it. According to

466 The use of the subjunctive mood is perfectly simple and intelligible if its proper and primary function be kept in view (§ 195). That function is, to indicate that the connexion between the subject and the predicate is not regarded as corresponding to any *actual, external* event or state of affairs, past, present, or future, independent of the thought of the speaker, but is dealt with simply as a *conception of the mind*, without being spoken of any *actual* objective reality.* Using the term *objective* for what has an existence of its own, independent of the thought of the speaker, and *subjective* for what exists (or is dealt with as existing) only in the thought of the speaker, we may say that the *indicative* is the mood of *objective predication* and the subjunctive the mood of *subjective predication*. The principal forms that such conceptions assume are indicated in § 195. The use of the subjunctive in hypothetical sentences is explained in §§ 435—440.

467 The subjunctive mood was employed more commonly by the older writers than is the case now. It was used, for example, in dependent questions (as " I adjure Thee that Thou tell us whether Thou *be* the Christ "); and in various forms of hypothesis relating to what is, was, or will be the fact (' If it be,' ' If it were,' &c.), where the speaker confines himself to treating the fact supposed as a mere conception of the mind, although it might have been dealt with *objectively* by means of the indicative mood.†

468 *Sequence of Tenses.*—The tense of the verb in an accessory or dependent clause commonly depends upon that of the verb in the principal clause. A present or future in the principal clause requires a present or future indicative, or a present subjunctive, in the dependent clause. A past tense in the main clause requires a past tense in the dependent clause; *e.g.*, " He does this that he may please me "; " He will do this that he may please me "; " He has done this that he *may* please me "; ‡ " He did this that he might please me "; " He

---

this we ought to say, " Neither we nor John *is* rich "; " Either the pupils or their teacher *is* wrong "; " Neither the children nor I am hungry." To me all such sentences sound simply barbarous. It would be better to say, " Either the pupils are wrong, or their teacher is "; " Neither are we rich, nor is John," &c. Inasmuch, however, as it comes to much the same thing whether we say that something can be *asserted* of *neither*, or *denied* of *both*, good writers sometimes allow themselves the use of contraction with *neither—nor*, but treat the verb according to the rule of concord for subjects of different number or person connected by *and*, as, " Neither you nor I are in fault." (Compare " Hæc si neque ego neque tu fecimus." *Ter., And.* i., 2, 23.)

* It is altogether wrong to talk of the subjunctive mood as being *governed* by conjunctions. *If* or *unless* cannot possibly *govern* the subjunctive (*i.e.*, necessitate its being used), for they are followed quite as often by the indicative as by the subjunctive. Which mood is to be employed depends entirely upon the principle stated above If the subjunctive is uniformly employed after any particular conjunction (such as *lest*), it is because that conjunction, from its meaning, is incapable of introducing any sentence except one which denotes a mere conception of the mind.

† The modern use of the indicative is in many cases quite improper, as in " Take care that the child *does* not hurt himself." A purpose, *as such*, exists only in the mind itself. So also in putting a *general* case, such as " He that smiteth a man so that he *die*" (*Ex.* xxi. 12), the subjunctive is proper, because the indicative, by turning the result supposed into a *fact*, would deprive it of its *generality*, and render it no longer suitable for the *general definition* that is wanted. In such sentences as " *Come* what may "; " *Be* he who he may "; " *Come* life, *come* death," &c., we have (not the imperative, but) the subjunctive.

‡ Notice that *has done* is a *present* tense. (See § 207.)

says that he is better"; "He said that he was better," &c. But if the dependent clause states a *universal truth*, it is better to keep the present tense. Thus: "He allowed that all men *are* liable to error"; "He denied that God *exists*."

469 The Infinitive Mood may be used 1, as the simple subject or object of a finite verb (§§ 189, 191, 192, 385, 397). It sometimes has *to* before it in these cases, sometimes not. 2. Attached to a substantive, so that substantive and verb form a complex object of another verb (§ 397). 3. As an adverbial adjunct to another verb, or to an adjective. It is only the gerundial infinitive (§ 192) that can be thus used. The *to* retains its proper force (§§ 192, 372, 2). 4. As the complement of a verb of incomplete predication (§ 395).

470 The origin and construction of the gerund in *-ing* are explained in §§ 200, 201. When a verbal substantive in *-ing* is preceded by *the* or followed by *of*, it must be regarded as the representative of a verbal noun in *-ung*, as in "land suitable for the planting of trees"; "During the reading of the will," &c. When preceded by *the*, it should be followed by *of*. When the verbal noun in *-ing* has an object, like a verb, it is the gerund.*

471 Respecting the attributive and the predicative use of adjectives, see §§ 360, 391. As regards adjectives used substantively, and adjectives which have become substantives, see §§ 99-101. Adjectives and participles sometimes relate to the substantive which is *implied* in a possessive pronoun, as in "For *all our* sakes"; "It fills *my* mind waking and sleeping."

472 As a general rule the Article should be repeated before each of a series of nouns representing different things (as "I saw a horse, a cow, and a pig in the stable"; "An Act of Parliament requires the assent of the Queen, the Lords, and the Commons"), but not before each of several nouns describing the same thing † (as "He was the founder and patron of the institution"; "He slew the tyrant and destroyer of his country"), or before each of several adjectives attached to one noun (as "I dislike the long, rambling, and obscure sentences of that author"; "He delivered a short, pithy, and pun-

---

* The use of a participle where we ought to have a gerund, is a common error, as in, "I heard of *him running* away," instead of 'I heard of his running away'; "It is of no use you saying so," for 'It is of no use your saying so' (*i.e.*, 'It — namely, your saying so—is of no use'). At any rate the modern idiom tends towards the use of the gerund and the possessive, instead of the attributive participle. Still there are some expressions in which the latter is always used, as "You will oblige me by *all leaving* the room "; "I have my doubts as to this heing true"; "You seem to understand me by *each* at once her choppy finger *laying* upon her skinny lips" (*Macbeth*); and the best writers sanction the participial construction, as, "I then all smarting with *my wounds being* cold" (*Shaksp.*); "Upon *Nigel insisting*," &c. (*Scott*); "These circumstances may lead to your Ladyship quitting this house" (*Thackeray*); "He wolde resten after *the sunne goyng* down" (*Wicl., Gen.* xxviii. 11). It may be questioned whether this participial construction has not fallen into undeserved disrepute. Phrases like *post urbem conditam* (= *after the foundation of the city*) are quite common in Latin. On the whole, there is scarcely sufficient reason to reject such constructions as, "I have no doubt about the prisoner being guilty"; "There was a story of money having been buried there," &c.

† In "He was a better prose-writer than poet," the omission of *a* before *poet* results from the form of the sentence which is contracted: "He was a better prose-writer than [he was a good] poet."

gent address"). But certain infractions of the strict rule are allowable, when no ambiguity can possibly result. If the things spoken of are very closely connected together, one article often does double duty, as " We saw the King and Queen"; " The tables and chairs were in confusion"; " He gathered all the apples and pears"; " He built a coachhouse and stable." On the other hand the article may be repeated when it is impossible that more than one person or thing can be meant, as " He rose a sadder and a wiser man"; " You will find this road the shortest and the pleasantest."

473 When a noun is used attributively or predicatively with distinct reference to its *signification*, the article should not be used. Thus: " He became Chancellor of the Exchequer"; " John Smith, captain of the Petrel, next gave evidence."

474 Pronouns should agree in gender, number, and person with the nouns for which they stand. Their case is determined by the construction of the clause in which they occur. Thus: 'I do not like John (*obj.*); he (*nom.*) is an idle boy'; 'I know the man (*obj.*) whose (*poss.*) portrait hangs there,' &c. Even if the pronouns happen to *coincide* in case with the nouns to which they relate, this is not *grammatical agreement*, it is a mere accident.

475 The antecedent of a relative pronoun is sometimes disguised in the form of a possessive (adjective) pronoun, as " Whose is the crime, the scandal to be *theirs*." Repecting the omission of the antecedent or the relative, see §§ 160, 166, 409. The *continuative* relative (§ 413) can never be omitted.

476 When a relative refers to a noun which is in the attributive or predicative relation to a personal pronoun, the relative is sometimes made to agree in person with the pronoun, rather than with its actual antecedent. Thus: " I am .... a plain blunt man, that *love my* friend" (*Sh. J. C.* iii. 2); " Thou art the God that *doest* wonders" (*Ps.* lxxvii. 14). Still more commonly do we say," It is * I who *am* in fault," although the exact construction of the sentence is, ' It (the person) who *is* in fault, is I.' †

477 Respecting *it* used as the subject of impersonal verbs, see § 344. For *it* as a preparatory or anticipatory subject, see § 387. For *it* used as a vague cognate objective, see § 372, note. The sense of *it* is so vague, that it may relate to a plural, as " It is we who have won."

478 If two alternative nouns, differing in gender or number, are referred to by the pronoun *he, she, it*, we sometimes find the plural employed,‡ as, " If an ox gore a man or a woman, so that *they*

---

* In the older forms of the language the verb attached to the *it* was influenced by the following noun or pronoun. Thus in Chaucer we have, " It am I." " It *ben* nat ge that speken" (*Matt.* x. 20). In German we have *es sind*, if a plural follow.

† To such a question as, " Who is there ?" we might get such a reply as, " It is I, your uncle, who *am* come to see you." To such a question as, " Who is come to see me ?" we should expect such an answer as, " It is I, your uncle, who is come to see you." On this point I differ from Dr. Adams (*Eng. Lang.*, p. 208).

‡ Compare the ambiguous *each* in, "Let *each* esteem other better than *themselves*." Some repeat the alternative in the pronoun, " So that he or she die"; " build his or her pretensions," &c, Cobbett insisted upon this being the only correct method. His dictum was ridiculed in the ' Rejected Addresses' by the parody, " I take it for granted that every intelligent man, woman, and child, to whom I address myself, has stood severally and respectively in Little Russell Street, and cast their, his, her, and its eyes on the outside of this building" (*Rushton, Rules*, &c., p. 110). *Double* alternatives involve a rather violent application of the prin-

die" (*Ex.* xxi. 28); "Not on outward charms alone should man or woman build *their* pretensions to please" (*Opie*).

479 *They who*, or *they that* is just as legitimate as *he who*, or *he that*. The plural *they* is freely used in this way by the older writers, but now-a-days *those* is usually substituted for it.

480 It must be borne in mind that in constructing a sentence out of its elements, an adjunct which, for *grammatical* purposes, is attached *directly* to some word, may, with regard to the *logical* sequence of ideas, be connected with that word only after some other adjunct has been joined to it. The predicate usually applies only to the *logical* subject (§ 348). In 'The boy was nearly killed,' '*was killed*' can be attached to '*boy*' only after '*nearly*' has been joined to the verb. In 'The first king of Rome' '*first*,' and '*of Rome*' are not *co-ordinate* adjuncts. One is applicable only after the other has been attached.*

PUNCTUATION.

481 In speaking, the words of a sentence, especially if it be a complex one, are not uttered consecutively without any break. Certain pauses are made to mark more clearly the way in which the words of the sentence are grouped together.

In writing, these pauses are represented by marks called *stops* or *points*. Punctuation (derived from the Latin *punctum*, a *point*) means "the right mode of putting in points or stops."

The stops made use of are—1. The Comma (,). 2. The Semicolon (;). 3. The Colon (:). 4. The Full Stop or Period (.).†

As it is impossible to lay down perfectly exact rules for the introduction of pauses in speaking, so it will be found that in many cases the best writers are not agreed as to the use of stops in writing. All that can be done is to lay down the most general principles.

---

ciple of contraction, and approach dangerously near to the advertisement in the comedy: "Rats and gentlemen ketched and waited on." It is better to express the sentence in full (as, "If an ox gore a man so that he die, or gore a woman so that she die"), or change the form (as, "Not on outward charms alone should man build his pretensions to please, or woman hers"). But after all there is no great objection to the plural.

* A good deal of hypercriticism has been wasted on such phrases as "The three first verses of the chapter," &c. We are told that this is incorrect, because there is only one first verse. On this principle it is equally wrong to talk of 'The first hours of infancy,' or 'The last days of Pompeii,' for there is only *one* first hour, and *one* last day. Surely if there are several last days, their number may be specified. It would be the height of pedantry to alter "His two eldest sons went to sea" into "His eldest two sons went to sea"; yet strictly there can be only one eldest son. German writers see nothing wrong in such phrases as, "die drei ersten," "die zwei letzten," &c. All these superlatives admit of a little laxity in their application, just as *chief* and *extreme* admit of the superlatives *chiefest* and *extremest*. 'The three first verses' simply means 'The three verses before which there is no other.' Those who tell us to write 'The first three verses,' and so on, must do so on the hypothesis that the whole number of verses is divided into *sets* *of three*, of which *sets* the first is taken. But what, if the chapter only contains five altogether?

† These words (properly speaking) are names not of the *stops*, but of the portions of sentences which they mark off. *Comma* means a *clause*; *Colon*, a limb or member of a sentence; *Semicolon*, a half *Colon*; *Period*, a complete sentence.

482 The Full Stop is used at the end of a complete and independent sentence, but not at the end of a sentence which is followed by another *collateral* sentence (§ 419).

483 In simple sentences the comma is inserted—

1. Before the main verb, when the subject is accompanied by an attributive adjunct, which, with its adjuncts, forms a combination of words of considerable length. As, "The injustice *of the sentence pronounced upon this wise and virtuous man,* is evident." But if the adjunct is expressed briefly, the comma is not used; as, "The injustice *of the sentence* is evident."

2. Before and after any participle (not used as a mere qualitative adjective) or participial phrase; as, "The man, having slipped, fell over the cliff." "The general, having rallied his soldiers, led them forwards." "Undaunted, he still struggled on." "All night the dreadless angel, unpursued, through heaven's wide champaign winged his glorious way."

3. Before and after any attributive adjunct to the subject which consists of an adjective, or noun in apposition, when those are accompanied by other words standing to them in the attributive, objective, or adverbial relation. *E.g.,* "Bacon, the illustrious author of the 'Novum Organum,' declared," &c. "The soldier, afraid of the consequences of his insubordination, deserted."

4. Before or after a phrase or quotation which is either the subject or the object of a verb. Thus: "Nelson's watchword was, England expects every man to do his duty." "He said to his disciples, Watch and pray."

5. When the subject of a sentence consists of several substantives enumerated successively without having the conjunction *and* placed between them, they must be separated by commas. Thus: "John, William, James, and Henry took a walk together."

6. A comma is inserted after an adverbial phrase consisting of a noun (with its adjunct) used absolutely, or an infinitive mood (preceded by *to*) implying purpose, when it precedes the verb or its subject As, "To conclude, I will only say," &c. "The man being dead, his heirs took possession of his estate."

7. Other complex adverbial phrases also are frequently followed by commas, when they precede the subject of the sentence; as, "By studying diligently for five hours a day, he mastered the language in six months." Such phrases

should be both preceded and followed by commas when they come between the subject and the verb.

8. Nouns used in the vocative (or nominative of appellation) are separated by commas from the rest of the sentence; as, "John, shut the door." "I said, Sir, that I had not done that."

484 In compound sentences:—

1. A substantive clause used as the subject of a verb should be followed by a comma. Thus: "That the accused is innocent of the crime imputed to him, admits of demonstration." "How we are ever to get there, is the question."

If such a clause *follows* the verb (the latter being preceded by *it*), a comma does not usually precede the substantive clause. As, "It is of great importance that this should be rightly understood."

A substantive clause which is the object of a verb is not generally preceded by a comma, unless it is of considerable length. When it is short, it follows the main verb without any break. Thus: "He acknowledged that he had done this." "Tell me how you are." But: "In answer to these inquiries the messenger replied, that he had not been present when the engagement took place."

2. An adjective clause is not separated by a comma from the noun which it qualifies when it is an essential part of the designation of the thing signified; that is, when the thing or person signified is not sufficiently indicated by the antecedent noun. Thus: "The man who told me this stands here." "I do not see the objects that you are pointing out."

But if the designation of the person or thing meant is complete without the relative sentence, so that the latter only extends and defines that designation, then a comma must be introduced. Thus: "We are studying the reign of William Rufus, who succeeded his father A.D. 1087." "I will report this to my father, who is waiting to hear the news."

In accordance with the principle laid down in § 479, 1, an adjective sentence usually has a comma placed after it, when it is attached to the subject of the sentence, and always has a comma after it when it is followed by any adverbial adjuncts of the principal verb; otherwise it would not be clear whether such adjuncts belonged to the main sentence or to the adjective clause. Thus "He resisted the man who attacked him, with all his might"

3. Adverbial sentences are generally separated from the main sentence by commas, unless they are very short, and closely connected with what precedes. Thus: "When you have finished your work, tell me." "I will not reward you, unless you deserve it." But: "He ran away as soon as I saw him." "I could not catch him before he escaped."

485 Co-ordinate sentences are generally separated by commas when they are expressed at full length. Thus: "Next day they resumed their labours, and success soon crowned their efforts." "We were very tired, but we could not stop long." "Either he will succeed, or he will perish in the attempt."

Commas are also inserted between contracted co-ordinate sentences (§ 445), except when the portions that are expressed are very closely related to each other, and are connected by the conjunctions *and*, *or*, and *nor*. Thus: "We remained there that night, and set out early on the following day." "He searched diligently, but could not find it." But commas are not needed for such sentences as, "The infantry halted and formed a hollow square." "He struck and killed his brother." "Whether he win or lose does not concern us."

486 Collateral sentences (§ 449) are separated by commas when they are short, and by semicolons when they are of considerable length.

When collateral sentences are contracted, commas should be placed between those portions that remain. When a series of contracted sentences are partly collateral and partly co-ordinate, commas are inserted between the remains of the collateral sentences, but not between those of the co-ordinate clauses, provided these are closely connected together by means of the conjunctions *and* and *or* (see § 481). Thus: "He saw, wooed and won the daughter of the prince." "Early to bed and early to rise, makes a man healthy, wealthy and wise." "He gazed upon the earth, the sea, the sky." "He took leave of his father, his brother and his sister." "He paid his bill, mounted his horse and rode away." "He does not study either Greek or Latin."

487 The above are the chief rules for the insertion of the comma. But a stop may be placed in writing whenever a pause would be made in speaking, for the purpose of rendering the sense more clear. And, *vice versâ*, stops

may be omitted in writing where, in reading or speaking, the portions of a sentence, between which some rule would seem to require a stop, are pronounced together without any break.

488 A semicolon is used instead of a comma, when the sense of the passage requires that a longer pause should be made in uttering it than is usually indicated by a comma. No other more exact rules can be given for the use of this stop.

489 The colon represents a longer pause than the semicolon. It may be placed between collateral sentences, when the connexion between them is not very close. It is also frequently placed before a quotation.

490 Besides the stops, some other signs are employed in writing.

A note of interrogation (?) must be placed at the end of all direct questions, but not after indirect questions. Thus: "Have you written your letter?" But: "He asked me whether I had written my letter."

The note of admiration or exclamation (!) is placed after interjections, exclamations, and after nouns and pronouns used in addresses, when particular stress is to be laid upon them. This mark is also frequently placed at the end of a sentence which contains an invocation.

491 The parenthesis ( ) is used to enclose a clause, or part of a clause, which does not enter into the construction of the main sentence, but is merely introduced *by the way*. Words enclosed within a parenthesis do not require to be separated from the rest of the sentence by any other stop.

492 Double or single inverted commas '—', or "—", are used to mark quotations.

ANALYSIS OF SENTENCES.

493 a. The first stage in the analysis of a simple sentence is to separate the grammatical subject with its adjuncts from the predicate-verb with whatever is attached to it as object, complement, or adverbial adjunct. The grammatical subject with its attributive adjuncts forms the *logical* subject of the sentence; the predicate verb, with all that is attached to it, forms the *logical* predicate of the sentence (§ 348).

Examples.

Logical Subject. (Grammatical Subject with Attributive Adjuncts.)	Logical Predicate. (Predicate-Verb, with Objective and Adverbial Adjuncts.)
Our messenger	has not yet arrived.
We	will carry all our property with us.
The village preacher's modest mansion	rose there.
The wretched prisoner, overwhelmed by his misfortunes,	was on the point of putting an end to his existence.
A bird in the hand	is worth two in the bush.

493 b. The following example illustrates the separation of the logical subject into the grammatical subject and its attributive adjuncts (§ 348).

"The soldiers of the tenth legion, wearied by their long march, and exhausted from want of food, were unable to resist the onset of the enemy."

Logical Subject.		Logical Predicate.
Grammatical Subject.	Attributive Adjuncts of Subject.	
Soldiers	1. The 2. of the tenth legion 3. wearied by their long march 4. exhausted from want of food	were unable to resist the onset of the enemy.

SYNTAX—ANALYSIS OF SENTENCES.

493 c. In the following examples the logical predicate is separated into its component parts:—

Logical Subject.	Logical Predicate.		
	Predicate-Verb.	Object, with Adjuncts.	Adverbial Adjuncts.
The sight of distress	fills	a benevolent mind	1. always 2. with compassion.
We	will bend	our course	1. thither 2. from off the tossing of these fiery waves.

493 d. In the following example both the subject and the object of the verb are separated into the substantive and attributive adjuncts of which they are composed:—
"The mournful tidings of the death of his son filled the proud heart of the old man with the keenest anguish."

Subject.	Attributive Adjuncts of Subject.	Predicate.	Object.	Attributive Adjuncts of Object.	Adverbial Adjuncts of Predicate.
tidings	1. The 2. mournful 3. of the death of his son	filled	heart	1. the 2. proud 3. of the old man	with the keenest anguish.

493 e. The following examples show how a complex predicate (§ 391-395) may be separated into its components:—
"That hero was deservedly called the saviour of his country."

Subject, with Adjuncts.	Predicate.		Adverbial Adjuncts of Predicate.	
	Verb of Incomplete Predication.	Subjective Complement.	Adverbial Adjunct of Verb.	Adverbial Adjunct of Complement.
that hero	was called	the saviour of his country	deservedly	

"This misfortune will certainly make the poor man miserable for life."

Subject with Adjuncts.	Predicate.		Object with Adjuncts.	Adverbial Adjuncts of Predicate.	
	Verb of Incomplete Predication.	Objective Complement.		Adjunct of Verb.	Adjunct of Complement.
This misfortune	will make	miserable	the poor man	certainly	for life

493 *f.* The thorough analysis of a sentence is to be conducted in the following manner:—

i. Set down the subject of the sentence, which may consist (1) of a single substantive, or (2) of two or more substantives united by co-ordinative conjunctions, or (3) of an infinitive mood, or (4) of a quotation, or (5) of a subordinate substantive clause (see §§ 384-387).

ii. Set down the attributive adjuncts of the subject. These may consist (1) of an adjective or participle (with or without adjuncts of their own), or (2) of a noun, an infinitive mood, or a substantive clause in apposition to the subject, or (3) of a substantive (noun or pronoun) in the possessive case, or (4) of a substantive preceded by a preposition (including under this head an infinitive mood preceded by *to*), or (5) of an adjective clause (§ 362).

iii. Set down the predicate-verb. If the verb is one of incomplete predication, set down the complement of the predicate, and indicate that the verb and its complement make up the entire predicate (§§ 389-395).

iv. If the predicate be a transitive verb, set down the object of the verb. The object of a verb admits of the same varieties as the subject. If the predicate be a verb of incomplete predication, followed by an infinitive mood, set down the object of the dependent infinitive (§ 397).

v. Set down those words, phrases, or adjective clauses, which are in the attributive relation to the object of the predicate, or to the object of the complement of the predicate, if the latter be a verb in the infinitive mood (§ 389).

vi. Set down those words, phrases, or adverbial clauses which are in the adverbial relation to the predicate, or the complement of the predicate. These adverbial adjuncts may consist (1) of an adverb; or (2) of a substantive (or verb in the infinitive mood) preceded by a preposition; or (3) of a noun qualified by an attributive word; or (4) of a substantive (noun or pronoun) in the objective case, before which *to* or *for* may be understood; or (5) of a nominative absolute; or (6) of an adverbial clause (§ 372).

These various elements of the sentence may be arranged either in the mode adopted in the following examples, or in that indicated in the table at the end of the book.

Examples of the Analysis of Simple Sentences.

494 *a*. "Having ridden up to the spot, the enraged officer struck the unfortunate man dead with a single blow of his sword."

Subject,   'officer.'

Attributive adjuncts of subject,
   1. 'the' (§ 362, 1).
   2. 'enraged' (§ 362, 1).
   3. 'having ridden up to the spot' (§ 362, 1).

Predicate,
   Verb of incomplete predication, 'struck.'
   Complement of predicate (§ 395) 'dead.'

Object,   'man.'

Attributive adjuncts of object,
   1. 'the.'
   2. 'unfortunate.'

Adverbial adjuncts of predicate,
   1. 'on the spot' (§ 372, 2).
   2. 'with a single blow of his sword' (§ 372, 2).

494 *b*. "I saw a man with a sword." Here *with a sword* forms an *attributive* adjunct of the object *man*. It does not denote the manner or means of the action *saw* (§ 362, 4).

495   "Who are you?" *

Subject,   'you.'

Predicate,
   Verb of incomplete predication, 'are.'
   Complement of predicate, 'who.'

496   "Now the bright morning star, day's harbinger, comes dancing from the East."

Subject,   'star.'

Attributive adjuncts of subject,
   1. 'the' (§ 362, 1).
   2. 'bright' (§ 362, 1).
   3. 'day's harbinger' (§ 362, 3).

Predicate,
   Verb of incomplete predication, 'comes.'
   Complement of predicate, 'dancing'† (§ 391).

Adverbial adjunct of the predicate, 'from the East' (§ 372, 2).

---

* The construction of an interrogative or relative sentence is most easily seen by looking at that of the corresponding affirmative or demonstrative sentence. Thus, ' *Who are you?*' answers to "*I am he.*"

† It is much better to class this example with such phrases as "*looks fine*," "*grows tall*," "*smells sweet*," &c., than to treat *dancing* as an attributive adjunct of the subject, which in the order of ideas it certainly is not.

497 "He found all his wants supplied by the care of his friends."
Subject,   'he.'
Predicate,   { *Verb of incomplete predication*, 'found.'
               Complement of predicate, 'supplied' (§ 395)
Object,   'wants.'
Attributive adjuncts of object,   { 1. 'all' (§ 362, 1).
                             2. 'his' (§ 362, 3).

Adverbial adjunct of the complement of the predicate, 'by the care of his friends' (§ 372, 2).

(In the phrase "*by the care of his friends,*" we may also separate the words "*of his friends,*" as forming an attributive adjunct of the noun *care*.)

498 "A man of weak health is incapable of the thorough enjoyment of life."
Subject,   'man.'
Attributive adjuncts of subject,   { 1. 'a' (§ 362, 1).
                             2. 'of weak health' (§ 362, 4).
Predicate,   { *Verb of incomplete predication*, 'is.'
               Complement of predicate, 'incapable' (§ 393).

Adverbial adjunct of the complement of the predicate, 'of the thorough enjoyment of life.' (See the note on the last example.)

499 "And now, their mightiest quelled, the battle swerved, with many an inroad gored."
Subject,   'battle.'
Attributive adjuncts of subject,   { 1. *Article*, 'the.'
                             2. *Participial phrase*, 'with many an inroad gored' (§ 362, 1).
Predicate,   'swerved.'
Adverbial adjuncts of predicate,   { 1. *Adverb*, 'now.'
                               2. *Noun, with attributive adjunct, in the nominative absolute*, 'their mightiest quelled' (§ 372, 5).

500 "He gave him a letter to read." Here 'him' (*i.e.,* 'to him') and 'to read' (*ad legendum*, § 190) form adverbial adjuncts of the predicate.

501 It frequently happens that the attributive adjuncts of the subject or object have in their turn adverbial or other adjuncts of sufficient importance to be worth setting down separately. In that case they may be inserted in the analysis under a heading of their own. Thus :—

         "Hence, loathed Melancholy,
           Of Cerberus and blackest midnight born,
             In Stygian cave forlorn,
     'Mongst horrid shapes, and shrieks and sights unholy."

Subject,   'melancholy.'
Attributive ad-   ⎧ 1. *Adjective*, 'loathed.'
 juncts of subject, ⎩ 2. *Participle*, ' born.'
                    ⎧ 1. 'Of Cerberus and blackest midnight.'
Adverbial ad-   ⎨ 2. ' In Stygian cave forlorn.'
 juncts of 'born,'⎬ 3. ' 'Mongst horrid shapes, and shrieks, and
                    ⎩   sights unholy.'
Predicate (understood), 'go' (or depart).
Adverbial adjunct of predicate, ' hence.'

502*a* "All but one were killed."

Here 'but one' (A. S. *bútan ánum*) is an adverbial adjunct (§ 372, 2) of the verb. The sentence means 'all, leaving out one, were killed.'

502*b* "None but the brave deserve the fair."

That is, 'None, if we leave out the brave, deserve the fair.' ' *But the brave*' (like ' *but one* ' in the last example) is an adverbial adjunct of the predicate. (For another mode of explaining the construction of *but* in this instance, see § 289, note. It is easy to see that the filling up of the ellipsis there indicated is possible only after a negative.) "Who but a madman would act thus?" means, "Leaving out the class of madmen, who would act thus?" The phrase 'but a madman,' is, in any case, an adverbial adjunct of the predicate.

503   " But being charged, we will be still by land" (*Antony and Cleopatra*, iv. 11, 1).

Here ' but being charged' is a gerund, preceded by the preposition *but*, and means 'leaving out the case of being charged.' The phrase forms an adverbial adjunct to the predicate verb *will be*. The sentence means, " Unless we are attacked, we will make no movement by land."

504   " Whence, but from the author of all ill, could spring so deep a malice ?"

Here an adverbial phrase instead of a substantive seems to follow the preposition *but*. The use of the gerund after *but* in the last example, however, suggests that the full phrase should be *but springing from the author of all ill*, that is, " Without springing from the author of all ill," or, "If we leave out the case of springing from the author of all ill, whence could so deep a malice spring?" So, "Matchless but with the Almighty," is " Matchless but (being matched) with the Almighty."
A similar explanation may be given of such phrases as, " He never comes *but when he is not wanted*," i.e., 'but (*coming*) when he is not wanted;' so 'except when he is not wanted,' may be treated as ' *coming* when he is not wanted being excepted.' We do, however, find adverbs standing for qualified substantives, and preceded by prepositions. *Before now* is equivalent to *before the present time*.

505   " I can but lament the result."

In such sentences it seems as though *but* were an adverb, meaning *only*. It is, however, the preposition *but*, followed by a verb in the infinitive (or substantive) mood. In reality all such constructions have arisen from the improper omission of a negative.* In Chaucer we find, "I n'am but a loude compilatour;" "That I may l.ave not but my meat and drinke" (Wedgwood, *Dict. s. v.* 'but').

Examples of the Analysis of Complex Sentences.

506 When there are subordinate clauses, the analysis of the entire sentence must first be conducted as if for each subordinate clause we had some single word. When the relation of the several clauses to the main sentence and to each other has thus been clearly marked, the subordinate clauses are to be analysed on the same principles as simple sentences. Mere conjunctions (§ 286) do not enter into the grammatical structure of the clauses which they introduce. No combination of words forms a dependent sentence without a finite verb expressed or understood.

507 The relation of the parts of a complex sentence may be indicated by the following notation :—1. Let brackets of different kinds enclose the several clauses, and be so placed as to enclose *everything* that enters into the structure of the clause in question. If a clause contains other subordinate clauses within it, let these be enclosed in brackets of their own. A *principal* sentence need not be enclosed in brackets, unless it be one of two or more co-ordinate sentences. 2. Let a *principal* sentence be marked by a capital letter placed before it,† as (A), (B), &c. 3. Let each subordinate clause be marked by a *small* letter of its own prefixed to it (inside the brackets), a letter without a dash (a, b, &c.) denoting a substantive clause, a letter with a dash (c', d', &c.) denoting an adjective clause, and a letter with two dashes (m'', n'', &c.) denoting an adverbial clause. (Co-ordinate clauses may be denoted by the *same* small letter repeated and distinguished by numerals placed underneath, as a_1, a_2, b_1', b_2', b_3'.) This *single* letter would be enough to *denote* the clause for subsequent reference; but, to show more clearly the connection of the clauses, if one subordinate clause is contained within another, let the letter which denotes the contained clause be *preceded* by the letter or letters denoting the containing clause. Thus, let ($a'b$) denote a substantive clause (b) which is contained within an adjective clause (a'); let (ab'_2c'') denote an adverbial clause (c'') contained within the second (b'_2) of two or more co-ordinate adjective clauses contained within a substantive clause (a). Thus in the following example (C): "I have heard [(a) that my brother has lost at play the money {(ab'.) which was given to him ⊰ ($ab'c''$.) that he might pay his debts ⊱"}], the substantive clause marked a includes all from 'that my brother' to

---

* There are other instances in which negatives are improperly omitted in English. "Do not spend more than you can help," ought to be "Do not spend more than you cannot help." "He has lost ever so much money," should be, "He has lost never so much money," *i.e.*, "He has lost a quantity of money, and never before lost so much."

† This may be omitted if the sentence is an isolated one.

'debts.' The adjective clause beginning with 'which' is marked ab', because it is an adjective clause (b') contained within the substantive clause which is marked a; and the adverbial clause beginning with *that* is marked $ab'c''$, being an adverbial clause (c'') contained within the adjective clause marked ab'; all the clauses being parts of the principal sentence (C). The letters denoting the clauses may be enclosed within brackets of their own, or not, at discretion. If it is desired to indicate to which out of two or more co-ordinate sentences a clause belongs, carry out the notation by prefixing to the letter or letters placed before the clause the capital letter placed before the sentence.

1. Sentences containing Substantive Clauses.

508 (A) " He inferred from this [(a) that the opinion of the judge was {(ab) that the prisoner was guilty}]."

Analysis of (A).

Subject, 'he.'
Predicate, 'inferred.'
Object, { *Substantive clause,* [(a) 'That † the opinion of the judge was that the prisoner was guilty'] (§ 403).
Adverbial adjunct of predicate, 'from this' (§ 372, 2).

---

* The use of this notation is not at all essential in the analysis of sentences, but it will be found to add much to the clearness of the process. Instead of brackets enclosing the various clauses, lines of different sorts may be drawn under or over the clauses. A thick line may denote a substantive clause, a thin line an adjective clause, and a dotted line an adverbial clause, the small letters denoting the clauses being placed at the beginning of the several lines. Thus, " I have heard
(a) ▬▬▬▬▬▬▬▬▬▬▬▬▬▬▬▬▬▬▬▬▬▬▬▬▬▬▬▬▬▬
   that my brother has lost at play the money which was given to him
                                                 (ab') ─────────────────────
   that he might pay his debts." The degree of subordination of the various
($ab'c''$)·············
clauses would thus be obvious at a glance. If the use of these combinations of letters for denoting the subordinate clauses be thought too difficult, each clause, as it is reached in the analysis, may be denoted by a letter or mark of any kind, for subsequent reference, without bracketing and marking the clauses in the first instance. Thus (A), " He inferred that the opinion of the judge was that the prisoner was guilty ":—

Subject, 'he.'
Predicate, 'inferred.'
Object, { (*Substantive clause*), 'that the opinion of the judge was that the prisoner was guilty' (X).

Analysis of (X).
Subject and adjuncts, 'the opinion of the judge.'
Predicate, { *Verb of incomplete predication,* 'was.'
               Complement (*Substantive clause*), 'that the prisoner was guilty' (Y).

Analysis of (Y).
Subject and adjunct, 'the prisoner.'
Predicate, { *Verb of incomplete predication,* 'was.'
               Complement, 'guilty.'

† *That,* being a mere conjunction, does not enter into the structure of the clause which it introduces.

184   SYNTAX—ANALYSIS OF SENTENCES.

Analysis of (a).
Subject,   'opinion.'
Attributive ad-   { 1. 'the.'
juncts of subject,   { 2. 'of the judge' (§ 362, 4).
Predicate,   { *Verb of incomplete predication,* 'was.'
   { *Complement (Substantive clause)* {(ab) 'that the prisoner was guilty' }.

Analysis of (ab').
Subject (with Attributive adjuncts), 'the prisoner.'
Predicate,   { *Verb of incomplete predication,* 'was.'
   { *Complement,* 'guilty.'

509 (A) "Tell me [(b) who * you *think* that man is]."

Analysis of (A).
Subject (understood), 'you.'
Predicate,   'tell.'
Object,   { *(Substantive clause)* [(b) ' Who you think that man is'].
Adverbial adjunct of predicate, 'me.'

Analysis of (b).
Subject,   'you.'
Predicate,   'think.'
Object, (Substantive clause) {(bc) 'Who that man is' }.

Analysis of (bc).
Subject, with adjunct, 'that man.'
Predicate,   { *Verb of incomplete predication,* 'is.'
   { *Complement of predicate,* 'who.'

510 "The hope that I shall be successful sustains me."
   The substantive clause 'that I shall be successful,' may be termed an *enlargement* of the subject *hope,* to which it stands in a species of *objective* relation, *hope* being a noun denoting an active feeling directed towards some object (§ 450).

511   (1) "That he said that is not true."   (2) "It is not true that he said that."
   In the former sentence the subject is the substantive clause "that he said that." In the latter the subject is the pronoun *it,* to which the substantive clause, "that he said that," stands in apposition, forming an attributive adjunct to it (§ 362, 2).

---

* It is common in sentences of this kind to see the interrogative or relative pronoun put in the objective case. This is wrong (see note on § 495). "Whom do men say that I am" would be correct only if it were allowable to say, "Men say that I am him." The words *you think* are printed in italics because, although they belong to the entire substantive clause, they interrupt the consecutiveness of the contained clause, 'who that man is.'

512 (1) "I told him that he was mistaken." (2) "I convinced him that he was mistaken."

In the first sentence *him* answers to the Latin *dative* case, and is an adverbial adjunct to the predicate *told*, the *object* of which is the substantive clause "that he was mistaken." In the second sentence *him* is the direct object of the verb, and the substantive clause (like the Latin *Accusative of Limitation*) forms an adverbial adjunct of the predicate (§ 407). The first sentence is equivalent to "He was mistaken. I told him *that;*" the second to "He was mistaken. I convinced him *with respect to that.*"

513 "There was a report that you were dead."

Subject,   'report.'
Attributive ad-   { 1. 'a.'
  juncts of subject,   { 2. Substantive clause, 'that you were dead'
                           (§ 362, 2).
Predicate,   'was.'
Adverbial adjunct of predicate,   'there.'

614 (A) "Methinks* [(a) the lady doth protest too much "].
Subject, '[that] the lady doth protest too much' (a).
Predicate, 'thinks.'*
Adverbial adjunct of predicate, '[to] me.'

Analysis of (a).

Subject,   'lady.'
Attributive adjunct of subject, 'the.'
Predicate,   'doth protest.'
Object,   'too much.'

515 (B) "Him thought* [(a) his sorrowful heart would break '].

Here the substantive clause "[*that*] his sorrowful heart would break" is the subject of the verb *thought*.

516 "I should have forgiven him, but that he repeated the offence."

Here we have a substantive clause preceded by the preposition *but*, the whole phrase forming an adverbial adjunct of the predicate "should have forgiven" (§ 403).

517 (A) "Thieves are not judged, but† [(m) they are by to hear"].
    (B) "It shall go hard but ‡ [(n) I will better the instruction].

In these two sentences the substantive clauses that follow the preposition *but* are not introduced by the conjunction *that*. The combination of the preposition and substantive clause forms an adverbial adjunct to the predicate (§ 372, 2).

---

* *Thinks* and *thought* are the present and past indefinite tenses of the old English verb *thincan*, 'to appear.' (Compare the German *dünkt* and *däuchte*).
  † That is, "without their being by to hear," or "the case of their being by to hear being excluded."
  ‡ That is, "The case of my bettering the instruction being excluded, it shall go hard."

2. Sentences containing Adjective Clauses.

518 (A) "The cohort, {(a') which had already crossed the river, quickly came to blows with the enemy."

Subject,	'cohort.'
Attributive adjuncts of subject,	1. *Article,* 'the.' 2. *Adjective clause,* 'which had already crossed the river' (a').
Predicate,	'came.'
Adverbial adjuncts of predicate,	1. 'quickly.' 2. 'to blows.' 3. 'with the enemy.'

Analysis of (a').

Subject,	'which.'
Predicate,	'had crossed.'
Object,	'river.'
Attributive adjunct to object,	'the.'
Adverbial adjunct to predicate,	'already.'

519 (B) "**Give** me that large book {(a') that you have in your hand"}.

Here the adjective clause "that you have in your hand" is in the attributive relation to the object 'book.' The relative *that* is the object of *have*.

520 "Give me what you have in your hand."

Here the adjective clause, "what you have in your hand" is used substantively, that is, without having its antecedent *that* expressed. In the analysis we may either introduce the word *that*, the object of *give*, and set down the relative adjective clause as an attributive adjunct to it, or we may at once call the adjective clause itself the object of the verb.

Care must be taken not to confound adjective clauses like the above with substantive clauses beginning with the *interrogative what*, as " *Tell me what he said.*" (§ 410.)

521 "I return to view where once the cottage stood."

Here 'where once the cottage stood ' is an adjective clause qualifying the noun *place* understood, which forms the object of *view*.

522 "Who is there but admires such deeds?"

The verb *admires* requires a subject. If we supply *he*, the phrase *but [that] he admires such deeds* is an adverbial phrase qualifying the predicate, and consisting of the preposition *but*, followed by a substantive clause. If we supply *who* ('but who admires,' &c.), we also get an adverbial adjunct to the predicate, the sentence being equivalent to, " Who, if we leave out those who admire such deeds, is there?" *Who admires such deeds* is then an adjective clause used substantively, that is, without an antecedent expressed, and preceded by a preposition.

522 "His conduct is not such as I admire."
Here *as I admire* must be taken as an adjective clause co-ordina. with *such*, and (like it) forming a complement to the predicate *is*. *As* does duty for a relative pronoun, and is the object of *admire* (§ 412).

3. Sentences containing Adverbial Clauses.

(D) [(m″)] " When in Salamanca's cave
   Him listed his magic wand to wave,]
  The bells would ring in Notre Dame."

Analysis of (D).

Subject (*with attributive adjunct*), 'the bells.'
Predicate,   'would ring.'
Adverbial adjuncts of predicate, { 1. (*Adverbial clause*) [(m″)] 'when in Salamanca's —— wave'].
     2. 'in Notre Dame.'

Analysis of (m″).

Subject (*Infinitive phrase*), } 'to wave his magic wand.'
Predicate,   'listed.'
Adverbial adjuncts of predicate { 1. 'When.'
     2. 'in Salamanca's cave.'
     3. 'him.' *

525 (A) "He slept [(n′) while I watched]."
Subject,   'he.'
Predicate, 'slept.'
Adverbial adjunct of predicate, } (*Adverbial clause*), 'while I watched.'

Analysis of (n′).

Subject,   'I.'
Predicate,   'watched.'
'While' is a conjunction (§ 291e).

526 "He slept till I awaked him."
Here it must be observed that *till* is not adverbial in its force. It is usually called a conjunction, and such a clause as 'till I awaked him' is regarded as an adverbial clause. *Till* was originally a preposition, and was used with a substantive clause after it (§ 291e).

527 (B) {(x″) "If it were done† [(x″y″) when 'tis done]}, then it were well [(z) it were done quickly"].

―――――――――
* *Him* has here the force of a *dative*.
† *i.e.* If it were all over when 'tis done.

188   SYNTAX—ANALYSIS OF SENTENCES.

Analysis of (B).

Subject,   'it.'
Attributive ad-⎫   Substantive clause in apposition, (§387) [(z)
juncts of subject, ⎭   'it were done quickly'].
Predicate,   'were.'
Adverbial ad-⎧ 1. (*Adverbial clause of condition*) ⎰ x'' 'If it
juncts of predi-⎨   were done, when 'tis done'⎱
cate,   ⎩ 2. 'then.'
              ⎩ 3. 'well.'

Analysis of (x'').

Subject,   'it.'
Predicate,   ⎰ *Verb of incomplete predication*, 'were.'
                  ⎱ *Complement*, 'done.'
Adverbial adjunct ⎫ (*Adverbial clause of time*) [($x''y''$) ' when 'tis
of predicate,   ⎭   done.']

Analysis of ($x''y''$).

Subject,   'it.'
Predicate,   ⎰ *Verb of incomplete predication*, 'is.'
                  ⎱ *Complement*, 'done.'
Adverbial adjunct ⎫
of predicate,   ⎭ ' when.'

Analysis of (z).

Subject,   'it.'
Predicate,   (*Ordinary passive verb*) 'were done.'
Adverbial adjunct ⎫
of complement,   ⎭ 'quickly.'

528   (A) " He ran so fast {(a'') that I could not overtake him "}.
Subject,   'he.'
Predicate,   'ran.'
Adverbial ad-⎫
juncts of predi- ⎬ ⎰ 'fast,' *qualified by*—1. 'so.'
cate   ⎭   ⎱ 2. 'that I could not overtake him.'

Analysis of (a'').

(*Adverbial clause co-ordinate with* 'so.' § 424.)
Subject,   'I.'
Predicate,   ⎰ *Verb of incomplete predication*, 'could.'
                ⎱ *Complement*, 'overtake.'
Object,   'him.'
Adverbial ad-⎫
junct of predi-⎬ ' not.'
cate,   ⎭

[It seems natural, at first sight, to regard *that* in this sentence as the equivalent of the Latin connective adverb *ut* (*note* on § 291*f*). But the construction in reality sprang out of the use of a substantive clause used in apposition to a demonstrative pronoun ('to *that* [degree]'), which was afterwards replaced by the adverb *so*. The *that*, therefore, had better still be regarded as the subordinative conjunction (§ 424), though the substantive clause has become adverbial.]

529   "He spoke loud that I might hear him."

Here the clause "that I might hear him" is now an adverbial adjunct of 'spoke.' It was originally a substantive clause in apposition to some such noun as *order* or *end* in such a sentence as "He spoke loud in order that I might hear him," or "to the end that I might hear him," where the whole phrase, "in order that I might hear him," forms an adverbial adjunct to the verb *spoke*.

530   (A) [(*b″*) "Whatever the consequence may be] I shall speak the truth."

Analysis of (b″).

(*Adverbial clause of concession attached to* 'shall speak.')
Subject (*with attributive adjunct*),   'the consequence.'
Predicate,   { *Verb of incomplete predication,* 'may.'
              { *Complement of predicate,* 'be.'
              { *Secondary complement* (§ 393), 'whatever.'

531   (C) "He is not so wise [(*a″*) as he is witty]."
Subject,   'he.'
Predicate,   { *Verb of incomplete predication,* 'is.'
             { *Complement,* 'wise.'
Adverbial adjunct of predicate, 'not.'
Adverbial adjuncts of complement,   { 1. 'so.'
                                     { 2. 'as he is witty' (*a″*).

Analysis of (a″).

(*Adverbial clause qualifying* 'wise,' *and co-ordinate with* 'so.')
Subject,   'he.'
Predicate,   { *Verb of incomplete predication,* 'is.'
             { *Complement,* 'witty.'
Adverbial adjunct of complement, 'as.'

532   (X) "Beware {(*d″*) how you meddle with these matters"}.
Subject (*understood*), 'you.'
Predicate,   { *Verb of incomplete predication,* 'be.'
             { *Complement of predicate,* 'ware.'
Adverbial adjunct of complement,   { (*Substantive clause used adverbially,* § 407),
                                    {   'how you meddle with these matters'
                                    {   (*d″*).

Analysis of (d").

Subject,	'you.'
Predicate,	'meddle.'
Adverbial adjuncts of predicate,	{ 1. 'how.' { 2. 'with these matters.'

Examples of the Analysis of Compound Sentences.

533 Ordinary sentences of this kind require no special discussion. All that has to be done is to analyse each of the co-ordinate clauses separately, omitting the conjunctions by which they are connected.

534 There is, however, one class of co-ordinate clauses which require care, namely those in which the relative pronoun has a *continuative* force. (See § 413, and *Analysis of Sentences applied to Latin*, § 165).

535 [(A) "At last it chaunced this proud Sarazin
  To meete me wand'ring;] [(B) who perforce me led
  With him away] [(C) but never yet could win]."

Analysis of (A).

Subject, 'it.'
Attributive adjunct of subject
(infinitive phrase, } 'to meete me wand'ring.'
in apposition to
'it,')
Predicate, 'chaunced.'
Adverbial adjunct of predicate, 'this proud Sarazin.'

The analysis of (B) and (C) presents no difficulty. They are *principal* clauses co-ordinate with (A); *who* being *continuative* in its force (§ 413).

536 [(A) "This is now our doom], [(B) {(m') which if we can sustain and bear,} our supreme foe in time may much remit his anger "].

Here *which* is *continuative* in force (§ 413).

Analysis of (B).

Subject (with adjuncts), 'our supreme foe.'
Predicate, { *Verb of incomplete predication*, 'may.'
  { *Complement*, 'remit.'
Object (with adjunct), 'his anger.'
Adverbial adjuncts of predicate, { 1. (*Adverbial clause*) [(m") 'which —— and bear '].
  { 2. 'in time.'
  { 3. 'much.'

Analysis of (m").

Subject,   'we.'
Predicate,   { *Verb of incomplete predication,* 'can.'
               { *Complement,* 'sustain and bear.'
Object,   'which.'

Contracted Sentences.

537   Before a contracted sentence (§ 445) is analysed, the parts omitted must be expressed at full length.

538   "There has not been a better or more illustrious man than Africanus." In full —

[(A) 'There has not been a better man than Africanus.']
[(B) 'There has not been a more illustrious man than Africanus.']

539   "We perceive that these things not only did not happen, but could not have happened." In full—

[(A) 'We perceive that these things not only did not happen.']
[(B) 'We perceive that these things could not have happened.']

540   "Many instances were related of wise forethought, or firm action, or acute reply on his part, both in the senate and in the forum." In full—

[(A) 'Many instances were related of wise forethought on his part in the senate.']
[(B) 'Many instances were related of wise forethought on his part in the forum.']
[(C) 'Many instances were related of firm action on his part in the senate.']
[(D) 'Many instances were related of firm action on his part in the forum.']
[(E) 'Many instances were related of acute reply on his part in the senate.']
[(F) 'Many instances were related of acute reply on his part in the forum.']

541   "Every assertion is either true or false, either wholly or in part." In full—

[(A) 'Every assertion is true wholly.']
[(B) 'Every assertion is true in part.']
[(C) 'Every assertion is false wholly.']
[(D) 'Every assertion is false in part.']

542   When co-ordinate sentences or clauses are connected by *neither, nor,* the simple negative *not* may be substituted for each in the analysis, the *conjunctive* portion of the words being omitted.

"The man who neither reverences nobleness nor loves goodness, is hateful." In full—
[(A) 'The man who reverences not nobleness is hateful.']
[(B) 'The man who loves not goodness is hateful.']

543 "Whether he succeed or fail, it will not matter to me." In full—
[(A) 'If he succeed, it will not matter to me.']
[(B) 'If he fail, it will not matter to me.']

Elliptical Sentences.

544 An elliptical sentence is one in which something is omitted which is essential to the complete construction of the sentence, but which is readily supplied in thought, without being expressed in words.

545 Contracted sentences are one variety of elliptical sentences, in which what is common to two or more co-ordinate sentences is expressed only once. In the sentences now to be considered that which is omitted is not common to two or more clauses.

546 Relative pronouns and relative adverbs are sometimes omitted.
"That is the book I gave you." In full—"That is the book *which* I gave you."
"That is the house I live in." In full—"That is the house *which* I live in."
"That is the way I came." In full—"That is the way *which* (or *by which*) I came." (Here the *which* or *by which* will be in the adverbial relation to the verb *came*.)
"He left the day I arrived." In full—"He left the day *that* (or *on which*) I arrived." (In this sentence *the day* is in the adverbial relation to *left*; *that* (or *on which*) is in the adverbial relation to *arrived*; and the dependent clause *that I arrived* is an adjective clause qualifying *day*.)

547 The commonest (and the most troublesome) elliptical sentences are those which begin with *as* and *than*. In analysing them care must be taken to ascertain *what the predicate really is* in the dependent clause, and what word the adverbs *as* and *than* qualify. (See §§ 267, 420—422.)

548 "He is as tall as I am."* In full—"He is as tall as I am *tall*."

---

* Clauses beginning with *as* frequently come after the adverb *so* or the demonstrative *as*, with which they are co-ordinate (see § 422). When *as* answers to *so* or *as*, it qualifies a word (expressed or understood) expressing the same sort of idea as is expressed by the word which the *so* or *as* qualifies. This is best seen by the Latin usage. It is not uncommon to find such sentences as the following :—" Qui se oppido munitissimo tamdiu tenuit *quamdiu* in provincia Parthi fuerunt " (Cic. *Fam.* xii. 19)—" Who kept himself in a very strongly fortified town *so long as* the Parthians were in the province." We see from the Latin that the relative adverb *as* (answering to *quam*) really qualifies the word *long* understood (" as long as the

This sentence is analysed precisely in the same way as that in § 531. If we ask what the predicate in the dependent clause is (or what is predicated of *me*), the answer is, "*being tall;*" and moreover not *being tall* simply, but *being tall in a certain degree*, which degree is denoted by the relative adverb *as*, which qualifies *tall* (understood) in the adverbial clause, just as the demonstrative adverb *as* qualifies *tall* in the main clause.

549 "He is taller than I am." In full—(A) "He is taller [(a″) than I am tall"].

Subject,   'he.'
Predicate,   { *Verb of incomplete predication*, 'is.'
           { *Complement of predicate*, 'taller.'
Adverbial adjuncts of predicate,   { (*Adverbial clause*) [(a″) 'than I am tall'].

Analysis of (a″).

Subject,   'I.'
Predicate,   { *Verb of incomplete predication*, 'am.'
           { *Complement of predicate*, 'tall.'
Adverbial adjunct of predicate, 'than.'

It has been explained that the connective adverb *than* originally signified *when* (§ 204, *note*), and in this relative sense was employed to introduce the standard of comparison. The sentence in full is:—"He is taller when I am tall," *i.e.*, 'when my tallness is taken into account.'

550 "He is more industrious than clever." In full—"He is more industrious than *he is* clever."

Here again the way in which the sentence gets its meaning is quite intelligible when the original and proper signification of *than* is understood. It means:—'He is more industrious when he is clever,' *i.e.*, 'when his cleverness is regarded, or taken as a standard,'—'when he has cleverness to serve as a measure of his industry.' The *when* refers not so much to *time* as to *the circumstances of the case*.

Parthians kept themselves *long*, &c.). So again: "Nemo orator *tam multa* ne in Græco quidem otio scripsit, *quam multa* sunt nostra" (Cic. *Orat*. 30)—"No orator has written *so many* things, as our writings are *many*." "Tam magis illa fremens, et tristibus effera flammis, quam magis effuso crudescunt sanguine pugnæ" (Virg. *Æn*. vii. 788). In English we render *tam magis—quam magis* by *so much the more—as;* but the Latin shows that the *as* really qualifies the word *more* (understood). But it is the common practice in Latin (and the universal practice in English) to omit the word qualified by *quam* (English *as*), when it is a'ready expressed in the main clause; as, "Vixit tamdiu quam licuit in civitate bene beateque vivere" (Cic. *de Off*. ii. 12). The same principle is illustrated by such correlatives as *tantus—quantus*, and *talis—qualis*. If *tantus* means *so great, quantus* (though rendered only by *as*) must really mean *as great*.

It may be taken as a general rule that after the relative adverbs *as* and *than* we must supply a word of the same kind of meaning as the word qualified by the simple or demonstrative adverb in the main clause. In Anglo-Saxon we often find the word qualified by the relative adverb expressed, as: *Ic ne mæg swa fela gefon swa fela swa ic mæg gesyllan*: "I cannot catch so many as I can sell (many)" —*Aelf. Coll*.

O

551 "He has not written so much as I have." In full—"He has not written *so much as* I have written *much*." (See § 421, and note on § 549.)

The adverb *as* does not refer to the *manner* of my writing (i.e., it is not an adverb of *manner*, qualifying the verb *have written*), but refers to the *quantity* that I have written (i.e., it is an adverb of *degree*, qualifying the word *much* understood).

552 "He has lived as many years as you have lived months." In full—"He has lived *as many* years *as* you have lived *many* months."

In the adverbial clause *as* is an adverb qualifying *many* (understood), and the whole adverbial clause is co-ordinate with the demonstrative *as* in the main clause.

553 "He has written more letters than you." In full—"He has written more letters than you have written many letters."

It is clear that in the subordinate clause the object of the verb *have written* is not expressed, and yet is requisite to make the sense complete. A transitive verb must have an object (expressed or understood) as well as a subject. And as a comparison is drawn between the *number* of letters written in each case, the object *letters* (understood) must be accompanied by an adjective indicating number. The whole is attached to the predicate in the main clause, denoting the standard of comparison kept in view when the assertion of the main clause is made.

554 "He does not write so well as you." In full—"He does not write *so well* as you write *well*." The adverbial idea which is attached to the predicate in the subordinate clause is not the *manner* (speaking generally) of 'your writing,' but the *degree of goodness* that marks 'your writing.' The idea of *goodness* will be expressed by *well*, and the notion of *degree* by the adverb *as*, which qualifies *well*.

555 "I would as soon die as suffer that." Here it is clear that the word *as* in the subordinate clause does not mark the *manner* of the suffering referred to, but the *degree of readiness* with which 'I would suffer that.' Therefore *as* must qualify an adverb (marking *readiness*), understood. At full length the sentence is, "I would as soon die as (I would soon) suffer that."

556 "I would rather die than suffer that."

The analysis of the preceding sentence will guide us to that of the one before us. At full length it will be, "I would rather die than (I would soon) suffer that." Here *than* ($=$ *when*) qualifies the predicate *would suffer*, and the adverbial clause, '*than I would soon suffer that*,' qualifies the predicate in the main clause.

557 "I saw John as well as Thomas." In full—"I saw John as well as [I saw] Thomas [well]." Here the elliptical adverbial clause '*as Thomas*' qualifies and explains the *as* in the main clause, to which it is therefore in the adverbial relation.

558 "He is not so rich as you think." In full—(A) "He is not so rich [(a") as you think {(a"b) that he is rich "}].

Subject, 'he.'
Predicate, { Verb of incomplete predication, 'is.'
             { Complement of predicate, 'rich.'
Adverbial adjunct of predicate, 'not.'
Adverbial adjuncts of complement, { 1. 'so.'
                                   { 2. (Adverbial clause) [(a") 'as you think that he is rich'].

Analysis of (a").

"As you think that he is rich."
The construction of this clause is the same as though it were "You think that he is so rich." The relative adverb *as* qualifies the adjective *rich*, which is the complement of the predicate in the dependent substantive clause "*that he is rich.*"

559 "He is richer than you suppose." In full—(B) "He is richer [(x") than you suppose that he is rich]."

Subject, 'he.'
Predicate, { Verb of incomplete predication, 'is.'
             { Complement of predicate, 'richer.'
Adverbial adjunct of predicate, } Adverbial clause [(x") 'than you suppose that he is rich'].

Analysis of (x").

Subject, 'you.'
Predicate, 'suppose.'
Object (Substantive clause), { (x"y) 'that he is rich.'}
Adverbial adjunct of predicate, 'than' (= *when*).

Analysis of (x"y).

Subject, 'he.'
Predicate, { Verb of incomplete predication, 'is.'
             { Complement of predicate, 'rich.'

The separation of *than* or *as* from the clause to which it really belongs may be illustrated by such sentences as, "I told him how foolish I thought he was." "He asked me how I thought he looked."

56) "I had rather die than endure such disgrace." In full (C) "I had rather die [(c") than [I would soon] endure such disgrace"].

196   SYNTAX—ANALYSIS OF SENTENCES.

Subject,   'I.'
Predicate,   { *Verb of incomplete predication*, ' had.'
                { *Complement of predicate*, ' rather.' *
Object,   ' die.'
Adverbial adjunct of *the predicate*, 'than [I would soon] endure such disgrace' (c").

Analysis of (c").
Subject,   'I.'
Predicate, ' would endure.'

561 "I am not so foolish as to believe that." In full—(A) "I am not so foolish [(z") as I should be foolish to believe that "].

Here the clause, "As I should —— that," is co-ordinate with *so*, and in the adverbial relation to *foolish*. *As* is in the adverbial relation to the complement *foolish* understood. *To believe that* (i.e., *for believing* that, or *in believing that*) is an adverbial adjunct of the verb *should be*.

562 "I am not such a fool as to believe that." In full—(E) "I am not such a fool [(a") as I should be a fool to believe that "].

Here the elliptical adverbial clause (a") qualifies the adjective *such* The adverb *as* may be taken as qualifying the predicate *should be*.

563 "He looks as if he knew me." In full—"He looks as (he would look) if he knew me."

564 "I agree with you in so far as you adopt his opinion."
Here a comparison is instituted between *the extent* to which 'I agree,' and *the extent* to which 'you adopt his opinion.'
Each clause therefore involves a word denoting *extent*, qualified '

---

* The explanation of this construction is not easy. It is frequently said that *had* is a corruption of *would*. If this were so, the difficulty would vanish: but there is good reason for believing that *had* is quite correct. The analogous construction with *lief* is unquestionably genuine. *E.g.*, "*I had as lief not be, as live to be in awe of such a thing as I myself*"—(Shakspeare, *Julius Cæsar*, i. 2); as also that with the comparative *liefer* or *liever*. Thus we find in Chaucer: "*Ne never had I thing so lief, ne liever*"—(*Frank. Tale*). This last example gives us a good clue to the construction. *Lief* and *liever* are *adjectives* (not *adverbs*) agreeing with the object of the verb *have*, which in this construction is a verb of incomplete predication (*Gr.* 391, 395), so that *lief* and *liefer*, or *liever*, are its *complements*. (Compare the phrases *lieb haben* and *lieber haben*, in German.) At present the use of the phrase *to have lief* is restricted to cases where the object of the verb *have* is a verb in the infinitive mood, and the adjective *lief* is qualified by the adverb *as*. The use of the comparative *liefer* or *liever* is obsolete. Now, in old English, we find *rathe* (*early* or *ready*); comp. *rather*, superl. *rathest*, used as adjectives. Milton speaks of *the rathe primrose*, and Spenser of *the rather* (i.e., *earlier*) *lambs*. Thus, by taking *rather* as an adjective (giving the idea of *preference*, which easily springs out of the radical notion of the word), we get in the phrase *to have rather* a construction precisely analogous to that in *to have lief* (that is, to *hold* or regard as *dear* or *desirable*), or *to have liefer*: *have* being a verb of incomplete predication, *rather* its complement, and the dependent infinitive the object of *have*. Let it be observed that *I had sooner do so and so* is bad English. *Sooner* is not an adjective. We must say, *I would sooner*, &c. *I would rather* is good English, because *rather* is an adverb as well as an adjective. In the phrase *I had rather*, the verb *had* is in the subjunctive mood.

respectively by a demonstrative and a relative adverb of degree, by means of which the comparison is effected. At full length, therefore, the sentence will be, "I agree with you in so far as you adopt his opinion (far)."

565 "He knows that, inasmuch as I have told him." That is to say, the extent to which it is the fact that he knows that, is equivalent to the extent to which it is the fact that I have told him. The relative *as*, therefore, in the subordinate clause, qualifies a word (understood) denoting extent, and the whole adverbial clause is co-ordinate with the demonstrative *as* in the phrase *in as much*; the phrase *in as much* being in the adverbial relation to the verb *knows*.

566 "I cannot give you so much as five pounds." In full—"I cannot give so much as five pounds (are much)." (In Latin the correlatives *tantum* and *quantum* would be used; and *quantum* shows that the idea of quantity belongs as essentially to the dependent as to the main clause.)

567 "I cannot give you more than five pounds." The analogy of the preceding sentence shows that we must fill up the ellipsis thus:—"I cannot give you more than five pounds are much."

568 "Our habits are costlier than Lucullus wore."
Here again the original sense of *than* (=*when*) gives us an easy explanation of the ellipsis. 'Our habits are costlier than (when) Lucullus wore costly habits;' *i.e.*, 'Taking Lucullus's wearing of costly habits as a standard of comparison, our habits are costlier.'

569 "More than twenty men were killed." That is, "More men than twenty (are many) were killed." In other words:—"When twenty are many (or, if twenty are regarded as many), more were killed."

570 "Whether he likes it or not, I shall do it." This is a contracted elliptical sentence.
Whether is equivalent to *if either* (Latin, *sive*, i.e., *si vel*). At full length we get two co-ordinate sentences.
(A) "If he likes it, I shall do it."
(B) "If he does not like it, I shall do it."

571 a "He cannot so much as read." In full—"He cannot (do) much as (to) read (is much)." The elliptical adverbial clause '*read*' is co-ordinate with the adverb *so*, and the connecti adverb *as* qualifies *much* understood.

572 b "He was fond of all such amusements as cricket and rowing.'
As, in the elliptical clause *as cricket and rowing are*, must be taken a a substitute for a relative pronoun (§ 412), and so forming the comple ment of the verb of incomplete predication *are*. The whole clause is in the attributive relation to *amusement*, and is co-ordinate with *such*. It has been before explained that the proper correlative of *such* (= swa-lic) is *which* (= hwi-lic). It is for this *which* that *as* does duty,

572 c "Which when Beelzebub perceived, than whom, Satan except, none higher sat, with grave aspect he rose."

The objective case *whom* is anomalous, though the usage of the best writers sanctions it. If it were grammatically correct, it would also be correct to say, 'None sat higher than *him.*' In analysis 'than whom' must be treated as a mere *adverbial phrase*, it being impossible to supply the ellipsis so as to expand it into an adverbial clause.

572 d. "Let us go."

Here *let* is the second person plural of the imperative mood of the verb *let*, which is a verb of incomplete predication, having *us* for its object and *go* for its complement, the subject of the imperative being, as usual, understood. Just as in the case of the objective complement (§395), of which in fact this is one variety, we have an attributive notion (§294), denoted by the infinitive *go*, attached to the object *us*. It is a blending of the objective and the infinitive complement. The grammatical relations of the words in the imperative sentence, 'Let [ye] him go' are the same as in the assertive sentence 'I let him go' (§357). 'I let him go' does not differ (grammatically) from 'I made him go,' which is closely analogous to 'I made him angry,' the only difference being that the attributive idea attached to the object is expressed by a verb in the one case, and an adjective in the other. The class of attributive words includes both (§294).

PARSING.

573 The preceding system of analysis still leaves us with groups of words in many cases, into the mutual relations of which it does not enter. When a minute account of each word of a sentence is given, including not only its syntactical relation to other words, but also its etymological inflections and accidents, the process is termed *parsing*. Two or three examples will show the mode in which it should be performed better than any system of rules.

574 "I told him that I did not know who had taken the red book that lay on the table."

I.—Personal pronoun of the first person, singular number, in the nominative case, because it is the subject of the verb *told*.

told.—Transitive verb: in the active voice, indicative mood, past indefinite tense, first person, singular number: in the predicative relation to *I*, with which it agrees in number and person.

him.—Personal pronoun of the third person and the masculine gender; in the singular number and objective case, standing in the adverbial relation to the verb *told*, of which it is the indirect object.

that.—Subordinative conjunction, connecting the substantive clause, "*I did not know—table*," with the verb *told*.

I.—Personal pronoun of the first person, in the singular number and nominative case: subject of the verb *did*.

did.—Auxiliary verb, in the active voice, indicative mood, past indefinite tense, first person singular; in the predicative relation to *I*, with which it agrees in number and person.

not.—Adverb of negation, modifying the verb *did*.

know.—Transitive verb, in the active voice, infinitive mood, imperfect tense; depending on the verb *did*.

who.—Interrogative pronoun, in the singular number, third person, and nominative case, being the subject of the verb *had taken*.

had taken.—Transitive verb; in the active voice, indicative mood, past perfect tense, third person, singular number; in the predicative relation to the pronoun *who*, with which it agrees in number and person.

the.—Definite article, in the attributive relation to *book*.

red.—Qualitative adjective, in the positive degree of comparison; in the attributive relation to the noun *book*.

book.—Common noun, of the neuter gender; in the singular number and objective case, standing in the objective relation to the verb *had taken*.

that.—Relative pronoun, of the neuter gender, third person and singular number, to agree with its antecedent *book*, and in the nominative case because it is the subject of the verb *lay*.

lay.—Intransitive verb; in the active voice, indicative mood, past indefinite tense, third person, singular number, in the predicative relation to *that*, with which it agrees in number and person.

on.—Preposition governing the noun *table*.

the.—Definite article, in the attributive relation to the noun *table*.

table.—Common noun, of the neuter gender; in the singular number, objective case, governed by the preposition *on*.

EXERCISES.

The Numbers placed at the commencement of the Exercises are those of the Paragraphs in the Grammar to which they relate.

EXERCISES ON THE NOUN.

34   Write down the abstract nouns which correspond to the following adjectives :—

Pure, simple, good, bad, worthy, splendid, just, meek, temperate, large, wide, broad, slow, quick, red, blue, sour, sharp, sweet, distant, near, soft, able, innocent, durable, brilliant, merry, brief, white, long, able, humble, popular, obstinate, wicked, pious, poor, sad, infirm, jovial, silent, wise, prudent, abundant.

Write down the adjectives which correspond to the following abstract nouns :—

Nobility, stupidity, fickleness, suppleness, height, depth, acidity, dependence, sleepiness, greenness, rigidity, ductility, sonority, infirmity, patience, condescension, prosperity, wisdom, elegance, strength, valour, magnanimity, elevation, candour, durability, insipidity, heroism, monstrosity, grandeur, width, breadth, senility.

38   Write down in one column all the masculine nouns in the following list ; in another column all the feminine nouns ; in a third column all the neuter nouns ; and in a fourth column all the nouns of common gender :—

Cow, horse, dog, man, girl, ship, house, Robert, Jane, London, Thames, goose, hen, cock, bird, sheep, pig, boar, fox, uncle, nephew, John, vixen, lass, ox, form, desk, tree, servant, footman, maid, boy, nursemaid, baby, slate, gander, elephant, tiger, lioness, Maria, France, Napoleon, cart, infant, brother, lady, pen, lord, king, sovereign, queen, ruler, judge, author, cousin, sister, mother, aunt, box, speaker, William.

67   Write out the following sentences, and draw one line under the nouns which are in the possessive singular and two lines under those which are the possessive plural, one line over those in the nominative case, and two lines over those which are in the objective case.   Also point out on what nouns the possessive cases depend :—

He admires the lady's beauty.   He saw the queen's courtiers.

They live in kings' courts. The king's palace is large. The lady's robe was torn. I saw some ladies in the room. The ladies' dresses were handsome. The boys' exercises are badly written. I saw the boys at play. The boy's father has arrived. She made the women's dresses. Where is my wife's purse? The men slew their wives. The men heard of their wives' danger. Call the girls in. Give me the girls' books. Hold the horse's head. The horses are drinking water. The horses' hoofs are hard. He is paring the horses' hoofs. He stole John's sister's books. John stole his sister's books. The men's wages are due. My father's house is large. I saw John's brothers. He ran away from his father's house.

80. Write out the following sentences, and draw one line under the nouns which are the *direct* objects of verbs, and two lines under those which are *datives* or *indirect* objects:—

Give Mary an apple. He gave the dog a bone. He gave the dog to his cousin. My father sent John to school. My uncle sent John a cake. The policeman took the man to prison. The kind woman took the poor man a loaf. Mary fetched the beer. Fetch your mother a chair. John fetched Tom a slap on the head. He brought the runaway home again. My father brought my brother a watch from town. Pour the water into the basin. Pour your cousin out a glass of wine. He wrote his father a long letter. Sir Walter Scott wrote 'Marmion.' He handed the lady to her carriage. Hand that gentleman a glass.

EXERCISES ON THE ADJECTIVE.

85--98 Write down in a column the adjectives in the following sentences, and write opposite each the noun which it qualifies; also point out to which class each adjective belongs:—

Give me two shillings. He rides a black horse. Wise men never waste time. Twenty men were killed. He heard of the poor man's death. The fine ladies' dresses are torn. The ladies' fine dresses are torn. He cropped the black horse's tail. The brown horse has a black tail. That man has two horses. Every man has two ears and one mouth. They travelled the whole day. Several carriages have passed this house. Take another seat. All men admire generous actions. No man likes pain. Which dish do you prefer? What books have you read? We have read these books. Do not tell such lies. Such conduct deserves punishment. He succeeded the first time. Each man received the same sum. Much precious time was lost. Many brave men were killed. That sentence is on the second page of the third volume. What nonsense you talk.

87. In the following sentences point out whether the adjective is in the attributive or in the predicative relation to the noun which it qualifies, paying particular attention to the cases in which the noun is not expressed:—

There is a white cow. He gave me ten apples. The apples are ripe. Which boy is the cleverest? They seem happy. He feels ill. Idle boys must be punished. The tallest boys are not always the strongest. He has many kind friends. The days are short. The nights are longest in winter. It is hottest in summer. We have the coldest weather in winter. My cousin is named Jane. A man riding at full gallop has passed the house. The soldiers, wearied with the march, halted. The soldiers are weary. Who gave you that pretty book? It is the prettiest I ever saw. What news is there? The reports are alarming. The man spread an alarming report. These mistakes are vexatious.' The sleeping lion was aroused by the fierce dogs. The lion, sleeping in his den, was aroused. I saw the boys sleeping. The boys are sleepy. Those pears are the ripest. Those pears are ripe. When will the corn be ripe? Which is the way? Which wine is the best? The first volume is the best. The second volume is tedious. What time I am afraid I will trust in thee.

99 In the following sentences supply the nouns which are understood:—

I have read these books, but I have not read those. All go to one place. The meek shall inherit the earth. Which of these books have you read? Take this apple and give me that. He was punished for this. This is pretty. The poor suffer more than the rich. This picture is the prettiest. Which boy is the cleverest? Which of these two boys is the cleverer? My book is the prettiest. That is the prettiest book. John is the cleverest in the class. She is the prettiest of all my cousins. These are my children. That is John's hat. My apple is the biggest.

104—116 Write down the comparative and superlative degrees of the following adjectives, or their substitutes:—

Large, great, high, fierce, lovely, full, tame, rich, happy, handsome, common, merry, near, gay, cold, holy, healthy, bright, cold, big, red, rich, monstrous, winsome, sad, mad, beautiful, fresh, dull, hearty, quarrelsome, blithe, splendid, clever, idle, gentle.

Write down the positive degree of the following adjectives:—

Prettier, rudest, sweetest, justest, gentler, finest, steeper, tenderer, worst, slenderest, duller, sweetest, gentlest, wittier, slower, tidiest, wealthier, handsomest, sprightlier, mightiest, nastiest, rudest, brightest, crudest, better.

EXERCISES ON THE PRONOUNS.

128 Point out what nouns the pronouns are used for in the following exercise:—

The master praised the boy because he was attentive. Children are loved when they are good. The boys have lost their ball. If the thief is caught he will be punished. Jane has found her book. The horse ran away with his rider. Parents love their children. When the boys have learnt their lessons, they must say them to the master. The men will be paid when they have finished their work. The woman has lost her child. When the girl was old enough, her mother sent her to school. The girls have lost their needles; they will never find them again. The kitten was biting its mother's tail. If the man leaves his glove behind him, his dog will fetch it for him. The boy said that he had found the shilling. John cried out, 'I have found a bird's nest.' Jane said she had finished her task. George, you said you had learnt your lessons.

130 Write out the following sentences and draw one line under the substantive pronouns, and two lines under the adjective pronouns:—

I told him that. He heard that we had arrived. Who said so? Which wine do you prefer? Whose pen is this? Give me that book. I told him myself. Thou art the man. She is mad. What business is it of yours? One cannot but admire his perseverance. We ride every day. Who is that man whom you were speaking to? Our house was burned down. His father has come and is talking with mine. You may sit on either side.

129 Point out which of the adjective pronouns in the following sentences are used adjectively, and which are used substantively:—

On what day do you set out? I do not like this book; give me that. That is the style which I admire most. I could not find that book which you wanted. Will you have these or those? He gave twopence to each of them. I do not love either of them. That is what I said. I cannot eat this meat: have you no other? You may have whichever ball you like. What happiness is in store for you! Tell the others what I said. What lovely weather! Pay me the money which you owe me.

148—167 Write out the following sentences, and draw one line under the relative pronouns, and two lines under their antecedents:—

He who does wrong deserves punishment. Give this money to the poor man whose child was killed. They that seek me early shall find me. Whose is this book that I have found? Is that the man whom you spoke of? That is not the book which I gave you. You are not the person whom I expected. Which is the author whom you admire most? He departed the very day that I arrived. It is that that grieves me. It is this that I fear. That which you tell me is incredible. That which is false and mean should be despised. Those who love wisdom will find it. Come and see the pony that my father has given to my brother, who has just left the school at which he was for so many years. They are but faint-hearted whose courage fails in time of danger. Blessed is the man whose transgression is forgiven. Happy are they in whose midst peace reigns. He doth sin that doth belie the dead. Whose hatred is covered by deceit, his wickedness shall be showed before the whole congregation. He to-day that sheds his blood with me shall be my brother. "This is the priest all shaven and shorn that married the man all tattered and torn that kissed the maiden all forlorn that milked the cow with the crumpled horn that tossed the dog that worried the cat that killed the rat that ate the malt that lay in the house that Jack built."

166 Supply relative pronouns where they are understood in the following sentences :—

Pay me the money you owe me. Which was the road you took? Play me the tunes I love. Be reconciled with the man you have offended. That is not the book I gave you. I am come to pay for the goods I bought yesterday. He has not answered the letter I wrote him. Have you received the money I sent you? He is not the man I expected.

143, 144, 148 In the following sentences point out when *that* is a relative pronoun and when it is a demonstrative pronoun :—

There is that man again. "There is that scattereth and yet increaseth." He to-day that sheds his blood with me shall be my brother. That man is guilty. What was that noise that I heard? Who is that man? Is that the horse that you bought? Whose is that book that you have in your hand? Avoid that which is sinful. Write down the words that I dictate. You said that you did not know. That is not true. Who is he that wishes for more men? Tell that boy to be quiet All the goods that he sells are bad. Cease that noise. What was that that you were saying? It is that that I fear. That is the hope that supports me. Show me the man that dares to climb that height. The teacher says that that 'that' that that boy made use of was unnecessary.

–160 Write out the following sentences; draw one line under the relative pronouns, and two lines under the interrogative pronouns :—

Which is the shortest road? Have you read the book which I gave you? Do you know what he said? Whom did he refer to? Who said so? Is that the man who said so? Do you know who did this? Did you see which way he went? Is that what you said? Tell me what you said? I want to know who broke the window. They do not know what to do. What is the matter with you? Do you know what that means? Did you hear what I said? By what means can we succeed? On what day will you come? Why do you tell me what I know already? When did you receive what I sent you? Who is there? Do you know the gentleman who has just arrived? Whose hat is this? Can you tell me whose hat this is? Do you know the man whose house was robbed? Will you tell me whom I am to give this to?

Write out the following sentences; draw one line under the relative and interrogative pronouns which are in the nominative case, and two lines under those which are in the objective case :—

Where is the man who did this? He is a man whom I despise. Do not trust a man whom all shun. He is a man in whom I have no confidence. Where is the pen which I gave you? Who has taken the pen which lay on my desk? I will show you the horse which I bought yesterday. I do not like books that convey no instruction. This is the man whom I sent for. That is the book which I sent you for. Give me the book that I asked for. They that seek me early shall find me. Have you seen the ship which has just arrived? There is the ship of which my uncle is captain. To which of these persons did you refer? That is the book which I spoke of. He is the very man that I was looking for. I love them that love me. He purchased the house which his brother had built. He no longer possesses the estate which once belonged to him. He avoids everything that interferes with his studies. What did you ask for? What did he say? What ails you? What induced you to say so? Which of them is right? Which of these do you want? Which pleases you most? Take whichever you like best. I will do whatever I like. He likes whatever is manly. He likes everything that I like. He likes everything that pleases me. He likes everything that I am fond of. He admires whatever is pretty. Where are the flowers that you promised to send me? To whom did he sell the house that he built? He has lost everything that belonged to him. Repeat what I said. Tell me what you want. Tell me who did that. Tell me what ails you. Read what follows. Correct the mistake which he made. Correct the mistakes which occur in that sentence. Send me the cake which you promised me. Have you received the letter that I sent you? That is not a dress that becomes her.

EXERCISES ON THE VERB.

182 Make a list of twenty transitive, and of twenty intransitive verbs, and make sentences illustrating the use of them.

182, 183 In the following examples point out whether the verb is used transitively, intransitively, or reflectively :—

He speaks. He speaks French. He talks too loud. He is talking nonsense. He is eating. He is eating his dinner. He rides to town every day. I ride a black horse. He plays too eagerly. He plays the flute. He is working a sum. Yeast makes beer work. He strikes the ball. The snake twists and turns about. The earth turns round. He has twisted his ankle. He turned the man out of the room. The boy is spinning a top. The top spins round. I smell a rat. The rose smells sweet. He is resting. I am resting myself. He gave up the game. You had better give in. The town surrendered. The commandant surrendered the town. The undertaking promises well. He promised to come. His return rejoiced the hearts of his parents. We all rejoiced at his success. The ship struck on a rock. I struck myself with a hammer. He struck the ball hard. He has not shaved this morning. The barber shaved me yesterday. Get your umbrella. Get out of my way. I withdraw my claim. The deputation withdrew. Every one laughed. They laughed him to scorn. He ran a race. He ran a thorn into his finger. Keep where you are. Keep your place. Get up. He roused up at the sound. He launched out into all sorts of extravagance. The horsemen spread over the plain. The robbers soon dispersed.

186 Express the sense of each of the following sentences by

means of the passive voice of the verbs that are used; as, "He struck the boy," "The boy was struck by him."

The cat killed the mouse. The soldiers are defending the city. This does not surprise me. We love our parents. He hates meanness. The man has earned the reward. That surprised me. This will please you. I had not expected this. We shall refuse your request. We have received a letter. We heard the thunder. We are writing French exercises. He had cut his own throat. Idleness will clothe a man with rags. Did that boy make your nose bleed?

Express the sense of each of the following sentences by means of the active voice of the verbs that are used:—

We were overtaken by a storm. Has my letter been received by you? He was killed by the blow. The pig has been killed by the butcher. The letter was never received by us. Thou wilt be loved by all. I was being pushed by my neighbour. Has a new house been built by your brother? Was your coat torn by that boy? Mice are caught by cats. By whom has your coat been torn? By whom shall you be accompanied? By how many soldiers will the queen be escorted?

191, 192 Point out which verbs in the following sentences are in the infinitive mood, drawing one line under those in the simple infinitive, and two lines under those in the gerundive infinitive:—

Did you speak? Shall you go? We shall soon be there. Let me see it. Dare you say so? We heard him speak. You must depart. I let him go on. You need not stay. I cannot see. He could not reply. If I might but see him. You may be sure of it. Did you say that? I do not know. Do not let it fall. Do tell me his name. He does not hear. I can easily do that. I will try to do so. I long to depart. We hoped to succeed. To please you is our constant endeavour. We can but fail if we try.

192 Write out the following sentences. Draw one line under those gerundial infinitives which are the subjects of other verbs, two lines under those which are the objects of other verbs, and three lines under those which are used to denote the purpose or cause of some action or state:—

He came to fetch me. He went to see what was the matter. To be slothful in business is not the way to succeed. He hopes to hear from you soon. Show me how to do it. I desire to see you. It is all very well to say you can't, but you must try to do it. It is easy to see that he knows nothing about it. He dislikes to be kept waiting. We sent him to buy some bread. His object is to tire out my patience. That water is not fit to drink. Help me to carry this. I am happy to find you so much better. I am glad to hear it. The boys had a long task to do. I was not prepared to hear that news. He pretended to be asleep. He did his best to ruin me. He is anxious to do his duty. He delights to tease me. The master called the boy to say his lesson. I love to watch the return of spring. I am charmed to welcome you to my house. Have you come to stay with us? He is too clever to make such a mistake. Such a fellow is not fit to live. I am sorry to hear such an account of him.

193—195 Point out which verbs in the following sentences are in the indicative mood, and which are in the subjunctive mood:—

Oh that it were with me as in days that are past. How gladly would I have done it. He did so gladly. Though he slay me, yet will I trust in him. If this be granted, the proof easily follows. If this were true, he would not deny it. If he had said so, I should have believed him. He did not deny it. Unless you try hard, you will not succeed. Though hand join in hand, the wicked shall not go unpunished. I could not open the door when I tried. I could not open the door if I tried. Except ye repent, ye shall all likewise perish. He would not answer me when I called. He would persist in his contumacy, in spite of all I could say. If you would lend me fifty pounds, I should be much obliged to you. I would not go, even if they were to send for me. If that really happened, it was a great calamity. If you had the money when he asked for it, you ought to have paid him. If I had the money, I would give it to you. If that was the case, why did you not tell me?

197—202 Point out when the imperfect participle is used in the following examples, and when the gerund:—

I see a man riding on horseback. A man passed by, running at full speed. I like reading. He hates lying. A lying witness ought to be punished. He gained his ends by using false pretences. In keeping thy commandments there is great reward. The officer fell while leading his troops into action. See yonder bark, struggling against the wind and tide. The centre of the group was occupied by a figure holding a globe. We fell in with a ship sailing to America. We arrived there first by taking a shorter route. He is fond of improving his mind. He lives by begging from his friends. He went about, begging from his friends.

Make ten other sentences containing gerunds and ten containing imperfect participles.

206 Change the verbs in the following sentences successively into all the other eight primary tenses, without altering the voice of the verb:—

I am writing a letter. He sells the house. We spent the money. He will have finished his task. I had travelled from London to York. He buys corn. I was persuaded to give him permission. We shall be attacked by robbers. We had been led by a short road. Are you learning French? Is he not telling a falsehood? The money has been counted.

EXERCISES ON THE ADVERB,

THE PREPOSITION, AND THE CONJUNCTION.

262—264 Write down in separate columns the simple adverbs and the connective adverbs in the following list:—

Well, now, to-morrow, here, when, where, wherefore, how, therefore, yet, yes, quickly, as, so, quite, all, however, generally, enough, perhaps, often, early, little, twice, very, not, namely, above, whither, then, thither, once, immediately, why, thence, whereon, thus, while, within, that, than, wherein.

264—270 Distinguish the connective from the interrogative adverbs in the following sentences, and point out the verb which each adverb qualifies:—

When did you arrive? We came when you did. Where is your brother? I will tell you the news when I see you. How do you do? Whence did you get that report? He worked while we played. He asked me how I had travelled. Whither are you going? Whence came these? We visited the place where the great battle was fought. I will follow you whithersoever you go. How we got out again I scarcely know. That is the reason why I did not write sooner. Why do you tell such stories? Wherever he lives he will be happy. We came directly when we heard you call. When did you find it? Why did you not come sooner? How can one believe him? Wherefore did they leave the town? I will tell you why they left. Tell me how you arranged the matter. Where did you lose your purse?

269 Write out the following sentences, and draw one line under the adjectives, and two lines under the adverbs:—

Do not speak so fast. I am going by a fast train. The mill is fast by the brook. He is a fast runner. Go on faster. Run quicker. He advanced with quicker steps. What a hard lesson! He hits hard. The tree is hard by the pond. He tried hard. My bed is hard. He is a just man. We were just starting. He did just what I expected. That decision was right. He lay right across the doorway. They advanced right up the hill. He is the worst boy in the class. He writes worst. I love John best. He is my best friend. She is less beautiful than her sister. He received less money. He is the most studious boy I ever saw. John will get most praise.

283, 284 Write down in separate columns the prepositions that denote place, the prepositions that denote time, and the prepositions that denote causality.

In the following sentences point out the prepositions and the words that are governed by them, and state in each case whether the preposition marks the relation of a thing to a thing, of an action to a thing, or of an attribute to a thing:—

There is a horse in the meadow. I am fond of music. He

EXERCISES. 209

rejoices in iniquity. A man on horseback has just passed. He is afraid of the dog. He killed the man with a sword. There is a man with a cocked hat. He is merry without being rude. Those men quarrelled with each other. They bade adieu to each other. Do not stand before me. Do not place yourself between me and the light. He is just in all his dealings. Such a master will be served with readiness. Come away from the window. The book is under the table. I see a book under the table. I see a book lying under the table. They are going to church. Stand behind me. Get off that chair. His conduct is beyond all praise. Do not come near me. This is past bearing.

284 Distinguish the prepositions from the adverbs in the following sentences:—

He got up behind. There is a garden behind the house. Do not lag behind. I told you that before. He departed before my arrival. I came the day before yesterday. I could not come before. The earth turns round. Run round the table. Open that box, there is a book inside. You will find a book inside that box. He repeated that over and over. I see a picture over the chimney-piece. Sit down. He ran down the hill. Run after him. That comes after. Go along. He planted a row of trees along the river. That is above my reach. God reigns above. He is beneath my notice. From the summit of the hill we saw the villages lying beneath. The box was painted within and without. He met with troubles without end. That is the hill that he ran down. There is the church which we go to. Yonder is the village that he comes from. That is the piece which I cut off. That is the man whom I spoke of. That is the servant whom I packed off. Sing me the song that I am so fond of. Here is the box, but where is the book which I put inside? That is the number which I wrote down. Which is the tree that you climbed up? He knocked down the pillar which I had set up.

259, &c. Write out the following examples, and draw one line under the prepositions, two under the adverbs, and three under the conjunctions:—

Though I am poor, yet I am contented. He is rich, nevertheless he is unhappy. They are poor, because they are extravagant. He is industrious, and consequently he is successful. The man is neither wealthy nor wise. I believed, therefore have I spoken. Unless you try, you will not succeed. Except ye repent, ye shall all likewise perish. I will behave so as to please my parents. As you say so, I must believe it. Tell me why you did that? Where thou dwellest, I will dwell. He is rich and also generous. He cannot but grieve, for he has lost his best friend. I do not care whether you go or stay. Since you say so, I believe it. I have not seen him since last week. I have never heard of him since. This is for you. I honour him, for he is a brave man. He invited me, and accordingly I went. John came, and likewise William. If you do that, you will suffer for it. There is nobody but me at home. You may go, but I will stay.

143, 148, 288, 289 Point out when *that* in the following sentences

P

is a demonstrative pronoun, when it is a relative pronoun, and when it is a conjunction:—

He said that he had not done it. I heard that he had arrived. Look at that star. I am so troubled that I cannot speak. He does that that he may vex me. He is the very man that I want. I am sure that he said so. That is certain. He is so lazy that he never does anything. His indignation was such that he could scarcely speak. I am sure that you never read that book that I gave you that you might study it. He says that we shall never succeed in that attempt. I am afraid that he says that, that he may deceive me. It is very strange that none of them heard it. He went to London in order that he might find a situation.

Make twenty other sentences in which *that* is used at least twice in different senses.

362, 372 Distinguish the attributive adjuncts of substantives in the following examples from the adverbial adjuncts of verbs:—

I see a horse in the field. He gathered the primroses by the river. She laid the book on the table. She admired the book on the table. I called on my neighbour who lives over the way. Our neighbours over the way have been very kind. We rely on your promise. Reliance on his promises is useless. Put not your trust in princes. Do your duty to your neighbour. What is my duty to my neighbour? He adhered to his determination to make the attempt. He is too feeble to make the attempt. He is not rich enough to buy the house. He gave him his best wine to drink. The place abounds in good water to drink. He has neither food to eat nor raiment to wear. Do you see that man on horseback? He has given up riding on horseback. He rode to town on horseback.

Analysis of Simple Sentences.

493 a Divide the following sentences into two parts, the first part consisting of the logical subject (*i.e.*, the *grammatical* subject, with all the adjuncts belonging to it), the second of the logical predicate (*i.e.*, the verb and all that is attached to it).

The old church has fallen into ruins. The brave soldiers defended their post to the last. Fine, warm weather followed rain. A rich old uncle left him all his property. A stitch in time saves nine. The most difficult tasks are overcome by perseverance. The palace of the prince was set on fire. A horseman, wrapped in a huge cloak, entered the yard. The rent in his coat was made by an old nail. The laughing children sported round his knee. Place yourself in my situation. The horse, terrified by the lightning, ran away at full speed. Dismayed at the prospect, they beat a retreat.

493 b Take the preceding sentences, and separate the grammatical subject and its adjuncts in each. Specify also of what the

adjuncts consist (§ 390). Do the same with the following examples:—

The owner of that estate is a fortunate man. The man's abject misery moved my compassion. A man on horseback passed me. The ancestors of this family were renowned. Water for drinking was very scarce. Disgusted by so many acts of baseness, the man's friends all deserted him. Does your uncle, the doctor, know of this? Whence did the author of that book get his materials? Who in the world told you that? Every finite verb in a sentence must have a subject. John's account of the affair alarmed me. My brother John told me that. My cousin, the inventor of this machine, is dead.

Make or find twelve sentences in which the grammatical subject is enlarged (§ 388), and state in each case of what the enlargement consists.

9 3 c In the following sentences separate the logical predicate into its component parts:—

John gave me a shilling yesterday (§ 372, 4). I met the man in the street. I saw a man on horseback* just now. I saw the occurrence through a gap in the wall. To-day I shall help the men mowing the barley. I shall not go out of doors all day. Did you finish your Greek exercise during my absence? Send the fellow out of the house directly. I desire nothing better. I desire nothing more ardently. I told him my opinion pretty plainly. They have already tried the path over the mountains. He has already returned me all the money (§ 372, 4). Why have you kept this intelligence so long from me?

493 d Take the preceding sentences, and separate the objects of the verbs from their attributive adjuncts. Do the same with the following sentences:—

We heard the sound of the horn reverberating among the rocks. Everybody admires John's little sister. Who has not admired a noble ship sailing over the waves? Have you read this author's last work yet? The man struck the poor little boy on the head (§ 372, 2). The master praised the boy at the top of the class (§ 362, 4). I saw a soldier on horseback. I walked through the river on foot. The farmers want dry, warm weather for a month. He borrowed fifty pounds for a year. We have just bought a calf a month old. This general has just terminated a war of ten years' duration. Do you see that horse in the meadow?

e In the following sentences separate the complex predicate into its component parts, and specify whether the complement is a Subjective Complement, an Objective Complement, or an Infinitive Complement. (See §§ 393, 395).

---

* Observe that this does not indicate *where the act of seeing took place.*

He grew rich suddenly. He called the man a liar. They became very poor. The wine tastes sweet. I am not happy. He is called John. He is thought wise. We do not deem the occurrence unfortunate. That step was deemed imprudent. His friends thought him insane. The number cannot be reckoned. He ought not to say so. The tradesman was declared insolvent. Nothing is more hateful. Nothing can be more abominable. I wish the boy safe back again. You may play in the garden. You must not touch that. They cannot escape The prisoner was declared guilty. We consider this course expedient. He came laughing into the room. The dog ran away howling. She looks very pretty. He stood petrified with horror. We are wont to follow our own inclinations too much. He is said to have poisoned his brother. He lives happy enough in his poverty. His threats were rendered ineffectual by the measures adopted. I am sure of pleasing you in this.

Make a sentence with each of the following transitive verbs, and then enlarge the predicate, 1. With an object; 2. With an object and an adverbial adjunct. Thus: *He loves. He loves his parents. He loves his parents with all his heart.*

Strike. Speak. Love. Stretch. Help. Touch. See. Lead. Draw. Hate. Feel. Slay. Join. Build. Govern. Raise.

Take the sentences formed in the last exercise, and enlarge the object in each with two or more attributive adjuncts.

493 *f*, 494—505 Give the complete analysis of the following sentences :—

No complete survey of the country having been made, it is impossible to state accurately the amount of cultivated land. Did you ever hear a full account of that adventure? Virtue and happiness go hand in hand. Not being acquainted with the facts of the case, I must decline pronouncing an opinion. Full many a flower is born to blush unseen. In coming to a decision on this point, we must be guided solely by the evidence before us. The host himself no longer shall be found careful to see the mantling bliss go round. Teach erring man to spurn the rage of gain. Downward they move, a melancholy band. He used a strong stick to support his feeble steps. I have experienced nothing but kindness at his hands. We can but hope for the best. There is nothing but roguery to be found in villainous man. There live not three good men unhanged in England. For mine own part, my lord, I could be well contented to be there, in respect of my love to your house. Considering all this . (§ 283), the escape of so many is astonishing. Except my brother, no one was in the room at the time. I have too much to do* to stay here. He did not give the boys enough to eat. I am doubtful of the wisdom of this proceeding. It is impossible to understand† such nonsense. The heat of the climate renders it almost impossible

---

* *To do* forms an attributive adjunct of *much*. *To stay* is an adverbial adjunct of *have*.
† *To understand*, &c., is in apposition to *it*.

to work. I left him almost speechless. I found this flower in the hedge. I found him at the point of death. Who taught you those bad manners? (§ 372, 4). Fill me the goblet full. He plucked me ope his doublet. I should blush to be o'erheard and taken napping so (§ 192). To tell you the truth, I don't believe that How sweet the moonlight sleeps upon the bank! What can skill avail us? What can we do but wait? (§ 505). Who but a fool would talk like that? (§ 504). Let me die the death of the righteous (§ 372, 4). I have fought a good fight. Whose fault was that but his own? How like a fawning publican he looks!

Analysis of Complex Sentences

1. *Sentences containing Substantive Clauses.*

506—517 Analyse the following sentences, having first enclosed the substantive clauses in brackets:—

I know that your story cannot be true. That he was the instigator of the crime is most certain. I fear thou play'dst most foully for it. Thence it is, that I to your assistance do make love. It is scarcely to be expected that he will succeed in that attempt. Tell me how old you are. I wish to know when this message was delivered. It is my opinion that you ought to adopt a different plan. The fact that you vouch for the truth of this statement is enough for me. It is a question among doctors which mode of treatment is the most successful. But that I knew him to be a man of honour, I could not have believed the story (§ 517). He told me he knew all about it (§ 406). I will spend my last shilling but I will bring him to justice (§§ 403, 517). Tell me why you think so. Show me where you hid yourself. In case you succeed, write to me. Except ye repent, ye shall all likewise perish (§§ 283, 372, 5). Tell me what you think of all this. It is uncertain what the result will be. I hate him, for he is a Christian, but more for that in low simplicity he lends out money gratis. The fact that he was insolvent soon became known. I am not yet so old but I can learn. Try if you can decipher that letter. By Jacob's staff I swear I have no mind of feasting forth to-night. It must be owned he is a most entertaining companion. What his capacity is, signifies nothing. Where I live does not concern you. What does it signify how rich he is? What signifies what weather we have in a country going to ruin like ours? Methinks I know that handwriting (§ 514). That depends upon how you did it. O yet I do repent me of my fury, that I did kill them (§ 510). Anon methought the wood began to move (§ 514). Thou sure and firm-set earth, hear not my steps which way they walk, for fear the very stones prate of my whereabout.

2. *Sentences containing Adjective Clauses.*

408—413, 518, &c. Analyse the following sentences, having first enclosed the adjective clauses in brackets:—

That is the man who stole your purse. He that is down need fear no fall. They that will be rich fall into temptation and a snare It* was my brother who told me. I have lost the money you gave me (§ 409). Who steals my purse, steals trash. Pay the man what you owe him (§§ 372, 4, 410, 510). What I said was this. What he wants is to have his own way. What was the opinion of the judge who tried the case? I will repeat what I said to you. What do you think of the man who could do this? The reason why you cannot succeed is evident (§ 408). That is the place where I hid myself. The fortress whither the defeated troops had fled was soon captured. Blessed is he whose transgressions are forgiven. This is the only witchcraft I have used (§ 409). We can never recover the time we have mis-spent. Where is the book I gave you yesterday? In me thou seest the twilight of such day as after sunset fadeth in the west. His behaviour is not such as I like (§ 412). God's benison go with those that would make good of bad. He hath a wisdom that doth guide his valour to act in safety. Who can advise may speak. Infected be the air whereon they ride. Who was the thane lives yet, but under heavy judgment bears that life which he deserves to lose.

3. *Sentences containing Adverbial Clauses.*

414—442, 524—532 Analyse the following sentences, enclosing the adverbial clauses in brackets, and specifying to which of the various classes of adverbial clauses they belong:—

I will tell you the secret when I see you. When you durst do it, then you were a man. He still lay where he fell. He was so altered that I did not know him (§ 528). He is happy because he is contented. While he is here, we shall have no peace. If you do that, you will suffer for it. I must not give you the book, for it is not mine. He will go to ruin unless he alters his conduct. He did not pay me when I called on him, because he had no money. If this account is true, the man is much to be pitied. Whatever may be the consequence, I will do what I have said. He is not happy, although he is so rich; for his only son has taken to vicious courses. Wherever you go, I will follow you (§ 530). However dangerous such a course may be, it is the only one that we can adopt. I will walk in the garden until you return (§ 526). As the tree falls so it will lie. He left the room, that he might not be drawn into the quarrel. The mountain is so high that there is always snow on the top of it (§ 528). The higher you climb,† the wider will the prospect be (§ 270). She is as good as she is beautiful. I doubt not but to die a fair death for all this, if I escape hanging for killing that rogue.‡ A plague upon it when thieves cannot be true to one another. An I have not ballads

---

* In sentences of this kind *it* is equivalent to *the person*. The relative clause is in the attributive relation to *it*. Compare §§ 387, 511.

† This adverbial clause qualifies *wider*, and is co-ordinate with *the* which precedes *wider*.

‡ Mind that *for killing*, &c., is not an adverbial adjunct of *escape*, but an attributive adjunct of the substantive *hanging*.

made on you all and sung to filthy tunes, let a cup of sack be my poison. When we can entreat an hour to serve, we would spend it in some words upon that business, if you would grant the time. So * I lose not honour in seeking to augment it, I shall be counselled. I do not despair of the future, dark as it appears at present. When I am determined, I always listen to reason, because then it can do no harm. What signifies asking, when there's not a soul to give you an answer? The flighty purpose never is o'ertook, unless the deed go with it. I'll charm the air to give a sound, while you perform your antic round. The lady's fortune must not go out of the family; one may find comfort in the money, whatever one does in the wife.

507 In the following examples, substantive clauses contain other clauses within them. Enclose the containing and the contained clauses by brackets of *different* sorts. Prefix a properly marked letter to each clause, and then put the letter that denotes the *containing* clause before that which denotes the *contained* clause.

He heard that the Helvetii had burned all the corn except what they were about to take with them (§§ 283, 372, 5, 521). He said he would return the book when he had read it. I wish the boy would finish the task I set him. Tell me how old you were when your father died. Who told you that I built the house which you see? But that my foot slipped as I turned the corner, I should have won the race. He fears that his father will ask him where he has been. But that I told him who did it, he would never have known. Whatever I may have gained by folly, you see I am willing to prevent your losing by it. Go bid thy mistress when my drink is ready she strike upon the bell. Nor failed they to express how much they praised that for the general safety he despised his own. Who but felt of late (§ 522) with what compulsion and laborious flight we sunk thus low? Where they most breed and haunt I have observed the air is delicate.

Deal in a similar manner with the following adjective and adverbial clauses, which contain other clauses within them :—

The person who told you that I said so is mistaken. The child who does not mind when he is spoken to must be punished. He is not such a fool as I thought he was (§ 412). Scouts were sent out who were to see in what direction the foe had retreated. There are men who care not what they say. The house where I lived when I was in town has been pulled down. The man who does the best that he can deserves praise. Whoever maintains that genius by itself can accomplish everything, is mistaken. I have only done what I told you I would do. They fear what yet they know must follow. The time approaches that will with due decision make us know what we shall say we have, and what we owe. I should

---

* *So* qualifies *shall be counselled*, and the clause that follows *so* is in apposition to it, and explains it. It is thus equivalent to a hypothetical clause. See § 440, &c.

report that which I say I saw.* I have secret reasons, which I forbear to mention, because you are not able to answer those of which I make no secret. The time has been that when the brains were out the man would die. The right valiant Banquo walked too late, whom † you may say, if it please you, Fleance killed. The eighth appears, who bears a glass which shows me many more.

In the following examples each sentence contains a subordinate clause which contains another subordinate clause, which in its turn contains a third. Bracket and analyse them.

I was grieved when I heard how he had obtained the character which he bore among his neighbours. I know that he would never have spread such a report if he had not believed what your brother told him. Men who see clearly how they ought to act when they meet with obstacles are invaluable helpers. I will not excuse you unless you tell me who it was who was the author of that statement. It would be well if all men felt how surely ruin awaits those who abuse their gifts and powers. It was so hot in the valley that we could not endure the garments which we had found too thin when we were higher up among the mists. I need not tell you how glad I am that you have abandoned the design which you mentioned to me. I will give you no more money till I see how you use what you have.

Contracted Sentences.

445, 449, 452 Fill up and analyse the following sentences:—

You must either be quiet or leave the room. Neither John nor his brother was present. He wrote the exercise quickly, but well He pursued, but could not overtake the retreating enemy. The man left the house, but soon returned. The larynx, or rather the whole of the windpipe taken together, besides its other uses, is also a musical instrument. Let the rich deride, the proud disdain these simple blessings of the lowly train. I have not decided whether I will go or not. He yields neither to force nor to persuasion. It is uncertain whether he wrote the book, or not. He allowed no day to pass without either writing or declaiming aloud. So will fall he and his faithless progeny. Whose fault? Whose but his own? No man can be great unless he gives up thinking much about pleasures and rewards and gets strength to endure what is hard and painful. Wiles let them contrive who need, or when they need, not now. Who knows whether our angry foe can give it, or will ever? If you pursue this course, you will not injure me but you will ruin yourself. Our greatness will appear then most conspicuous when great things of small, useful of hurtful, prosperous of adverse we can create. Our purer essence then will overcome the noxious vapour of these raging fires, or, inured, not feel.

---

* The construction of the sentence "which I say [that] I saw" is the same as that of "I say that I saw this."
† See last note.

Sentences containing Elliptical Clauses.

453, 544, &c. Analyse the following sentences, having first supplied the words that are understood:—

He looks as stupid as an owl. He is not so clever as his brother. He is as rich as his brother. He is richer than I am. To prevaricate is as bad as lying. He is not so wise as he thinks. I had rather die than endure such a disgrace. It is not so bad to suffer misfortune as to deserve it. Better is a dinner of herbs where love is, than a stalled ox and hatred therewith. I will do as you desire. He is not so rich as he once was. He is better to-day than yesterday. It is better to die than to live in such misery. I am not such a fool as to tell him my secret. This is better than if we had lost everything. He looked as if he could kill me. I'd rather be a dog, and bay the moon, than such a Roman. He told me that wisdom was better than wealth; as if I did not know that before. I would give a thousand pounds an I could run as fast as thou canst. I'll shed my dear blood drop by drop in the dust, but I will raise the down-trod Mortimer as high in the air as this unthankful king. An 'twere not as good a deed as drink to turn true man and leave these rogues, I am the veriest varlet that ever chewed with a tooth. What can be worse than to dwell here driven out from bliss? Rather than be less, he cared not to be at all. For mine own part, if I were as tedious as a king, I could find it in my heart to bestow* it all on your worship. He has no redeeming qualities whatever.† How could you make such a blunder as to suppose I did it? My companion understood the art of managing money matters much better than I. What if I don't tell you? I have as good a right to the money as you. You will comply with my wishes, won't you? I never attend to such requests; do you? His wages as a labourer‡ amount to twenty shillings a week. Tell me which is the better, this or that. He accompanied me as far as to the end of the street. As for me, I will have nothing to do with it. As to your proposal, I cannot assent to it. As to what you tell me, it passes belief. The author is no other than my old friend Smith (§ 264, *note*). With other notes than to the Orphean lyre I sang of chaos and eternal might (§ 264, *note*).

---

* The infinitive phrase *to bestow*, &c., is in apposition to *it*, the object of *find*.
† In full: "Whatever redeeming qualities there are."
‡ In full: In phrases like this, *as* introduces an elliptical hypothetical clause, the connective *as* having replaced the demonstrative *so*. "As a labourer" is in full: "As (= if) he is a labourer." "As for me" is "As (= if) the matter is for me." See §§ 442, and notes.

APPENDIX A.

Anglo-Saxon Forms of some Important Words.

1. The demonstrative and relative pronoun was thus declined:—

	Singular.			Plural.
	Mas.	*Fem.*	*Neut.*	*M. F. & N.*
Nom.	se (þe)	seo (þeó)	þæt	þâ
Gen.	þæs	þǣre	þæs	þâra (þǣra)
Dat.	þam (þæm)	þære	þam (þæm)	þâm (þǣm)
Acc.	þone (þæne) þâ		þæt	þâ
Abl.	þŷ, þe	—	þŷ þê	—

As a demonstrative, this pronoun answered to the Latin *is, ea, id*.

2. There was another demonstrative word, answering to the Latin *hic, haec, hoc*, which was declined as follows:

	Singular.			Plural.
	Mas.	*Fem.*	*Neut.*	*M. F. & N.*
Nom.	þes	þeós	þis	þâs
Gen.	þises	þisse	þises	þissa
Dat.	þisum	þisse	þisum	þisum
Acc.	þisne	þâs	þis	þâs
Abl.	þeós	—	þeós	—

3. The following are the forms of the personal pronouns:—

	First Person Sing.	Second Person Sing.	Third Person Sing.		
			M.	*F.*	*N.*
Nom.	ic	þû	he	heó	hit
Gen.	mîn	þîn	his	hire	his
Dat.	me	þe	him	hire	him
Acc.	me (mec)	þe (þec)	hine	hî (hig)	hit

	Dual.	Plural.	Dual.	Plural.	Plural.
Nom.	wit	we	git	ge	hî (hig)
Gen.	uncer	ûre (ûser)	incer	eówer	hira (heora)
Dat.	unc	ûs (ûsic)	inc	eów	him (heom)
Acc.	unc (uncit)	us	inc (incit)	eów (eówic)	hî (hig)

It is worthy of notice that in Anglo-Saxon there was a *dual* number in the pronouns of the first and second persons, and that the Dative and Accusative forms are not always the same. The genitive plural *ure* has probably lost the letter *n*; *ouren* (for *of us*) is found in Wiclif. Chaucer uses *they* for the nominative plural, but *her* and *hem* for *their* and *them*.

APPENDIX.   219

4. The interrogative pronoun *hwa* was thus declined:—

	M.	F.	N.
Nom.	hwá		hwæt
Gen.	hwæs		hwæs
Dat.	hwám (hwæm)		hwam (hwæm)
Acc.	hwone (hwæne)		hwæt
Abl.			hwi

5. Declension of Nouns.

FIRST DECLENSION.

(Nouns ending in essential a *and* e.)

	Singular.			Plural.
	Masc.	*Fem.*	*Neut.*	*(All Genders.)*
Nom.	nam-a	tung-e	eag-e	-an
Gen.	nam-an	tung-an	eag-an	-ena
Dat. } Abl. }	nam-an	tung-an	eag-an	-um
Acc.	nam-an	tung-an	eag-e	-an

SECOND DECLENSION.

(Nouns ending in a Consonant, and Masculines in -e.)

	Masc.		*Fem.*		*Neut.*	
	Sing.	Plural.	Sing.	Plural.	Sing.	Plural.
Nom.	hund	-as	spræc	-a	word	(as in Sing.)
Gen.	hund-es	-a	spræc-e	{-a, -ena}	word-es	-a
Dat. } Abl. }	hund-e	-um	spræc-e	-um	word-e	-um
Acc.	hund	-as	spræc-e	-a	word	(as in Sing.)

The Third Declension presents no additional forms of special importance.

6. Declension of Adjectives.

Adjectives preceded by a demonstrative word had their three genders declined like the masculine, feminine, and neuter nouns of the first declension.

When not preceded by a definitive word, adjectives were declined as follows:—

	Singular.			Plural.	
	Masc.	*Fem.*	*Neut.*	*M. and F.*	*Neut.*
Nom.	gód	gód	gód	góde	gódu
Gen.	gódes	gódre	gódes	gódra	gódra
Dat.	gódum	gódre	gódum	gódum	gódum
Acc.	gódne	góde	gód	góde	gódu
Abl.	góde	gódre	góde		

7. Conjugation of Verbs.

A. Verbs of the Weak Conjugation.

First Class.—Nerjan (*to preserve*).

Inf.—nerjan. *Imp. Part.*—nerjende. *Perf. Part.*—(ge)nered.

Indicative Mood.

Present Tense.		*Preterite Tense.*	
Sing.	*Plural.*	*Sing.*	*Plural.*
1. nerje	nerjað	1. nerede	neredon
2. nerest	nerjað	2. neredest	neredon
3. nereð	nerjað	3. nerede	neredon

Subjunctive Mood.

Present Tense.		*Preterite Tense.*	
Sing.	*Plural.*	*Sing.*	*Plural.*
1, 2, and 3. nerje	nerjen	1, 2, and 3. nerede	nereden

Imperative.—*Sing.*, nere. *Plural.*, nerjað.

Second Class.—Lufjan (*to love*).

Inf.—lufjan. *Imp. Part.*—lufjende ('lufigende').
Perf. Part.—(ge)lufod.

Indicative Mood.

Present Tense.		*Preterite Tense.*	
Sing.	*Plural.*	*Sing.*	*Plural.*
1. lufje (lufige)	lufjað (lufigeað)	1. lufode	lufodon
2. lufast	lufjað (lufigeað)	2. lufodest	lufodon
3. lufað	lufjað (lufigeað)	3. lufode	lufodon

Subjunctive Mood.

Present Tense.		*Preterite Tense.*	
Sing.	*Plural.*	*Sing.*	*Plural.*
1, 2, and 3. lufje (lufige)	lufjen (lufigen)	1. lufode	lufoden

Imperative.—*Sing.*, lufa. *Plural.*, lufjað.

Third Class.—Hýran (*to hear*).

Inf.—hýran. *Imp. Part.*—hýrende. *Perf. Part.*—(ge)hýred.

Indicative Mood.

Present Tense.		*Preterite Tense.*	
Sing.	*Plural.*	*Sing.*	*Plural.*
1. hýre	hýrað	1. hýrde	hýrdon
2. hýrest	hýrað	2. hýrdest	hýrdon
3. hýreð	hýrað	3. hýrde	hýrdon

APPENDIX. 221

Subjunctive Mood.

	Present Tense.		Preterite Tense.	
	Sing.	Plural.	Sing.	Plural.
1, 2, and 3.	hýre	hýren	hýrde	hýrden

B. VERBS OF THE STRONG CONJUGATION.

Niman (to take).

Inf.—niman. *Imp. Part.*—nimende. *Perf. Part.*—(ge)numen.

Indicative Mood.

Present Tense.		Preterite Tense.	
Sing.	Plural.	Sing.	Plural.
1. nime	nimað	1. nâm	nâmon
2. nimest	nimað	2. náme	nâmon
3. nimeð	nimað	3. nâm	nâmon

Subjunctive Mood.

	Present Tense.		Preterite Tense.	
	Sing.	Plural.	Sing.	Plural.
1, 2, and 3.	nime	nimen	nâme	nâmen

Creópan (to creep).

Indicative Mood.

Present Tense.		Preterite Tense.	
Sing.	Plural.	Sing.	Plural.
1. creópe	creópað	1. creap	crupon
2. crýpst	creópað	2. crupe	crupon
3. crýpð	creópað	3. creap	crupon

The Verb 'to be' (See § 251).

Inf.—beón, wesan. *Imp. Part.*—wesende. *Perf. Part.*—(ge)wesen.

Indicative Mood.

Present Tense.

	1	2	3
Sing.	beóm (beó)	bist (býst)	býð
	com	eart	is (ys)
Plural.	beóð	beóð	beóð
	sindon (sind)	sindon (sind)	sindon (sind)
	aron	aron	aron

Preterite Tense.

	1	2	3
Sing.	wæs	wære	wæs
Plural.	wæron	wæron	wæron

APPENDIX.

Subjunctive Mood.

Present Tense.

	1	2	3
Sing.	beó síe (sî, seó) wese	beó síe (sî, seó) wese	beó síe (sî, seó) wese
Plural.	beón síen (sin) wesen	beón síen (sin) wesen	beón síen (sin) wesen

Preterite Tense.

Sing.	wǣre	wǣre	wǣre
Plural.	wǣren	wǣren	wǣren

Imperative.

Sing.	beó	wes
Plural.	beóð	wesað

The foregoing are the leading inflections of the Anglo-Saxon, or *First Period* of English. (See *Preliminary Notice*, p. 5.)

In the *Second Period* we find a weakening of the broad vowels (*a, o,* and *u*) in suffixes to *e*, and a tendency to drop some suffixes altogether. The use of *-es* as a plural suffix increases. *Es* also begins to be used as a genitive suffix in feminine nouns. Some suffixes properly belonging only to particular declensions begin to be used indiscriminately in all. In adjectives of the strong declension suffixes do not always appear in their full form. In the weak declension they are often replaced by *-e*, a change which in the Northern dialect applied to the strong declension as well.

The inflections of the demonstrative or relative pronoun *se, seo,* þæt (now þe, þeo, þæt) are sometimes dropped, so that we get an uninflected form *the*, which, as a demonstrative, is the modern definite article. The neuter relative *thet* or *that* was used with antecedents of any gender.

In verbs the gerundial infinitive often ended in *-en* or *-e*, instead of *-enne* or *-anne*, in place of which *-inde* is also found. *Shall* and *will* began to come into use as ordinary auxiliaries. The old prefix *ge* of perfect participles was weakened to *i*, and frequently dropped, as was also the *-n* of the suffix.

The simplification of the grammar is especially observable in the Northern dialect.

The *Third Period* exhibits a continued weakening of the old forms, spoken sounds and their written representatives being both in an unsettled state. The influence of two opposed systems of accentuation is traceable (§ 27); grammatical and natural gender begin to coincide, and differences of declension connected with differences of gender cease.

In nouns the inflections have dwindled down to the plural suffix *-s, -es, -is,* or *-ys*, used without regard to gender or ancient modes of declension (*-en* being however still used in a large number, and a few plurals being formed by the suffixes *er, re,* or *e*, or by a change of vowel); the ordinary genitive suffix *-s, -es,* or *-is* (curiously dropped in the case of the family names *father, mother, brother* and *sister*, and of several feminine nouns, but found in plural genitives like *mennes*); and the occasional genitive plural suffix *-ene*. Traces of a dative singular in *-e* are still found. Both cases are often expressed by means of prepositions.

In adjectives the only suffix is *-e*, which is used partly after demonstratives, and partly to denote the plural. The duals of the personal pronouns disappear. *Sche, sho,* or *ho,* replaces the feminine *heo*.

As regards verbs, various strong verbs get the weak inflection; *-e* in the first person singular present is often dropped, and in the second *-est* is sometimes changed to *-ist* or *-yst*. In the plural *-ath* or *-eth* is sometimes replaced by *-en*, of which the *-n* is sometimes dropped. In the preterite of the strong conjugation the change of vowel which marked the second person singular and the plural disappears, and the suffix *-est* or *-ist* comes in to mark the second person singular in this tense as well as in the present. Sometimes *-es* is found for *-est*. The *n* of the plural is sometimes dropped, and is rarely used in the subjunctive mood. In weak verbs *-ed* replaces *-od*, where the latter termination had been used. The final *n* of the infinitive is commonly dropped, so that the mood ends in *-e*. The *g* or *j* of the connecting syllable in such Anglo-Saxon verbs as *lufjan* or *lufigan* was sometimes retained in the form of *i* or *y*, giving rise to such infinitives as *makie, answerye*.* The participial suffix *-inde* or *-ynd* is often replaced by *-ing* or *-yng*.

In the *Fourth Period*, the Midland section of the Northern dialect becomes predominant. In nouns the dative suffix entirely disappears. Plurals in *-en*, or with a modified vowel, become merely exceptional cases. The names of relationship (*father, mother,* &c.) are less commonly used without their genitive suffix. The inflections of adjectives are much the same as in the preceding period. The *substantive* use of the genitive cases of the pronouns disappears, the possessive sense being expressed by the pronominal adjectives, and all other senses by means of prepositions. *They* (*thei*) is used for the nominative plural of the demonstrative of the third person, but *here* and *hem* still maintain their ground as genitive and dative. The plural *tho* (= *those*) is still sometimes used. The short form *I* (often written *i*) for *ich* or *ic*, though found in the preceding period, becomes more common in this.

In verbs the Weak Conjugation becomes more and more common. The plural suffix *-eth* is usually replaced by *-en*, the *n* of which is often dropped. In the imperative mood the suffix *-eth* is usually, but not invariably employed. As the period advances, the infinitive more and more frequently drops its suffix.

E is a common adverbial termination. As compared with the preceding period, this is one of settlement and reconstruction.

In accentuation a reaction against the French system sets in, and numerous French words are brought under the laws of the English system.

The *Fifth Period*, that of *Modern English*, is marked by a still further simplification of the accidence, and the gradual settlement of the orthography and accentuation of words, resulting in that form of the language which is now in vogue.

* In Somersetshire such infinitives as *sewy, reapy, nursy,* are still heard.

APPENDIX B.

I. A List* of some Celtic Words preserved in English.

bag	crock-ery	gown	lath	rug
bard	crag	griddle	mattock	size
basket	crowd (fiddle)	gruel	mesh	smooth
barrow	cudgel	grumble	mop	soak
bog	dainty	gyve	muggy	solder
bran	darn	hawker	pail	tackle
camp	flannel	hem	pan	tall
button	fleam	hog	peck	tinker
bug-bear	flaw	knell	pitcher	trudge
cabin	funnel	knock	rail	welt
clout	fur	knoll	rasher	whip
coble	glen	lad	ridge	wicket
cock-boat	goblin	lass	rim	wire

The following geographical names are of Celtic origin :—*Rivers :*— Avon, Dee, Don, Ouse, Severn, Stour, Thames, Trent. *Hills :*—Cheviot, Chiltern, Grampian, Malvern, Mendip. *Islands :*—Arran, Bute, Man, Mull, Wight. *Counties :*—Devon, Dorset, Kent. *Towns :*—Liverpool, Penrith, Penzance.

The following Celtic elements are found in some geographical names† :—*Aber* (mouth of a river), as, ' Aberdeen, Aber-brothwick, Aberwick (Berwick) ;' *Auchin* (field), as ' Auchindoir, Auchinleck ;' *Ard* or *Aird* (high, projecting), as, ' Ardnamuchan, Ardrishaig ;' *Bal* (village), as, ' Balmoral ;' *Ben* or *Pen* (mountain), as, ' Ben Nevis, Penmaenmawr ;' *Blair* (field clear of wood), as, ' Blair Athol ;' *Brae* (rough ground), as, ' Braemar ;' *Caer* (fort), as, ' Caerleon (Carlisle) ; *Combe* or *Comp* (valley), as, ' Compton, Ilfracombe, Appuldurcombe ;' *Dun* (hill), as, ' the Downs, Dumbarton ;' *Inch* (island), as, ' Inchkeith, Inchcape ;' *Inver* (mouth of a river), as, ' Inverness, Inverary ;' *Kill* (cell, chapel), ' Kilmarnock ;' *Lin* (deep pool), ' Linlithgow, King's Lynn ;' *Llan* (church), ' Llandaff, Launceston ;' *Tre* (town), ' Coventry (town of the convent), Oswestry ;' *Strath* (broad valley), ' Strathfieldsaye.'

II. Scandinavian Words and Elements in English.

The most important of these are found in some geographical names‡ :—

| ark | (temple or | Arkholm | beck (brook), Caldbeck |
| argh | altar) | Grimsargh | by (town), Whitby |

---

* This list is mainly extracted from a longer one given by Mr. Garnett in the 'Transactions of the Philological Society,' vol. i., p. 171
† See Angus, *Handbook*, &c., p. 18; Bain, *English Grammar*, p. 124
‡ This list is taken from a larger one given by Dr. Adams (*Eng Lang.* p. 6.)

APPENDIX. 225

dal (valley), Dalby
ey, a (island), { Orkney / Grimsa
fell (rocky hill), Scawfell
ford } (inlet) { Seaford / Seaforth / Holmfirth
forth
firth
force (waterfall), Mickleforce
garth } (enclosure) { Dalegarth / Fishguard
guard
gill (valley), Ormesgill

holm (island), Langholm
ness (headland), Skipness
scar (steep rock), Scarborough
skip (ship), Skipwith
thing } (place of meet- { Thingwall / Tingwall / Dingwall
ting   ing)
ding
thorp } (village) { Grimsthorpe / Milnthrop
throp
toft (small field), Lowestoft
with (wood), Langwith

III. Elements handed down from the Anglo-Saxon stage of English.

[Nothing more is attempted here than a brief classification, with a few examples.]

1. The pronouns, numerals, prepositions, conjunctions, adjectives of irregular comparison, and the auxiliary, defective, and (so-called) irregular verbs.

2. Monosyllabic derivatives formed by a modification of the root vowel or of the final consonant, as *ditch* (from *dig*), *bless* (from *bliss*) and the majority of the words formed by strictly English suffixes.

3. Most words denoting common natural objects and phenomena, as—

cloud	evening	light	silver	sun
dale	flood	moon	snow	thunder
dawn	ground	morning	spring	water
day	heat	night	star	wind
dew	hill	noon	stone	world
earth	ice	rain	stream	winter
east	iron	sea	summer	year
egg	lead			

4. Words relating to the family, household, and farm, as—

brother	bath	door	chaff	scythe
child	beam	dough	cheese	wheat
daughter	bed	home	corn	ash
father	bolster	hearth	cow	beech
friend	besom	kettle	delve	berry
husband	bread	loaf	harvest	brick
kin	brew	oven	hay	fir
mother	broth	roof	hemp	grass
sister	cloth	thatch	honey	oak
wife	comb	barley	milk	oats
widow	cook	barn	plough	tree, &c.
bake	cradle	calf	rake	

5. The names of most of the parts of the body, as—

beard	brain	oar	foot	heel
body	breast	eye	hair	knee
bone	breath	finger	hand	leg
bosom	brow	fist	heart	lip
blood	chin	flesh	head	mouth,

Q

6. The names of common animals, as—

ape	dove	hare	man	ruddock
bear	fish	hawk	owl	throstle
bee	foal	horse	ox	turtle
beetle	fowl	hound	sheep	weevil
bird	fox	lamb	raven	worm
deer	goose	lark		

7. Terms for common qualities and actions, as—

bold	high	ask	buy	find
blind	low	hear	chaffer	fly
bright	holy	bid	chew	get
broad	hot	bind	come	give
cold	old	bite	dip	go
dark	quick	blaze	do	have
dead	rough	bleach	drink	kill
deaf	sock	blow	eat	love
good	smooth	bring	fear	look
hard	pretty	burn	fill	make, &c.

8. Names of common things—weapons, tools, clothes, &c.—

awl	bridge	hat	name	bow
bank	food	knife	ship	arrow
book	fire	meat	sword	bill
boat	hook	nail	spear	

IV. The Classical Element in English.

The greater part of the abstract terms in English, and words relating to religion, law, science, and literature, are of Latin or Greek origin. Most words of three or more syllables are of classical origin, and a very large number of those of two syllables, the exceptions being mostly words formed by *English* suffixes, from monosyllabic roots. Most monosyllabic words in English are of Teutonic origin, but many are derived from Latin and Greek, the greater part having come to us through the French.* The following belong to this class † :—

ace (*as*)	aunt (amita)	brace (brachium)
age (*uetaticum*), *Old Fr.* édage)	bail (bajulus)	brief (brevis)
	balm (balsamum)	broach (brochus)
aid (adjutum)	base (bassus)	bull (bulla)
aim (aestimare)	beast (bestia)	cage‡ (cavea)
air (aer)	beef (boves)	camp (campus)
aisle (ala)	blame (blasphemia)	cane (canna)
alms (ελεημοσυνη)	boil (bullire)	car ⎫
arch (arcus)	boon (bonus)	carry ⎬ (carrus)
ark (arca)	bowl (bulla)	charge ⎭

---

* It is, however, a great mistake to suppose that a word taken from the French language is necessarily of *classical* origin. Some writers forget that the Franks and Normans were of Teutonic origin.

† The words from which they are derived are appended. Those in italics are of a post-classical age.

‡ The change of a *b*, *p*, or *v* between vowels into the sound of soft *g* is found in several words.

APPENDIX.

cape (caput)
cash (capsa)
cease (cessare)
chafe (calefacere)
chain (catena)
chalk (calx)
chair (cathedra)
chance (*cadentia*)
chant (cantare)
charm (carmen)
chase (*captiare*)
chief (caput)
clang (clangor)
claim (clamare)
coast (costa)
coin (cuneus)
cook (coquus)
coop (cupa)
couch (collocare)
count (comes)
count (computare)
core (cor)
cork (cortex)
cost (constare)
coy (quietus)
crape (crispus)
cup (cupa)
croak (crocitare)
cue (cauda)
cull (colligere)
dame (domina)
date (datum)
daunt (*domitare*)
dean (decanus)
die (*dadus*)
desk } (discus)
dish }
dose (δοσις)
doubt (dubitare)
dress (dirigere)
due (debitum)
duke (dux)
face (facies)
fail (fallo)
fair (feria)
faith (fides)
fan (vannus)
fay (fata)
feast (festus)
feat (factum)

feign (fingere)
fence (defensum)
fierce (ferus)
fife (pipare)
fig (ficus)
file (filum)
flame (flamma)
flour } (flor-os)
flower }
flute (flatus)
foil (folium)
force (fortis)
forge (fabrica)
found (fundere)
fount (fons)
frail (fragilis)
frock (floccus)
frown (frons)
fruit (fructus)
fry (frigere)
fuse (fundere)
glaive (gladius)
glut (glutire)
gorge (gurges)
gout (gutta)
gourd (cucurbita)
grant (*credentare*)
grease (crassus)
grief (gravis)
gross (grossus)
gulf (κολπος)
heir (heres)
host (hospit-)
hulk (ὁλκας)
inch (uncia)
jaw (gabata)
jest (gestum)
jet (jactum)
join (jungo)
joy (gaudium)
juice (jus)
lace (laqueus)
lease (laxare)
liege (*legius*)
lounge (longus)
mace (massa)
mail, *armour* (macula, *mesh*)
male (masculus)
mass (missa)

mix (misceo)
mood (modus)
mop (mappa)
mount (mons)
niece (neptis)
noise (noxia)
noun (nomen)
nurse (nutrix)
ounce (uncia)
pace (passus)
pain (poena)
paint (pingere)
pair (par)
pale (palleo)
paunch (pantex)
pay (pacare)
peace (pax)
peach (persica)
pierce (pertusum)
place (platea)
plait (plectere)
plea } (placitum)
plead }
plum (prunum)
plunge (*plumbicare*)
point (punctum)
poise (pensum)
poor (pauper)
porch (porticus)
pound (pondus)
praise (pretiare)
pray (precari)
preach (praedicare)
prey (praeda)
priest (presbyter)
print (premere)
prize } (pretium)
price }
proof (probare)
push (pulsare)
quire (chorus)
quite (quietus)
rage } (rabies)
rave }
ray (radius)
rear (retro)
rest (restare)
rill (rivulus)
river (riparius)
roll (rotulus)

228   APPENDIX.

round (rotundus)   space (spatium)   test (testis)
rule (regula)   spice (species)   toast (tostus)
safe (salvus)   spoil (spolium)   toll (telonium)
sage (sapiens)   spouse (sponsus)   tour ⎱ (tornare)
saint (sanctus)   sprain (exprimo)   turn ⎰
sauce (salsus)   spy (specio)   trace ⎱ (tractus)
scan (scandere)   squad, square (ex-   trait ⎰
scent (sentire)   quadrare)   treat (tractare)
scarce (ex-scarptus) stage (staticus)   try (terere)
scourge (corrigere) stain (stinguo)   tune (tonus)
seal (sigillum)   strain (stringo)   vault (voluta)
search (circare)   strange (extraneus)   vaunt (vanitare)
seat (sedes)   strait (strictus)   veal (vitulus)
short (curtus)   street (strata)   veil (velum)
siege (assedium)   sue, suit (sequor)   vice (vitium)
sir (senior)   sure (securus)   view (videre)
sluice (exclusis)   taint (tinctus)   void (viduus)
soar (exaurare)   task (taxare)   voice (vox)
soil (solum)   taste (taxitare)   vouch (vocare)
sound (sonus)   taunt (temptare)   vow (votum)
source (surgere)   tense (tempus)   waste (vastus)

The above list does not include a large number of monosyllables, the Latin origin of which is obvious, such as *cede* (*cedo*), *long* (*longus*), &c. Some of the less obvious etymologies are taken from Müller's admirable " Etymologisches Wörterbuch der Englischen Sprache."

Besides words like the above, which with many others have been distinctly *imported* from the classical languages into English, there are numerous instances in which a word or root is common to several of the Aryan languages, without having been borrowed by any one from another, all having received the word in common from some more primitive source. In tracing the variations which such words assume, a very remarkable relation between the consonants is found, which is commonly known as 'Grimm's Law.' The substance of the following statement of this law is taken from Max Müller (Lect. ii. 199, &c.) and Helfenstein (*Comp. Gr.*, p. 99).

If the same roots or the same words exist (1) in Sanskrit, Greek, Latin, &c., (2) in Gothic or the Low German dialects, * and (3) in Old High German, then I. When the first class have an aspirate,† the second have the corresponding soft check (*i.e., flat* or *middle* mute), the third the corresponding hard check (*i.e., sharp* or *thin* mute). II. When the first class have a soft check (*flat* or *middle* mute), we find the corresponding hard check (*sharp* or *thin* mute) in the second class, and the corresponding aspirate in the third. III. When the

---
    * Of which English is one.   † See §§ 18, 19.

first class have a hard consonant (*sharp* or *thin* mute), the second have the aspirate, and the third the soft check (*flat* or *middle* mute). In this third section of the rule, however, the law holds good for Old High German only as regards the *dental* series of mutes, the middle (or flat) guttural being generally replaced by *h*, and the middle (or flat) labial by *f*.*

The three branches of the law given above may be easily remembered in the following way :—Take a circular disc of cardboard, and mark on it three radii, inclined each to each at an angle of 120°. Mark these radii (1), (2), and (3), corresponding respectively to the three classes of languages above referred to—(1) denoting Sanskrit, Greek, Latin, &c.; (2) denoting Gothic and Low German dialects (including English); and (3) denoting Old High German. Place the disc on a sheet of paper, and write *Aspirate* opposite the end of radius (1), *Middle* or *Flat* opposite the end of radius (2), and *Thin* or *Sharp* opposite the end of radius (3). The disc may be shifted, so that radius (1), instead of pointing to *Aspirate*, may point to the other two classes of mutes in succession. In each position of the disc, each radius will point to the class of mutes that may be expected to characterize any word that is common to all three classes of languages, provided that one radius points to the class of mutes which the word in question exhibits in that group of languages which that radius represents.

The following are a few instances of the application of this law :—

I.

	Greek.	Latin.	Sanskrit.	English. (Ang. Sax.)	Gothic.	Old High German.
1.	χήν χεές χόρτος	(h)anser heri hortus	hansa hyas	goose gestrandaeg garden	gans gistra gards	kans kestar karto
2.	θυγάτηρ θύρα ἀήρ θαρσεῖν	fera	dhrish	daughter door deer dare	daughtar daur dius ga-daur-san	tohtar tor tior tarran
		medius	madhya	middle		mitte
3.	φέρω (φράρpα) φηγός φύω	fero frater fagus fu-i	bhri bhratri bhavâmi	bear brother beech be (be om)	baira bróthar bóka	piru pruoder puocha pim

* The above is the law in its general form. It is subject to special modifications and exceptions, which will be found treated at length by the authors referred to.

II.

	Greek.	Latin.	Sanskrit.	English. (Ang. Sax.)	Gothic.	Old High German.
4.	γνῶμι γένος γόνυ μέγας ἐγώ	gnosco genus genu mag-nus ego	jnâ jâti jânu mah-at	know kin knee A.S. micel A.S. ic	kan kuni kniu mih-ils ik	chan chuni chniu mih-il ih (G. ich)
5.	ποδ-ός δέκα δύω ὀδόντ-ος	ped-is decem duo dent-is	dasan daut-as	foot ten two tooth	taihun twai tunth	vuoz zehan zwei
6.	κάνναβις			help hemp	hilfa	hilfu hanaf

III.

	Greek.	Latin.	Sanskrit.	English. (Ang. Sax.)	Gothic.	Old High German.
7.	κεφαλή καρδία (κός)	caput cord-is qui-s	kapâla hridaya	A.S. heafod heart A.S. hwa	haubith hairto hvas	houpit (herza)
8.	τύ τρεῖς ἕτ-ερος	tu tres alter	twam trayas ant-ara	thou three other	thu threis anthar	du dri andar
9.	πατήρ ὑπέρ πλέος	pater super ple-nus piscis pellis	pitri upari pûrna	father over full fish fell	fadar ufar fulls fisks	ubar

General Table of Grimm's Law.

		I.			II.			III.		
		1	2	3	4	5	6	7	8	9
1.	Sanskrit	gh (h)	dh (h) $bh(h)$		g	d	b	k	t	p
	Greek	χ	θ	ϕ	γ	δ	β	κ	τ	π
	Latin	$h, f(g, v)$	$f(d, b)$	$f(b)$	g	d	b	c, qu	t	p
II.	Gothic,&c.	g	d	b	k	t	(p)	$h, g, (f)$	th, d	f, b
III.	O.H.Ger.	k	t	p	ch	z	$ph(f)$	h, g, k	d	f, v

APPENDIX C.

A List* of some of the most important Anglo-Saxon Words which are still preserved in English.

Prepositions.

æft, æfter; after
æt; at
ær; ere
andlang; along
be, bí, big; by
beforan; before
begeondan; beyond
behindan; behind
beneoðan; beneath
betweonum, betwynan; between
betweox, betwux; betwixt
búfan; above
bútan, búton (without); but
feor; far from
fram; from
for; for
in; in
neah; near
of; off, of
ofer; over
on; on, in
ongean; against
to; to, too
under; under
up, uppan; up
út, útan; out
wið (against); with, (as in withstand, angry with, &c.)
þurh; through

Numerals.

án; one
twegen; two, twain
þrí; three
feówer; four
fíf; five
six; six
seofon; seven
eahta; eight
nigon; nine
tyn; ten
endlif, endlufon; eleven
twelf; twelve
þreótyne; thirteen
feówertyne; fourteen, &c.
twentig; twenty
teóntig; one hundred
enlufontig; one hundred and ten
twelftig; one hundred and twenty

Words relating to the Common Objects of Nature.

ác; oak, acorn (i.e. ac-corn)
æpl, æpel; apple
æsc; ash
æmette; emmet
æspen; aspen
bitel; beetle
bár; boar
beofer; beaver
berige; berry
beo, bio; bee
birce; birch
blæd (branch); blade
bóc; beech
brǽr; briar
bremel; bramble
brid (the young of an animal); bird
bróc; brook
catt; cat
clæg; clay
clam (mud); clammy
clawu; claw
coc; cock
comb (valley); in names, as Alcomb, Compton
crán; crane
dæg; day
dagian; to dawn
deaw; dew
denu (valley); den (in names, as Tenterden)
deór (animal); deer
eá (water); island (i.e. eáland)
efen; evening
coðre; earth
fæðer; feather
fisc; fish
fleax; flax
flód; flood

---

* This list does not pretend to be exhaustive; it is intended to show the kind of words that have maintained their ground in English, and the principal changes of form that have occurred in them.

frosc; frog
fugel (*bird*); fowl
gós; goose
hæð; heath
hafoc; hawk
hagol; hail
hran; *raindeer* or *reindeer*
lawere; laverock, lark

lencten (*the spring*); Lent
leoht; light
móna; moon
pabol; pebble
regen; rain
sǽ; sea
snaw; snow

spearwa; sparrow
stær; stare, starling
stán; stone
sumer; summer
sunne (*fem.*); sun
treow; tree
wæter; water
woruld; world

Words relating to the House and Farm.

a-bacan; to bake
acer, æcer; acre
aeg (*pl.* aegru); egg, eyry
æsce; ashes
æmyrie; embers
bæð; bath
bæst (*inner bark*); bast-mat
bere; barley
bere-ern (ern=*place*); barn
berewe; barrow
besem; besom
bin (*manger*); corn-bin
bolla; bowl
bolster; bolster
bórd; board
bræc; breeches
bread (*fragment*); bread
búan (*to till*); boor
buc; buck-et
bulluca (*calf*); bullock
byt; butt, bottle
camb; comb
ceaf; chaff
cealf; calf
cese, cyse; cheese
cetel; kettle

clucge (*bell*); clock
cnedan; to knead
cóc; cook
cod (bag); peascod
cóte, cýte; cot, cottage
cradol; cradle
cract; cart
croc (*pot*); crock-cry
cú; cow
cwearn (*mill*); quern
delfan (*dig*); to delve
dic; dike, ditch
ealo; ale
efese (*fem. sing.*); eaves
ele; oil
erian (*to plough*): to ear
feauh (*little pig*); farrow
feld; field
feorm (*food*); farm
flocc; flock
fóda; food
furh; furrow
fýr; fire
gád; goad
gærs; grass
gát; goat
geard (*hedge*); yard, garden

geát; gate
grút (*meal*); groats, grouts
hærfest; harvest
heorð; hearth
hlæfdige; lady
hlaford; lord
hláf; loaf
hóf (*house*); hovel
hróf; roof
hund; hound
hús; house
hwǽte; wheat
hweol; wheel
lám (*mud*); loam
mǽd; mead-ow
meolc; milk
ófen; oven
ortgeard (*yard for worts or vegetables*); orchard
oxa; ox
ricg; rick
sceáp; sheep
spúca; spoke (*of a wheel*)
wǽgen; wagon, wain
wudu; wood
þæc; thatch
þerscan; to thresh

Words relating to Family and Kindred.

bróðor; brother
brýd; bride
cild (*pl.* cildra); child
cnápa, cnáfa (*boy*); knave

cyn; kin
dóhtor; daughter
fæder; father
husbonda (*householder*); husband

módor; mother
nefa; nephew
widuwa; widower
widuwe; widow
wíf (*woman*), wife

Words relating to the Parts of the Body and Natural Functions.

ancleow; ankle
bælg (*bag*); belly,
  bulge, bellows
bán; bone
blæddre; bladder
blód; blood
bodig (*stature*), body
bosm (*fold*); bosom
bræð; breath
bræw; brow
breost; breast
ceaca; cheek
ceówan; to chew
cin; chin
cneow; knee
cnucl; knuckle
eáge; eye

eár; ear
earm; arm
elboga; elbow
finger; finger
flǽsc; flesh
fót; foot
fýst; fist
gesiht; sight
góma; gum
hǽr; hair
hand; hand
heáfod; head
heals (*neck*); halter
hél; heel
heorte; heart
hlist (*the sense of hearing*); listen

hoh (*heel*); hough
hricg (*back*); ridge
hrif (*bowels*); midriff
lim; limb
lippe; lip
maga (*stomach*); maw
mearg; marrow
múð; mouth
nægl; nail
nasu; nose
sculder; shoulder
seón; to see
toð; tooth
tunge; tongue
tusc; tusk
þeoh; thigh, thews
þróte; throat

Words relating to Handicrafts, Trades, &c.

adesa; adze
anfilt; anvil
angel (*hook*); to angle
ár; oar
árewe; arrow
bát; boat
bil; bill

bræs; brasss
bycgan; to buy
bytel; beetle
ceáp (*bargain, sale*);
  cheap, chaffer,
  chapman
ceol (*small ship*); keel

cláð; cloth
craeft (strength)
craft
hamor; hammer
mangian (*to traffic*);
  monger

Words denoting Common Attributive Ideas.

báld; bold
biter; bitter
blæc; black
blác (*pale*); bleach
bleo; blue
brád; broad
brún; brown
calu (*bald*); callow
ceald; cold
ból; cool

deare; dark
deóp; deep
deóre; dear
eal; all
eald; old
efen; even
fægr; fair
fætt; fat
fúl; foul
geolo; yellow

grǽg; grey
gréne; green
heáh; high
heard; hard
hefig; heavy
hwít; white
rud (red); ruddy,
  ruddle, ruddock (*the
  robin-redbreast*)

Words referring to Common Actions and Feelings.

acan; to ache
acsian; to ask
béran; to bear
agan; to own
áth; oath
beatan; to beat
beódan; to bid

berstan; to burst
biddan; to bid
{ bítan; to bite
{ bitt; bite, bit
blédan; to bleed
bliðe; blithe
brecan; to break

ceorfan (to cut)
  carve
ceósan; to choose
clænan; to clean
cráwan; to crow
creópan; to creep
cuman; to come

cunnan (*to know, to be able*); ken, con, can, cunning, uncouth (=*unknown*)
cwelian, cwellan; to kill, to quell
dǽd; deed
dón; to do
drǽdan; to dread
drencan; to drench
drincan; to drink
dreógan (*to work*); drudge

ac, eac (*also*); eke
adl (*pain, sickness*); addle
æfre; ever
æmta (*leisure*), æmtig; empty
ænlic; only
ǽr, *superl.* ǽrost; ere, early, erst
æþel (*noble*); Atheling, Ethelred
bǽr; bier
bǿtan (*to curb*); bit
bana (*killer*); bane, rats-bane
beacen; beacon
beacnian; to beckon
bealu (*woe*); bale-ful
béd *prayer*); bedesman
behefe (*gain*); behoof
besittan (*to sit round*); beset
beorht (*brightness*); *Albert*, &c.
bisegu (*business*); busy
blæst; blast
bláwan; to blow
bland (*mixture*); to blend
bletsian (*from* blót, *sacrifice*); to bless
blowian; to blow
blóstma; blossom

dýnan; to dine
dyppan; to dip
etan; to eat
feallan; to fall
fédan; to feed
félan; to feel
fleógan; to fly
folgian *or* fyligean; to follow
gifan; to give
gitan; to get
gleó; glee

Miscellaneous Words.

bóc; book
bocsum (*flexible*); buxom
boga (*arch*); bow
borgian (*from* borgpledge); to borrow
bót (*remedy, from* betan, '*to make better*;') boot-less, to boot
bród; brood
bryeg; bridge, brig
brydel; bridle
bryne (*burning*); brimstone
brysan; to bruise
brytan (*to break*); brittle
bugan; to bow
búr (*cottage*); bower
burh (*fort*); borough
bylgian; to bellow
byrðen; burthen
byre (*mound*); byre
byrian; to bury
carl (*male*); Charles
carl-fugel=male bird
cearu; care
cearcian; to creak
ceorl; churl
cirps (*curled*); crisp
cleafan; to cleave
clypian (*to speak, call*); y-clept
cnáwan; to know

grafan (*to dig*); engrave
habban (þú hæfst =*thou hast*); to have
hæft (*holding*); haft
heorcnian; to hearken
hýran; to hear
leógan; to lie
luf; love
sorh; sorrow
sprécan; to speak

cniht (*youth, attendant*); knight
cnoll; knoll
cnott; knot
cnucian; to knock
cos, cyss; kiss
crafian; to crave
cric; crutch
crincan (*to be weak*), cringe
crump (*crooked*); crumple
crydan; to crowd
cuc, cwic (*alive*); quick
cwealm (*destruction*) qualm
cwén (*female*); queen, quean
cwénfugel; hen bird
cweðan (*to say*); quoth
cýð (*acquaintance*); kith
cyning; king
déefe (*fit*); deftly
dǽl (*part*); deal, dole
dearran; to dare
déman (*to judge*), dóm; deem, doom
deofan (*to sink*); dive
dohtig; doughty
dol (*foolish*); dolt
dreórig (*bloody, sad*), dreary

APPENDIX. 235

drífan; to drive
drígan (to dry); drug, drought
dwínan (to pine); dwindle
dýne (thunder); din
dysig (foolish); dizzy
dýnt (stroke); dint
eác (also); eke
ealdor; elder, alderman
ecg; edge
eorl (man of valour); earl
eornest; earnest
fadian (to set in order); fiddle-faddle
faegen glad); fain
faran (to go); fare, ford
fealo (yellow); fallow (ground), fallow-deer
feoh (cattle, money), fee
feohtan; to fight
feor; far
ficol; fickle
fiðele; fiddle
fleot (bay); Northfleet, &c.
fleotan; to float
folc; folk
forhtian; to frighten
fóster (food); foster
{ freó; free
{ freón (to set free, love); friend
fretan (to gnaw); to fret
gaderian; to gather
gál (merry), galan (to sing); nightingale
gamen (pleasure); game
gán, gangan (to go); go, gang, gangway
gár (dart); to gore
gást; ghost, gas
geáp (wide); gape, gap

gear; year
geara; yore
gearo (ready); yare
geleafa; belief
{ geong; young
{ geogoð; youth
geála (merry feast); yule
geond; yonder
georn (desirous), geornian; to yearn
geótan (to pour); gutter
geréfa (companion); reeve, sheriff, landgrave
glisnian; to glisten
glitian; to glitter
gnagan; to gnaw
{ gód; good
{ god-spell: gospel,
{ (spell=message)
grápian (to lay hold of); grab, grapple, grope
grétan; to greet
guma (man); bridegroom
gyldan (to pay); to yield, guild
gyrsta; yester-day
hád (state or condition); Godhead, child-hood, &c.
hæcce; hook
hæfen; haven
hǽlan; to heal
hǽst; (hot); hasty
{ halig; holy
{ halgian; to hallow
hám; home, Cobham, &c.
hás; hoarse
healdan; to hold
healf; half
hebban; to heave
hélan (to hide); hell
heonan; hence
heord (flock, treasure); herd, hoard

here (army); harbour (i.e., refuge for an army, from beorh or beorga), herring (the army- or shoal-fish
hingrian; to hunger
hiw (form, fashion); hue
hládan (to pump up); ladle
hloð (band of robbers, booty); loot
hóc; hook
hóf; hoof
holm (river island); Langholm, &c.
hræd; ready
hraðe (soon); rathe, rather
hreósan; to rush
hreówan (repent); to rue
hriddel (sieve); to riddle (with holes)
{ hwæt (sharp); to whet
{ hwytel (knife); to whittle
hwearf (turning, exchange, barter); wharf
hweorfan (to turn); warp
hwíl (time); while
hýd (skin); hide
hýð (shore, port); Greenhithe, &c.
lǽr (doctrine); lore
lǽran (teach); learn (still vulgarly used in the sense of teaching)
hláford; lord
leas (false, void); leasing, -less (as in harm-less)
leod (people); lewd (belonging to the common people)
leóf (dear); lief

APPENDIX.

líc (*corpse*); lich-gate
licgan; to lie
lín (*flax*); linen, linnet (*the flax-finch*)
lystan (*to please, to take pleasure, used impersonally*); 'him listed,' listless
mægen (*strength*); might and main
magan (*be able*); may
mǽl (*time, portion*), mǽlum (*in parts*); piecemeal (so stæpmǽlum, *step by step*)
manig; many
maðu (*worm*); moth
max, masc (*noose*); mesh
mengian (*to mix*); mingle, among
mersc; marsh
metsian (*to feed*); mess, messmate, meat
midde; mid, middle
mód (*mind*); mood
morð (*death*); murther
morgen; morn, morrow
mót (*assembly, from* métan *to meet*); shire-moot
mycg; midge
nacod; naked
næddre (*serpent*) adder (*an adder = a nadder*)
næs *or* næsse; naze, -ness (in Furness, &c.)
neah (*comparat.* near); nigh
nearo; narrow
neód; need
neb (*break*); nib
neaðan; be-neath
niesan; to sneeze
niht; night

niðer (*down*); nether
ordǽl (or=*free from*, dǽl = *part, partizanship*); ordeal
ost; cast
pic; pitch
pinewincle, periwinkle
píp; pipe
pocca; pouch, pocket
prætig (*crafty*); pretty
pýle; pillow
rǽcan; to reach
rǽdan (*interpret*); to read
rép, ráp; rope
reác; (*smoke*); reek
reáfa (*robber*); reiver
reáfian; be-reave
réc (*care*); reckless
rein (*clean*); rinse
ríc (*dominion*); bishop-ric
rip (*harvest*); ripe, reap
ród (*cross*); rood
sæd (*sated*); sad
sǽl (*good luck*); sǽlig (*lucky*); seely (*old Engl.*), silly (i.e., *blessed*)
sár; sore, sorry, sorrow
scacan; to shake
scádu, sceado; shadow
scafan (*scrape*); to shave
sceaft (*a scraped pole*); shaft
scanca; shank
scapan, sceapan *a form, create*; make (*From this comes the suffix* scipe *or* scype = -ship)
sceacga (*a bush or bunch*); shaggy
ic sceal (*I owe*); I shall

sceéran; to shear, to share, short
sceaðan (*to steal, injure*); scatheless
sceáwian (*to look*); show
sceoh (*perverse*); askew
sccofan, scufan; shove, shuffle, scuffle
scéorp (*clothing*); scarf
scinan; to shine
scip; ship, skipper
scir (*pure, clear*); sheer
scir; shire
scir-gerefa; sheriff
scólu (*band*); shoal
scrincan; to shrink
scrúd (*garment*); shroud
sealt; salt
secg; sedge
secgan; to say
seld; seldom
segel; sail
sencan; to sink
seóc; sick
scolfer; silver
slǽp; sleep
slecge (*hammer*); sledge
slóp (*frock, loose outer dress*); slop shop
sluma; slumber
sméru (*grease*); smear
snican (*creep*); sneak
sóð (*truth*); soothsayer
spǽtan; to spit
spéd (*prosperity*); speed
spell (*tale*); gospel (i.e., good-spell)
spiwan; to spew
sprengan; to sprinkle
stæf; staff
stǽger; stair
stearc (*strong*); stark
starch

stelan; to steal
stenc; stench, stink
stcopan (*to bereave*);
step-son (*i.e., or-
phan son*) step-
father (*orphan's
father*)
steorra; star
sticce (*portion*); stick,
steak
stician; to stick, stitch
stigan (*to mount*); stir-
rup (i.e., stig-ráp
= *mounting rope*)
stóc (*place*); names
in — stoke
stów (*place*); to
stow away, stew-
ard (*guardian of a
mansion*), names in
— stow
streowian; to strew
sum (*a certain —*);
some-body, &c.
suð · south
sweart (*black*); swar-
thy
swelgan; to swallow
sweltan (*to die*); swel-
ter
sweord; sword
swerian; to swear,
answer (*from* and
= *against*)
swifan (*to move quick-
ly*); swift
syllan (*to give*); sell
tǽcan; to teach
tǽsan (*to pluck*);
tease
tendan (*to kindle*);
tinder
teoða (*tenth*); tithe
tíd (*time*); tide
tilian (*to prepare*); till
{ treówian (*to trust*);
  to trow
  treówð (*confi-
  dence*); truth, trust
trog (*tub, boat*);
trough

tumbian (*to dance*);
tumble
tún (*enclosed ground*);
town
twegen (*two*); twain,
twin, between,
twenty
wacan, wacian; to
wake, watch
wǽd (*garment*);
widow's weeds
wǽpen; weapon
{ wǽr (*cautious*);
  ware, wary
  warnian; to warn
wǽscan; to wash
{ wana (*lack*); want
  wanian; to wane
wandrian; to wander
wealcan (*to roll, turn*);
walk
weald (*forest*); Weald,
Wold
wealdan (*to rule*);
wield, Bretwalda
(*governor of the
Britons*)
wealh (*foreign*);
Welsh, walnut
weard (*guard*); ward
wed (*a pledge*); to
wed
wel, bet, betst; well,
better, best
wendan (*to turn*);
to wend one's way
wén (*hope*), wénan
(*to expect*); ween,
overweening
weorc; work
weorpan (*to throw, to
change*); to warp,
mouldwarp (*i.e.,
mould-caster*).
weorð; worth
weorðan (*to become*);
'woe worth the
day,' i.e., 'woe be
to the day'
wesan (*to be*); was,
&c.

wic (*dwelling*); Aln-
wick, Greenwich,
&c.
wicca, wicce; witch,
wicked
wilcuma (*a desired
guest*); welcome
wiht (*thing, creature*);
wight, whit
win (*war*); Baldwin,
Godwin
{ witan (*to know*); to
  wit, I wot
  witnes (*knowledge*);
  witness
wið (*against*) with-
stand; to be angry
with, &c.
wolcen (*cloud*); wel-
kin
wóp (*weeping*);
whoop
worð (*farm*); Tam-
worth, &c.
wós (*juice*); ooze
wræstan (*to twist*):
wrest, wrestle
wrécan (*to afflict*);
wreck, wreak,
wretch
wrégan (*to accuse*):
bewray
wríða (*band*); wreath
to wreathe, writhe
wyn (joy); winsome
wyrd (*fate*); weird
wyrhta (*workman*);
wright
weor (*bad*) wyrse,
wyrrest; worse,
worst
yfel (*bad*); evil, ill
yrman (*to afflict*);
harm
yrman; to run
{ þencan; to think
  þincan (*to seem*),
methinks (*i.e., seems
to me*), methought
(*i.e., seemed to me*)
þeóf; thief

þirel (*hole*); drill, þweor (*oblique*; a- þringan (*to press*);
nostril (i.e., *nose-* thwart throng
hole { þyrr; dry þræl (*slave*); thral-
{ þyrst; thirst dom

Specimens of Words that have remained unaltered, or nearly so.

bindan	gift	miss-ian	spring-an
box	gleam	mist	stand-an
brand	gold	nest	stepp-an
bring-an*	grim	norð	sting-an
bristl	grind-an	oft	storm
climb-an	grip-an	open	spurn-an (*to*
corn	grów-an	oðer	*strike with*
crib	great	ram	*the heel*)
croft	heáp	rascal (*a lean*	stre´am
crop	helm	*deer*)	sup-an
deaf	help-an	rest	swing-an
deað	hem	sand	tell-an
dim	hilt or hylt	seám	timber
drag-an	horn	send-an	turf
dumb	hors	sett-an	twig
dust	hunt-ian	side	wan
east	ídel	sing-an	web
elf	inn	sitt-au	west
elm	land	slinc-an	will-an
end-e	leaf	slip-an	wind
fell	lust	slit-an	winter
find-an	man	sot	wit
forð	melt-an	spend-an	word
full	mere (*lake*)	spill-an	þing [þorn

A List of the principal Latin Words from which Derivatives are formed in English.†

Acer (*sharp*), acidus (*sour*), acerbus (*bitter*) ; acrid, acerbity, acrimony, acid.
Acuo (*I sharpen*) ; acute, acumen.
Aedes (*house*) ; edifice, edify (*literally, to build up*).
Aequus (*level*) ; equal, equation, equator, adequate, equity, iniquity, equivocate, equinox.
Aestimo (*I value*) ; estimate, esteem, aim.   Aestus (*tide*) ; estuary.
Aeternus, *i.e.*, aeviternus (*of endless duration*); eternity, eternal.
Aevum (*age*) ; coeval, primeval.   Agger (*heap*) ; exaggerate.
Ager (*field*) ; agriculture, agrarian.

* The infinitive termination *an* is no longer used.
† In most cases only a few samples of the English derivatives are given.

APPENDIX. 239

Ago (*I set in motion, drive, do*); agent, act, agile, agitate.
Alacer (*brisk*); alacrity.
Alius (*other*), alter (*other of two*); alien, alibi, alter, alternate.
Alo (*I nourish*); alimony, aliment. Altus (*high, deep*); altitude, exalt.
Ambitio (*going round, courting favour*); ambition, ambitious.
Ambulo (*I walk*); amble, somnambulist (*i.e., sleep-walker*).
Amo (*I love*), amicus (*friend*), amor (*love*); amour, amorous, amicable, amiable.
Amoenus (*pleasant*); amenity. Amplus (*large*); ample, amplify,
Ango (*I choke*), anxius, anxious, anxiety, anguish.
Angulus (*corner, bend*); angle.
Anima (*breath*), animus (*mind*); animate, animal, magnanimous, animosity.
Annulus (*ring*); annular. Annus (*year*); annual, anniversary.
Anus (*old woman*); anile. Aperio (*I open*); April, aperient, aperture.
Apis (*bee*); apiary. Appello (*I call*); appellation, appellant, appeal.
Aptus (*fitted*), apto (*I fit*); adapt, apt.
Aqua (*water*); aqueous, aquatic, aqueduct.
Arbiter (*umpire, go-between*); arbitrate, arbitrary.
Arbor (*tree*); arbour. Arca (*chest*); ark. Arcus (*bow*); arc, arch.
Ardeo (*I burn*); ardent, ardour, arson. Arduus (*steep*); arduous.
Arena (*sand*); arena, arenaceous. Argentum (*silver*); argent.
Argilla (*clay*); argillaceous. Arguo (*I prove*); argue, argument.
Aridus (*dry*); arid, aridity. Arma (*fittings, arms*); arms, arm, armour.
Aro (*I plough*; arable, earing. Ars (*skill*); art, artist, artifice.
Artus (*joint*), articulus (*little joint or fastening*); articulate, article.
Asinus (*ass*); asinine. Asper (*rough*); asperity, exasperate.
Audax (*bold*); audacious, audacity. Audio (*I hear*); audience, audible.
Augeo (*I increase*); augment, auction, author, authority.
Aurum (*gold*); auriferous.
Auspex (*one who takes omens from birds*); auspicious, auspices.
Auxilium (*help*); auxiliary.
Avarus (*greedy*); avarice, avaricious. Avidus (*eager*); avidity.
Avis (*bird*); aviary. Auris (*ear*); aurist, auricular.
Barba (*beard*); barb, barbed, barber. Beatus (*blessed*); beatitude.
Bellum (*war*); belligerent, rebel. Bene (*well*); beneficent, benediction.
Benignus (*kind*); benign. Bestia (*beast*); beast, bestial.
Bini (*two by two*) binary. Bis (*twice*); bissextile, bisect.
Blandus (*coaxing*); bland. Brevis (*short*); brief, brevity.
Caballus (*horse*); cavalry.
Cado, sup. casum (*I fall*); cadence, ac-cident, oc-casion, casual.
Caedo, caesum (*I cut*); suicide, regicide, incision, concise, cement (*i.e., caedimentum*).
Calamitas; calamity. Calcitro (*I kick*); recalcitrant.
Calculus (*pebble*); calculate. Calx; chalk, calcine.
Callus (*hard skin*), callosus; callous. Campus (*plain*); camp, encamp.
Candeo (*I burn or shine*), candidus (*white*); candid, incandescent, incendiary, candle, candour.
Canis (*dog*); canine. Canna (*reed or tube*), canalis; canal, channel.
Canto (*I sing*); chant, incantation.
Capillus (*hair*): capillary. Carmen (*song*); charm.

Capio (*I take*), captus (*taken*); captive, capacity, accept, conception, recipient, anticipate.
Caput (*head*); cape, capital, captain, chapter, decapitate, precipitate.
Carbo (*coal*); carbon, arboniferous.   Carcer (*prison*); incarcerate
Caro, carnis (*flesh*); carnal, incarnate, charnel-house, carnival.
Carpo (*pluck*); carp.   Carus (*dear*); charity.
Castigo (*restrain*); castigate, chastise.   Castus (*pure*); chaste.
Casus (*falling*); case, casual.   Causa; cause; excuse, accuse.
Caveo, cautum (*I take care*); caution.
Cavus (*hollow*); cave, cavity, excavate.
Cedo (*I go*); cede, precede, proceed, cession.
Celeber (*frequented*); celebrate, celebrity.
Celer (*quick*); celerity.   Celo (*I hide*); conceal.
Censeo (*I judge*); censor, censure.   Centum (*hundred*); cent, century; centre, concentrate, centrifugal.
Cerno, cretum (*I distinguish*); discern, concern, discreet, secret.
Certus (*resolved*); certain, certify.   Cesso (*I loiter*); cease, cessation.
Charta (*paper*); chart, charter, cartoon.
Cingo (*I gird*); cincture, succinct, precincts.
Circum (*round*), circus (*a circle*); circle, circulate, circuit, circumference.
Cista (*box*); chest.   Cito (*I rouse*); citation, excite.
Civis (*citizen*); civil, civic, city (*from* civitas).
Clamo (*I shout*), clamor; claim, exclaim, clamour.
Clarus (*bright*); clear, clarify.   Classis; class, classic.
Claudo, clausum (*I shut*); close, enclose, exclude, preclude, include.
Clemens (*mild*); clemency, inclement.
Clino (*I bend*); incline, recline, declension.
Clivus (*sloping ground*); declivity.   Coelebs (*bachelor*); celibacy.
Coelum (*heaven*); celestial.   Cogito (coagito—*I think*); cogitate
Cognosco (*I examine, know*); recognize, cognizant.
Colo, cultum (*I till*); culture, cultivate, colony.
Color; colour.   Columna; column.
Comes (*companion*); concomitant, count.
Commodus (*convenient*); commodious, commodity, incommode.
Communis; common, community.   Contra (*against*); counter.
Copia (*plenty*); copious.   Copulo (*I join together*); copulative.
Coquo, coctum (*I boil*); cook, decoction.
Cor, cordis (*heart*); cordial, concord, record.   Corona; crown, coronation
Corpus (*body*); corps, corpse, incorporate, corporeal, corpulent.
Cras (*to-morrow*); procrastinate.
Credo (*I believe*); creed, credulous, incredible, credit.   Creo; create.
Cresco, cretum (*I grow*); increase, accretion, crescent.
Crimen (*charge*); crime, criminal.   Crispus (*curled*); crisp.
Crudus (*raw*), crudelis; cruel, crude.   Crusta; crust.
Crux (*cross*); crusade, crucify, excruciate.
Cubo, cumbo (*I lie*); succumb, recumbent.
Cubitus (*a bend, elbow*); cubit.   Culpa (*fault*); inculpate, culpable.
Culter; coulter.   Cumulus (*heap*); accumulate.
Cupidus (*eager*); cupid, cupidity.
Cura (*care*); cure, curator, curious, procure, secure.
Curro, cursum (*I run*); concur, discursive, current, curricle, succour, course.

APPENDIX. 241

Curvus (*bent*); curve.   **Custodia** (*guard*); custody.
Damno; damn, condemn.   **Debeo, debitum** (*I owe*); debt, debit.
Debilis (*weak*); debility.   **Decem** (*ten*); December, decimal, decimate.
Decens (*becoming*), decor, decorus; decent, decorous.
Densus; dense, condense.
Dens, dentis (*tooth*); dentist, trident, indent.
Desidero (*I long for*); desire, desiderate.
Deus (*God*); deity, deify, deodand (*to be given to God*).
Dexter (*right*); dexterous, dexterity.
Dico, dictum (*I say*); contradict, predict, diction, dictate.
Dies (*day*); diary, diurnal.
Digitus (*finger*); digit, digital.   **Dirus**: dire.
Dignus (*worthy*); condign, dignity, dignify.
Disco (*I learn*); disciple, discipline.
Divido; divide, division.   **Divinus**; divine, divination.
Do, datum (*I give*); dative, add, addition, date.
Doceo (*I teach*); docile, doctor, doctrine.
Dolor (*grief*), doleo, (*I grieve*); dolorous, condole.
Domo (*I tame*); indomitable.   **Dono** (*I present*); donation, condone.
Domus (*house*); domicile, domestic, dome.
Dominus (*master*); dominate, dominant, domineer.
Dormio (*I sleep*); dormant, dormitory, dormouse (?)
Dubius (*doubtful*); doubt, dubious, indubitable.
Duco, ductum (*I lead*), dux (*leader*); conduct, duke, adduce, seduce, educate.
Duo (*two*); dual, duet, duel.
Durus (*hard*), duro (*I harden*); endure, durable, indurate.
Ebrius (*drunken*); ebriety, inebriate.   **Edo** (*I eat*); edible, esculent.
Ego (*I*); egotist.   **Emo** (*I buy*); redeem, exempt.
Eo, ivi, itum (*I go*); exit, initial, transit, perish.
Equus (*horse*), eques (*horseman*); equine, equerry, equitation.
Erro (*I wander*); err, error, erroneous, erratic, aberration.
Esca (*food*); esculent.   **Examino** (*I weigh*); examine.
Exemplum; example, sample.   **Exerceo**; exercise.
Expedio (*I set free*); expedite, expedition.
Experior (*I try*); experiment, expert, experience.
Faber (*mechanic, engineer*); fabric, fabricate.
Fabula (*little story*); fable, fabulous.   **Facetus** (*clever*); facetious.
Facies (*make or appearance*); face, facial, superficial.
Facilis (*easy*); facile, facility, difficulty, faculty, facilitate.
Facio (*I make, do*); fact, faction, affect, infect, defect, deficient, benefactor, manufactory, perfect.
Fallo (*I deceive*); false, fail, fallible.
Fama (*report*); fame, infamous.   **Familia**; family, familiar.
Fans (*speaking*), fatum (*what is spoken or decreed*); infant, fate, fatal.
Fanum (*temple*); fane, profane, fanatic.   **Fastidium** (*loathing*), fastidious.
Fatuus (*tasteless, silly*); fatuous, infatuated.   **Faveo**; favour.
Febris; fever, febrifuge, febrile.   **Fecundus** (*fertile*); fecundity.
Felis (*cat*); feline.   **Felix** (*happy*); felicity.
Femina (*woman*); feminine, effeminate.

R

APPENDIX.

Fendo (*I strike*) ; defend, offend, offence, fence.
Fero (*I bear*) : fertile, infer, defer, circumference ; *part*. latus ; dilate, translate.
Ferox ; ferocious, ferocity.   Ferrum (*iron*) ; ferruginous.
Ferveo (*I boil*) ; fervent, fervid, effervesce.
Festus (*solemn, joyful*) ; festive, feast.   Fibra ; fibre.
Fides (*faith*), fido (*I trust*) ; fidelity, confide, perfidy, defy.
Figo, fixum (*I fasten*) ; fix, crucifix.   Filius (*son*) ; filial, affiliate.
Findo, fissum (*I cleave*) ; fissure, fissile.
Fingo, fictum (*I shape*) ; fiction, figure, feign.
Finis (*end*) ; final, finite, finish, confine, define, infinitive.
Firmus ; firm, confirm, affirm.   Fiscus (*treasury*) ; fiscal, confiscate.
Flaccidus ; flaccid.   Flagellum (*scourge*) ; flagellation.
Flagitium(*disgrace*); flagitious. Flagro (*I burn*); flagrant, conflagration
Flamma; flame, inflammation.   Flo, flatum (*I blow*); inflate, flatulent.
Flecto (*I bend*) ; deflect, inflect, flexible, circumflex.
Fligo, flictum (*I strike*) ; afflict, conflict, profligate.
Flos, floris (*flower*) ; flora, florid, floral, effloresce.
Fluo, fluxum (*I flow*), fluctus, (*wave*) ; flux, fluxion, influence, superfluous, fluctuate, fluid.
Fodio, fossum (*I dig*) ; fosse, fossil.
Folium (*leaf*) ; foliage, folio, exfoliate, trefoil.
Fons ; fount, font, fountain.   Forma ; form, reform, inform.
Formido (*fear*) ; formidable.   Fors, fortuna ; fortune, misfortune.
Fortis (*strong*) ; fort, fortify, fortitude, fortress.
Frango, fractum (*I break*) ; fragile, frail, infringe, infraction, refraction, refractory, fragment, fracture.
Frater (*brother*) ; fraternal, fratricide.   Fraus, fraudis ; fraud.
Frequens ; frequent.   Frico (*I rub*) ; friction.
Frigus (*cold*) ; frigid, refrigerate.   Frivolus ; frivolous.
Frons ; front, affront, frontispiece.   Frugalis ; frugal.
Fruges, fructus (*fruit*), fruor (*I enjoy*) ; fruit, fructify, fruition.
Frustra (*in vain*) ; frustrate.   Fugio (*I flee*) ; fugitive, refuge.
Fulgeo (*I lighten*) ; refulgent.   Fulmen (*thunderbolt*) ; fulminate.
Fumus (*smoke*) ; fumigate, fume.
Fundo (*I pour*) ; found, foundry, refund, confound, confuse, refuse..
Fundus (*bottom*) ; found, foundation, fundamental, profound.
Fungor (*I discharge*) ; function, defunct.   Funus ; funeral.
Fur (*thief*) ; furtive.   Futilis ; futile.
Garrio (*I prattle*) ; garrulous.
Gelu (*ice*) ; gelid, congeal, jelly, gelatine.   Gemma ; gem.
Gens (*race*), gigno (*root gen-*), *I beget* ; genus (*kind*); gentile, generate, generation, gender, degenerate, general, gentle, genteel.
Germen (*bud*) ; germinate.
Gero, gestum (*I bear*) ; gesture, suggest, belligerent, vice-gerent.
Glacies (*ice*) ; glass, glacial, glazier.   Glans (*kernel*) ; gland, glandular.
Gleba (*clod*) ; glebe.
Globus (*ball*), glomero (*I make into a ball*) ; globe, conglomerate.
Gloria ; glory.
Gradus (*step*), gradior, gressum (*I walk*) ; grade, degrade, digression, congress, transgress, aggression.

APPENDIX. 243

Grandis (*large*); **grand**, aggrandize.   Granum; grain.
Gratia; **grace**, gratuitous, gratis.   Gratus; grateful, gratitude.
Gravis (*heavy*); grave, gravitation, grief.
Grex (*flock*); gregarious, congregate.   Guberno (*I pilot*); govern.
Habeo, habitum (*I have*); have, habit, prohibit.
Habito (*dwell*); habitation, inhabit.
Haereo (*I stick*); adhere, adhesion, **hesitate.**
Haeres or heres (*heir*); inherit, hereditary.
Halo (*I breathe*); exhale, inhale.   Haurio, haustum (*I draw*); **exhaust.**
Herba; herb, herbaceous.   Hibernus (*wintry*); hibernate.
Histrio (*actor*); histrionic.   Homo (*man*), humanus; human, homicide.
Honestus; honest.   Honor; honour, honourable, honorary.
Horreo (*I shudder*), horror, horridus; horror, horrid, horrify, abhor.
Hortor; exhort.   Hortus (*garden*); horticulture.
Hospes (*guest*); hospitable, hospice, host.   Hostis (*enemy*); hostile,
Humeo (*I am wet*); humid, humour.
Humus (*ground*); exhume, humble, humiliate.
Ignis (*fire*); ignite, igneous.   Ignoro; ignore, ignorant.
Imago; image, imagine.   Imbecillis (*weak*); imbecile.   Imbuo; imbue.
Impero (*I command*), imperium; empire, emperor, imperious, imperative.
Index, indico (*I point*); indicate, indicative.
Inferus (*low, placed underneath*); inferior, infernal.
Ingenium (*talent, disposition*); ingenious.
Ingenuus (*native*); ingenuous, ingenuity.   Insula (*island*); insular, insulate.
Integer (*whole, sound*); integral, integrate, integrity.
Intelligo (*I perceive*); intelligent, intellect.   Invito; invite.
Ira (*anger*); ire, irate, irascible.   Irrito (*I provoke*); irritate.
Irrigo; irrigate.   Iterum (*again*); reiterate.
Iter, itineris (*journey*); itinerant.
Jaceo (*I lie down*); adjacent.
Jacio, jactum (*I throw*); eject, reject, object, adjective, conjecture, subject.
Jocus; joke, jocular.   Jubeo, jussum (*I order*); jussive.
Judex; judge, judicious, adjudicate, prejudice.
Jugum (*yoke*); conjugal, conjugate, subjugate.
Jugulum (*collar bone*); jugular.
Jungo, junctum; join, joint, juncture, conjunction, injunction,
Juro (*I swear*); conjure, jury, perjury.
Jus (*justice*), justus (*just*); just, unjust, injury, justify, jurisdiction.
Juvenis (*young*); juvenile, junior.   Labor; labour, laborious, laboratory.
Labor, lapsus sum (*I slide*); lapse, elapse, collapse.
Lac, lactis (*milk*); lacteal, lactic.   Lacero (*I mangle*); lacerate.
Lacrima (*tear*); lacrimose.   Lacus; lake.
Laedo, laesum (*I dash or hurt*); lesion, elide, elision, collision.
Lamentor; I lament.   Langueo, languidus; languid, languish.
Lapis, lapidis (*stone*); lapidary, dilapidate.   Largus; large.
Lassus (*weary*); lassitude.   Lateo (*I lie hid*); latent.
Latus (*broad*); latitude.   Latus, lateris (*side*); lateral, equilateral.
Laus, laudis (*praise*); laud, laudation, laudable.
Lavo (*I wash*); lavatory, lavation, lave.   Luxus (*loose*); lax, relax.
Lego (*I send* or *depute*): legate, allege, legacy.

Lego, lectum (*I gather, choose*); collect, select, elect, recollect, lecture, college, legion.
Lenis (smooth); lenity.   Lentus (*flexible*); relent.
Levis (*light*), levo (*I lift*); levity, alleviate, relieve, elevate.
Lex, legis (*law*); legal, legitimate, legislate.
Liber (*free*); liberal, liberate, deliver.   Liber (*book*); library, libel.
Libo (*I pour*); libation.   Libra (*balance*); deliberate, libration.
Licet (*it is lawful*); licence, illicit.   Lignum (*wood*); ligneous.
Ligo (*I tie*); ligament, religion, league, allegiance, oblige.
Limen (*threshold*); eliminate.   Limes, limitis (*boundary*); limit.
Linea; line, lineal.   Lingua (*tongue*); linguist, language.
Linquo, lictum (*I leave*); relinquish, relict, delinquent.
Liquor, liquidus; liquor, liquid, liquefy.
Litera; letter, literal, illiterate.   Lividus (*dark blue*); livid.
Locus (*place*), loco (*I place*); locate, local, locomotion.
Longus; long, longitude, elongate.
Loquor, locutus, (*I speak*), loquax; elocution, loquacious, colloquy, eloquent.   Lucrum (*gain*); lucrative, lucre.
Ludo, lusum (*I play*); elude, prelude, illude, illusion, ludicrous.
Lumen (*light*); luminous, illuminate.   Luna (*moon*); lunar, lunatic.
Luo, lutum (*I wash*); dilute, ablution, diluvial.
Lustrum (*purification*); lustre, lustrous, lustration, illustrate.
Lux (*light*); lucid, elucidate.
Machina; machine,   Macula (*spot*); immaculate.
Magister (*master*); magistrate, magisterial.
Magnus (*great*), major (*greater*); magnitude, majesty, majority, mayor.
Malus (*bad*); malice, malignant, maltreat, malady.
Mamma (*breast*); mamma, mammalia.
Mando (*commit, enjoin*); mandate, command, commend, remand.
Maneo, mansum (*I remain*); mansion, remain, remnant, permanent, imminent.
Manus (*hand*); manual, manufactory, manuscript, maintain, manacle, emancipate, manumit.   Mare (*sea*); marine, maritime, mariner.
Mars; martial.   Massa; mass, massive.
Mater (*mother*); maternal, matricide, matron, matrix, matriculate, matrimony.   Materia (*timber, stuff*); matter, material.
Maturus (*ripe*); mature, immature, premature.
Medeor (*I heal*), medicina; remedy, medicine, medical.
Medius (*middle*); mediator, mediocrity, immediate.
Mel (*honey*); mellifluous.   Melior (*better*); ameliorate.
Membrum; member, membrane.
Memor (*mindful*), memini (*I remember*); remember, memory, memorial, memoir, commemorate, comment.   Mendax (*lying*); mendacious.
Mendicus (*beggar*); mendicant, mendicity.
Mendum (*fault*); amend, mend, emendation.
Mens, mentis (*mind*); mental, vehement.   Mereo meritum (*I deserve*); merit.
Mergo, mersum (*I plunge*); immerse, merge, emergency.   Merus; mere.
Merx (*wares*), merchant, commerce, mercer, market,
Metior, mensus sum (*I measure*); immense, mensuration, measure.
Migro (*I change my abode*); migrate.

Miles, militis (*soldier*) ; military, militia.
Mille (*thousand*); mile, millenium, million.
Minister (*servant*); minister, ministry.
Minor (*less*), minuo (*I lessen*); diminish, minor, minority, minute.
Mirus (*wonderful*) miror (*I admire*) ; admire, miracle.
Misceo, mixtum, (*I mix*) ; miscellany, promiscuous.
Miser (*wretched*) ; miser, miserable, misery commiserate.
Mitigo; mitigate.
Mitto, missum (*I send*); emit, admit, permit, promise, mission, missile.
Modus (*measure*) ; mode, mood, model, moderate, modest, modulation.
Mola ; mill-stone, meal, molar, immolate, emolument (*the miller's perquisite*). Mollis (*soft*); emollient, mollify, mollusk.
Moneo, monitum (*I warn*) ; admonish, monument, monster, monitor.
Mons, montis ; mount, mountain, surmount, dismount, promontory.
Monstro (*I show*); demonstrate. Morbus (*disease*); morbific, morbid.
Mordeo, morsum (*I bite*) ; remorse, morsel.
Mors, mortis, (*death*) : mortal, mortuary. Mos, moris (*custom*) ; moral.
Moveo, motum (*I move*), mobilis, momentum ; move, motive, moment, mobility, emotion. Mula : mule.
Multus (*many*); multitude, multiform, multiple, multiply (plico, -plex).
Mundus (*world*) ; mundane.
Munio (*I fortify*) ; munition, ammunition, muniment.
Munus, muneris (*gift, share*) ; remunerate, immunity.
Murus (*wall*) ; mural, intramural.
Musa (*muse*); music, amuse, museum. Mutilus (*maimed*) ; mutilate.
Muto (*I change*) ; mutable, mutation, commute, transmute.
Narro ; narrate, narrative. Nasus (*nose*) ; nasal.
Nascor, natus sum (*I am born*) ; nascent, natal, native, nation, cognate, nature, natural.
Navis (*ship*); naval, navigate, navy. Nauta (*sailor*); nautical, nautilus.
Necesse ; necessary, necessitude, necessity.
Necto, nexum (*I tie*) : connect, annex. Nefas (*wickedness*) ; nefarious.
Nego (*I deny*); negation, renegade. Negotium, (*business*) ; negotiate.
Nervus (*string*); nerve, enervate. Neuter (*not either*); neuter, neutral.
Niger (*black*) ; negro. Nihil (*nothing*) ; annihilate.
Noceo (*I hurt*) ; innocent, noxious, innocuous.
No-sco, notum (*I know*) ; no-men (*name*), no-bilis (*noble*) ; noun, name, nominate, nominal, noble, ignoble, ignominy, note, notation, notion, notice. Non (*not*) ; non-entity, non-age.
Norma (*rule*) ; normal, enormous. Novem (*nine*) ; November.
Novus (*new*) ; novel, innovate, renovate, novice.
Nox, noctis (*night*) ; nocturnal, equinox.
Nubo (*I marry*) ; nuptial, connubial. Nudus (*naked*) ; nude, denude.
Nullus (*none*) ; nullity, nullify, annul.
Numerus (*number*) ; numeral, enumerate.
Nuntio (*I announce*) ; nuncio, announce, renounce, renunciation.
Nutrio (*I nourish*) ; nutritious, nutriment. Nutrix, nurse.
Nympha : nymph. Oblivio (from liv-idus) ; oblivion.
Obliquus: oblique. Obscoenus: obscene. Obscurus (*dark*) ; obscure.
Occulo, occultum (*I hide*) ; occult.
Occupo (*I lay hold of*) ; occupy, occupation.

Octo (*eight*); octave, octavo, October.
Oculus (*eye, bud*); ocular, oculist, inoculate.
Odium (*hatred*); odious, odium.
Odor (*smell*), oleo (*I smell*); odour, odorous, redolence, olfactory.
Officium (*duty, business*); office, officious.   Oleum (*oil*); oleaginous
Omen; ominous, abominate.
Omnis (*all*); omnipotent, omnibus (*for all*).
Onus, oneris (*load*); onerous, exonerate.   Opacus (*shaded*); opaque.
Opinor (*I think*); opine, opinion.   Optimus (*best*); optimist.
Opto (*I desire*); option, adopt.   Opus, operis (*work*); operate.
Orbis (*circle*); orb, orbit, exorbitant.
Ordo, ordinis (*order*); ordinate, ordain, ordinary.
Orior, ortus sum (*I rise*); orient, origin, abortive.
Oro (*I speak*); orator, oracle, adore, inexorable.
Os, oris (*face*); oral.   Osculor (*I kiss*); oscillate.
Ovum (*egg*); oviparous, oval.
Paciscor, pactus sum (*I make an agreement*); pact, compact.
Pagina; page.   Pagus (*village*); pagan, peasant.
Pallium (*cloak*); pall, palliate.
Pallor (*paleness*); palleo, (*I am pale*); pallor, pallid.   Palma; palm.
Palpo (*I stroke*); palpable, palpitate.
Palus (*stake*); pale, palisade, impale.
Pando, pansum and passum (*I spread*); expand, expanse, compass.
Pango, pactum (*I fasten*); compact, impinge.
Panis (*bread*); pantry.   Par (*equal*); parity, peer, compare.
Parco, parsum (*I spare*); parsimony.   Pareo (*I appear*); apparent.
Pario (*I bring forth*); parent, viviparous.
Paro (*I prepare*); impair, repair, prepare, compare, comparative.
Pars, partis (*part*); partition, impart, party, particle, participle, parse, particular, bipartite.   Pasco, pastum (*I feed*); pasture, repast, pastor.   Passus (*stride*, see *pando*); pace.
Pateo (*I lie open*); patent.
Pater (*father*); paternal, patron, patrimony, patrician, patristic.
Patria (*country*); patriot, expatriate.
Patior, passus sum (*I suffer*); patient, passion, passive.
Pauper (*poor*); pauper, pauperism.   Pavio (*I ram tight*); pave, pavement.
Pax, pacis (*peace*); pacific.
Pecco (*I sin*); peccant, impeccable, peccadillo.
Pectus, pectoris (*breast*); pectoral, expectorate.
Peculium (*private property*); peculiar, peculation.
Pecunia (*money*); pecuniary.   Pellis (*skin*); peltry.
Pello, pulsum (*I drive*); compel, repel, repulse, pulse, pulsation.
Pendeo (*I hang*), pendo, pensum, (*I hang* or *weigh*); depend, expend, pension, pensive, recompense, pendulum, compensate, perpendicular, pensile.   Pene (*almost*); peninsula.
Penetro (*I pierce*); penetrate.
Penuria (*want*); penury, penurious.   Perdo (*I lose*); perdition.
Persona (*mask*); person.
Pes, pedis (*foot*); pedal, pedestrian, impede, expedite, biped.
Pestis (*plague*); pest, pestilence.
Peto, petitum (*ask, seek*); petition, compete, repeat, appetite.

Pingo, pictum (*paint*) ; depict, picture, pigment, Picts.
Pilo (*I steal*) ; pillage, compile.   Piscis (*fish*) ; piscatory.
Pius (*dutiful*) ; pious, piety, pity, expiate.
Placeo (*I please*) ; placid, placable, complaisant, pleasant.
Plango ; com-plain, plaint.   Planta ; plant, plantation.
Planus (*level*) ; plane, plain, explain.
Plaudo (*I clap*) ; applaud, applause, plaudit, plausible.
Plebs (*commonalty*) ; plebeian.
Plecto, plexus (*I weave*) ; complex, perplex.
Pleo (*I fill*), plenus (*full*) ; plenary, complete, replete.
Plico (*I fold*) ; implicate, apply, application, comply, reply, supplicate, suppliant, duplicity, double, complex, pliable, surplice, accomplice.
Ploro (*I weep*) ; deplore, explore.   Pluma ; plume.
Plumbum (*lead*) ; plumber, plummet.
Plus, pluris (*more*) ; plural, surplus.
Pœna (*fine*) ; penal, punitive, punish, repent, penance, penitent.
Polio ; polish, polite.
Pondus, ponderis (*weight*) ; pound, ponderous, preponderate, ponder.
Pono, positum (*I place*) ; impose, repose, deposit, compound, position, component.   Pons (*bridge*) ; pontoon.
Populus (*people*) ; popular, depopulate, public, publish.
Porcus (*hog*) ; pork.
Porta (*door*) ; portal, portico, porthole.
Porto (*I carry*) ; export, portable, support.   Portus ; port.
Possum (*I can*) ; possible, potent.
Post (*after*) ; posterity.   Postis ; post.   Postulo (*I demand*) ; postulate.
Præda (*plunder*) ; predatory, depredation, prey.
Pravus (*crooked*) ; depraved.
Precor (*I pray*) ; deprecate, precarious (*depending on entreaty*).
Prehendo (*I grasp*) ; apprehend, apprehension.
Premo, pressum (*I press*) ; express.
Primus (*first*) ; prime, primitive, primeval, primrose.
Princeps (*prince*) ; principal, principle.   Pristinus ; pristine.
Privo (*I deprive, make separate*) ; deprive, private, privacy, privy.
Probo (*I approve, make good*) ; prove, probe, probation, probable, reprobate.
Probus (*honest, good*) ; probity.   Probrum (*a shameful act*) ; opprobrious.
Promptus, from promo (*ready*) ; prompt, promptitude.
Pronus ; prone.   Propago ; propagate.
Prope (*near*), proximus (*nearest*) ; propinquity, proximate, proximity.
Proprius (*one's own*) ; proper, property, propriety, appropriate.
Prurio (*I itch*) ; prurient.   Pudor (*shame*), pudet ; impudent.
Puer (*boy*) ; puerile.   Pugil (*boxer*) ; pugilist.
Pugna (*fight*), pugno (*I fight*) ; pugnacious, impugn, repugnance.
Pulmo (*lungs*) ; pulmonary.   Pulpa ; pulp.
Pungo, punctum (*I prick*) ; pungent, puncture, punctuation, expunge, point, appoint.   Puppis (*stern*) ; poop.
Pupus, pupulus, pupillus (*a little boy*) ; puppet, pupil.
Purgo (*I cleanse*) ; purge, purgatory.
Purpura ; purple.   Purus ; pure, purify.
Puto (*I cut, calculate, think*) ; amputate, compute, count, repute, depute, putative.   Putris (*rotten*) ; putrid, putrefy.

Quaero, quaesitum (*I seek*); question, inquire, require, query, quest, exquisite, inquest.   **Qualis** (*of which kind*); quality, qualify.
Quantus (*how great*); quantity.
Quatio, quassum (cutio, cussum *in compounds, I shake or strike*) quash, percussion, discuss.
Quatuor (*four*), quartus (*fourth*), quadra (*square*); quart, quarto, quarter, quadrature, quadrant, quadratic.
Queror (*I complain*); querulous.   **Quies, quietis** (*rest*); quiet, acquiesce.
Quinque (*five*); quintessence.   **Radius** (*rod, ray*); radius, radiate.
Radix, radicis (*root*); radish, radical, eradicate.
Rado, rasum (*I scrape*); erase, razor, abrade.
Ramus (*branch*); ramification.
Rapio, raptum (*I snatch*); rapid, rapture, rapine, rapacious, ravish, ravage, raven, ravenous.   **Rarus** (*thin*); rare, rarefy.
Ratio (*reckoning, calculation, proportion*); reason, ratiocination, rational, ration.   **Ratus** (*reckoned, fixed*); ratify, rate.
Rego, rectum (*I make straight*); regular, direct, erect, regent, regimen, regiment, rector, rectify.
Rex, regis (*king;* not the same root as the last); regal, regicide: Regnum; reign, regnant, interregnum.
Reperio (*I find*); repertory.   **Repo** (*I creep*); reptile.
Res (*thing*); real, republic.   **Rete** (*net*); retina, reticule.
Rideo, risum (*I laugh*); deride, risible, ridicule, ridiculous.
Rigeo (*I am stiff*); rigid, rigour.
Rigo (*I water*); irrigate, irriguous.   **Ritus**; rite, ritual.
Rivus (*brook*), rivalis (*having the same brook in common*); river, rival, derive, arrive, rivulet.
Robur (*oak, strength*); robust, corroborate.
Rodo, rosum (*I gnaw*); corrode, corrosion.
Rogo (*I ask*); arrogate, derogate, rogation, prorogue.   **Rosa**; rose.
Rota (*wheel*); rotate, rotary.   **Rotundus**; round, rotund, rotundity.
Rudis (*untaught*); rude, erudite, rudiment.   **Ruga** (*wrinkle*); corrugate.
Ruminare (*to chew the cud*); ruminate.   **Rumor**; rumour.
Rumpo, ruptum (*I break*); rupture, abrupt, eruption, corrupt, bankrupt.
Ruo (*I rush*); ruin.   **Russatus** (*dyed red*); russet.
Rus, ruris (*country*); rustic, rural.   **Saccus**; sack.
Sacer (*sacred*), sacerdos (*priest*); sacred, sacrament, sacrifice, consecrate, sacerdotal, sacristan.
Sagax (*knowing*); sage, sagacious, presage.
Sal; salt, saline, salary (*properly an allowance for salt*).
Salio, saltum, *in compounds*, sultum (*I leap*); salient, assail, assault, salmon (*the leaping fish*), desultory, exult, insult, saltatory.
Salus, salutis (*safety*); salute, salutary.
Saluber; salubrious.   **Salvus** (*safe*); salvation, salve, salvo, saviour
Sancio, sanctum (*I consecrate*); sanction.
Sanctus (*holy*); saint, sanctify.
Sanguis, sanguinis (*blood*); sanguinary, sanguine, consanguinity.
Sano (*I make sound*); sanative, sanatory.

APPENDIX. 249

Sanus (*sound*); sane, sanity, sanitary.
Sapio (*I taste, am wise*), sapor (*taste*); savour, sapient, insipid.
Satelles (*attendant*); satellite.
Satis (*enough*), satur (*full*), satio (*I fill*); satiate, satiety, saturate, satisfy.
Scando (*I climb*); scan, scansion, ascend, descend, condescend.
Scindo, scissum (*I split*); rescind, abscissa, scissors.
Scintilla (*spark*); scintillate.
Scio (*I know*); science, prescience, omniscience, conscious.
Scribo, scriptum (*I write*); scribe, describe, scripture, postscript.
Scrupulus (*a little pebble*); scruple, scrupulous.
Scrutor (*I examine*); scrutiny, inscrutable.
Seco, sectum (*I cut*); sect, section, insect, dissect, segment, secant.
Seculum (*age, world*); secular.
Sedeo, sessum (*I sit*), sido (*I set*), sedo (*I settle*); session, sedentary, sedulous, sediment, assess, possess, preside, subside, assiduous, consider, sedate.
Semi (*half*); semicircle.   Senex (*old-man*); senile, senior, senate.
Sentio (*I feel, think*), sensus (*feeling*); scutient, scent, sentence, assent, sense, sensual, sensitive.
Sepelio (*I bury*), sepulcrum; sepulture, sepulchre.
Septem (*seven*); September, septennial.
Sequester (*an umpire*); sequestrate, sequestered.
Sequor, secutus (*I follow*), secundus (*following*); sequence, sequel, consequent, persecute, second.
Sero, sertum (*I set in a row*); insert, exert, desert, series, sermon.
Semen (*seed*); seminary, disseminate.   Serus; sere.
Servus (*slave*), servio (*I serve*), servo (*I watch or preserve*); serf, servile, servitude, servant, servitor, preserve, observe, deserve.
Sidus (*star*); sidereal.
Signum; sign, signify, signal, resign, design, assignation.
Sileo (*I am silent*); silent, silence.   Silva (*wood*); sylvan.
Similis (*like*); similar, assimilate, resemble, semblance, simulate.
Simul (*together*); simultaneous, assemble.   Sincerus; sincere.
Singuli (*one by one*); single, singular.   Sinister; sinister.
Sinus (*bend*); sine, sinuous.
Sisto (*I stop, I stand*); consist, insist, resist, assist.
Socius (*companion*); social, society.   Sol (*sun*); solar, solstice.
Solemnis (*annual, festive*); solemn.   Solidus; solid, solder.
Sollicito; solicit.   Solor; con-sole, solace.
Solum (*ground*); soil. Connected perhaps with this, is the root *sul* or *sil* in exsul (*exile*); consul (*consul*); counsel. The root is really identical with *sed* or *sid* in sedeo and sido.
Solus (*alone*); solo, solitude.
Solvo, solutum (*I loosen*); solve, solution, dissolute.
Somnus (*sleep*); somnolent.   Sopor (*sleep*); soporific.
Sonus; sound, sonorous, consonant.   Sordes (*dirt*); sordid.
Spargo, sparsum (*I strew*); sparse, disperse.
Spatium; space, spacious, expatiate.
Specio, spectum (*I look*), species (*appearance, kind*); special, specious, respect, aspect, spectator, speculate, despise, suspicion.

Sperno (*I reject*); spurn.   Spero (*I hope*); despair, desperate.
Spiro (*I breathe*), spiritus (*breath*); spirit, aspire, conspire.
Splendeo (*I shine*); splendour, splendid.   Spolium; spoil, spoliation.
Spondeo, sponsum (*I promise, bargain*); sponsor, spouse, respond,
response, despond.   Stagnus (*standing*); stagnant, stagnate.
Stella (*star*); constellation, stellar.   Sterilis; sterile.
Sterno, stratum (*I throw down, spread*); prostrate, consternation.
Stilla (*drop*); distil.   Stilus; style.   Stimulus (*goad*); stimulate.
Stipendium (*pay*); stipend, stipendiary.   Stirps (*root*); extirpate.
Sto, statum (*I stand*); station, stature, stable, distant, obstacle, superstition, armistice, substance, substantive.
Statuo (*I set up*); statue, statute, constitute.   Strenuus; strenuous.
Stringo, strictum (*I tighten*); stringent, strain, constrain, strict, strait.
Strangulo (*I strangle*).
Struo, structum (*I pile up*); construct, destroy, destruction, construe.
Studium (*zeal, eagerness*), studeo (*I am eager*); study, student.
Stupeo (*I am amazed*); stupid.
Suadeo, suasum (*I advise*); suasion, persuade.
Sublimis (*raised aloft*); sublime, sublimate.   Subtilis; subtile, subtle.
Sudo (*I sweat*); exude.
Sum (*I am*), root es, ens (*being*); entity, present, absent.   Futurus (*about to be*); future.   Summus (*highest*); sum, summit, consummate.
Sumo, sumptum (*I take*); assume, consume, consumption.
Super (*above*), superus (*upper*), supremus (*highest*); superior, supreme, supernal.   Supinus (*on the back*); supine.
Surgo, surrectum (*I rise*); surge, resurrection, insurrection.
Tabula (*board*); table, tablet, tabular, tabulate.
Taceo (*I am silent*); tacit, reticence, taciturn.   Taedium (*disgust*); tedious.
Tango, tactum (*I touch*); tact, contact, tangible, contagion, contiguous, attain, pertain, attach.   Taxo; tax, taxation.
Tardus (*slow*); retard, tardy.
Tego, tectum (*I cover*); protect, integument, detect.
Temere (*rashly*); temerity.   Temno (*I despise*); contemn, contempt.
Tempero (*I moderate*); temperate, temper.
Templum; temple, contemplate.
Tempus, temporis (*time*); temporal, temporary, tense.
Tendo, tensum (*I stretch*); contend, intend, tense, intense, tension.
Teneo, tentum (*I hold*); tenant, tenure, tenaceous, tenour, retain, contain, content, retinue, tendril, continuous.   Tener; tender.
Tento *or* tempto (*I try*); tempt, attempt, temptation.
Tenuis (*thin*); tenuity.   Tepeo (*I am warm*); tepid.
Terminus (*boundary*); term, terminate, exterminate, determine.
Tero, tritum (*I rub*); trite, contrition, attrition, detriment.
Terra (*earth*); terrestrial, terrene, inter, terrier, terrace.
Terreo (*I frighten*); terrify, terrible, terror, deter.
Testis (*witness*); testify, testimony, attest, detest, protest.
Texo, textum (*I weave*); text, context, texture, textile.
Timeo (*I fear*); timid.   Torpeo (*I am numb*); torpid.
Torqueo, tortum (*I twist*); torsion, contort, contortion, torture, torment.
Torreo, tostum (*I parch*); torrid, toast.   Totus (*whole*); total.
Traho, tractum (*I draw*); tracto (*I handle*); treat, tract, contract, attract, tractable, tractate.   Tranquillus; tranquil.

Tremo (*I tremble*); tremour, tremulous, tremendous.
Trepido (*I am in disorder*); trepidation.
Tres, tria (*three*); trefoil, trident, trinity.   **Tribuo** (*I assign*); tribute.
Tribus; tribe, tribune.   **Triumphus**; triumph.
Trudo, trusum (*I thrust*); extrude, intrusion. **Truncus**; trunk, truncated.
Tueor (*I protect*); tuition, tutor.
Tumeo (*I swell*); tumid, tumour, tumult, contumely, tomb.
Tuber (*a swelling*); protuberance, tubercle.
Tundo, tusum (*I thump*); contusion.
Turba (*mob*); turbulent, turbid, disturb.   **Turpis** (*foul*); turpitude.
Uber (*udder*), exuberant.   **Ubique** (*everywhere*); ubiquity.
Ulcus, ulceris (*sore*); ulcer, ulceration.
Ultra (*beyond*), ulterior (*further*), ultimus (*furthest*); ulterior, ultimate, penult.   **Umbra** (*shade*); umbrage, umbrageous, umbrella.
Uncia (*a twelfth part*); ounce, inch, uncial, unciary.
Unguo, unctum (*I anoint*); unguent, ointment, unction.
Unda (*wave*), undare (*to rise in waves*); abound, redound, abundant, inundate.
Unus (*one*); union, unity, unit, triune, uniform, universe, universal, unique.
Urbs (*city*); urban, urbane, suburb.
Urgeo (*I press*); urge, urgent.   **Urna**; urn.
Uro, ustum (*I burn*); combustion.
Utor, usus sum (*I use*); use, usage, utility, usury, usurp.
Uxor (*wife*); uxorious.   **Vacca** (*cow*); vaccine, vaccination.
Vaco (*I am unoccupied*); vacant, vacation, vacate, vacuum, evacuate.
Vado, vasum (*I go*); invade, evade, invasion, wade.
Vagor (*I wander*), vagus (*wandering*); vague, vagrant, vagabond, extravagant.
Valeo (*I am strong*); valid, valour, value, avail, prevail, prevalent, valedictory.
Vallis; vale, valley.   **Vallus** (*stake*); circumvallation.
Vanus (*empty*); vain, vanity.   **Varius**; various, variegate.
Vapor (*steam*); vapour, evaporate.   **Vas** (*pot*); vessel, vascular.
Vastus (*desolate*); vast, waste, devastate.
Veho, vectum (*I carry*); convey, convex, inveigh, vehicle.
Vello, vulsum (*I pluck*); convulse, revulsion.
Velum (*covering*); veil, reveal, develop, envelop.   **Vena**; vein.
Vendo (*I sell*); vend, venal.   **Venenum** (*poison*); venom.
Veneror (*I worship*); venerate, revere.
Venio, ventum (*I come*); convene, venture, convent, advent, prevent, revenue, convenient, covenant.
Venter (*belly*); ventral, ventriloquist.   **Ventus** (*wind*); ventilate.
Verbum (*word*); verb, verbal, proverb.
Vergo (*I incline*); verge, converge. **Vermis** (*worm*); vermicular, vermin.
Verto, versum (*I turn*); verso (*I turn*); verse, version, convert, divorce, adverse, advertise, perverse, universe, vortex, vertical.
Verus (*true*); verity, verify, aver.
Vestis (*garment*); vest, vesture, vestry, 'avest.
Vetus (*old*); inveterate, veteran.
Vexo (*I harass*); vex, vexation.   **Vibro**; vibrate.

Via (*road*); deviate, obviate, pervious, trivial.
Vicis (*change*); vicissitude, vicar, vicarious, viceroy.
Vicinus (*neighbour*); vicinity.
Video, visum (*I see*); visible, vision, provide, revise, visage, prudence, providence, survey, invidious, envy.
Vilis (*cheap*); vile, vilify.　　Villa (*country house*); villa, village.
Vinco, victum (*I conquer*); victor, vanquish, victim, convince, convict.
Vindex (*avenger*); vindicate, vindictive.
Vir (*man*), virtus (*manliness*); virtue, virago, triumvir, virile.
Vis (*force*); violent.　　Viscus; viscera, eviscerate.
Vita (*life*); vital.　　Vitium (*fault*); vice, vicious, vitiate.
Vitrum (*glass*); vitreous, vitrify, vitriol.
Vivo, victum (*I live*); revive, vivify, vivacious, victuals.
Voco (*I call*), vox (*voice*); voice, vocal, vocation, invocate, convoke, provoke, vowel, vocabulary.　　Volo (*I fly*); volatile.
Volo (*I will*); voluntary, volunteer, benevolent, volition.
Volupis (*delightful*); voluptuous.
Volvo, volutum (*I roll*); revolve, volume, revolution, voluble, volute.
Vomo; I vomit.　　Voro (*I devour*); voracious, devour, carnivorous.
Voveo, votum (*I vow*); vote, votive, votary, devote, devout.
Vulgus (*common people*); vulgar, divulge, vogue, vulgate.
Vulnus (*wound*); vulnerable.

List of the principal Greek Words Derivatives from which have been adopted into English.

Αγγελος (angelos, *messenger*); angel, evangelist.
Αγιος (*sacred*); hagiology. Αγωγη (*leading*); synagogue.
Αγων (*struggle*); agony, antagonist. Αδαμας (*steel*); adamant, diamond.
Αηρ (*air*); aeronaut, acrostation. Αθλον (*contest*); athlete, athletic.
Αιθηρ (*sky*); ether, ethereal. Αιμα (*blood*); haemorrhage.
Αινιγμα (*riddle*); enigma. Αιρησις (*choice*); heresy, heretic.
Αισθησις (*perception*); aesthetics. Ακαδημεια; academy.
Ακμη (*point*); acme. Ακολουθεω (*I follow*); acolyte *or* acolyth.
Ακουω (*I hear*); acoustics. Ακροαομαι (*I listen*); acroamatic.
Ακρος (*top*); acropolis. Αλλος (*other*); allopathy.
Αλληλοι (*one another*); parallel. Αλφα (*a*); alphabet.
Αμφι (*on both sides*); amphibious, amphitheatre.
Ανεμος (*wind*); anemometer. Ανθος (*flower*); anthology.
Ανθραξ (*coal*); anthracite. Ανθρωπος (*man*); anthropology, philanthropy.
Αξιωμα (*claim, demand*); axiom. Αρκτος (*bear*); arctic.
Αριθμος (*number*); arithmetic. Αριστος (*best*); aristocracy.
'Αρμονια; harmony. Αρτηρια; artery.
Αρχη (*rule, beginning*); monarch, archangel, architect.
Ασκεω (*I exercise*); ascetic. Αστηρ (*star*); astral, asteroid, astronomy.
Αω (*I breathe*); asthma, atmosphere. Αυτος (*self*); autograph, autocrat.
Βαλλω (*I throw*), βολη, βλημα; hyperbole, parable, emblem, symbol.
Βαπτω, βαπτιζω; baptize. Βαρβαρος (*not Greek*); barbarous.
Βαρος (*weight*); barometer. Βασις (*treading, support*); base, basis.
Βιβλιον (*book*); Bible, bibliopole. Βιος (*life*); biography, amphibious.
Βλασφημια; blasphemy. Βομβυξ (*silk-worm*); bombazine.
Βοτανη (*grass*); botany. Βρογχος (*windpipe*); bronchitis.
Γη (*earth*); apogee, geography, geology. Γαλα (*milk*); galaxy.
Γαμος (*marriage*); bigamy. Γαστηρ (*belly*); gastric, gastronomy.
Γενος (*race*); genealogy. Γιγας; giant, gigantic.
Γλωσσα (*tongue*); gloss, glossary. Γλυφω (*carve*); hieroglyphic.
Γνωμων (*pointer*); gnomon, physiognomy.
Γραφω (*I write*); grammar, telegraph, graphic, paragraph.
Γυμναζω (*I exercise*); gymnastic. Γυνη (*woman*); misogynous.
Δακτυλος (*finger*); dactyl. Δαιμων (*divinity*); demon.
Δειγμα (*pointing*); paradigm. Δεκα (*ten*); decalogue.
Δενδρον (*tree*); dendrology. Δημος (*people*); democracy.
Διαιτα (*way of living*); diet. Διδασκω (*I teach*); didactic.
Διπλωμα (*anything folded*); diploma. Δογμα (*opinion*); dogma, dogmatic
Δοξα (*opinion, glory*); orthodox, doxology.
Δραω (*I act*); drastic, drama. Δρομος (*running*); hippodrome.
Δυναμις (*power*); dynamics, dynasty. 'Εδρα (*seat*); cathedral.
Εθνος (*race*); ethnic, heathen, ethnology. Εθος (*custom*); ethics.
Ειδος (*form*); kaleidoscope, cycloid, &c.
Ειδωλον (*image*); idol, idolatry. Εικων (*image*); iconoclast.
Ειρωνεια (*dissimulation*); irony. Ελαστικος (*that may be driven*); elastic.
Ελεημοσυνη (*pity*); eleemosynary. 'Ελλην (*Greek*); Hellenic.
'Εν (*one*); hyphen. Ενδον (*within*); endogenous.
Εντερα (*entrails*); dysentery. 'Εξ (*six*); hexagon.

APPENDIX.

Εξω (*outside*); exoteric.   'Επτα (*seven*); heptarchy.
Εργον (*work*); energy, metallurgy.
Ερημος (*solitary*); eremite, hermit.
'Ετερος (*other*); heterodox, heterogeneous.   Ετυμος (*true*); etymology
Ευ (*well*); eulogy, euphony.   Εχω (*I hold*); epoch.
Ζωνη (*girdle*); zone.   Ζωον, ζωδιον (*animal*); zoology, zoophyte, zodiac.
'Ηγησις (*leading*); exegesis.   Ηλεκτρον (*amber*); electricity.
'Ηλιος (*sun*); heliacal, heliotrope.   'Ημερα (*day*); ephemeral.
'Ημι (*half*); hemisphere.   'Ηρως; hero.
Ηχη, ηχω (*sound*); echo, catechize.
Θεαομαι (*I behold*); theatre, theory, theorem.
Θαυμα (*wonder*); thaumatrope.   Θεος (*God*); theology, theism, enthusiast.
Θερμος (*heat*); thermometer, isothermal.
Θεραπευω (*I heal*); therapeutics.
Θεσις, θεμα (*placing*); anathema, antithesis, epithet, theme.
Θηκη (*box*); hypothecate, apothecary.   Θυμος (*mind*); enthymeme.
Ιδεα (*form*); idea.
Ιδιος (*peculiar*); ιδιωτης, ιδιωμα; idiom, idiot. idiosyncrasy.
'Ιερος (*sacred*); hierarch, hieroglyphic.   'Ιλαρος (*cheerful*); hilarity.
'Ιππος (*horse*); Philip, hippopotamus.
Ισος (*equal*); isomorphous, isochronous, isosceles (σκελος = leg).
Ιστορια (*investigation*); history, story.   Ιχθυς (*fish*); ichthyology.
Καλεω (*I call*); εκκλησια; ecclesiastic.
Καλος (*beautiful*); καλλος (*beauty*); calligraphy, calotype, calisthenic.
Καλυπτω (*I hide*); apocalypse.   Καθαρος (*pure*); cathartic.
Κακος (*bad*); cacophonous.   Κανων (*rule*); canon, canonical.
Καυστικος (*burning*); caustic.   Κεντρον (*point*); centre.
Κλιμα (*slope*); climate.   Κλιμαξ (*ladder*); climax, climacteric.
Κλινω (*I bend*); incline, enclitic.   Κοινος (*common*); epicene.
Κογχη (*cockle*); conchology.
Κοσμος (*world*); cosmical, microcosm.   Κομητης (*long-haired*); comet.
Κρανιον (*skull*); cranium.   Κρατος (*strength*); autocrat, democrat.
Κρινω (*I judge*); κρισις, κριτικος; critic, crisis, hypocrisy.
Κρυσταλλος (*ice*); crystal.   Κρυπτω (*I hide*); apocrypha, crypt.
Κυκλος (*circle*); cycle, cycloid, cyclopaedia.
Κυλινδρος (*roller*); cylinder.   Κυβος; cube.   Κυων (*dog*); cynic.
Κυριακος (*belonging to the Lord*); church.   Κωμος (*festivity*); encomium.
Κωνος; cone.   Λεγω (*say, choose*); eclectic.
Λεξις (*speech*); lexicon, dialect.   Λαμβανω (*I take*); epilepsy, syllable.
Λειπω (*I leave*); ellipse, eclipse.   Λειχην; lichen.
Λειτος (*belonging to the people*); liturgy.
Λιθος (*stone*); lithography, lithic.
Λογος (*speech, reason*); logic, dialogue, syllogism.
Λυρα; lyre, lyric.   Λυω (*loosen*); paralysis.   Μαγος; Magian, magic
Μακρος (*long*); macrocosm.   Μαθημα (*learning*); mathematics.
Μαρτυς (*witness*); martyr.   Μελας (*black*); melancholy.
Μελος (*tune*); melody.   Μεταλλον; metal.
Μετρον (*measure*); meter, barometer.   Μητηρ (*mother*); metropolis.
Μηχανη (*contrivance*); mechanics.   Μιαινω (*I pollute*); miasma.
Μικρος (*small*); microscope.   Μιμος (*imitator*); mimic.
Μισος (*hatred*); misanthrope.   Μνημων (*remembering*); mnemonic.

APPENDIX 255

Μονος (*only*); monarch, monogamy, monotheism.   Μοναχος; monk.
Μορφη (*form*); amorphous.   Μυστηρια; mystery.
Ναυς (*ship*); nautical, nausea (sea-sickness).
Ναρκοω (*I benumb*); narcotic.   Νεκρος (*dead*); necropolis, necromancy.
Νεος (*new*); neology, neophyte.   Νευρον (*string, nerve*); neuralgia.
Νησος (*island*); Polynesia.
Νομος (*law*); antinomian, astronomy, gastronomy.
Νοσος (*disease*); nosology.   Οβελισκος; obelisk.
Ὁδυς (*way*); exodus, method, period.   Οικος (*house*); economy.
Οικησις (*dwelling*); οικεω (*I inhabit*); diocese, oecumenical.
Ὁλος (*whole*); catholic, holocaust.   Ὁμοιος (*like*); homoeopathy.
Ὁμος (*same*); homogeneous.
Ονομα, ονυμα (*name*); synonymous, patronymic.
Οξυς (*sharp*); oxygen, paroxysm.
Οπτικος (*belonging to sight*); optics, synopsis.   *Οραω (*I see*); panorama.
Οργανον (*instrument*); organ.   Ορθος (*straight*); orthodox, orthography.
Ὁριζω (*I define*); horizon, aorist.   Ορνις (*bird*); ornithology.
Ορφανος; orphan.   Ορχηστρα (*dancing-place*); orchestra.
Οστεον (*bone*); osteology.   Οφις (*serpent*); ophicleide.
Οφθαλμος (*eye*); ophthalmia.   Παλαιος (*ancient*); palaeography.
Παν (*all*); pantheism, pantomime.   Παν (*Pan*); panic.
Παθος (*suffering, affection*); pathos, sympathy, pathetic.
Παις (*boy*); pædagogue.   Πανηγυρις (*assembly*); panegyric.
Παιδεια (*instruction*); cyclopaedia.   Πατεω (*I walk*); peripatetic.
Παυσις (*stopping*); pause.   Πειρα (*trial*); empirical.
Πεντε (*five*); pentagon.   Πεντηκοστος (*fiftieth*); pentecost.
Πεταλον (*leaf*); petal.   Πετρα (*rock*); petrify, Peter.
Πεπω (*digest*); dyspeptic.
Πλασσω (*I mould, daub*), πλαστικος; plastic, plaster.
Πλανητης (*wandering*); planet.   Πλησσω (*strike*); apoplexy.
Ποιεω (*I make*); poet.   Πολεμος (*war*); polemic.
Πολος (*bowl, pole*); pole, polar.
Πολις (*city*); polity, policy, metropolis.
Πυλυς (*many*), polygon, polygamy, polytheism.
Πομπη (*procession*); pomp, pompous.   Πους (*foot*); antipodes, tripod.
Πρασσω (*I do*); practice, pragmatical.
Πρεσβυτερος (*elder*); presbyter, prester, priest.
Πρισμα (*something sawn*); prism.   Πρωτος (*first*); prototype.
Πτωμα (*fall*); symptom.   Πυρ (*fire*); pyrotechnics, empyrean.
Πωλεω (*I sell*); monopoly.
Ῥεω (*I flow*), ρευμα; catarrh, rheum, rheumatic.
Ῥηγνυμι (*I break*); cataract.   Ῥητωρ (*orator*); rhetoric.
Ῥις (*nose*); rhinoceros.   Ῥυθμος (*measured motion*); rhythm.
Σαρξ (*flesh*); sarcophagus.   Σαρκαζω (*I tear the flesh*); sarcastic.
Σβεννυμι (*I extinguish*); asbestos.   Σιφων (*tube*); siphon.
Σιτος (*food*); parasite.   Σκανδαλον (*stumbling-block*); scandal.
Σκηνη (*tent, stage*); scene.   Σκηπτρον (*staff*); sceptre.
Σκοπεω (*I look*), σκοπος; episcopal, bishop, scope, telescope, microscope.
Σπαω (*I draw*); spasm.   Σπερμα (*seed*), σπορα; spermatic, sporadic.
Σπειρα (*coil*); spire, spiral.
Στασις (*standing*); apostasy, ecstasy, system.
Στελλω (*I despatch*): epistle, apostle.   Στενος (*narrow*); stenography.

APPENDIX.

Στερεος (*solid*); stereoscope, stereotype.
Στιγμα (*brand*); stigma.   Στιχος (*line*); distich, acrostic.
Στρατος (*army*); strategy.   Στροφη (*turning*); catastrophe, apostrophe
Συκος (*fig*); sycophant.   Σφαιρα (*ball*); sphere.
Σφυζω (*I throb*); asphyxia.   Σχημα (*form, make*); scheme.
Σχιζω (*I divide*); schism.   Σχολη (*leisure*); school, scholar.
Ταφος (*tomb*); epitaph.   Ταξις (*arrangement*); syntax.
Τονος (*stretching, pitch*); tone, tonic, monotony.
Τομη (*cutting*); atom, epitome, entomology.
Τευχος (*implement, book*); pentateuch.
Τηλε (*far off*); telescope, telegraph.
Τοπος (*place*); topography, topic.   Τροπος (*turning*); tropic, trope.
Τυπος (*shape*); type.   Τυραννος; tyrant.
Ύγρος (*moist*); hygrometer.
Ύδωρ (*water*); dropsy, hydrate, hydrostatics, hydrogen, hydrophobia.
Ύμνος; hymn, anthem.   Ύπνος (*sleep*); hypnotic.
Ύστερος (*womb*); hysteria, hysterical.
Φαγω (*I eat*); sarcophagus.
Φαινω (*I show*); phenomenon, phantom, phase.
Φαρμακον (*drug*); pharmacy.
Φερω (*I bear*); phosphorus, metaphor.
Φημι (*I say*) emphasis, prophecy.   Φθογγη (*voice, vowel*); diphthong
Φθισις (*wasting*); phthisic.   Φιλος (*fond of*); philosophy, Philip.
Φλεβς (*vein*); phlebotomy.
Φλεγμα (*inflammation, slimy humour*); phlegm.
Φοβος (*fear*); hydrophobia.   Φραγμα (*fence*); diaphragm.
Φρασις (*saying*); phrase.   Φρην (*mind*); phrenology.
Φυσις (*nature*); physics, physiology.   Φυτον (*plant*); zoophyte.
Φωνη (*voice*); phonetic, phonography.   Φως (*light*); photography.
Χαος (*empty space*); chaos.   Χαρακτηρ (*something engraved*); character.
Χαρις (*thanks*); eucharist.   Χειρ (*hand*); chirography, chiromancy.
Χιλιοι (*thousand*); kilogramme.
Χιμαιρα (*a fabulous monster*); chimerical.   Χολη (*bile*); melancholy.
Χονδρος (*cartilage of the breast*); hypochondriac.
Χορδη (*string*); chord.   Χορος (*dance*); chorus, choir.
Χρονος (*time*); chronology.   Χριω (*I anoint*); Christ, Christian.
Χρωμα (*colour*); achromatic.   Χυμος, χυλος (*juice*); chyme, chyle.
Χωρος (*place*); chorography.   Ψαλλω (*I play the lyre*); psalm.
Ψευδος (*falsehood*); pseudonym.   Ψυχη (*soul*); psychology.
Ωδη (*song*); ode, monody, parody.   Ων, οντος (*being*); ontology.
Ώρα (*hour*); horology, horoscope.   Ωσμος (*thrusting*); endosmose.

The above list does not include a large number of scientific terms employed in botany, medicine, zoology, &c.

The following table of the Greek alphabet is inserted for the use of those who are unacquainted with the Greek character:—

A, α = a.   B, β = b.   Γ, γ = g.   Δ, δ = d.   E, ε = ĕ.   Z, ζ = z.
H, η = ē.   Θ, θ = th.   I, ι = i.   K, κ = k or c.   Λ, λ = l.
M, μ = m.   N, ν = n.   Ξ, ξ = x.   O, ο = ŏ.   Π, π = p.   P, ρ = r.
Σ, σ = s.   T, τ = t.   Υ, υ = u.   Φ, φ = ph.   X, χ = ch.
Ψ, ψ = ps.   Ω, ω = ō.

Miscellaneous Words adopted from Foreign Languages

French.—Beau, belle, bon-mot, bouquet, congé, depot, éclat, ennui. envelope, foible, naïve, environs, etiquette, penchant, picquet, soirée, toilette, trousseau, &c.

Italian.—Akimbo, alarm (all' arme), alert (all' erta, *from Lat.* erectus), ambassador (*ultimately from the Gothic* andbahts, '*servant*'), avast (*It.* basta), bass (*Lat.* bassus, '*fat, squat*'), bassoon, baluster (*vulgarly* banister), balustrade, bandit (*root* 'ban'), bravo, brigade, brigand, brigantine, brocade, bronze, burlesque, bust, cameo, cannon ('*a great tube*,' from *Lat.* canna), canto, canteen, cape (*from* caput), caper (*from Lat.* caper), captain, caravel, caricature ('an exaggeration,' *from* caricare, 'to load'), cartel, cartoon (*Lat.* carta; cartone = *large or thick paper, pasteboard*), charlatan, citadel, companion ('*a comrade*,' *one who shares your bread, from* con *and* panis), concert, concerted (*probably from* concertare), conversazione, cosset (*It.* casiccio, '*a lamb brought up by hand in the house*'), cupola, ditto, dilettante, domino, dram, farrago (*mixed food, from* 'far'), folio, fresco, gabion, gala, gallant, garnet, gazette, granite, gondola, grate, grotto, harlequin, improvisatore, incognito, influenza, inveigle, lava, lupine, macaroni, manifesto, madrigal, mezzotint, motto, opera, paladin, pantaloon, piazza, palette, parapet (*from* petto, '*the breast*'), parasol, pigeon (piccione), pilgrim (pelegrino, *from* peregrinus), pistol, policy (*of insurance,* &c., polizza, *a corruption of* polyptychum, '*a memorandum book of many leaves*'), porcupine (porcospino), portico, proviso, regatta, scaramouch, sketch, soprano, stanza, stiletto, stucco, studio, tenor, terra-cotta, torso, umbrella, virtue, virtuoso, vista, volcano.

Spanish.—Alligator (el lagarto), armada, barricade, battledore (batador), caparison, capon, cargo, caracole (caracol, '*a winding staircase*'), castanets, chocolate, cigar, clarion, clarionet, cochineal, cork (corcho, *from* cortex), creole, desperado, discard, dismay (desmayar, '*to faint*'), don, duenna, embargo, embarrass, filigree, filibuster, flotilla, grandee, jade (ijada, '*the flanks*,' ijadear, '*to pant*'), javelin (*a boar-spear, from* jabali '*wild boar*'), jennet, lawn (lona, *transparent texture*'), mulatto, negro, pamphlet (*perhaps from* papelete, '*a note*'), pawn (peone, '*a labourer*'), pedestal, pillion, pint (pinta, '*a mark*'), platinum, punctilio, renegade (*corrupted into* runagate), savannah, sherry (Xeres), tornado, verandah.

Portuguese.—Caste, cocoa, commodore (commendador), fetish, mandarin (mandar, '*to have authority*'), marmalade (marmelo '*quince*'), palaver (*derived from* parabola '*parable*'), porcelain.

Dutch.—Boom, sprit, reef, schooner, skate, sloop, stiver, taffrail, yacht (jaghten, '*to chase*').

s

Arabic.—Admiral (*properly* ammiral), alchemy, alcohol (al-kohl, '*the fine powder of antimony*'), alembic, algebra (al-gebr, '*union or combination*'), alkali, almanac, amber, amulet, arrack (araq, '*sweat*'), assassin (*eater of* hashish), azimuth, cadi, caliph, camphor, carat, cipher, coffee, cotton, dragoman, elixir, emir, fakir, gazelle, giraffe, harem, hazard, jar, lute, magazine, mameluke, minaret, monsoon, moslem, mosque, mufti, mummy, nadir, naphtha, salaam, simoom, sirocco, sofa, sugar, sultan, syrup, talisman, tamarind, vizier, zenith, zero.

Hebrew.—Abbot, amen, behemoth, cabal, cherub, ephod, hallelujah, hosanna, jubilee, leviathan, manna, sabbath, seraph, shibboleth.

Persian.—Azure, balcony, bashaw *or* pasha, bazaar, caravan, checkmate (shahmat, '*king dead*'), chess, dervish, hookah, jackal, lilac, musk, orange, paradise, scimitar, shawl, sherbet, taffeta, turban.

Hindustani.—Buggy, bungalow, calico, chintz, chutnee, coolie, cowrie, curry, jungle, lac, mulligatawny, nabob, pagoda, palanquin, pariah, punch, pundit, rajah, rupee, sepoy, suttee, toddy.

Chinese.—Bohea, caddy, congou, gong, hyson, junk, nankeen, pekoe, tea.

Malay.—Amuck, bamboo, caoutchouc, gutta-percha, orang-outang, sago.

Turkish.—Bey, chibouk, janissary, sash, tulip, seraglio.

Polynesian.—Taboo, tattoo, kangaroo.

North and South American Indian.—Condor, hammock, lama, maize, mocassin, pampas, pemmican, potato, squaw, tobacco, tomahawk, tomata, wigwam.

Most of the words in this section will be found in the lists given by Dr. Adams, Dr. Angus, Mr. Bain, &c., and are treated in detail in the best etymological dictionaries, especially those by Wedgwood, Müller, and Stormonth.

ADDENDUM.

[See Anglo-Saxon numerals, p. 231.]

The numerals *one*, *two*, and *three* were the most fully declined; those from *four* to *twelve* being partially declined.

The syllable *lif* in *endlif* (Gothic *ainlif*) and *twelf* is in reality a word meaning *ten*, and is another form of *tig*. (Instances of the interchange of *l* with *d* or *t*, and of a guttural with *b* or *v* are not uncommon. Compare *odor* with *oleo* in Latin; *lacrima* with δάκρυ; *glans* with βάλανος; the pronunciation of *laugh* with its spelling, &c.) *Eleven* is therefore *one* + *ten*, *twelve* is *two* + *ten*.

walking
having
or mo
ted in
ntally,

plement

INDEX.

The references (except in a few instances) are to the paragraphs of the Grammar.

A, various sounds of, 16
  feminine suffix, 45
  weakened form of *on*, 123 note, 267, 268
  adverbial prefix, 267, 268
  feminine suffix, 45
  short form of *an*, 122
  for *he*, 141 *note*
Absolute nominative and objective, 282, 372 5
Accent, 26
  kinds of, 26
  Teutonic, 27
  French, 27
  influence of, 27
  distinguishes verbs from nouns, 339
Accusative, *see* Objective
Accusative case replaced by dative, 83 *note*
Active voice, 185, 186
  conjugation of, 257
Adjective, definition of, 85, 86
  not a name, 86 *note*
  used attributively, 87, 362, 471
  used predicatively, 87, 391
  test, 87
  not used as subject or object, 88
  qualitative, 90
  quantitative, 91
  demonstrative or definitive, 98
  pronominal, 98
  used substantively, 99, 100

Adjective become substantive, 101
  inflected, 103, App. A
  uninflected, 102
  comparison of, *see* Positive, Comparative, Superlative
  compound, 302
  derived, 317
Adjective clause, 362, 401, 408. 518-522
Adverbs, definition, 259, 260
  classification of, 265
  simple, 262
  conjunctive *or* relative, 262, 264, p. 116 *note*
  differ from conjunction, 263, 291*f*
  compound, 271, 290, 304
  derived, 267, 268, 269, 270
  with suffix omitted, 269 *note* †
  identical in form with prepositions, 271
  of affirmation and negation, 272
  after prepositions, 273
  used attributively, 362
  used for relative pronoun, 408
  comparison of, 274-276
Adverbial relation, 371
  adjuncts, 369 *note*, 371-375
  clauses, 414-440, 524-532, 547-572
  suffixes, 267-270
After, 281, 289 *note*

Alms, 60
Alphabet, 11, 13
An, *see* Indefinite Article
Analysis of sentences, 493a, &c.
    examples of, 494-572
And, 287, 288
    joining the mem¹rs of a compound subject, 386 *note*, 387 *note*
Angles, p. 1
Anglian dialects, p. 2
Anglo-Saxon, p. 2
    characteristics of, p. 2
    alphabet, 12
    accidence, App. A
    words and forms, App. B, App. C.
Antecedent to relative, 146, 475, 478
    omitted, 160
Any, 91, 170
Apostrophe in possessive case, 70, 71, 73, 74
Apposition, 362, 460, 461
Articles, 120, *see* Indefinite Article *and* Definite Article
    position with *such*, *so*, and *too*, 127
    repetition of, 472
Aryan languages, p. 1
As, adverb, 264 *note*, 290, 548, 551, 552, 554, 555, 558, 561-572
    used for relative pronoun, 167
Aspirated mutes, 20
Attributive relation, 360
    adjuncts, 362-365, 369 *note*, 493b
    adjuncts, position of, 365
    adjuncts, definitive and descriptive, 365c
Aught, 160
Auxiliary verb, *see* Verb

Be, conjugation of, 250, 226 8, 251
    a test verb, 252
    verb of incomplete predication, 391
    ben, bin, p. 87 *note*
Because, 291e
Before, 281, 288c, 289 *note*
Better, best, 114, 276
Both, 97, 288b
Bridegroom, derivation of, 45

Britons, language of, p. 1
Brothers, brethren, 55
But, p. 108 *note*, 288b, 288c, 289 *note*, 502, 505
By, 284

Can, could, 242
Case, definition, 63, 64
    number of cases in English, 83
    number of cases in Anglo-Saxon, p. 2, 64 *note*, App. A.
    nominative, *see* Nominative case
    possessive, *see* Possessive case
    objective, *see* Objective case
    endings, 64, 70, 72, 73, 75, 77
Celtic, *see* Keltic
Classical element in English, App. B.
Classification of words and forms, 294
Cognate objective, 372
Collateral sentences, 449, 450
Comma, use of, 479-484
Comparative degree, 106, 107, 108
    suffixes, 106 *note*, 115
    double comparatives, 118
Comparatives become positive, 119
Comparison of Adjectives
    degrees of, 104. *See* Positive, Comparative, Superlative
    irregular, 114
    expressed by *more* and *most*, 116
    when not allowable, 113
Comparison of Adverbs, 274-276
Comparison of Attributes, 109
Complement of predicate, 391-394
    subjective, 393
    objective, 395
    infinitive, 395
Composition of words, 297
Compound nouns, 300
    adjectives, 302
    pronouns, 302b
    verbs, 303
    adverbs, 304
    sentences, 443, 533-536
Con, 243
Concord of verb and subject, 376 383, 462-465
    of adjective and noun, 102
    of pronoun and noun, 474, 478

INDEX. 261

Conjugation of verbs, 219, 257
  strong conjugation, 220, 221, 225
  weak conjugation, 222, 224, 226
Conjunctions, definition of, 285, 286
  different from conjunctive adverbs, 263
  contrasted with prepositions, 287
  co-ordinative, 288*b*, 447
  subordinative, 288*c*
  developed out of prepositions, 289 *note*
  wrongly so called, 291*f*, 450
Consonants, 14, 19, 20
  doubled, 22, p. 92
Continuative use of relative, 413
Contracted sentences, 287 *note*, 445, 537, 465
Copula, 347
Cunning, 243

Danish element in English, p. 3
Dare, durst, 246
Dative case replaces accusative, 83 *note*
Daughter, derivation of, 44
Declension, 63, 84
Defective Verbs, 227-253
Definite article, 98, 124, 125, 126
  inflected, 126, App. A.
  thet *or* that, 126
Demonstrative pronouns, 98, 129, 138-151
Dental mutes, 19, 20
Derivation of words, 305, 341*b*
Dies, dice, 55
Digraphs, 17
Diphthongs, 17
Distributive pronouns, 98, 173-175
Disyllable, 21
Do, conjugation of, 253
  preterite formed by reduplication, 220, 253
  auxiliary of preterite in the weak conjugation, 222
  in interrogative and negative sentences, 255
  used to give emphasis, 254
  used to repeat preceding verb, 255
  = put, 254

Do = make, 254
Drake, derivation of, 44
Dual number, 47 *note*, App. A.
Duck, derivation of, 44

E, sounds of in English, 16
Each, 173, 174
Eaves, 60
Either, 175, 288*b*
Elder, eldest, 114 *note*
Elliptical sentences, 453, 544-572
Else, 268
En, plural suffix, 52
  adjective suffix, 318
  suffix of perfect participle, 221
English, the language of the Angles and Saxons, p. 1
  a low-German language, p. 1
  constituents of modern English, pp. 4-6
  development of, pp. 4, 5, App. A
Er, comparative suffix, 106
  plural suffix, 52
Ere, erst, 119, 276, 288*c*
Es, plural suffix, 48
  suffix of third person singular, p. 91
Ess, feminine suffix, 45
Est, st, suffix of second person singular, p. 91
Eth, suffix of third person singular, p. 91
Etymology, 8, 28, &c.
Every, 174
Except, 282, 291*e*

Far, 114 *note*
Farther, farthest, 114 *note*, 276
Father, derivation of, 44
Feminine gender, 38, 44-46
  suffixes, 44 *note*, 45
Few, 92
Final consonant doubled, 22
First, 114
For, meanings traced, 284*c*
  conjunction, 289 *note*
  prefix, 328
Foreign words adopted in English, App. C.
Former, 117
Fortnight, 62
Further, furthest, 114 *note*, 276

Ge, prefix in Anglo-Saxon, 173

262 INDEX.

Gender, definition of, 38, 39
  natural and grammatical, 39 *note*
  distinguished from sex, 37, 43
  how denoted, 44-46
  masculine, 38, 44, 45, 46
  feminine, 38, 44-46
  feminine suffixes, 44 *note*, 45
  neuter, 38
  common, 41
  of animals, 42
  in pronouns, 137
  Anglo-Saxon suffixes for, 45 *note*
Genitive, *see* Possessive
  in Anglo-Saxon, 72, App. A
  after numerals, 91 *note*, 62 *note*
  adverbial, 267, 268
Gerund, 192, 200, 201, 470
Gerundial infinitive, *see* Infinitive
Grammar, definition of, 3
Greek words in English, p. 3, App. C
  suffixes, 340
Grimm's law, App. C
Guttural mutes, 19, 20

Have, conjugation of, 248
  auxiliary of perfect tenses, 198
He, demonstrative pronoun, 138, App. A
Hence, here, hither, 270
Hight, 220, 247
His, 140
Husband, derivation of, 44
Hwa, hwæt, 152, App. A
Hwyle, 154
Hweðer, 155
Hybrids, 341*b*
Hypothetical sentences, 427, &c.

I, sounds of, 16
I, personal pronoun, 132, 136, App. A
If, 291
Imperative mood, 194, 256, p. 93 *note*
Imperfect participle, 197
  in Anglo-Saxon, 197 *note*
Imperfect tenses, 205, 206, 207, 212, 216
Impersonal verbs, 247, 387 *note*, 344 *note*, 382 *note*

Indefinite article, 121, 122, 123 *note*
Indefinite pronouns, 98
  who, what, which, 156, 157
  one, 168
  aught, 169
  any, 170
  other, 171
  some, 172
Indefinite tenses, 205, 206, 210, 215 216
  ambiguous in the passive, 215
Indicative mood, 193, 466
Indirect object, 80, 186
Indirect questions, 403, 410
Ine, feminine suffix, 45
Infinitive mood, 189-192
  without 'to' 191, 192, 368
  with 'to' (gerundial infinitive) 192, 372, 395 *note*
  object *or* subject, 189, 191
  tense in, 211
  syntax of, 469
Ing, suffix of participle, 197
  suffix of gerund, 200
  suffix of verbal nouns, 200 *note*, 470
Interjections, 293
Interrogative pronouns, 98, 152-155
Interrogative sentences, 255, 356
Intransitive verbs, 182, 183, 186, 187
  followed by a preposition, 186 *note*
It, pronoun, 140, App. A
  anticipatory subject, 387, 404, 477
  anticipatory object, 398
  cognate object, p. 147 *note* †
I wis, 245 *note*

Keltic languages, p. 1
  words in English, p. 2, App. B

Labials, 19
Last, latest, 114 *note*, 276
Latin words in English, p. 3, App. B, App. C
  prefixes, 335
  suffixes, 337-339
Lesser, 114 *note*
Lest, 291*b*
Let, 256
Like, adjective and adverb, 269 *note*

Liquids, 19
Mc-lists, 247
Little, less, least, 92, 114
    adverbs, 268
Lord, lady, derivation of, 44
Ly, adjective and adverbial suffix, 269

Man, 44
Many, 92
Masculi:e ddistinguished from
    male, 43
Masculine gender, 38, 44–46
May, 235–238
Means, 60
Monosyllable, 21
Moods, 188-196
Môtan, mote, 239
Mother, derivation of, 44
Mow, mowe, mought, 237
Much, 92, 114 *note*, 276
Mute *e*, 24
Mutes, 19
    sharp and flat, 20

Nam, nart, nis, nas, 251
Nat, niste, 245
Near, a comparative, 114 *note*, 276, 281
Negative particles, 272
Negative sentences, 255
Neither, 175, 288*b*
Nephew, niece, derivation of, 44
Neuter gender, 38, 39, 40, 42
    suffix 't,' 140, 153
Nill, 234
No, *see* None
No, nay, 272
Nominative case, definition of, 65
    derivation of, 64 *note*
    how ascertained, 66
    absolute, 373 *note*, 499
    syntax of, 456, 457
None, no, 94, 95, 168
Norman French, introduction and
    effects of, pp. 3, 6
Not, 272
Nouns, definition of, 29
    common, 30, 31
    proper, 31
    collective, 33
    abstract, 34
    gender of, 38
    numeral, 62 *note*

Nouns, general names, 35
    derived, 309–316
Number, definition of, 47
    how denoted, 47, 48–56
    singular, 47
    plural, 48–56
    plural suffixes, 48, 49, 54
    dual 47 *note*, App. A
    in verbs, 217
Numeral nouns, 91
    adjectives, 91, 98, App. C
    adjectives used as nouns, 62 *note*

O, sounds of, 16
Object of verb, 79, 81, 185
    use of term, 366
    simple, 397
    compound, 397
    complex, 397
    completing, 366 *note*
    replaced by prepositional phrase, 372
    enlarged, 399
Objective case, definition of, 79, 366
    how determined, 81
    form in nouns, 82
    denoting indirect object, 80, 372
    absolute, 372 *b*
    position of, 82
    governed by prepositions, 79
    objective for nominative, 177 *note*
    cognate objective, 372
    adverbial relation of, 80, 372
    syntax of, 459
Objective relation, 366, 370
Older, oldest, 114 *note*
One, 96, 168
Only, 90 *note*
Orthography, 7
Orthographical system, English, 25
    imperfections of, 25
Other, 171, 173, 288*b* *note*
Ought, 244
Owe, 244

Parsing, 573
Participles, 90, 197–199
    used absolutely, 282, 372 *b*
    miscalled prepositions, 282

Parts of speech, 6, 28
Passive voice, 185, 186, 187, 214
  conjugation of, p. 95, &c.
  of intransitive verbs, 186 *note*
  in Anglo-Saxon, 214 *note*
Pennies, pence, 55
Perfect participle, 197–199, 221, 223
  in the strong conjugation, 221
  in the weak conjugation, 223
  final 'd' of, sounded like 't,' 258
Perfect tense, active, 198, 205–209, 216
  in the strong conjugation, 220
  in the weak conjugation, 222
  in Latin, 220 *note*
Periods of the English language, p. 5, App. A
Person, in pronouns, 132, 133
  in verbs, 218
  origin of personal inflections, 218 *note*
Personal pronouns, *see* Pronoun
Personification, its influence on gender, 40
Plural, definition, 47
  suffixes of, 48, 49, 52, 54
  formed by vowel-change, 53
  same as singular, 56
  of proper names, 32
  of foreign words, 54
  used as singular, 58, 60, 62
  different in meaning from singular, 55, 61
  of compound names, 62
  double forms, 55
  words only used in, 61
  in Anglo-Saxon, 50, App. A.
  in *-ics*, 58
  of address, 134
  in pronouns, 137, 139
  suffix of, in present tense of verbs, p. 91 *note*
Positive degree, 105, 108
Possessive case, definition of, 67
  formation, 70, 71
  supposed derivation from 'his,' 72 *note*
  in feminine nouns, 73, App. A.
  of complex names, 75
  replaced by 'of,' 77
  used objectively, 78
  in names of things, 78

Possessive case of personal pronouns, 135, 142, 178
  attributive force of, 362
Predicate, 346, 347, 348, 356, 359, 376, 379, 389, 395
  simple, 390
  complex, 391, 392, 493*a*
  complement of, 391
  logical and grammatical, 34⁹ 493*e*
Predicative relation, 359, 379
Prefixes, Latin, 335
  Greek, 336
  Teutonic, 309, 319, 323, 327, 328
Prepositions, definition of, 277
  origin of, 279
  primary function of, 65 *note*, 279, 280
  simple, 281
  derived, 281
  same in form as adverbs, 279, p. 112
  relations indicated by, 283
  contrasted with conjunctions, 287
  become conjunctions, 289 *note*
Present used for future, 210, 213 *note*
  historic, 210
Preterite or past indefinite tense, *see* Perfect tense
  in the strong conjugation, 220
  in the weak conjugation, 222
  used as a present, 227
  final 'd' of, sounded like 't,' 258
  periphrastic forms of, p. 94
Pronominal adjectives, 178
Pronouns, definition of, 98, 128
  subdivision and classification of, 128, 130
  adjective, 129, 135, 178
  personal, 131–142, App. A.
  demonstrative, 138–151, App. A.
  relative, 146–167, App. A.
  interrogative, 152–155, App. A.
  distributive, 173-175
  reflective, 176, 177
  possessive, 98, 135, 178
  compound, 302*b*
  derived, 321*b*
Proposition in Logic, 347 *note*, 348
Punctuation, rules for, 474–492

INDEX.

Qualitative adjectives, 90
Quantitative adjectives, 91-97
Quoth, 247

Reduplication in the preterite tense, 220
Reflective pronouns, 98, 176, 177
Reflective verbs, 183
Relative pronouns, 98, 146-167
   that, 146-151
   who, 152, 156, 159
   what, 153, 159, 156, 157
   which, 154, 159, 156
   whether, 155
   whoso, &c., 158
   understood, 166, 409
   used continuatively, 413
   concord of, 474, 476
Riches, 60

S, plural suffix, 49, 50
'S, suffix of possessive case, 70
Aryan suffix, 76
   adverbial suffix, 267, 268
Saxons invade Britain, p. 1
Saxon dialect becomes predominant, p. 5
Scandinavian element in English, p. 3
Se, seo, thæt, 126, 141, App. A.
Second person sing. of verbs without suffix, 233, 243, p. 91 *note*
Self, 176, 177
Semi-vowels, 18
Sentence, definition of, 5, 343, 346
   simple, 355, 493, 505
   complex, 355, 400, 402, 442, 506-532
   compound, 355, 533-536
   contracted, 445, 486, 537-543
   collateral, 449
   elliptical, 544-572
   affirmative, 356
   imperative, 356
   optative, 356
   interrogative, 356
Sequence of tenses, 468
Shall, 206c, 212, 213
   conjugation of, 228, 229
   originally a preterite, 229
Sibilants, 19
Since, 291e
Singular number, 47
   like plural, 56

Singular number used as plural, 60
   used in multiplication, 62 *note*
Some, 172, 91
Ster, feminine suffix, 44 *note*
Subject of verb, 65, 218 *note*, 345, 350, 376-381
   understood, 383
   simple, 385
   compound, 381, 386, 287 *note*, 464
   complex, 387
   enlarged, 388
   logical and grammatical, 348, 493b
Subjunctive mood, 195, 196, 435-440, 466, 467
   conjugation of, p. 93, p. 97
Subordinate clauses, 401
Substantive clauses, 401, 403-406, 508-517
Substantives classified, 352
Such, 163
Suffixes, once independent words, 222 *note*
   in nouns, *see* Declension
   in verbs, *see* Conjugation
   in adverbs, 266, &c.
   plural, 48, 49, 54
   feminine, 45
   possessive, 70-76
   in derivatives, 305, &c.
   Latin, 337-339
   Greek, 340
Summons, 60
Superlative degree, definition of, 110, 111, 112
   how formed, 110-117
   formed from comparatives, 119
Syllables, 21 *note*
Syntax, definition of, 9, 342

T, suffix of second person singular, 228 *note*, 233, 236, p. 87 *note*
   offgrowth of 's' 281 *note*, 291e
Tenses, 203-216
   present, past, and future, 205-210
   imperfect, 205, 206, 208
   perfect, 205, 206, 207, 209
   indefinite, 205, 206, 208, 212, 215, 216
   in the infinitive, 211

Tenses, formed by inflection, 212, 221, 223
   auxiliaries, 212, 213, 214
   comparative table of, 216
Teutonic languages, p. 1
Thar, 264 *note*, 549, 550, 553, 556, 559, 560, 567, &c., 572
That those, 143, 144
That, rel. pron. 146-151
   difference between 'that' and 'who,' 149, 151, 165
   conjunction, 289, 424, 426, 528, 529
The, definite article, 124, 126
   before 'which,' 162
   adverb, þy, 270
Ther, comparative suffix, 106 *note*, 155, 171
There, thence, thither, 270
They, 141, 142, 479
Me-thinks, 247
This, these, 143, 144
Thou, 133, 136
   use of singular and plural forms, 134
Though, 291*d*
Thus, 270
To, meaning of, traced, 284
   before infinitive, *see* Infinitive
Transitive verbs, 182, 183, 186
Trix, feminine suffix, 45
Twelvemonth, 62

U, sounds of, 16
Uncouth, 243
Unless, 291*c*

Verbs, definition of, 179, 181, 353, 354, 359
   transitive and intransitive, 182, 183
   reflective, 183
   impersonal, 387 *note*, 247, 382 *note*, 344 *note*
   active voice and passive voice of, 185-187
   moods, 188-196
   participles, 197-199, 221 223

Verbs, gerund, 200, 201
   tenses, 203-216, *see* Tenses
   number, 217
   person, 218, 257
   conjugation, 219, 257
   regular verbs, 226
   defective verbs, 227-253
   compound verbs, 303
   derived verbs, 322
   verbs of incomplete predication, 391
   auxiliary, 212, 222, 196, 187, 228-238, 391
   concord of verb and subject 376-383
   intransitive verb and preposition not equivalent to a transitive verb, 372
Vowels, 14
   vowel sounds, 16
   vowel scale, 15

W, semi-vowel, 18
We, 132, 136, App. A
Wert, p, 87 *note*
What, which, whom, whether, *see* Relative pronoun
When, where, whence, whither how, why, 262-264, 270
Where, for preposition and 'which, 164
While, 291*e*.
Who, *see* Relative pronoun
Will, 212, 213, 230 234
(To) wit, 245
Witch, gender of, 44
With, 284
Wizard, derivation of, 44
Woman, derivation of, 44
Wont, 247
Worse, worst, 114 *note*, 276
Worth, weorthan, 247

Y, semi-vowel, 18
   pure vowel, 18
Ye, you, 133, 134
Yea, yea, 272

EXAMINATION QUESTIONS.

PUBLIC SCHOOL TEACHERS' EXAMINATION.

The following papers are made up of questions on Grammar and Etymology selected from amongst those set since 1871 at the Examination for Public School Teachers conducted by the Central Committee for the Province of Ontario :—

FIRST CLASS.

I.

1. Give reasons for regarding the article as an adjective.
2. Remark on the grammatical peculiarities of the following words or expressions:—"Children,"."alms," "gander," "songstress," "The more the merrier," "He is gone a-hunting," "The house is building."
3. Give as fully as you can the syntax of the subjunctive mood.
4. Give some examples of families of words from a common root.
5. To what great family of languages does the English belong? Under what subdivision is it properly classed? Mention the languages of the same subdivision.
6. Give instances of Celtic, Latin, and Danish remains in the English language, and state for what classes of words we have adopted chiefly Greek, Latin, and French derivatives.
7. Give specimens of spondee, dactyl, and anapest, and describe the Spenserian stanza.
8. Explain the figures Syncope, Paralepsis, and Pleonasm, indicating the class to which each belongs, and distinguish between Barbarism and Solecism, Simile and Metaphor.

II.

1. When may proper nouns be regarded as common, and when are common nouns equivalent to proper?
2. Indicate the various uses of the pronoun "it," and account for the curious change of gender in the following sentence :—" Death hath not only lost the sting, but *it* bringeth a coronet in *her* hand."—*Jeremy Taylor.*
3. (*a*) What may be regarded as the characteristic property of the verb? Does it ever include, besides, the property of the adjective? (*b*) Exhibit the origin of the termination "d" or "ed" in the past tense. (*c*) What value do you attach to inflection as a mode of indicating number and person in English verbs?

4. Enumerate the various uses of "but." Is such a construction as "Princes are but men" inconsistent with the grammatical definition of the adverb?
5. (a) Illustrate the primary and secondary use of the preposition. (b) Draw up a table exhibiting the relations expressed by prepositions.
6. Latham speaks of Etymology in the wide and in the limited sense of the word; explain his meaning.
7. (a) What proportion do words of Anglo-Saxon origin bear to those from classical sources? (b) Show that this proportion is not maintained in the language of ordinary intercourse.
8. Scan the following lines :—

> The proper study of mankind is man.
> Not a drum was heard, not a funeral note.

III.

1. "Orthographical expedients are resorted to on account of the imperfections of the English alphabet, which may be characterized as deficient, redundant, and ambiguous"—*Authorised Spelling Book.*

    Explain clearly the meaning of the term "Orthographical Expedient," and show in what respects the English alphabet is deficient, redundant, and ambiguous.
2. Explain the meaning of Orthöepy, Idiom, Dialect, and Metaphor, and give the best definition you can of "letter," "syllable," and "word."
3. Define Adjective and Pronoun; state how you classify adjectives and pronouns; show where you draw the line between these parts of speech; and explain your views with regard to the parsing of "his," "each," "this," "all," "another," "what," and "some," in the various constructions.
4. Explain with the aid of examples the meaning of Grammatical Equivalent and Conjunctive Adverb.
5. What argument does Max Müller regard as establishing conclusively that the English language is a branch of the great Teutonic stem of the Aryan form of speech?
6. (a) Mention some of the Celtic elements of the English language. (b) Name the two branches of the Celtic stock of languages. (c) Which of these was most probably the language of ancient Gaul? Confirm your answer by pointing out affinities.
7. Point out the difference between Barbarism and Solecism, and explain the figures Pleonasm, Metonymy, Paragoge, and Synecdoche, giving examples and indicating the class to which each belongs.
8. Give specimens of Iambus, Trochee, and Amphibrach.

IV.

1. Give the origin of the termination "ess" as a mode of expressing the feminine gender.
2. The termination "er" is common to adjectives of the comparative degree; to some other adjectives, as "upper," "under," &c.; and to certain pronouns, prepositions, and adverbs, as "either," "over," &c. What common idea underlies this identity of termination?
3. Define Relative Pronoun, Verb Impersonal (Proper and Improper), and Conjunctive Adverb.
4. Show how the Indicative and Potential Moods differ in their declarative force.
5. Some grammarians have given it as a rule that "verbs substantive govern the Nominative Case." Is this correct? Investigate the rule.
6. "Conjunctions connect not words but propositions." Show that this assertion can be maintained even with sentences like these: "John and Thomas carry a sack to market;" "Three and three make six."
7. What is meant by Service Metre and Alexandrines? Give specimens of each.
8. Compare words of Anglo-Saxon and Anglo-Norman origin for the purpose of explaining the preference given to either element in the choice of words.

V.

1. Do you consider "chicken," "riches," "alms," and "summons" to have been originally singular or plural? Give the grounds for your opinion.
2. Give examples of the indefinite relative. To what restrictions is it subject?
3. To what parts of speech is the termination "ing" common? Show fully how they are to be distinguished.
4. Give Latham's opinion in regard to the question of concord when two or more pronouns of different persons and of the singular number follow each other disjunctively.
5. Though all English comparatives end in "r," no superlative ends in "rt." How has this happened?
6. Illustrate the influence of Onomatopœia in the formation of words.
7. Give the derivation of the following words, tracing the history of the meaning wherever you can:—Muslin, currant, hymeneal, bursar, coercion, rill, priest, deed, bishopric, urbanity, universe, here, inoculate, religion, gentry, chestnut, vulgate, preposterous, rival, romance, health, legend, fancy.
8. When and under what circumstances did the principal elements which enter into the composition of the English language severally take their places in it?

VI.

1. Name the inflected parts of speech; state the inflections to which they are subject; and give an example of every inflectional form in the language. Give all the inflectional forms of "abbot," "me," "was." Are "fatherly," "happen," and "acknowledgment" inflectional forms? Explain the forms "his" and "whose."
2. Some grammarians consider the article and participle distinct parts of speech. State your own views, with reasons.
3. Give examples of sentences in which it is more appropriate to use "that" than "who" or "which." Explain the reason in each case.
4. Show to what extent we are to receive the statement that "the passive voice expresses passively the same thing that the active voice does actively."
5. Give as fully as you can the syntax of the Possessive Case.
6. Of words which have disappeared from our literary dialect mention (1) some which modern authors of note have endeavoured to revive; (2) others which survive only as provincialisms; and (3) others which pass for Americanisms, but which are really Old English.
7. Explain the figures Hyperbaton, Apocope, and Apostrophe, indicating the class to which each belongs.
8. What is meant by Historical Etymology?

VII.

1. Mention the causes of diversity in Orthography, and state in what respects the English alphabet is deficient, redundant, and inconsistent.
2. Give the best definition of Gender you know. State why you consider it the best, and point out its defects.
3. "The construction of English Infinitives is two-fold: (1) objective; (2) gerundial."—*Latham.*
Explain fully and exemplify this statement.
4. Name the verbs which specially belong to the class called "copulative," and explain their office in analysis. How would you deal in analysis with the Imperative and the Absolute?
5. Illustrate fully the adjective in predicate.
6. Derive the following words: — Mechanics, politics, cambric. meander, tantalize, April, Thursday, furlong, fathom, pilgrim, vintage, sarcasm, gazette, scarlet, tulip, tobacco, almanac, jubilee, caravan, sonnet, skate, ballast, calico, caricature, alligator.
7. Give the force of each of the affixes: Hood, ling, some, ric. aye, and less; illustrate by examples.
8. Give examples of Synæresis, Syncope, Paralepsis, Hyperbole.

VIII.

1. Define Logical Subject, Grammatical Subject, Case, Mood, Middle Voice, Predicate, Copulative Conjunction, and Disjunctive Conjunction.
2. Give a list of defective verbs.
3. "Substantives signifying the same thing agree in case." Point out the defects of this rule for apposition, and define "Apposition."
4. Give an etymological analysis of the following words, mentioning in each case prefix or affix, root, literal meaning, and ordinary signification :—Discussion, expressed, adventure, condolence, hypocrite, expedite, atonement, accuracy, cemetery, extravagant, trespass, dilapidation, advocate, adherent, disparity, colloquial, ambitious, transgression, degeneracy, declension (connect grammatical sense with root), dissection, pilgrimage, inarticulate, compunction.
5. Mention English words related in derivation to "speak," "sorrow," "choose," "what," "bequeath," "death," and "barren."
6. Which parts of speech are all of Saxon growth?
7. What traces of Danish occupancy do we find in local English names?
8. Write half a dozen lines on any subject you choose, using only words of Anglo-Saxon origin.

IX.

1. (*a*) Explain "strong" and "weak" preterites. (*b*) Cite instances to show that the tendency has been for some time to exclude the "strong" forms, quoting also some of the very few instances in which the reverse has taken place.
2. Define Middle Voice, Copulative and Disjunctive Co-ordination, and explain Dativus Ethicus, Adverbs of Deflection, and Equivocal Reflective.
3. Specify and exemplify the various constructions in which the sign of the possessive case is omitted.
4. Give examples of different cases which may arise in the application of the principle: "A verb must agree with its nominative in number and person," and state the special rule applicable to each case.
5. Distinguish between "common" and "mutual;" "stationery" and "stationary;" "feminine" and "effeminate;" "sanitary" and "sanatory;" "persecute" and "torment;" "loiter" and "linger."
6. What information about the following articles may be obtained from the names they bear :—Port (wine), sherry, nankeen, ammonia, bayonet, cherry, currants?
7. Give the derivation of :—Blame, metaphysics, peripatetics, synod, lord, ma'am, fee, villain, anathema, premature, retrograde, extravagant, rather, treacle, lass, comfort, epitaph, paper, executor, save, depose, mode, serve, paste, cover, lesson, meaning, fur, impostor, insolent.

8. Write etymological notes on:
   (a) In like manner also that women adorn themselves in modest apparel with *shamefacedness* and sobriety :—L Tim. ii. 9.
   (b) Woe *worth* the chose. woe *worth* the day.—*Scott.*
   (c) Come Fate into the list And champion me to the *utterance.*—*Shakespeare.*

SECOND CLASS.

I.

1. In what words is the aspirate rightly dropped when it stands as their first letter?
2. State the various uses of the pronoun "it."
3. Show that the perfect is a present tense, and write sentences to exhibit the violation of the "sequence of tenses" in connection with that tense.
4. Explain the construction of the objective case in each of the following sentences :—(a) He waited all night; (b) The book is worth a shilling; (c) Full many a league they rode; (d) They dreamt the future flight.
5. Give the different powers of the prefixes "be" and "en" or "em."
6. Make a list of five words from each of the Latin verbs ago, curro, jacio, fero, video, and rego.
7. Give words—two in each case—derived from these Greek roots: Charis, cratos, metron, phone, pathos.

II.

1. Investigate the statement that "mine" and "thine" are the possessive case of the personal pronoun, whilst "my" and "thy" are the possessive adjective.
2. "A verb is a word that makes an assertion." Discuss the defects of this definition.
3. What prepositions should follow "glad," "true," "insinuate," and "intervene"?
4. What are the Latin and Greek prefixes meaning "from," "beyond," "without"?
5. Derive the following words, giving the etymological analysis where you can :—Where, ephemeral, alone, before, river, rapturous, current, month, pain, blood, generally, number, agency, vicious, diabolical, wrote, stenography, pagoda.
6. Make a list of words derived from "lego," including four from the Latin and four from the Greek verb.
7. In the following groups of verbs of similar signification, indicate the appropriate use of each verb :—Esteem, estimate, appreciate; grant, allow, bestow, concede; build, erect, construct; usurp, arrogate, assume.

III.

1. Give examples of verbs of strong and of weak conjugation.
2. State the rule relating to "sequence of tenses" in connection with the conjunction "that," and quote Latham's reason to show that the rule must necessarily be absolute.
3. Illustrate the use of the adjective in predicate, and state clearly its force and relation.
4. Define and give examples of adverbial sentence and complex sentence, and form or quote a sentence containing a dependent proposition which is the subject of a verb.
5. Enumerate the affixes denoting state, condition, or quality, and give examples of each in combination.
6. Convert, by the help of prefixes or suffixes, the following adjectives into verbs :—Large, just, humble, strong ; and convert the following verbs into nouns :—Weave, compel, receive, dig think. Explain the law which governs each change.
7. Trace the following to Latin or Greek roots :—Venison, sample, maintain, livery, human, hermit, sarcophagus, volume, tautology, technical, phylactery, blasphemy.

IV.

1. What are the principal parts of "travel," "smell," "benefit"?
2. Give examples of the different uses (*a*) of words ending in "ing," and (*b*) of "but."
3. Give instances of infinitives and infinitive phrases used as the objects of a verb.
4. Give a detailed analysis of the following passage and the full syntactical parsing of all the italicised words : " *Strange as it* may seem *to find* a song-writer put forward *as* an active *instrument* of union among his fellow-Hellens, it is not *the* less true that those poets whom we have briefly passed in review, *by enriching* the common *language and* by circulating from town to town either in person or in their compositions, *contributed to fan* the flame of pan-Hellenic patriotism at a time *when there were few circumstances to co-operate* with them, and when the causes tending to perpetuate isolation seemed in the ascendant."—*Grote*.
5. (*a*) Explain the term "Hybridism," and illustrate by examples.
   (*b*) Show that "icicle" is hybrid in appearance only.
6. Give examples of (*a*) Derivatives formed by merely changing the radical vowel ; (*b*) Primitive words formed on the principle of imitation ; and (*c*) Derivatives from dotos, hodos, laos, pingo, olo or olesco, linquo, fligo, arceo, tero, and vello.
7. Trace the following to Latin roots :—Egregious, lateral, illusion, annex, complex, pulverize, quotient, satisfy, scripture, extortion, adult, monument.

V.

1. Write the plural of hidalgo, no, chimney, colloquy, Livy, vinculum, 3, w, appendix, Lord Gordon, court-martial.
2. Classify pronouns, enumerating those under each head.
3. Give the principal parts of hew, fly, flee, stride, rive, crow.
4. Give a classification of conjunctions.
5. K. RICH.   Of comfort no man speak ;
   Let's talk of graves, of worms, and epitaphs ;
   Make *dust* our *paper,* and *with* rainy eyes,
   Write sorrow on the bosom of the earth.
   Let's choose executors, and talk of wills ;
   And *yet not so—for what* can we bequeath
   Save our deposed bodies *to* the ground ?
   Our lands, our lives, and all, are *Bolingbroke's,*
   And nothing can we call *our own* but death
   And that small *model* of the barren earth
   Which serves *as paste* and cover to our bones."
   (a) Divide the above extract into propositions, stating their relations to each other, and analysing them ; (b) Parse the italicised words ; (c) Make a list of the words of classical origin in the passage.
6. Give words—two in each case—derived from these Greek roots: Ago, biblos, martur, deka, skopeo, tupos.
7. Give words of Latin and English origin corresponding with apology, catalogue, democracy, eulogize, mystery, prophesy, sympathy.

VI.

1. Give abstract nouns of the same derivation as "brief," "true," "common," "needy," "poor."
2. Give examples of the different constructions in which "as" is used, and tell in which of them it may be replaced by "that."
3. Distinguish :   May I go   from   Can I go.
                    Shall I go   "   Will I go.
                    Were I to go   "   Was I to go.
                    Would I have gone "   Should I have gone.
4. Give adjectives of Latin origin corresponding to the following nouns :—Dog, head, house, friend, step, light, law, rest.
5. Trace the following words to Greek roots :—Rhetoric, crypt, nautical, cosmogony, ephemeral, asteroid, polity, telegraph.
6. Give words—two in each case—derived from the Latin roots faber, fruor, integer, licet, plico, salio, voveo
7. What do you understand by the "imperfect incorporation" of words introduced from a foreign language ? State the principles which characterize it, and give examples.

VII.

1. What do you understand by "gender" in grammar? Show that your definition applies to each of these words: Lady, seamstress, man-servant, testatrix, mistress, heroine, margravine.
2. Write the past tense, present participle, and past participle of "flow," "fly," "singe," "die," "loose," "lay," and "hear."
3. Give accurate rules for the use of "shall" and "will."
4. Form or quote sentences to illustrate (1) the restrictive and the connective force of the relative pronoun, and (2) the twofold use of the cognate object.
5. Parse the italicised words in the following quotations:—(a) In spite *of* such a *man* as *Gibbon's* opposition; (b) They are not the same *that* they have been; (c) He did it in the *Geography* class; (d) They are very *much* in the style of Milton's Sonnets; (e) That is the way *that* boys begin.
6. Trace the following words to Latin and Greek roots, distinguishing those from each language:—Autumn, biscuit, disastrous, epidemic, autocratic, linen, analyse, amnesty, fanatic, optics, infant, verdict, oxygen, frantic, empyrean, federal, isothermal, carnival, polygon, system, fossil.
7. Give adjectives formed from Latin or Greek roots corresponding to the following English nouns:—Brother, forest, breath, beginning, husband, cloud, leg, eye, hand, rule, ship, tooth, fist, glass, disease, marriage, art.

VIII.

1. What parts of speech perform a double function? Give full explanatory examples.
2. Explain "Conjunctive Adverb," and write sentences containing the various forms of the "Adverbial Phrase."
3. Give rules for the right use of the subjunctive mood, with examples.
4. In each of the following pairs of sentences, point out the difference in meaning:—(a) He was the first *that* came. He was the first *who* came. (b) He would make a better statesman than lawyer. He would make a better statesman than *a* lawyer. (c) He arrived *safe*. He arrived *safely*.
5. Parse the italicised words in the following sentences:—
    (a) Did "religion," when our language was translated, mean *godliness*?
    (b) Thus shall mankind his guardian care engage, The promised *father* of a future age.
    (c) In Christian hearts, O for a pagan zeal! A needful but opprobrious *prayer*!
    (d) He is busy *thrashing*.
6. Derive "foliage," "atone," "demagogue," "lieutenant," "remnant," "jelly," "closet."
7. Mention words—two in each case—derived from these Latin roots: Arceo, caro, colo (are), falx, fiscus, gelu, grex, orior, sinus, tueor.

THIRD CLASS.

I.

1. Define Abstract Noun, Relative Pronoun, Verb Transitive and Intransitive, Adverb, Preposition.
2. Name and define those parts of speech which are inflected.
3. Name and distinguish plurals of nouns which have two forms of plural with different signification.
4. Give any six examples of irregular comparison of adjectives, and state the classes of adjectives which do not admit of comparison.
5. What changes for the sake of euphony do the following prefixes undergo :—Ad, con, sub, syn ?
6. Mention prefixes—each in combination with some word—which denote rest or motion forward and backward in place and time.
7. Give words in which the following affixes appear, and state the force of each :—Ard, eer, ory, dom, sy, ment, ship, ism, ule, ose, ish.

II.

1. Name the four great divisions of Grammar, and state the province of each.
2. Write the plurals of : Stuff, potato, canto, grotto, attorney, seraph, cousin-german, medium, stamen, appendix, thesis, chrysalis, cargo, tyro, echo, chimney, criterion, axis, genius, index, aide-de-camp.
3. Name the distributive and indefinite pronouns.
4. How is the verb inflected ? Name the moods and state the force of each.
5. In what cases is the final consonant doubled before an affix ?
6. Illustrate by examples the use of each of the prefixes denoting negation or destitution, and of each of the affixes denoting manner and rank, office, or dominion.
7. Give the different forms assumed by the prefixes "in" and "ad" in composition, illustrating your answer by examples.

III.

1. Write the plural of "cheese," "policy," "soliloquy," and "phenomenon ;" the singular of "species," "apparatus," and "indices ;" and the feminine of "beau," "earl," "lad," "stag," and "ram."
2. Explain the terms Declension, Conjugation, Case, Mood, Tense, Voice, Person, and Participle, illustrating your answer with examples.
3. Form the past tense and past participle of the following verbs :— Rid, rend, shed, dive, lean, light, wed, speed.
4. Show the different ways in which the words "there," "it," and "but" are employed.

5. Parse the following sentence, and change the form so that it shall contain a Nominative Absolute :—" When fresh troops had arrived, the battle was resumed."
6. Compose or quote a sentence containing the words "bail" and "bale" properly used, and another illustrating the different meanings of the word "crew."
7. What is the force of the following affixes :—Age, ry, ice, dom, ness, ock, ic, ose, ish, en ? State in regard to each of them whether it is of Anglo-Saxon or classic origin.

IV.

1. What is meant by Inflection, Gender, Predicate, Complement, Impersonal Verb, Interjection, Conjunction ?
2. What is the Passive Voice ? When may a verb in the Passive Voice be followed by the Objective Case ?
3. Give a list of Auxiliary Verbs.
4. How many tenses are there in the Potential Mood ? Give the signs of each.
5. Parse the following sentence, and change the active into the passive construction :—" His love of change drove him a pilgrim to the Holy Land."
6. Compose a complex sentence containing an example of Apposition.
7. What are the meanings of the prefixes : Para, meta, ob, be ; and of the affixes : Ness, by, dom ?

V.

1. Quote any two special rules for the formation of the plural of nouns, and write the plural of the following : Wharf, folio, spoonful, Mussulman, cherub, memorandum, miasma, alumnus.
2. Compare such of the following adjectives as are capable of comparison :—Cool, late, happy, perpendicular, many, triangular.
3. Inflect the Present Indicative of the verb "to strike" in all its three forms.
4. Define the terms Subject and Predicate.
5. Change the construction of the following sentence so as to introduce a Nominative Absolute, and parse the latter half :— " Having completed his arrangements for the battle, Napoleon beheld the vast array defile before him."
6. Form or quote a sentence containing a dependent proposition equivalent to an adverb.
7. Attach roots to the following prefixes, exhibiting when possible the change made in the prefix for the sake of euphony :—Ad, re, inter, trans, con, in, syn, amphi, hyper, sub.

VI.

1. Form Abstract Nouns from the following adjectives :—Pure, brief, slow, dear, intricate.
2. Write the plural of "pea," "attorney," "stratum," "lens," "focus," "Mussulman," "Henry," "sixpence," "seraph," "cameo," "index," "crisis ;" and the masculine or feminine form, as the case may be, of "widow," "czar," "testator," "witch," "duke," "sultan," "earl."

3. Give rules for forming the degrees of comparison of adjectives.
4. Write the past tense, present participle, and past participle of the following verbs :—Loose, bear, come, eat, flow, fly, go, dye, singe, die.
5. Re-write the following sentences so as to change the grammatical construction, but express the same meaning :—(a) To me the case seems to stand thus ; (b) In arguing about field sports, I was arguing with people whose doings were open to the world ; (c) He speaks the truth.
6. Explain the different uses of the objective case, giving an example of each.
7. Write Latin or Greek prefixes signifying "aside," "across," "against," "down," "together," "change," "near to," with examples.

VII.

1. Explain the inflection's in the Possessive case, and give examples of the appositive to the possessive.
2. Give a list of comparatives which want the positive.
3. What rules are laid down to regulate the use of the relative "that"?
4. Distinguish between Transitive and Intransitive verbs, giving an example of each.
5. Give the rule for the construction of the Predicate noun, and state with what verbs it is most frequently connected.
6. What is a sentence ? Write specimens of simple, compound, and complex sentences.
7. Give words in which the following affixes appear, and state the force of each affix :—Ling, all, ster, ness, acy, ure.

VIII.

1. Write a sentence containing an example of every part of speech properly used.
2. (a) What are the various modes of distinguishing the masculine and feminine genders ? (b) Give the feminine of "stag," "marquis," "buck," "executor."
3. Write the past tense, past participle and present participle of the following verbs :—Set, flee, seethe, cleave (to split), bear (to bring forth), shear, shoe, job, lie down, omit, prefer, wink, chew.
4. How may a simple subject be changed to a complex one ?
5. (a) Show that intransitive verbs are sometimes rendered transitive. (b) Give the transitive forms corresponding with "rise," "lie," "sit," "fall."
6. Show by examples how a verb may be modified by a word, by a phrase, and by a subordinate sentence.
7. Give words in which the following affixes appear, and state the force of each :—Ster, mony, ric, ion, ency, tude.

HIGH SCHOOL EXAMINATIONS.

The following papers, with the exception of the two Intermediate ones for 1876, are made up of questions set since 1873 for entrance into the High Schools and Collegiate Institutes of Ontario :—

I.
1. Define Noun, Pronoun, Verb, Mood, Tense.
2. Give the plurals of new, staff, folio, penny, index.
3. Give the feminines of earl, friar, hero, marquis, stag, ram, baron, peacock, preceptor; and the masculines of witch, roe, empress, niece, lass, maid, filly.
4. Of the following adjectives compare those that admit of comparison : Good, near, happy, beautiful, many, perpendicular, old, eternal.
5. Inflect the Personal Pronouns.
6. Give the past tense and past participle of the following verbs :—Flow, go, cleave (to split), get, smite, weave, crow, blow, mow, fall, call, tear, may, shoe, drink.
7. Analyse and parse : " The sun rose pleasantly over the scene that lay before us."

II.
1. Define Transitive Verb, Active Voice, Finite Verb, Adverb, Preposition.
2. Give the plurals of deer, family, foray, potato, half, beau, German, Frenchman.
3. Give the positive forms corresponding to "most," "first," "next," "eldest."
4. Give adverbs corresponding with "quick," "good," "little."
5. Write out in full, in the ordinary form, the indicative mood of the singular.
6. Give the past tense and past participle of slide, stoop, hide, hurt, wink, swim, set.
7. Analyse :
   " Full many a gem of purest ray serene
   The dark unfathomed caves of ocean bear."

And parse the italicised words in the following sentence :
   " *Where is the man that* will not fight for his country " ?

III.
1. Define Conjunction, Subject, Case, Person, Personal Pronoun, Verb.
2. Write the plural nominative of sheep, species, beau, solo, cherub, Mr.; the possessive singular and plural of chimney, sky, lass ; the comparative and superlative degrees of many, tedious, holy ; and the past tense, present participle, and past participle of rear, beseech, singe, dun, die, ply.

3. Give the third singular present indicative, third singular present subjunctive, present participle, and past participle of the following verbs: Dig, swim, flee, pay, pry, deal, thrust, threaten, shrink.
4. Express the following fractions by means of words.—

$\frac{2}{3}$ $\frac{5}{6}$ $\frac{1}{8}$ $3\frac{1}{32}$ and $\frac{10}{41}$.

5. Name three adjectives that are irregularly compared, and compare them.
6. Into what classes are pronouns divided? Give an example of each class.
7. Analyse :—"Saint Augustine ! thou well hast said
   That of our vices we can frame
   A ladder, if we will but tread
   Beneath our feet each deed of shame."
And parse :—" Scott, the famous author, who was an early riser, usually worked four hours in his study before breakfast."

IV.

1. Write the singular of potatoes, pence, swine, clauses, ties, pies, spies, lies, cries ; the possessive plural of who, lady, gentleman ; all the persons in the singular of the present and the past indicative of *will*, the principal verb, and all the persons in the singular of the present and the past of *will*, the auxiliary verb ; and the present and past participles of fulfil, sue, shine.
2. What is meant in Grammar by "qualify," "proposition," "gender" ?
3. Classify adjectives, and give an example of each class.
4. Give the rule for the use of the pronoun "that."
5. Give the masculine or feminine forms, as the case may be, of hero, sultana, countess, executor ; the plural of money, lily, folio, gas, brother, pea, cargo ; the comparative and superlative degrees of far, ill, funny ; the past tense and past participle of lead, sit, loose, pay, stay, shoe.
6. Analyse:
   " They buried him darkly at dead of night,
   The sods with their bayonets turning,
   By the struggling moonbeams' misty light,
   And the lanterns dimly burning."
7. Parse : "John studies two hours daily, but James, his brother, passes his time in playing chess."

V.

Correct where necessary the following sentences, giving reasons for any changes made :—
1. Neither James nor John do their work well.
2. You and me do not read those sort of books.
3. Every good pupil strives to please his teacher.

4. The toast was drank in silence.
5. It makes no difference to either you or I.
6. Neither John nor James is coming.
7. The burning of the *Bavarian* was one of the most dreadful accidents that has happened for many years.
8. My sister and my sister's child,
   Myself and children three,
   Will fill the chaise, so you must ride
   On horseback after we.
9. *A* or *an* is styled an indefinite article.
10. He is great, but truth is greater than us all.
11. There are a great many people in town.
12. Ten-elevenths are equal to twenty twoes.
13. The river has raised six inches since morning.
14. Of the two Henries this is the youngest.
15. I seen him a good ways up the street.

INTERMEDIATE EXAMINATION, JUNE, 1876.

" The signet-ring young Lewis took,
With deep respect and altered look ;
And said :—' This ring our duties own ;
And pardon, if to worth unknown,
In semblance mean obscurely veiled,   5
Lady in aught my folly failed.
Soon as the day flings wide his gates,
The King shall know what suitor waits.
Please you, meanwhile, in fitting bower
Repose you till his waking hour ;   10
Female attendance shall obey
Your hest, for service or array.
Permit I marshal you the way.'
But, ere she followed, with the grace
And open bounty of her race,   15
She bade her slender purse be shared
Among the soldiers of the guard."
      —*The Lady of the Lake, Canto VI.*

1. Divide vv. 9-17 into propositions, and fully analyse them.
2. Parse "pardon," "to," and "unknown," l. 4 ; "soon," ' as," and "wide," l. 7 ; "you," l. 10 ; "for," l. 12 ; "you," l. 13 ; "with," l. 14 ; "purse," l.16.
3. Give the derivation of "signet," "respect," "alter," "duty," "semblance," "lady," "aught," "folly," "repose," "obey," "marshal," "grace," "bounty," "service."
4. Explain the meaning of line 3, of " signet," and of "hest."

5. The syllables *et, re, be, per, tend, ance*, occur in many English words. State the meaning and explain the origin of each.
6. Render the passage in prose.
7. Give an account of the different uses of "it."
8. On what basis are verbs classified into strong and weak? State which of the verbs in the passage at the head of this paper are strong.

INTERMEDIATE EXAMINATION, DECEMBER, 1876.

1. "Harp of the North, farewell! The hills grow dark,
    On purple peaks a deeper shade descending;
    In twilight copse the glow-worm lights her spark,
    The deer, half-seen, are to the covert wending.
    Resume thy wizard elm! the fountain lending,
    And the wild breeze thy wilder minstrelsy—
    Thy numbers sweet—with Nature's vespers blending,
    With distant echo from the fold and lea,
    And herd-boys' evening pipe, and hum of housing bee."

    (1) Divide into propositions, state their kind, explain their connection, and fully analyse them.
    (2) Parse "dark" (l. 1); "half-seen" (l. 4); "wizard" and "fountain" (l. 5); and "pipe" (l. 9.)
    (3) Name the stanza and explain its structure. Scan and name the last two lines. Mention any long poem written throughout in this stanza.
    (4) Explain the meaning of "wizard elm" (l. 5), and "pipe" (l. 9).
    (5) Make a list of the words of classical origin that occur in the stanza, giving their roots when you can.
2. Parse the italicised words in the following extract:—

    "To hero *boune* for *battle* strife
    Or bard of martial lay,
    'Twere *worth* ten *years* of peaceful life
    One *glance* at their array!
    Their light armed archers *far* and *near*
    Surveyed the tangled ground,
    Their centre ranks *with* pike and spear
    A twilight *forest* frowned,
    Their barbed horsemen in the rear
    The stern *battalia* crowned."

    Explain the meaning of 'barbed' (l. 9), and "battalia" (l. 10).
3. Express, in as many different ways as you can, the fact that *John taught James grammar*, using not only the same but different words.

4. Combine the simple sentences in the following paragraph into compound sentences, where it is necessary, so as to produce a continuous narrative :—
The polar bear is of a white colour. It is found in the Arctic regions. It leads an almost entirely aquatic life in these regions. Its body is long. Its head is flat. Its muzzle is broad. Its mouth is peculiarly small. The paws are very large. They are covered on the under side with coarse hair. From the coarse hair it derives security in walking over the slippery ice. The fur is long. The fur is woolly. It is of fine texture. It is of considerable value.
5. Define the meaning of the grammatical terms : *Strong Conjugation, Gender, Degree of Comparison, Regimen, Adjective Sentence.*
6. What is an auxiliary verb ? Explain the use and meaning of each of the English auxiliary verbs.
7. Name the relative pronouns, and give examples of their respective uses.
8. Criticize the following sentences, making corrections where necessary :—
He is a better philosopher than a statesman.
The tenth and the eleventh boys in the class.
This is one of the most successful works that ever was executed.
Death has come to all, greater, wiser, better than I.
This wonderful steam walking man was invented and patented by John Blank, of Blanktown, after spending thousands of dollars and several years experimenting in steam walking machines, has at last accomplished a perfect steam man, five feet in height, and walks as natural as a living man.

CANADIAN LITERARY INSTITUTE, WOODSTOCK, ONTARIO.

ENTRANCE EXAMINATIONS.

1. Define Person, Voice, Case, Mood, and Tense.
2. Define the following parts of speech, and give an example of each in a short sentence :—Abstract Noun, Demonstrative Adjective, Distributive Pronoun, Indefinite Pronoun.
3. What part of speech is each of the "that's" in the following sentence ? Give reasons for your decision :—"I told John *that that* man *that* he saw reading *that* great book was not the learned person *that* he would have us think him to be."

4. Give the feminine of *duke, hunter, Sultan, friar, wizard*; the masculine of *niece, lass, peeress, bride, actress*; and the plural of *cargo, chimney, staff, flagstaff, story, pea, penny.*
5. Vary the structure of the following sentences by changing the Active into Passive, and the Passive into Active :—(*a*) Whatever is offensive in our manner is corrected by gentleness. (*b*) Every summer we may observe the mischievous effects of the rapacity of birds in the vegetable kingdom.
6. State clearly the uses of the Present Tense.
7. Quote the rules of Syntax which the following sentences are severally intended to exemplify :—
    (*a*) John gave *me* a book.
    (*b*) It cost a *shilling*.
    (*c*) "Others said, He is like *him*."
8. Analyze the following sentences, and parse the italicized words :—
    "*Night*, sable *goddess*, from *her* ebon throne,
    In rayless majesty, *now stretches* forth
    Her *laden* sceptre, o'er a slumbering world."

    "*Who* steals my purse *steals* trash."

FIRST YEAR.

1. Define *word, phrase, clause, sentence.* Give an example of each in a short sentence.
2. State clearly the distinction between *Simple, Complex*, and *Compound* sentences.
3. Name the essential terms of a sentence and the subdivisions of each. Analyze: "This skull has lain *you* in the ground these three *years*."—*Shakespeare.* Parse *you, years.*
4. Analyze the following sentence and parse the italicized words :—
    "*Full many a gem* of purest ray serene,
    The dark unfathomed *caves* of ocean bear."—*Gray.*
5. Correct or justify the following expressions, giving your reasons for corrections :—(*a*) Three and two *is* five. (*b*) The *two eldest* of the family. (*c*) The *first three* Gospels. (*d*) 'He made a better soldier than a poet.' "No laws are better than English laws."
6. In the following hypothetical sentence, distinguish the *Protasis* from the *Apodosis*, and point out clearly the four different senses in which "it" is used :—"If 'twer done when 'tis done, then 'twere well it were done quickly."—*Shakespeare.*

SECOND YEAR.

1. Give the meaning of the prefixes of the following words, with the corresponding prefixes in two other languages:—Homœopathy, retrospect, thoroughfare, synod, sidings.
2. Give the same with respect to the suffixes of the following :—Lawyer, monastery, earldom, beauteous, troublesome.

3. State and illustrate the logical use of compound words.
4. Give three examples of each of the following :—(a) Compound words indicating the place whence ; (b) incomplete compounds ; and (c) apparent compounds.
5. Give and analyze the compound diminutive terminations of Saxon origin.
6. Give a strict definition of "number," and show how the English language departs from this in respect to nouns, pronouns, and to verbs.
7. Analyze the following words :—Hence, mine, him, more, worse, farther, innermost, amidst.
8. Define the following figures, giving two examples of each : Prothesis, metathesis, syncope, aphæresis, elision.

McGILL NOMAL SCHOOL, MONTREAL.
MODEL SCHOOL CLASS.

I.

1. What is meant by inflection? Give an account of inflection in the English Language as compared with inflections in other languages.
2. Give the past tense and past participle of the following verbs :— Shear, lie, lade, be, chide, freight, cleave, thrive, swing, slide, spring, swim.
3. Point out the defect in the following sentence, and show how that defect may be avoided :—" When we see the beautiful variety of colour in the rainbow, we are led to enquire its cause."
4. Give the chief rules with reference to the position of the adjective.
5. Explain clearly the use of the participles ; account for the expressions *a fishing, a going, a hunting, a running ;* and show that a participle while used as a noun may be modified in all respects as a verb.
6. Explain the use of each of the words in italics in the following :—
   (a) Not *only* the men, but the women *also* were present.
   (b) I, *even* I, do bring a flood, &c. (c) *There* came to the beach a poor exile, &c. (d) She looks *cold.* (e) He arrived *safe.* (f) The milk turns *sour.*
7. State clearly what is meant by an adverbial phrase ; give a few examples of adverbial phrases, and state what you know of their origin.
8. Show that the infinitive mood may be the subject of a verb, the object of a verb, the predicate nominative after a copulative verb, in apposition with a noun, and the object of a preposition.

9. Verbs signifying *to name, choose, appoint, constitute,* and the like, generally govern two objectives: the *direct* and the indirect. Give examples of this.
10. Give examples of the different uses of the present tense of the indicative mood.

II.

1. Explain the use of each word in italics in the following:—(a) Do it at *once*. (b) *To think* that she should be so foolish! (c) You were silent when accused—a clear *confession* of guilt. (d) I am sorry, and *so* is he. (e) I shall expect you this *day* three *weeks*. (f) *It* was then that the cavalry charged. (g) *Granting* that you are right, what do you infer from this? (h) A friend of *mine* is here.
2. Explain what is meant by defective verbs. Give a list of them, and show how they may be used.
3. Sometimes the antecedent term of a *preposition*, and sometimes the subsequent, is omitted. Give examples.
4. State clearly what is meant by nouns in apposition. Show their various uses in the construction of sentences.
5. *Concerning, excepting, regarding, respecting, save,* and *except,* are found in the list of prepositions; in what other ways may they be considered? How may compound prepositions be explained?
6. Explain fully by examples the use of conjunctive adverbs. Why is it said that a few adverbs are sometimes used as adjuncts to nouns and pronouns?
7. Give a few examples illustrating the use of adverbial sentences.
8. Show clearly the use of the participle as a verbal noun.

ELEMENTARY SCHOOL CLASS.

I.

1. What is meant by adjectives not susceptible of comparison?
2. Give the plural of each of the following:—Chrysalis, bandit, virtuoso, ignis-fatuus, genus, fungus, oasis.
3. Show that the pronoun "*it*" is used in a variety of ways in the English language.
4. What is meant by the antecedent of a relative pronoun? Give examples of different antecedents.
5. State clearly what is meant by the restrictive use of a relative pronoun.
6. Explain the use of the word "*as*" in the following sentence:— Shun such *as* are vicious.
7. Transitive verbs have two voices, active and passive. Show the difference between them in construction and use.

8. Annex to each of the following the Latin word from which it is derived: fête, defy, endorse, duplicity, disdain, ducuna, ragout, germ, progeny, elite, lavender, elate.

II.

1. Show clearly the insufficiency and redundancy of the English Alphabet.
2. Write out the past tense of the verb to lie (repose).
3. For what purposes are verbs inflected?
4. Give the plural of each of the following:—focus, calx, erratum, magus, radius, hypothesis, stratum, miasma.
5. Show clearly the construction and use of the passive voice of transitive verbs in the English language.
6. What is meant by the office of the Relative being sometimes descriptive, and sometimes restrictive? Give examples.
7. State clearly the use and construction of compound relative pronouns.
8. How would you explain to a class the use of the words in italics in the following:—(a) It often happens *that* the good are unrewarded. (b) Give *but* one kind word. (c) The ship went *ashore*.
9. What is meant by the irregular comparison of adjectives?
10. Annex to each of the following the Latin word from which it is derived:—Filter, mallet, courage, malicious, religion, claret, bivalve, alarm, suffer, commerce, pantry, abominable.

BRITISH COLUMBIA TEACHERS' EXAMINATIONS.

I.

1. Name the words beginning with the letter "h," in which it is silent.
2. Explain the various uses of the different parts of speech.
3. Classify and name each part of speech in the following sentence:
"The power of speech is a faculty peculiar to man, a faculty bestowed on him by his beneficent Creator, for the greatest and most excellent uses; but, alas! how often do we pervert it to the worst of purposes!"
4. What is the distinguishing peculiarity between articles and adjectives?
5. Why are personal pronouns the only real pronouns?
6. What are the variations in the termination of an English verb? Give examples.

7. As words ending in "ing" are frequently used both as nouns and adjectives, how do you find to which class they belong?
8. Name one or two prepositional phrases.
9. How are words which are used both as adverbs and adjectives distinguished?
10. Define the participle, and how formed.
11. What is "case" in grammar? Give examples of the three cases.
12. Name the classes into which verbs are divided, with respect to their form; and their distinguishing marks, with respect to their signification.

II.

1. What does English Grammar signify?
2. Define Orthography, Etymology and Syntax.
3. Define the following, simply but fully: Noun, Adjective, Verb, Preposition, Conjunction, giving examples of each.
4. Name the parts of which a sentence may consist, and the different kinds of sentences.
5. What is a Proposition in logic, and of how many parts does it consist? Point them out in the following sentence:—"Virtue alone is happiness below."
6. Name the following parts of the verb To read: Imp. Potential; Plural Imperative; First Future Indicative; Third Plural Imp. Subjunctive.
7. Define a Participle and a Participial Adjective. Is the Participial form ever used for the Infinitive Mood?
8. What is meant by Inflexion? Of what may inflexions consist?
9. What is meant by Cases? Define them, giving an example of each.
10. In the sentence "And they feared when they heard that they were Romans," what part of speech is when? Give the reason.

III.

1. Give examples of Primitive, Derivative, Simple and Compound words.
2. Into how many parts is English Grammar divided; and of what does each treat?
3. Explain the use of each part of speech, giving examples.
4. What is meant by Case of Nouns, and what does each denote?
5. Name the classes into which Pronouns may be subdivided, giving one of each class.
6. When is the word "what" a compound relative—an interrogative Relative Pronoun—an Adjective Pronoun—an Interjection?
7. Illustrate by examples the kinds of Nouns, and their persons.
8. State the different kinds of Verbs, in regard to the manner of their action and their different forms, giving an example of each mood.

9. When is a verb called irregular? Name the present and imperfect tenses; also the perfect participle of *awake, choose, rise, write.*
10. How many tenses has each mood: and what words are the signs of them?
11. What is a participle derived from; and how are participles formed?
12. What parts of speech do adverbs qualify? Give two or three adverbial phrases.
13. Name the Prepositions which occur to you; and by what part of speech must a Preposition be followed?

FREDERICTON NORMAL SCHOOL, NEW BRUNSWICK.

I.

1. Classify the words *sweet, before, lead, till, deep, us.*
2. Give the inflections of *lion, tree, wrote, went, soon, good.*
3. Name the various kinds of extension of the predicate, and give an example of each.
4. Analyze in the prescribed form the following sentences:—
    "Heaven *hides* nothing from thy view."
    " He *with* his horrid crew
    Lay vanquished rolling in the fiery gulf."
    " Him the Almighty
    Hurl'd headlong flaming from the ethereal sky
    With hideous ruin and combustion *down*
    To bottomless perdition."
5. Parse in tabular form the words in italics.
6. Give the past tense and past participle of all the irregular verbs in the passage.
7. The same verb expressing the same action is sometimes transitive and sometimes intransitive; give examples, and point out the difference in meaning.
8. Name the different kinds of subordinate clauses, and give an example of each.
9. Explain the terms voice, mood, and case.

EXAMINATION QUESTIONS.

II.

1. Classify the words light, round, square, die, use, farther, so.
2. Give all the inflexions of lion, be, he, I, go, pretty, went, came.
3. Write the plural of lady, man, pea, chimney, hoof, wharf, cherub, genius, axis, penny.
4. What is a complex sentence? In how many relations may a substantive clause stand in a sentence? Give an example of each relation.
5. Define the term *case*. What seems to be the present tendency with respect to the use of the possessive case? Give examples in support of your answer. Explain the different uses of the objective case, and give an example of each.
6. Discuss the Number of the following words:—Physics, politics, bellows, scissors, riches, alms, news.
7. Explain the function of *than* in comparative sentences. What is its office in the preceding passage? What words in the passage do you regard as participles? Why? How can you distinguish participles from adjectives?
8. Give a short explanation of the nature and use of the *verb* and the *preposition*. Criticise the method in which the prescribed text-book on Grammar treats these parts of speech.

EXAMINATION PAPERS IN ARITHMETIC

By J. A. McLellan, M.A., LL D., *Inspector of High Schools,*
and Thomas Kirkland, M.A., *Science Master,*
Normal School, in two parts, containing

1st.—Chapter on the UNITARY METHOD, with solutions showing its application to every variety of problems.

2nd—Examination Papers in the elementary rules, vulgar and decimal fractions.

3rd—Examination Papers similar to those given for entrance examinations.

4th—Examination Papers similar to those given for third-class certificates.

5th.—Examination Papers similar to those given for second-class certificates, and the Intermediate Examination.

6th.—Examination Papers similar to those given for first-class certificates.

Adam Miller & Co., Publishers, Toronto.

Part 1. 60 cts. Complete Edition, 1.00. Hints and answers 50 cts.

ELEMENTARY STATICS.

By Thomas Kirkland, M.A., Science Master
Normal School, Toronto.

PRICE $1.00.

The following are the chief characteristics of this work:—

1st - It requires from the Student only a knowledge of Euclid, B. I., and Simple Equations in Algebra.

2nd—It contains chapters on the Parallelogram of Forces, Resolution of Forces, Moments, Centre of Gravity, Mechanical Powers, Virtual Velocities &c.

3rd—It contains a very large number of Exercises, many of them solved, and hints for the solution of all the more difficult ones.

4th—It is expressly adapted for Candidates for First and Second Class Certificates, and for the Intermediate Examination in High Schools and Collegiate Institutes.

ADAM MILLER & CO., Publishers.

BOOK-KEEPING,
FOR USE IN PUBLIC & HIGH SCHOOLS,

By S. G. BEATTY, Principal Ontario Business College, Belleville, and SAMUEL CLARE, Teacher of Writing and Book-keeping, Normal School, Toronto.

(Authorized for use in Schools.)

Price .. .. 70 cents.

GEORGE WALLACE, B.A , Head Master, High School, Weston,—Students preparing for Provincial Certificates will do well to read this Manual on Book-keeping.

V. SWITZER, B.A., Head Master Colborne High School.—I believe it to be better adapted to school work than the books in common use.

JOHN J. MAGEE, B.A., High School, Uxbridge.—Believe it to be more suitable for Public and High Schools than any hitherto published.

A. ANDREWS, Head Master Niagara High School.—It is a simple, lucid, and very practical unfolding of the principle involved in the science of accounts

ADAM MILLER & CO.

Canadian Copyright Edition.

HAMBLIN SMITH'S ALGEBRA,
With Appendix by ALFRED BAKER, B.A.,
Mathematical Tutor, University College, Toronto.
(Authorized for use in Schools.)

Price .. .. 90 Cents.

GEO. DICKSON, B.A., Head Master Collegiate Institute, Hamilton.—Arrangement of subjects good; explanations and proofs exhaustive, concise and clear; examples for the most part from University and College examination papers, and are numerous, easy and progressive. There is no better Algebra in use in our High Schools and Collegiate Institutes.

WM. R. RIDDELL, B.A., Mathematical Master, Normal School, Ottawa.—The Algebra is admirable and well adapted as a general Text Book.

ADAM MILLER & CO.

www.ingramcontent.com/pod-product-compliance
Lightning Source LLC
Chambersburg PA
CBHW022108230426
43672CB00008B/1316